Table of Cases

vii

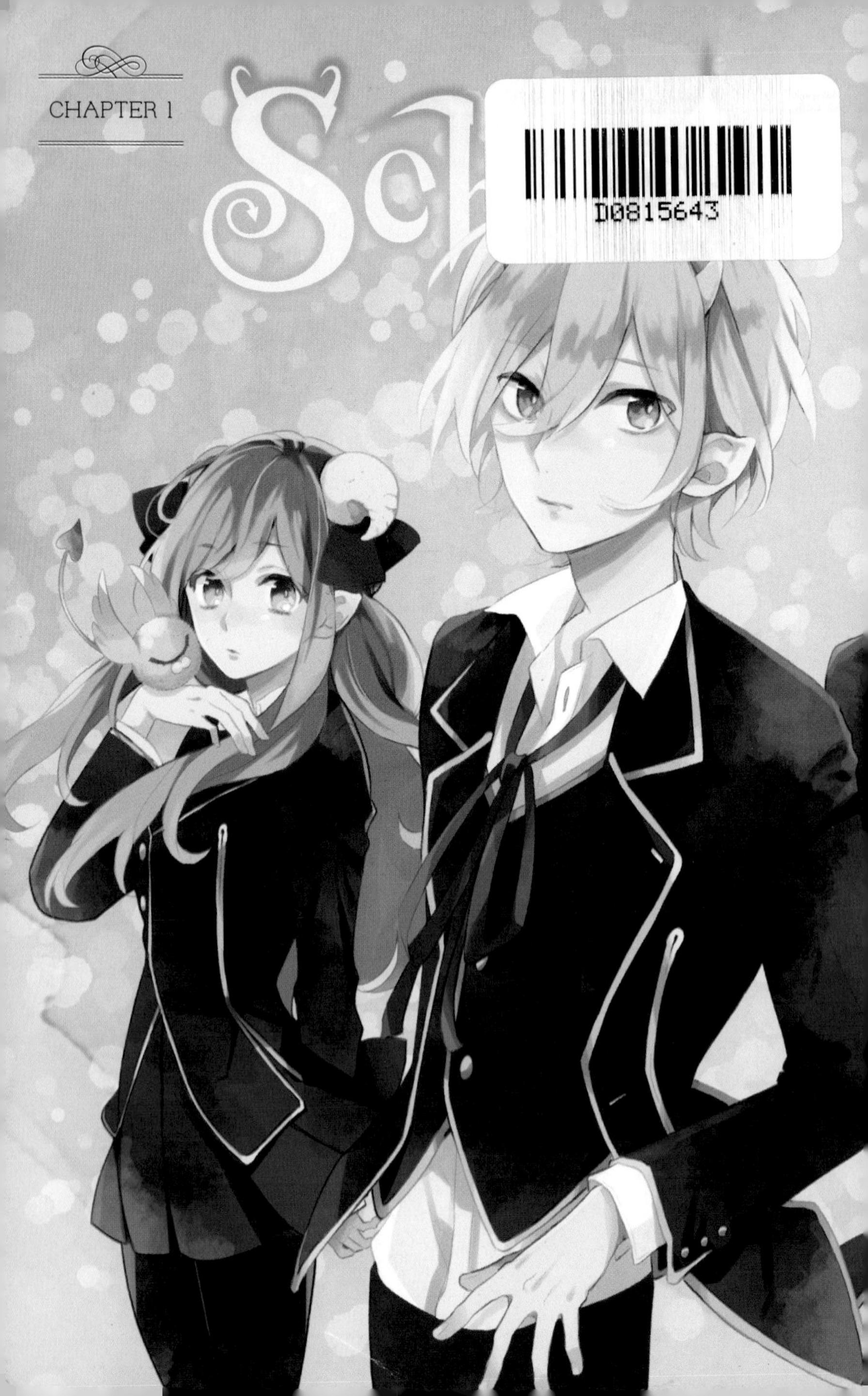
CHAPTER 1

CONTENTS

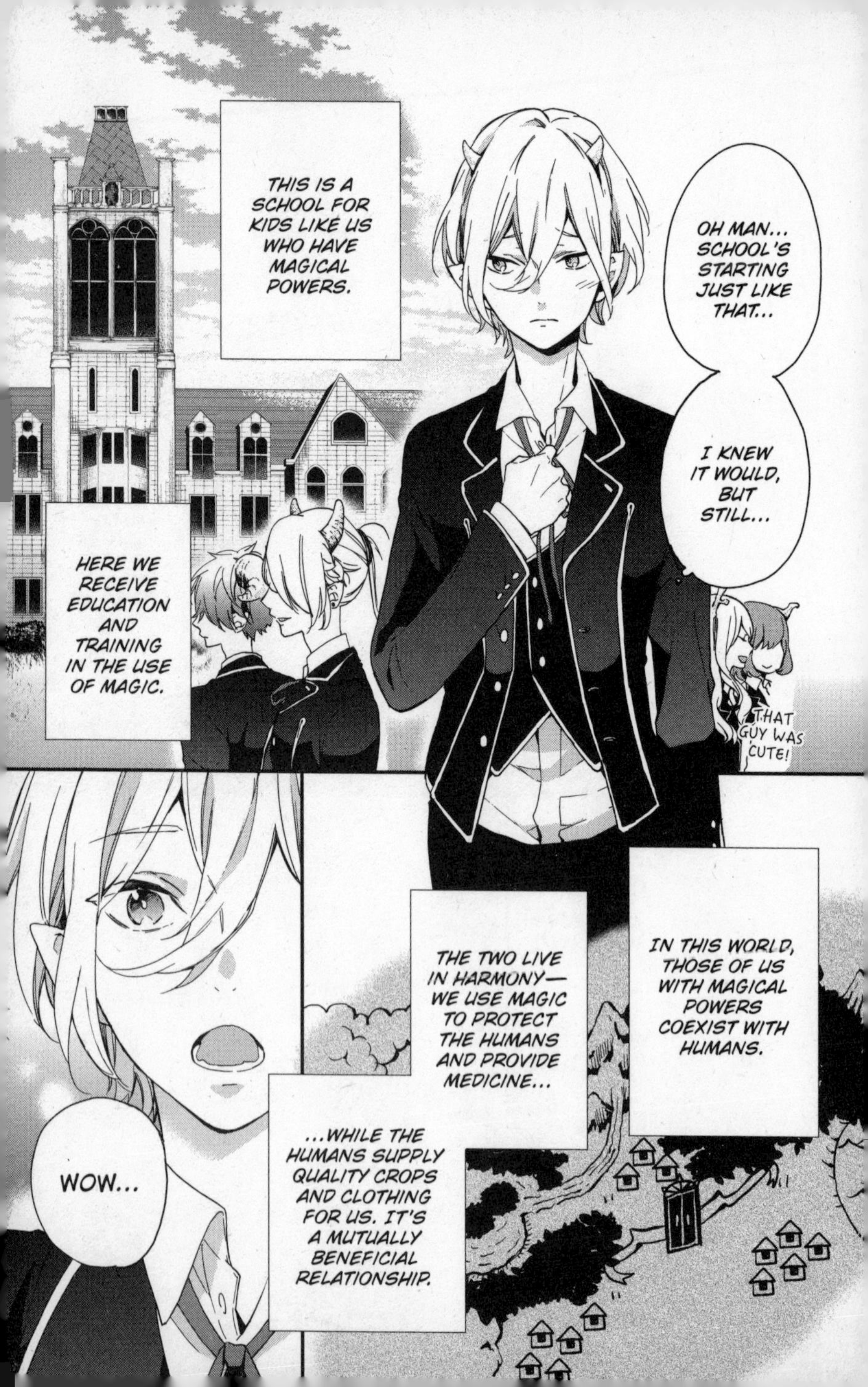
OH MAN... SCHOOL'S STARTING JUST LIKE THAT...
I KNEW IT WOULD, BUT STILL...
THIS IS A SCHOOL FOR KIDS LIKE US WHO HAVE MAGICAL POWERS.
HERE WE RECEIVE EDUCATION AND TRAINING IN THE USE OF MAGIC.
THAT GUY WAS CUTE!
IN THIS WORLD, THOSE OF US WITH MAGICAL POWERS COEXIST WITH HUMANS.
THE TWO LIVE IN HARMONY—WE USE MAGIC TO PROTECT THE HUMANS AND PROVIDE MEDICINE...
...WHILE THE HUMANS SUPPLY QUALITY CROPS AND CLOTHING FOR US. IT'S A MUTUALLY BENEFICIAL RELATIONSHIP.
WOW...

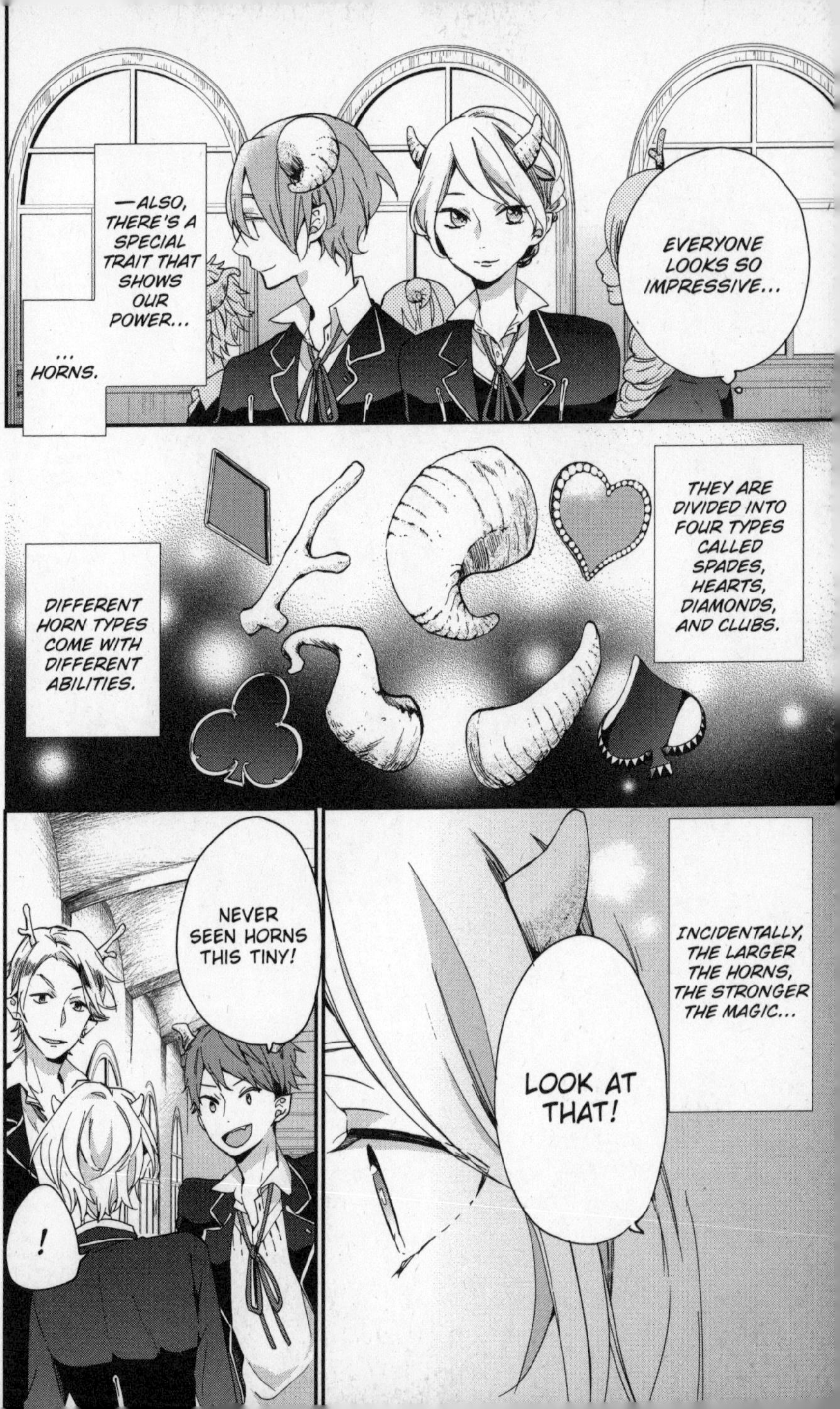
EVERYONE LOOKS SO IMPRESSIVE...
—ALSO, THERE'S A SPECIAL TRAIT THAT SHOWS OUR POWER...
... HORNS.
THEY ARE DIVIDED INTO FOUR TYPES CALLED SPADES, HEARTS, DIAMONDS, AND CLUBS.
DIFFERENT HORN TYPES COME WITH DIFFERENT ABILITIES.
INCIDENTALLY, THE LARGER THE HORNS, THE STRONGER THE MAGIC...
LOOK AT THAT!
NEVER SEEN HORNS THIS TINY!
!

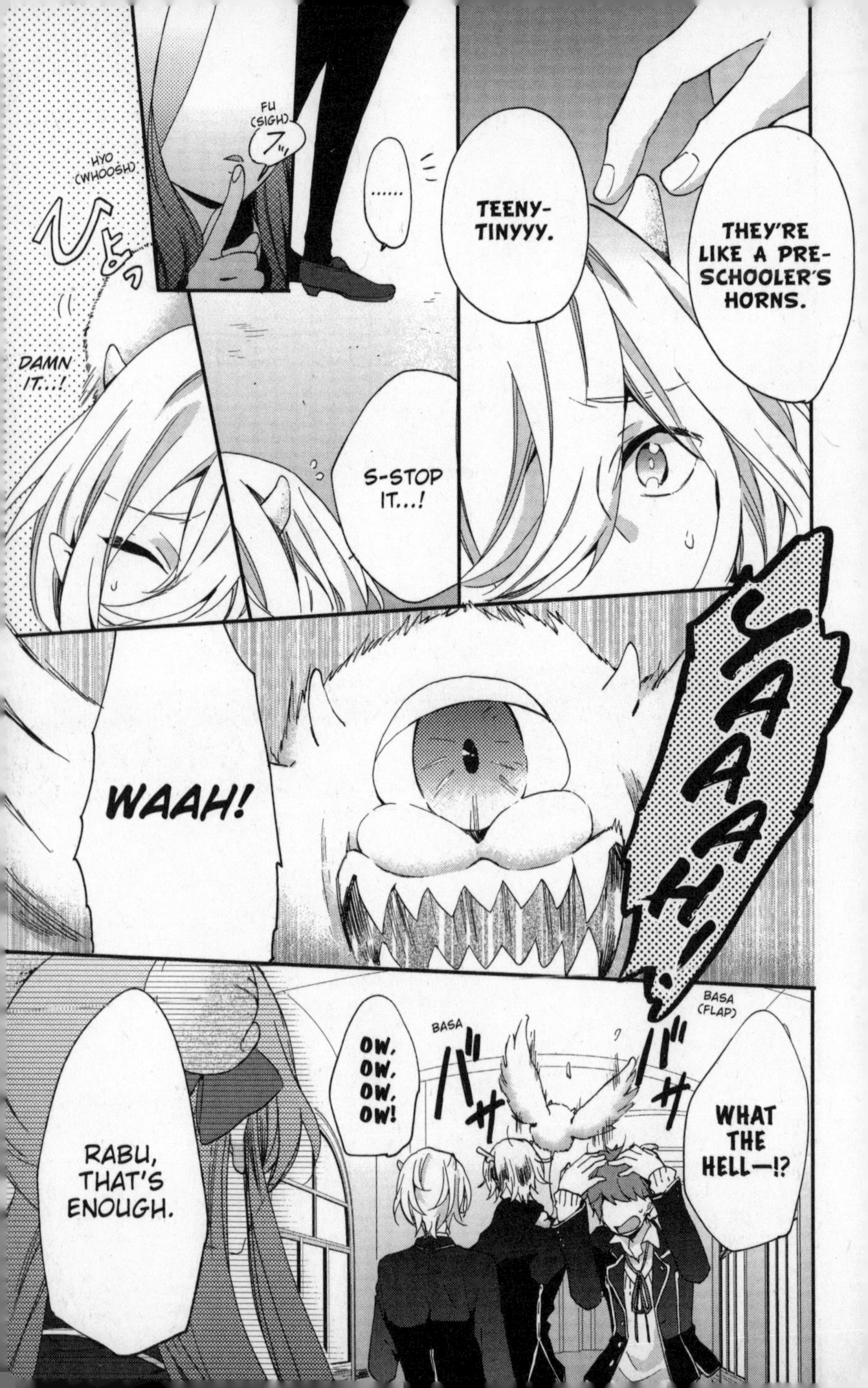
THEY'RE LIKE A PRE-SCHOOLER'S HORNS.
TEENY-TINYYY.
......
S-STOP IT...!
FU (SIGH)
HYO (WHOOSH)
DAMN IT...!
YAAAAH!
WAAH!
BASA (FLAP)
WHAT THE HELL—!?
BASA
OW, OW, OW, OW!
RABU, THAT'S ENOUGH.

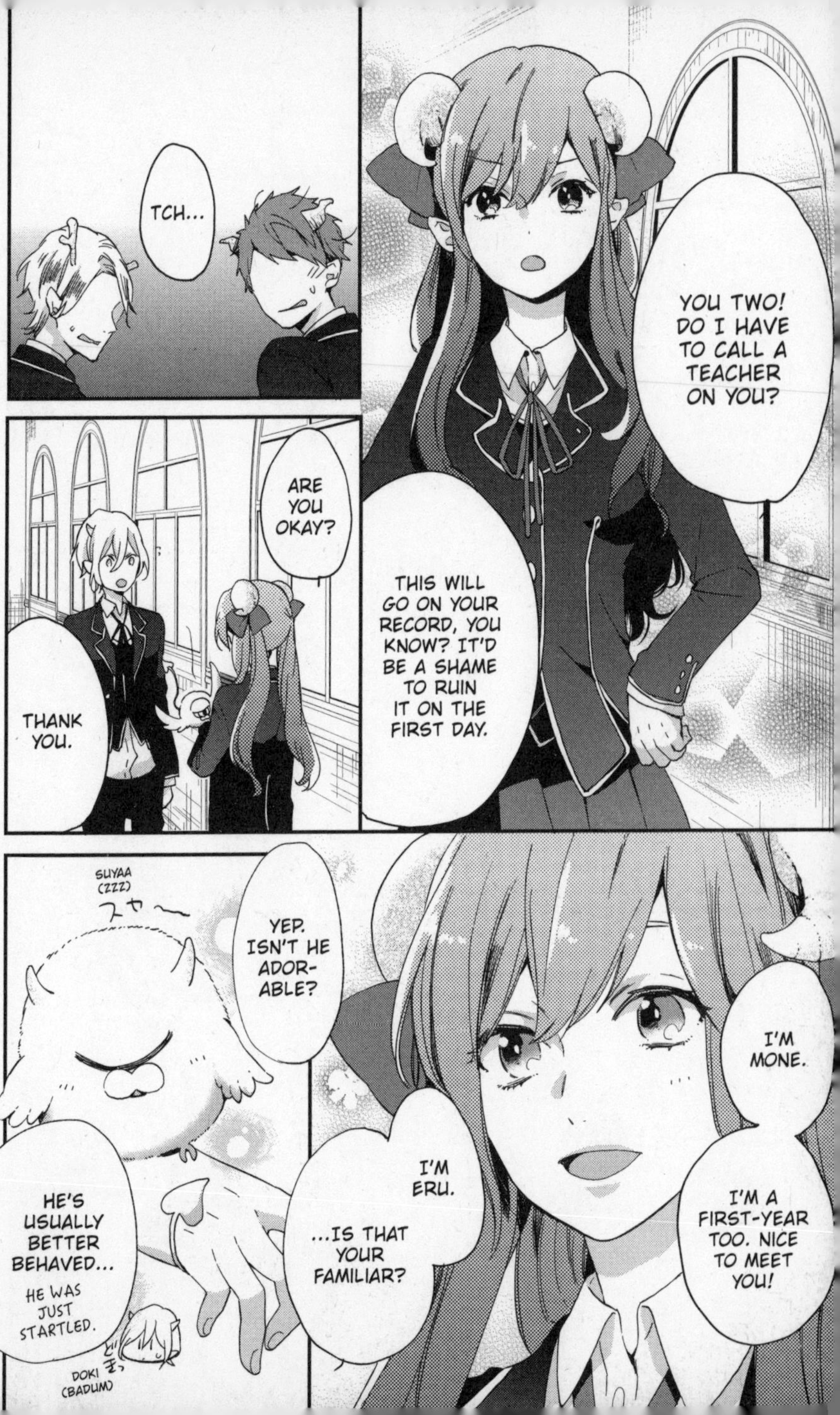
YOU TWO! DO I HAVE TO CALL A TEACHER ON YOU?
THIS WILL GO ON YOUR RECORD, YOU KNOW? IT'D BE A SHAME TO RUIN IT ON THE FIRST DAY.
TCH...
ARE YOU OKAY?
THANK YOU.
I'M MONE.
I'M A FIRST-YEAR TOO. NICE TO MEET YOU!
I'M ERU.
...IS THAT YOUR FAMILIAR?
YEP. ISN'T HE ADORABLE?
SUYAA (ZZZ)
スヤ～
HE'S USUALLY BETTER BEHAVED...
HE WAS JUST STARTLED.
DOKI (BADUM)

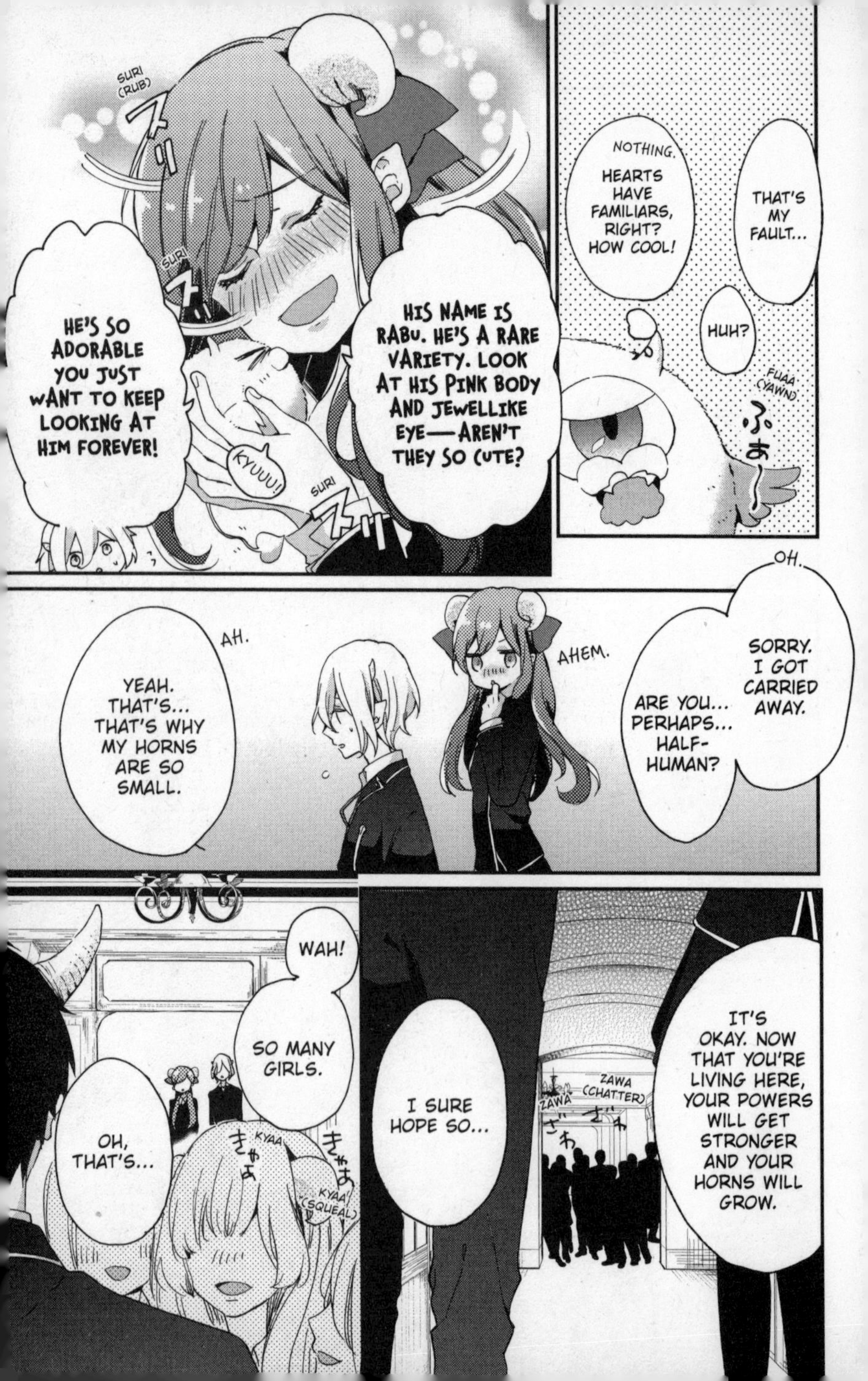

THAT'S MY FAULT...
NOTHING.
HEARTS HAVE FAMILIARS, RIGHT? HOW COOL!
HUH?
FUAA (YAWN)
ふあ〜
SURI (RUB)
HIS NAME IS RABU. HE'S A RARE VARIETY. LOOK AT HIS PINK BODY AND JEWELLIKE EYE—AREN'T THEY SO CUTE?
SURI
HE'S SO ADORABLE YOU JUST WANT TO KEEP LOOKING AT HIM FOREVER!
KYUUU!
SURI
OH.
SORRY. I GOT CARRIED AWAY.
ARE YOU... PERHAPS... HALF-HUMAN?
AHEM.
AH.
YEAH. THAT'S... THAT'S WHY MY HORNS ARE SO SMALL.
IT'S OKAY. NOW THAT YOU'RE LIVING HERE, YOUR POWERS WILL GET STRONGER AND YOUR HORNS WILL GROW.
ZAWA (CHATTER)
ZAWA
ざわ
I SURE HOPE SO...
WAH!
SO MANY GIRLS.
KYAA (SQUEAL)
KYAA
きゃあ
OH, THAT'S...

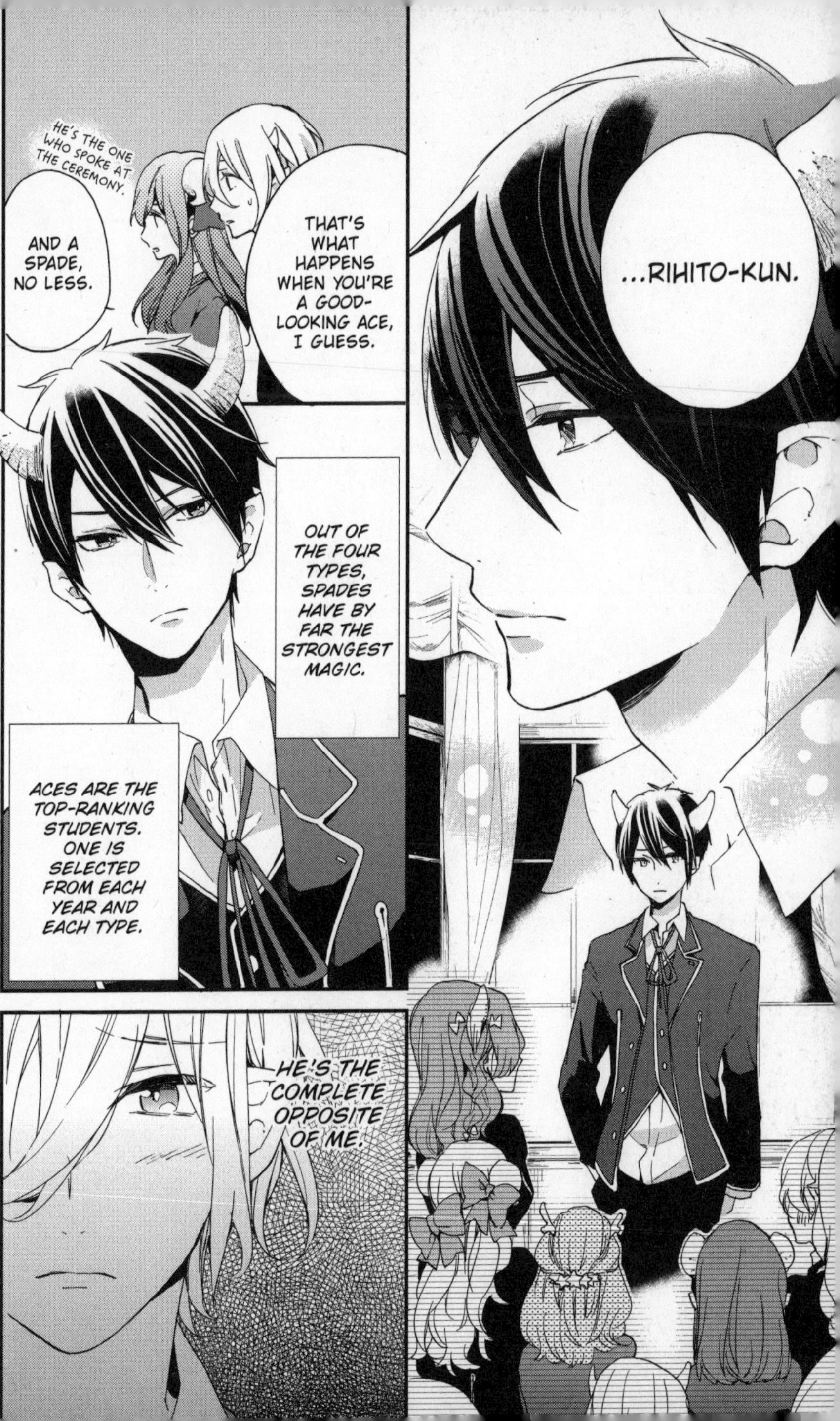
...RIHITO-KUN.
THAT'S WHAT HAPPENS WHEN YOU'RE A GOOD-LOOKING ACE, I GUESS.
HE'S THE ONE WHO SPOKE AT THE CEREMONY.
AND A SPADE, NO LESS.
OUT OF THE FOUR TYPES, SPADES HAVE BY FAR THE STRONGEST MAGIC.
ACES ARE THE TOP-RANKING STUDENTS. ONE IS SELECTED FROM EACH YEAR AND EACH TYPE.
HE'S THE COMPLETE OPPOSITE OF ME.

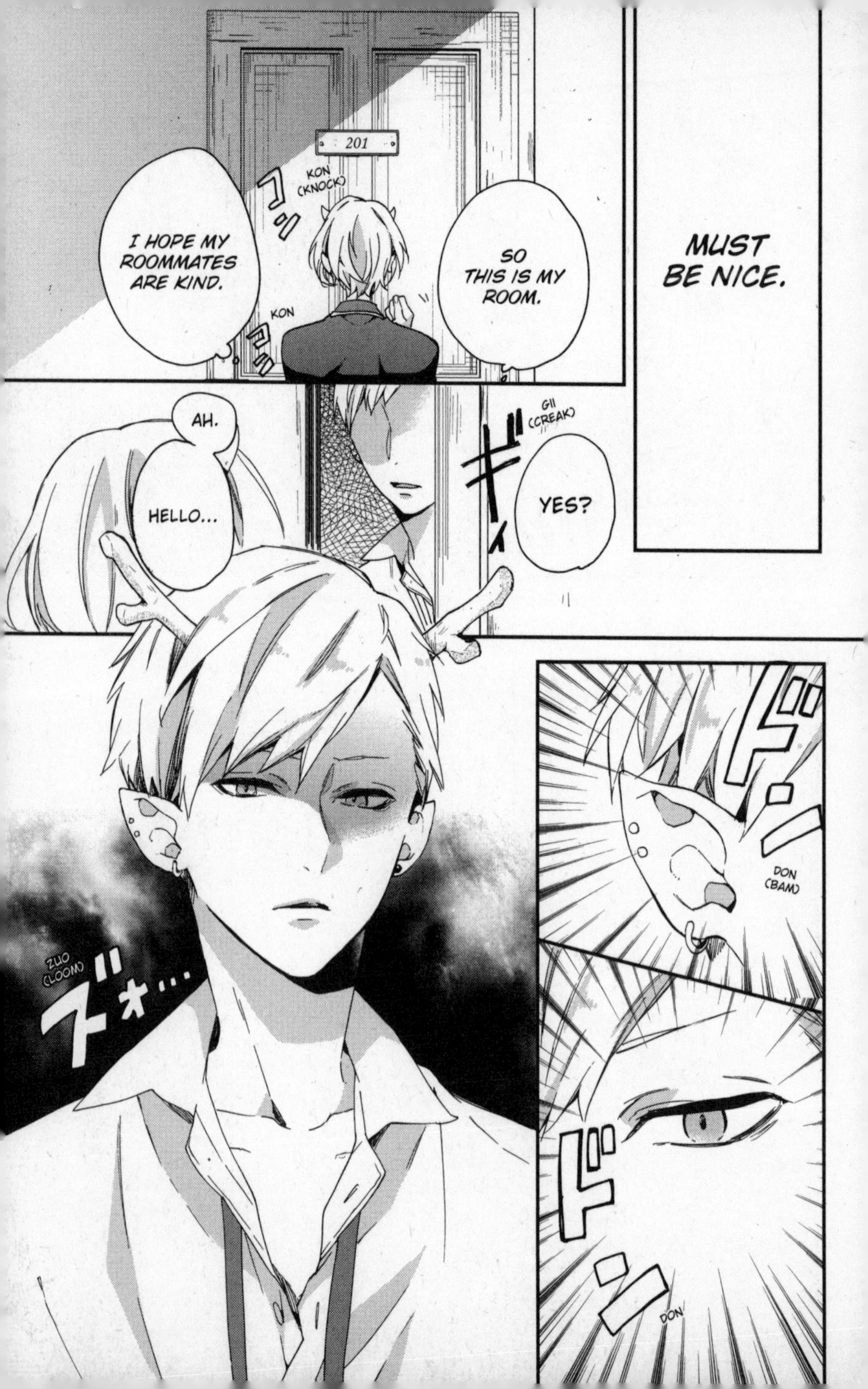
MUST BE NICE.
KON (KNOCK)
SO THIS IS MY ROOM.
I HOPE MY ROOMMATES ARE KIND.
KON
GII (CREAK)
YES?
AH.
HELLO...
DON (BAM)
DON!
ZUO (LOOM)

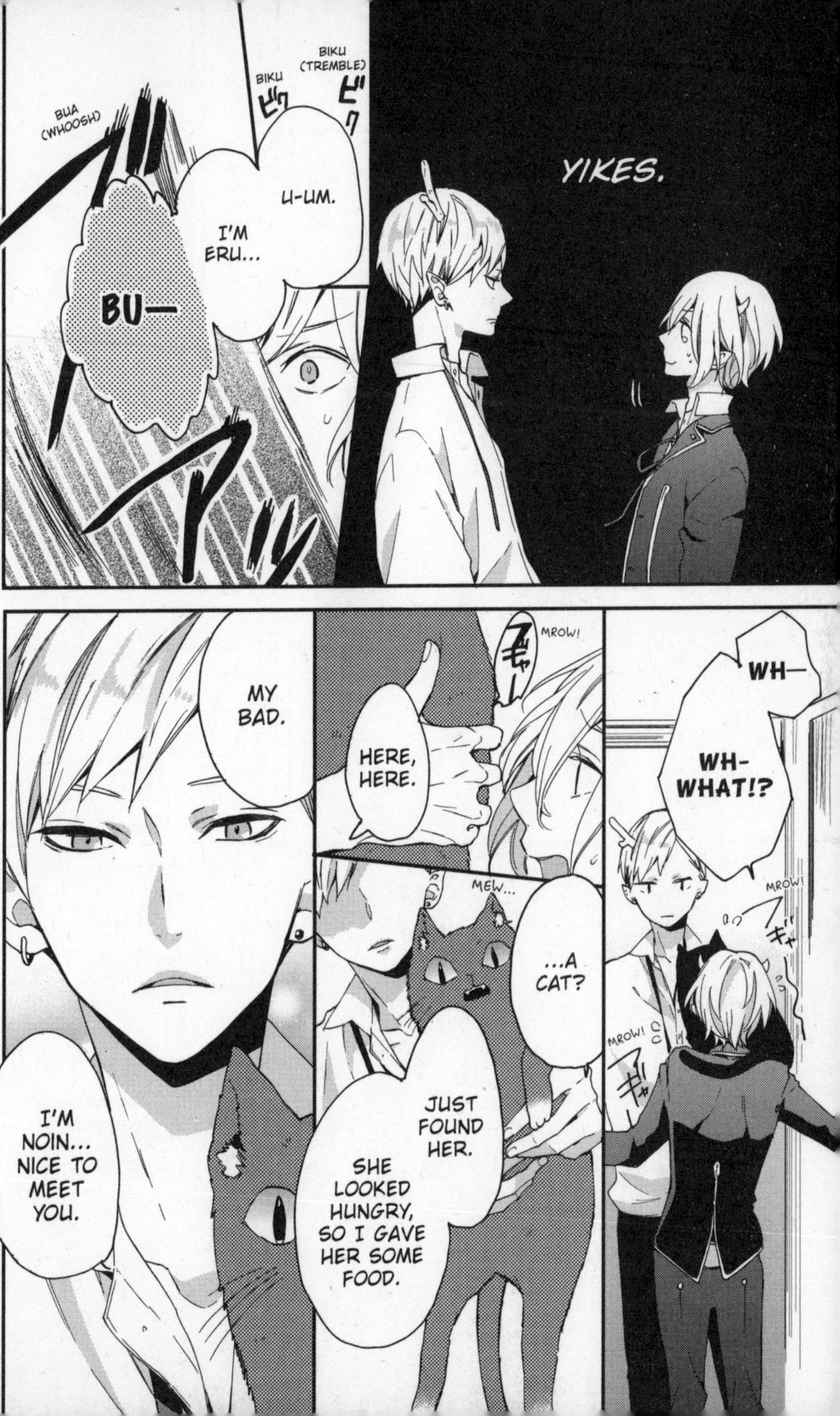
YIKES.
BIKU (TREMBLE)
BIKU
U-UM.
I'M ERU...
BUA (WHOOSH)
BU—
WH—
WH-WHAT!?
MROW!
MROW!
MROW!
HERE, HERE.
MEW...
...A CAT?
JUST FOUND HER.
SHE LOOKED HUNGRY, SO I GAVE HER SOME FOOD.
MY BAD.
I'M NOIN... NICE TO MEET YOU.

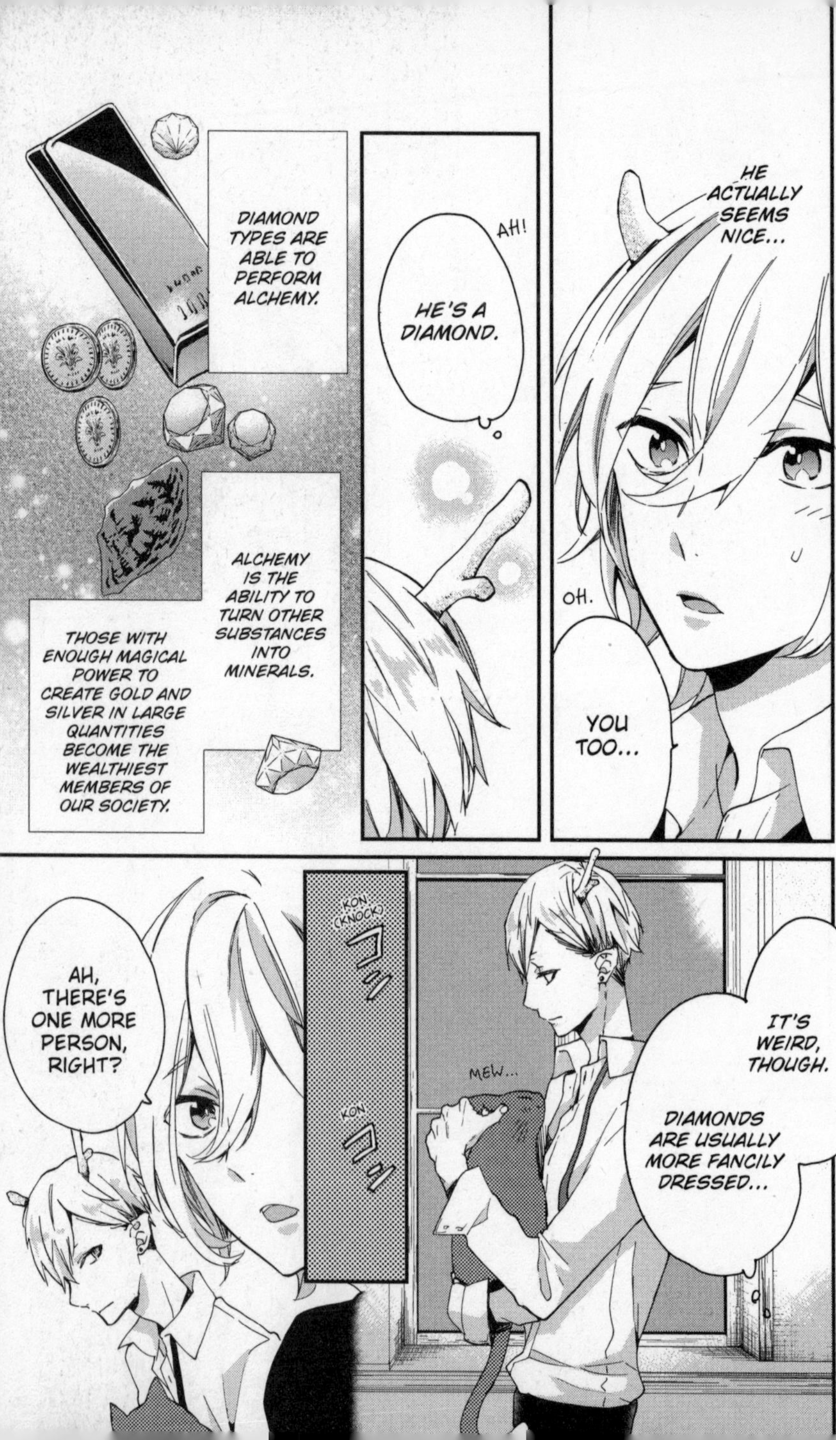
HE ACTUALLY SEEMS NICE...
OH.
YOU TOO...
AH!
HE'S A DIAMOND.
DIAMOND TYPES ARE ABLE TO PERFORM ALCHEMY.
ALCHEMY IS THE ABILITY TO TURN OTHER SUBSTANCES INTO MINERALS.
THOSE WITH ENOUGH MAGICAL POWER TO CREATE GOLD AND SILVER IN LARGE QUANTITIES BECOME THE WEALTHIEST MEMBERS OF OUR SOCIETY.
IT'S WEIRD, THOUGH.
DIAMONDS ARE USUALLY MORE FANCILY DRESSED...
MEW...
KON (KNOCK)
KON
AH, THERE'S ONE MORE PERSON, RIGHT?

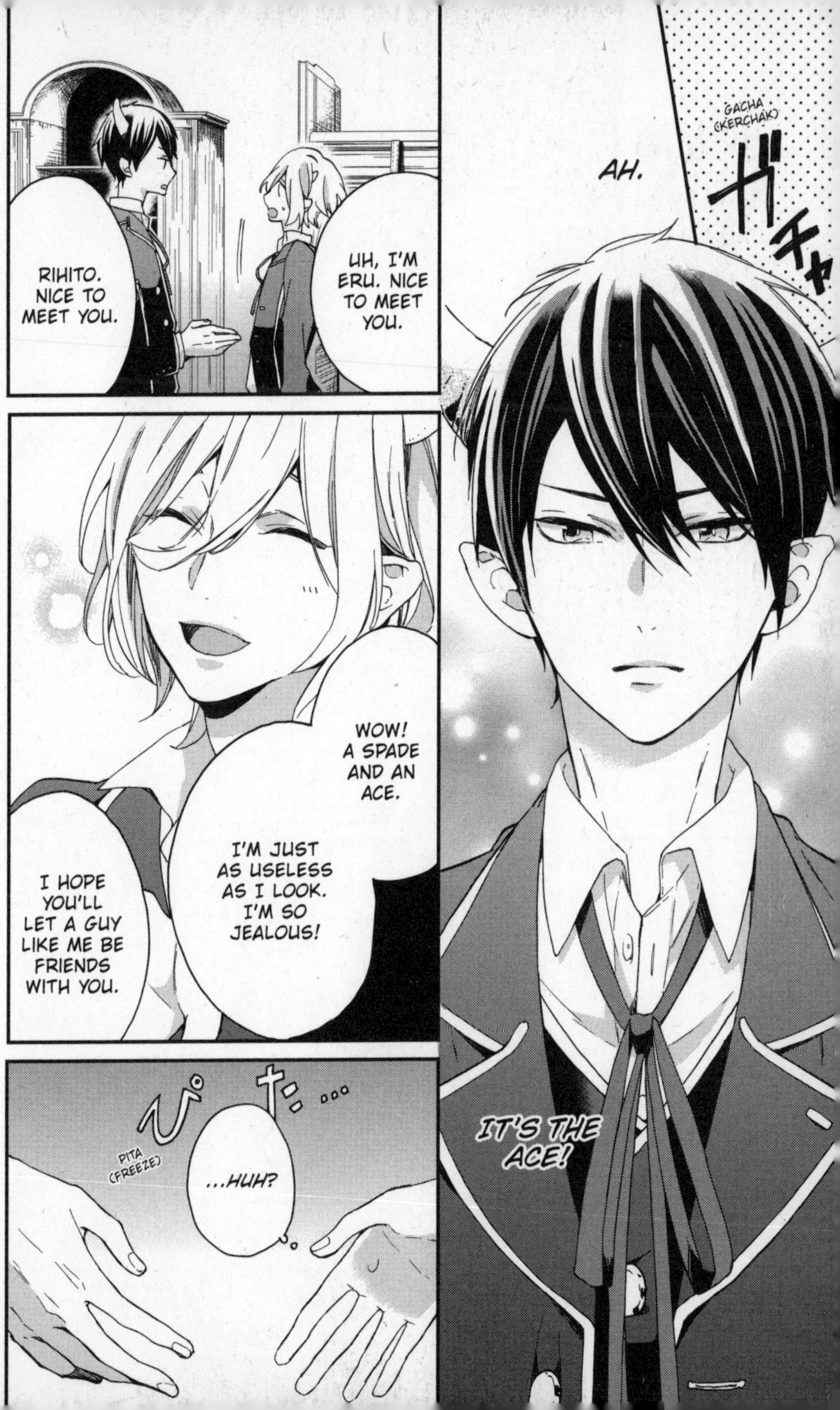
GACHA (KERCHAK)
ガチャ
AH.
IT'S THE ACE!
UH, I'M ERU. NICE TO MEET YOU.
RIHITO. NICE TO MEET YOU.
WOW! A SPADE AND AN ACE.
I'M JUST AS USELESS AS I LOOK. I'M SO JEALOUS!
I HOPE YOU'LL LET A GUY LIKE ME BE FRIENDS WITH YOU.
ぴた…
PITA (FREEZE)
...HUH?

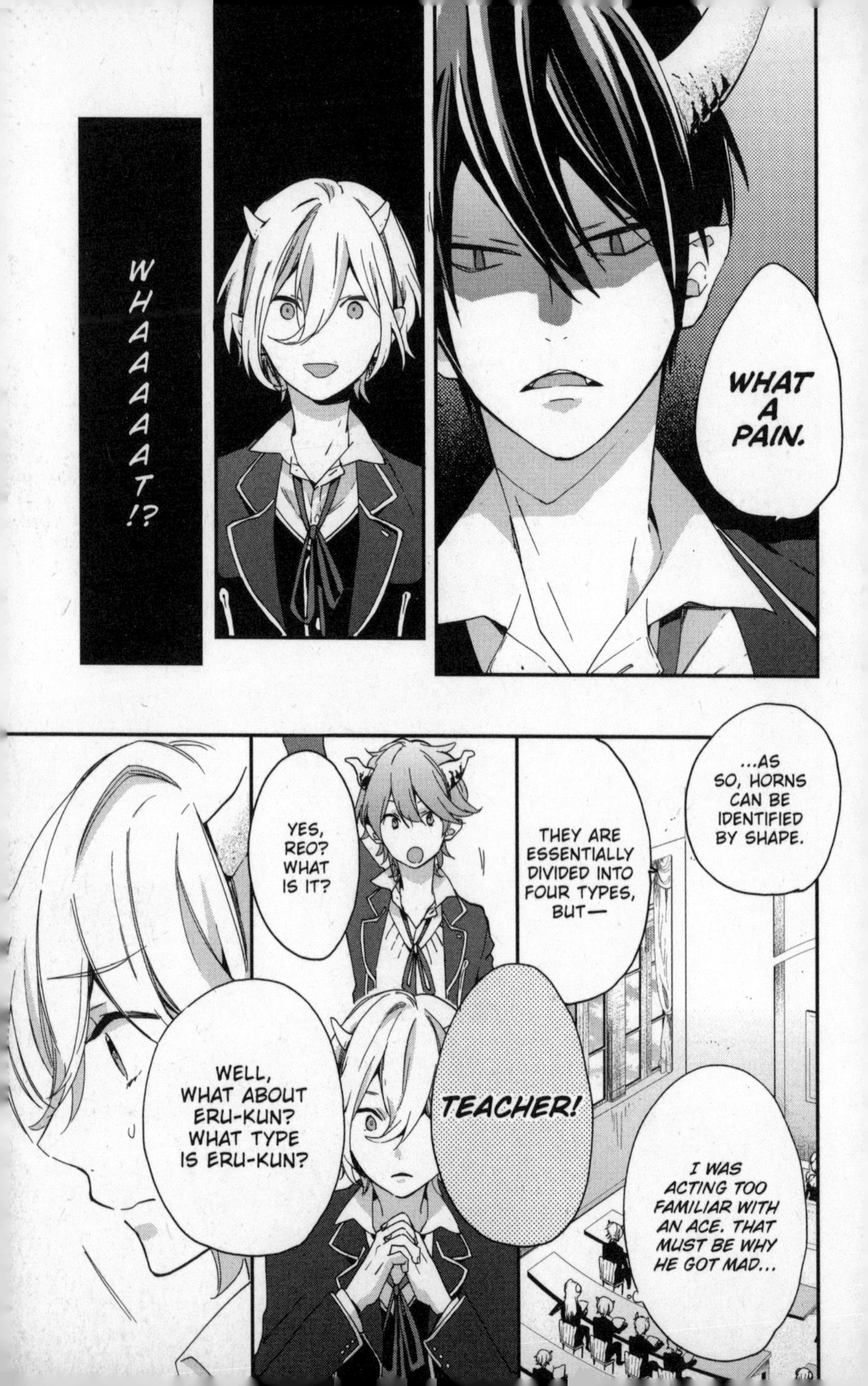
WHAT A PAIN.
WHAAAAAAT!?
...AS SO, HORNS CAN BE IDENTIFIED BY SHAPE.
THEY ARE ESSENTIALLY DIVIDED INTO FOUR TYPES, BUT—
I WAS ACTING TOO FAMILIAR WITH AN ACE. THAT MUST BE WHY HE GOT MAD...
TEACHER!
YES, REO? WHAT IS IT?
WELL, WHAT ABOUT ERU-KUN? WHAT TYPE IS ERU-KUN?

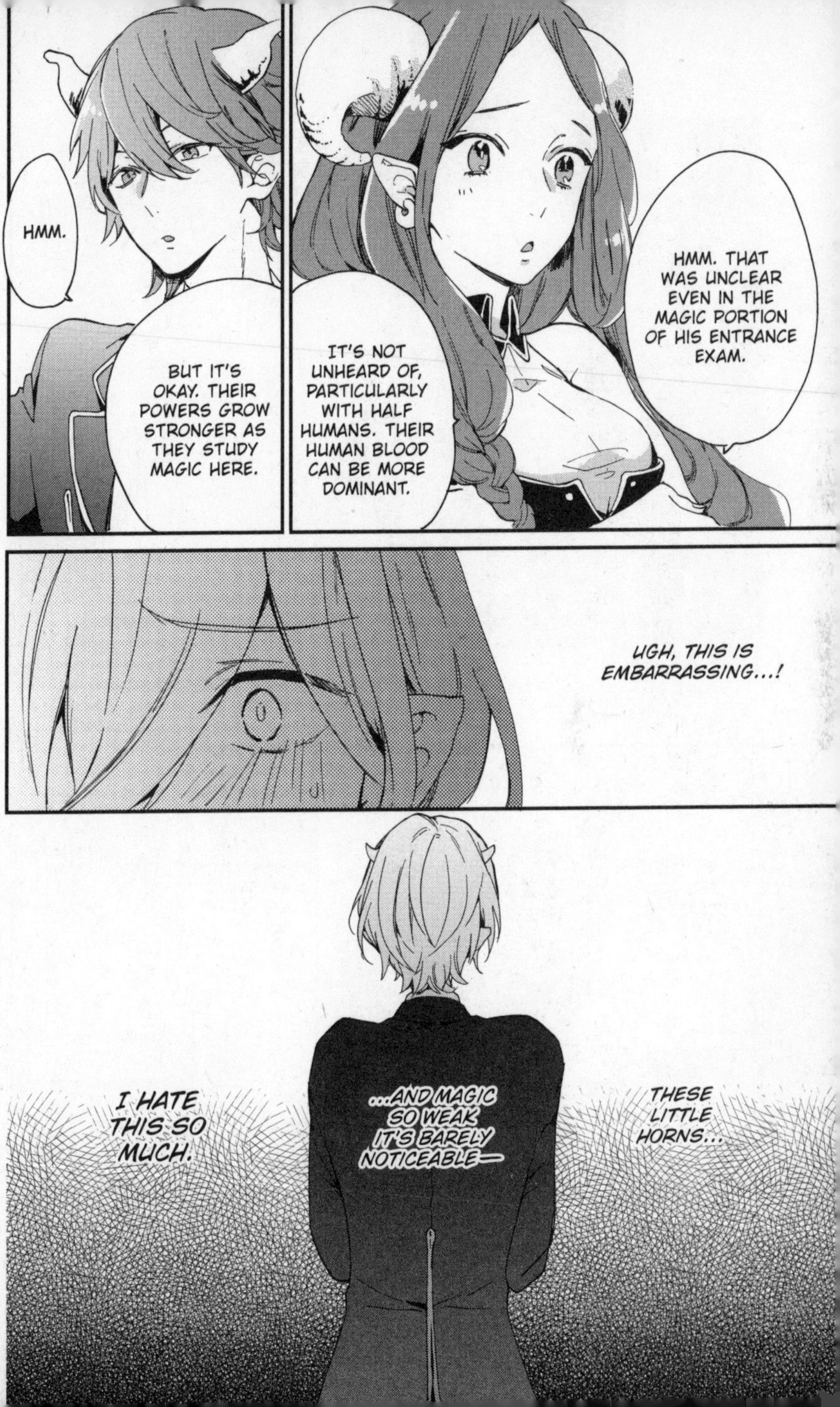
HMM. THAT WAS UNCLEAR EVEN IN THE MAGIC PORTION OF HIS ENTRANCE EXAM.
IT'S NOT UNHEARD OF, PARTICULARLY WITH HALF HUMANS. THEIR HUMAN BLOOD CAN BE MORE DOMINANT.
HMM.
BUT IT'S OKAY. THEIR POWERS GROW STRONGER AS THEY STUDY MAGIC HERE.
UGH, THIS IS EMBARRASSING...!
THESE LITTLE HORNS...
...AND MAGIC SO WEAK IT'S BARELY NOTICEABLE—
I HATE THIS SO MUCH.

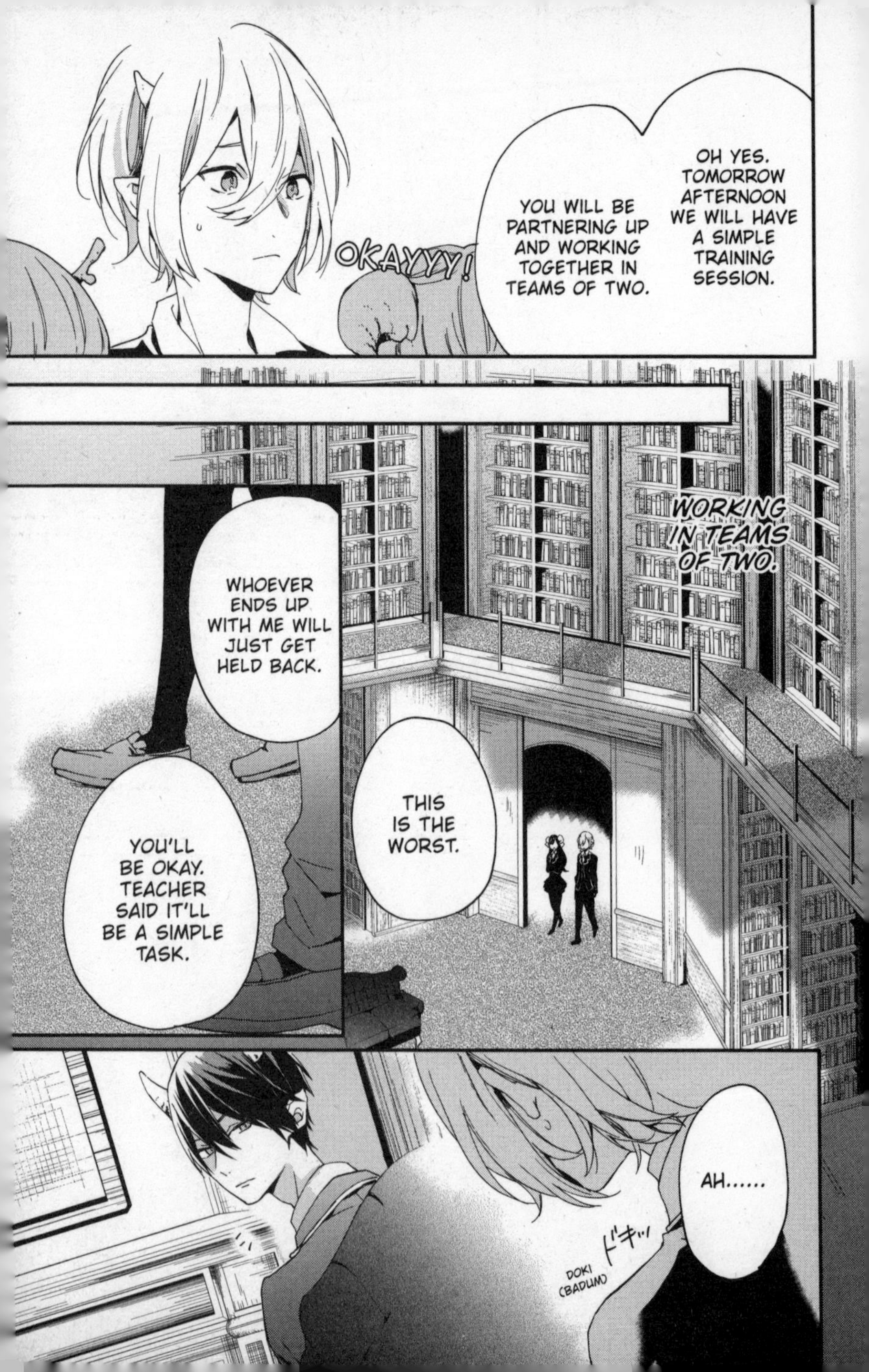
OH YES. TOMORROW AFTERNOON WE WILL HAVE A SIMPLE TRAINING SESSION.
YOU WILL BE PARTNERING UP AND WORKING TOGETHER IN TEAMS OF TWO.
OKAYYY!
WORKING IN TEAMS OF TWO.
THIS IS THE WORST.
WHOEVER ENDS UP WITH ME WILL JUST GET HELD BACK.
YOU'LL BE OKAY. TEACHER SAID IT'LL BE A SIMPLE TASK.
AH......
ドキッ
DOKI (BADUM)

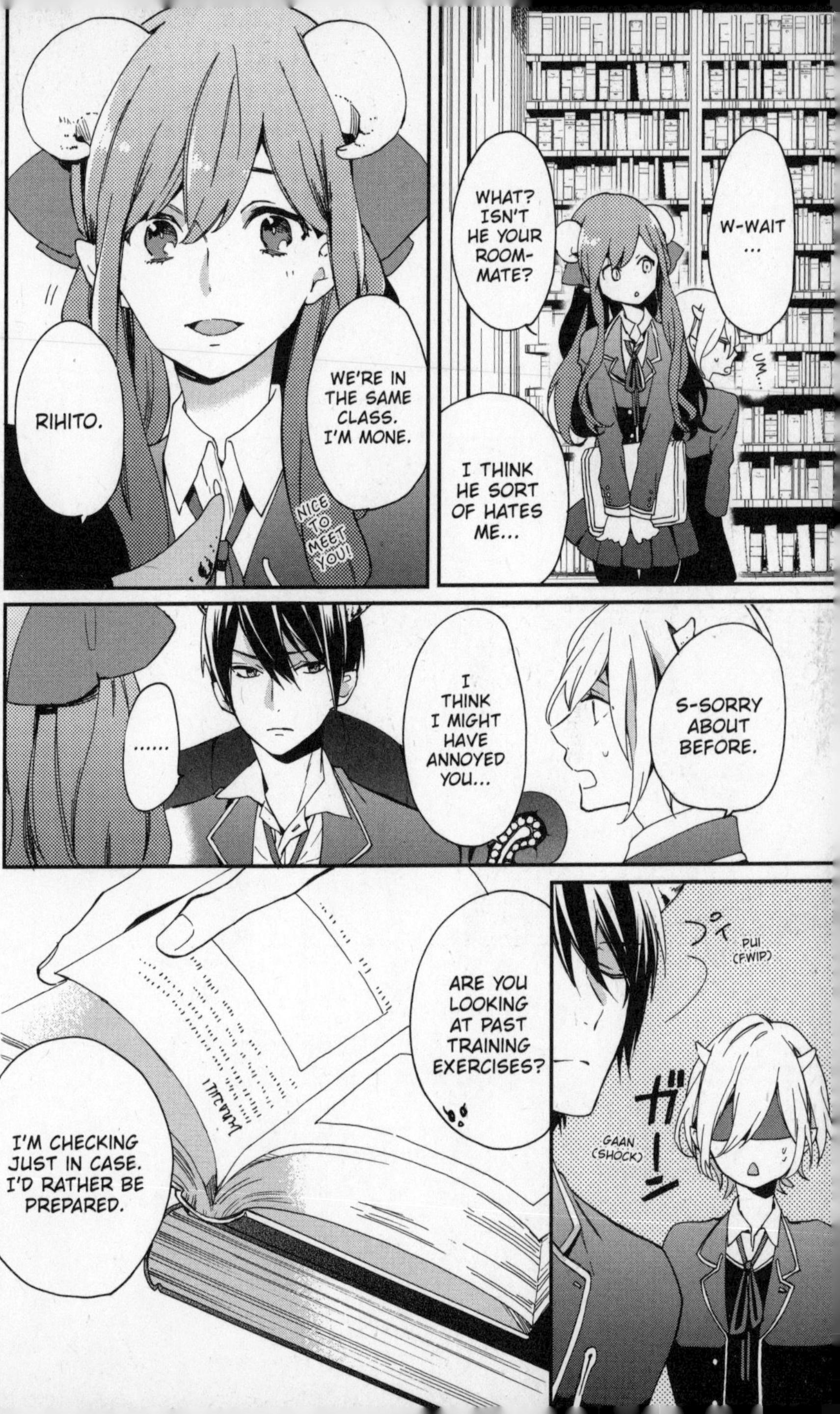
W-WAIT...
UM...
WHAT? ISN'T HE YOUR ROOM-MATE?
I THINK HE SORT OF HATES ME...
WE'RE IN THE SAME CLASS. I'M MONE.
NICE TO MEET YOU!
RIHITO.
S-SORRY ABOUT BEFORE.
I THINK I MIGHT HAVE ANNOYED YOU...
......
PUI (FWIP)
GAAN (SHOCK)
ARE YOU LOOKING AT PAST TRAINING EXERCISES?
I'M CHECKING JUST IN CASE. I'D RATHER BE PREPARED.

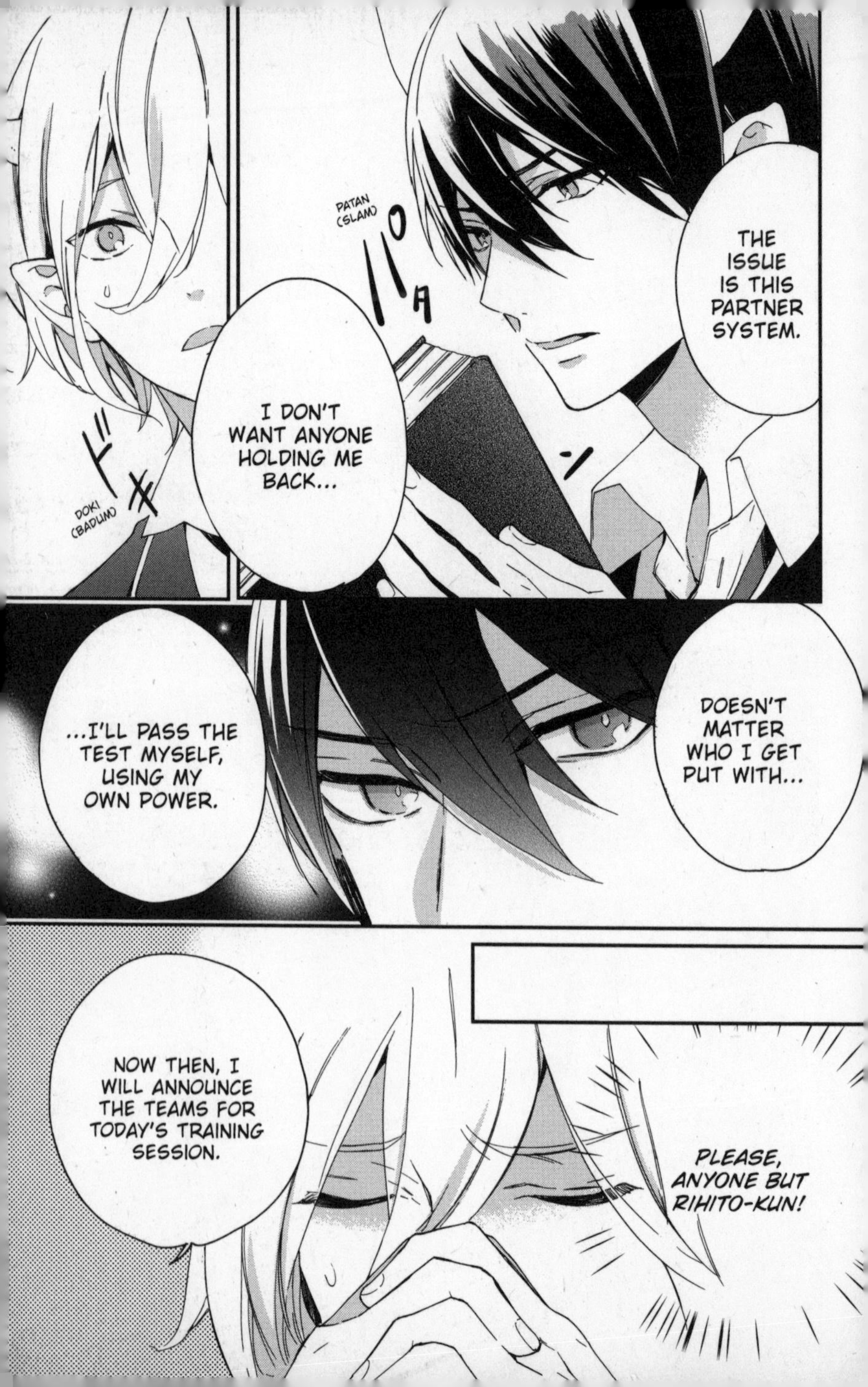
THE ISSUE IS THIS PARTNER SYSTEM.
PATAN (SLAM)
I DON'T WANT ANYONE HOLDING ME BACK...
DOKI (BADUM)
DOESN'T MATTER WHO I GET PUT WITH...
...I'LL PASS THE TEST MYSELF, USING MY OWN POWER.
NOW THEN, I WILL ANNOUNCE THE TEAMS FOR TODAY'S TRAINING SESSION.
PLEASE, ANYONE BUT RIHITO-KUN!

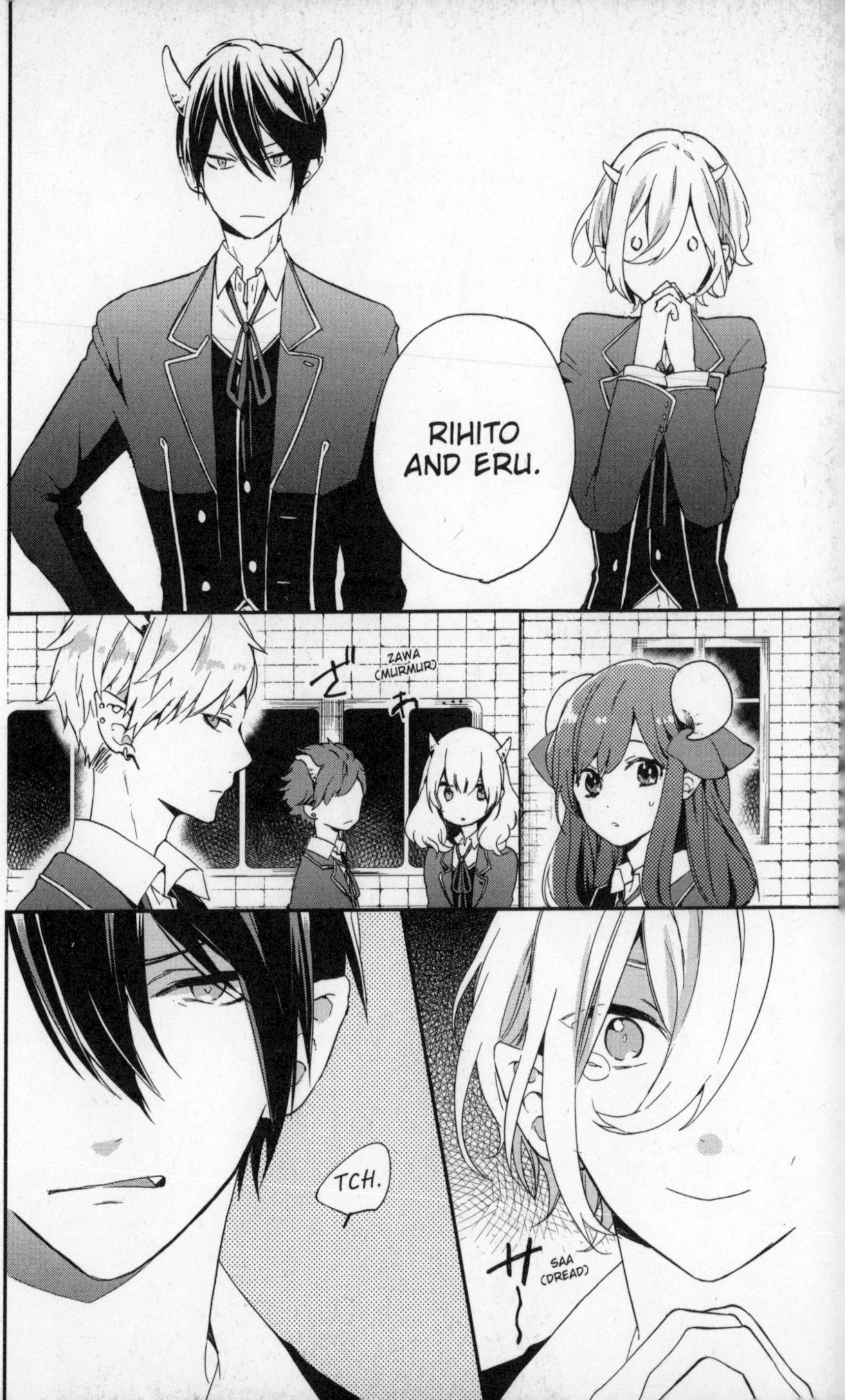
RIHITO AND ERU.
ZAWA (MURMUR)
TCH.
SAA (DREAD)

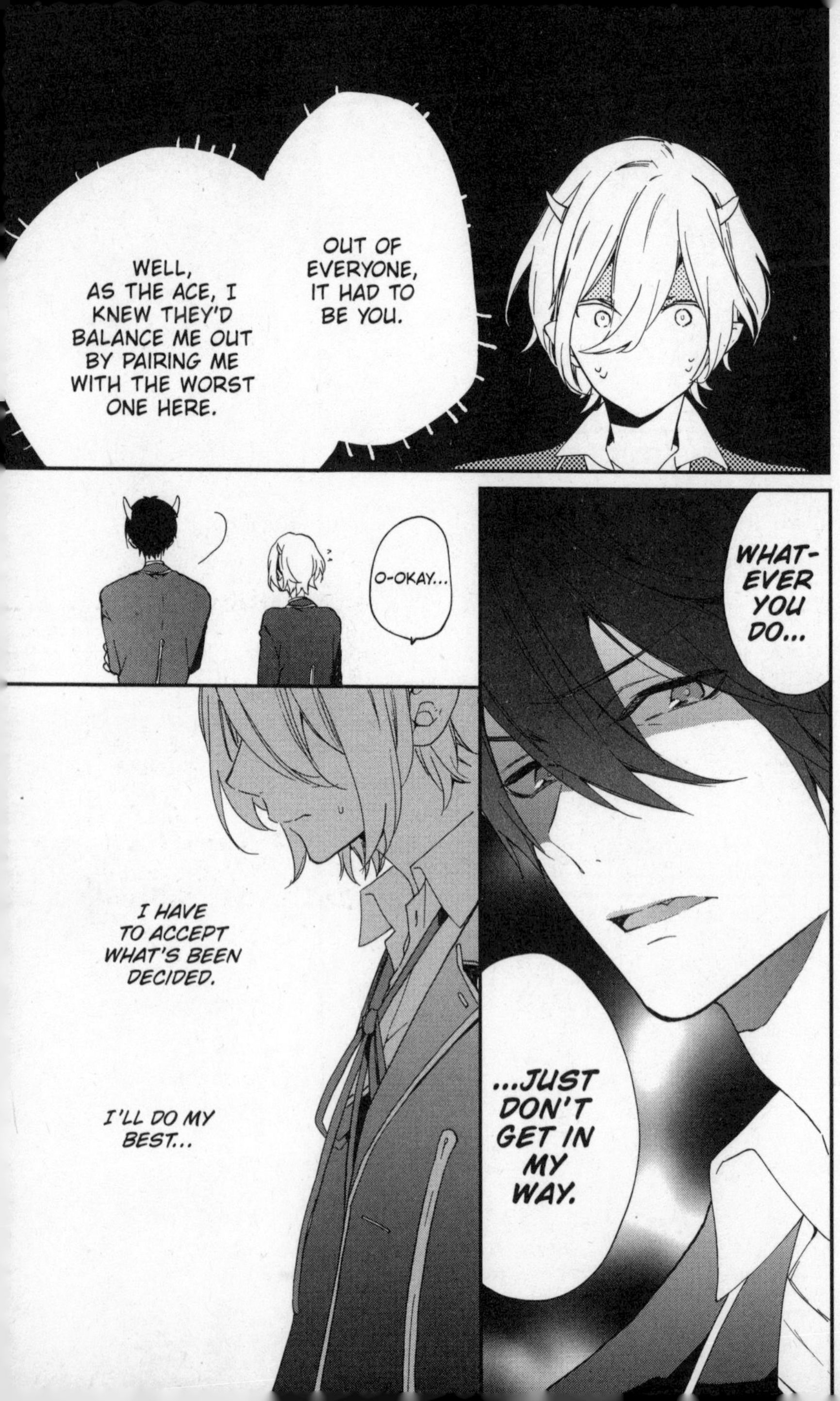
OUT OF EVERYONE, IT HAD TO BE YOU.
WELL, AS THE ACE, I KNEW THEY'D BALANCE ME OUT BY PAIRING ME WITH THE WORST ONE HERE.
WHAT-EVER YOU DO...
...JUST DON'T GET IN MY WAY.
O-OKAY...
I HAVE TO ACCEPT WHAT'S BEEN DECIDED.
I'LL DO MY BEST...

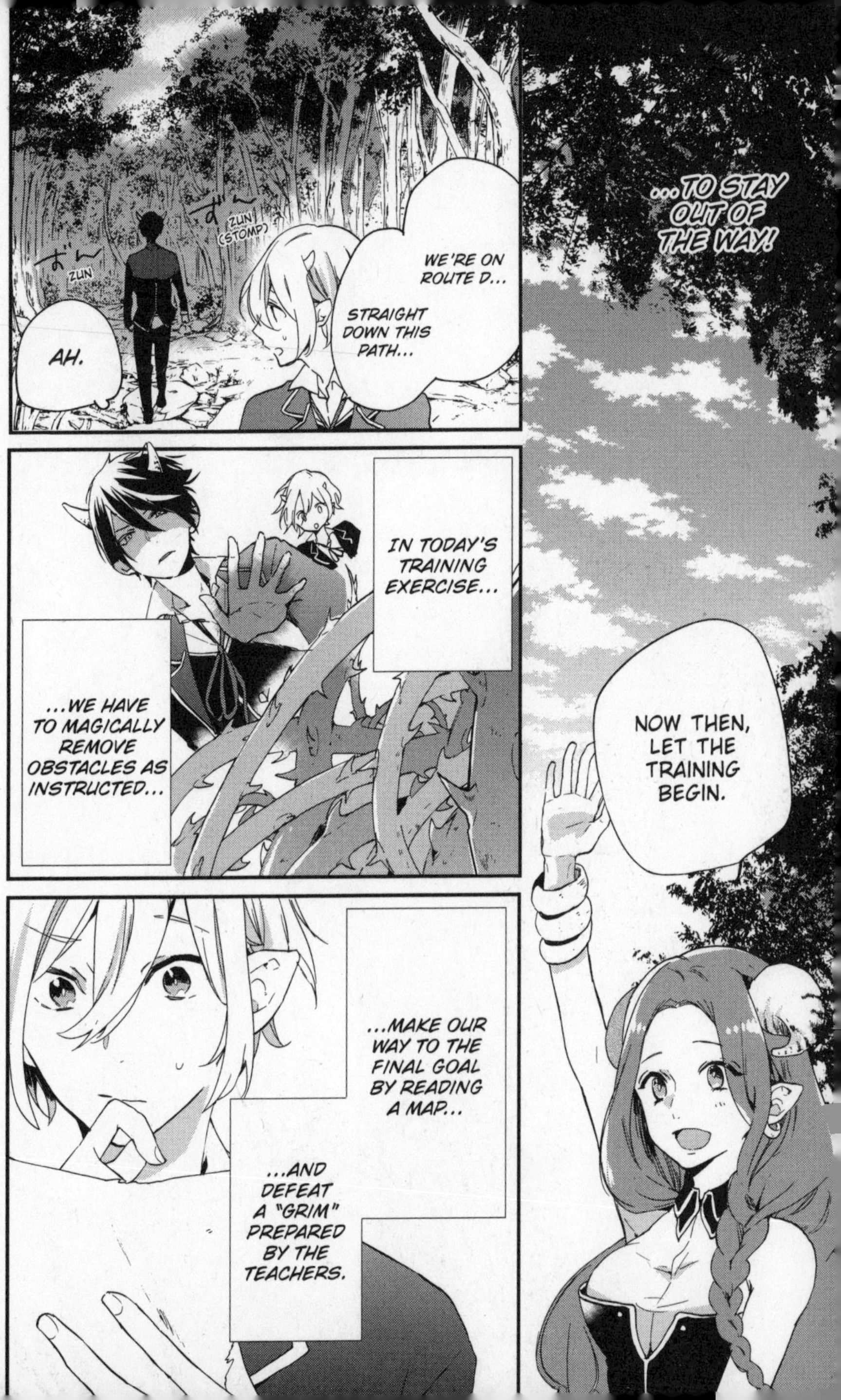
...TO STAY OUT OF THE WAY!
NOW THEN, LET THE TRAINING BEGIN.
WE'RE ON ROUTE D...
STRAIGHT DOWN THIS PATH...
ずん
ZUN (STOMP)
ずん
ZUN
AH.
IN TODAY'S TRAINING EXERCISE...
...WE HAVE TO MAGICALLY REMOVE OBSTACLES AS INSTRUCTED...
...MAKE OUR WAY TO THE FINAL GOAL BY READING A MAP...
...AND DEFEAT A "GRIM" PREPARED BY THE TEACHERS.

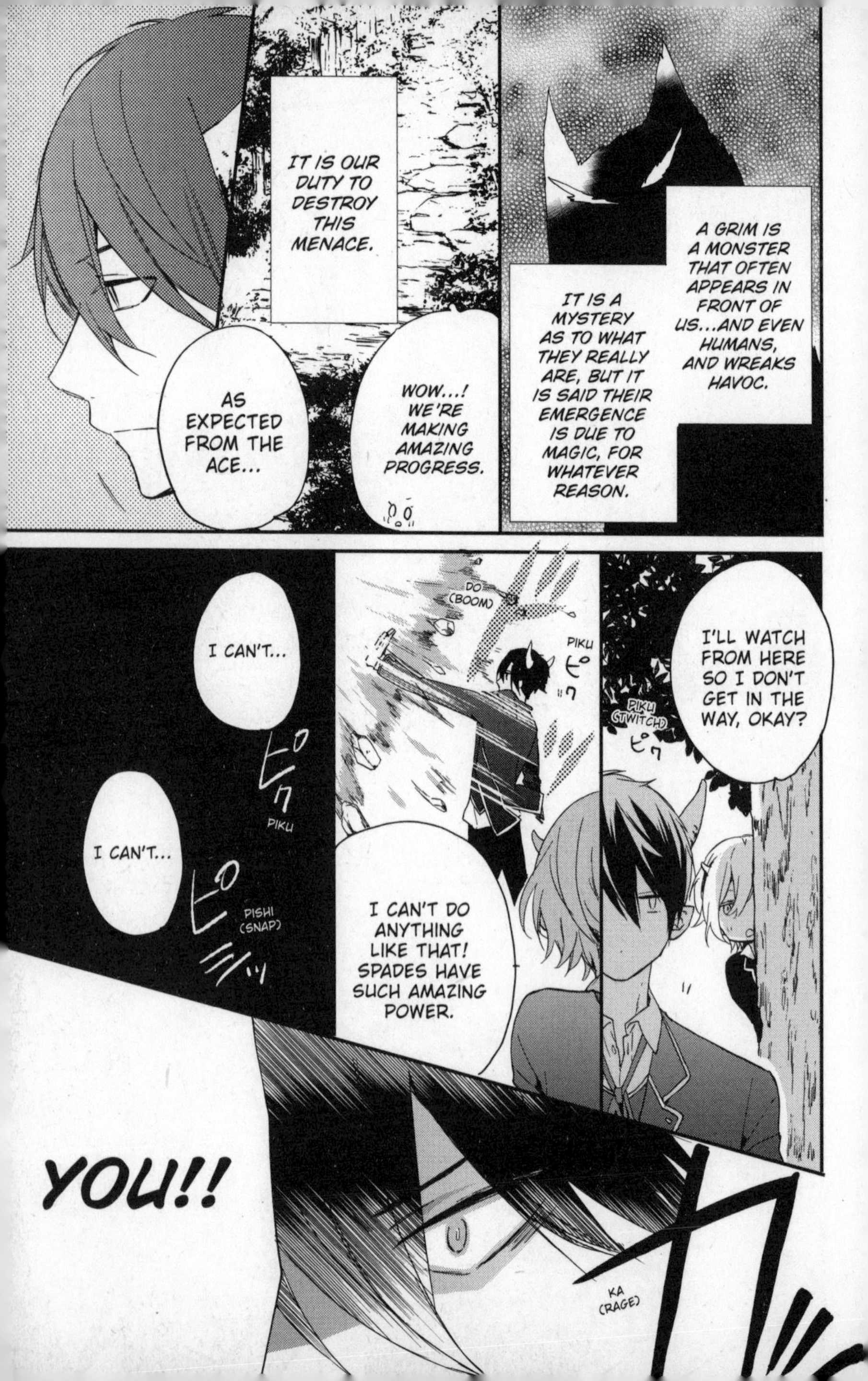
A GRIM IS A MONSTER THAT OFTEN APPEARS IN FRONT OF US...AND EVEN HUMANS, AND WREAKS HAVOC.
IT IS A MYSTERY AS TO WHAT THEY REALLY ARE, BUT IT IS SAID THEIR EMERGENCE IS DUE TO MAGIC, FOR WHATEVER REASON.
IT IS OUR DUTY TO DESTROY THIS MENACE.
WOW...! WE'RE MAKING AMAZING PROGRESS.
AS EXPECTED FROM THE ACE...
I'LL WATCH FROM HERE SO I DON'T GET IN THE WAY, OKAY?
PIKU (TWITCH)
DO (BOOM)
PIKU
I CAN'T DO ANYTHING LIKE THAT! SPADES HAVE SUCH AMAZING POWER.
I CAN'T...
PIKU
I CAN'T...
PISHI (SNAP)
KA (RAGE)
YOU!!

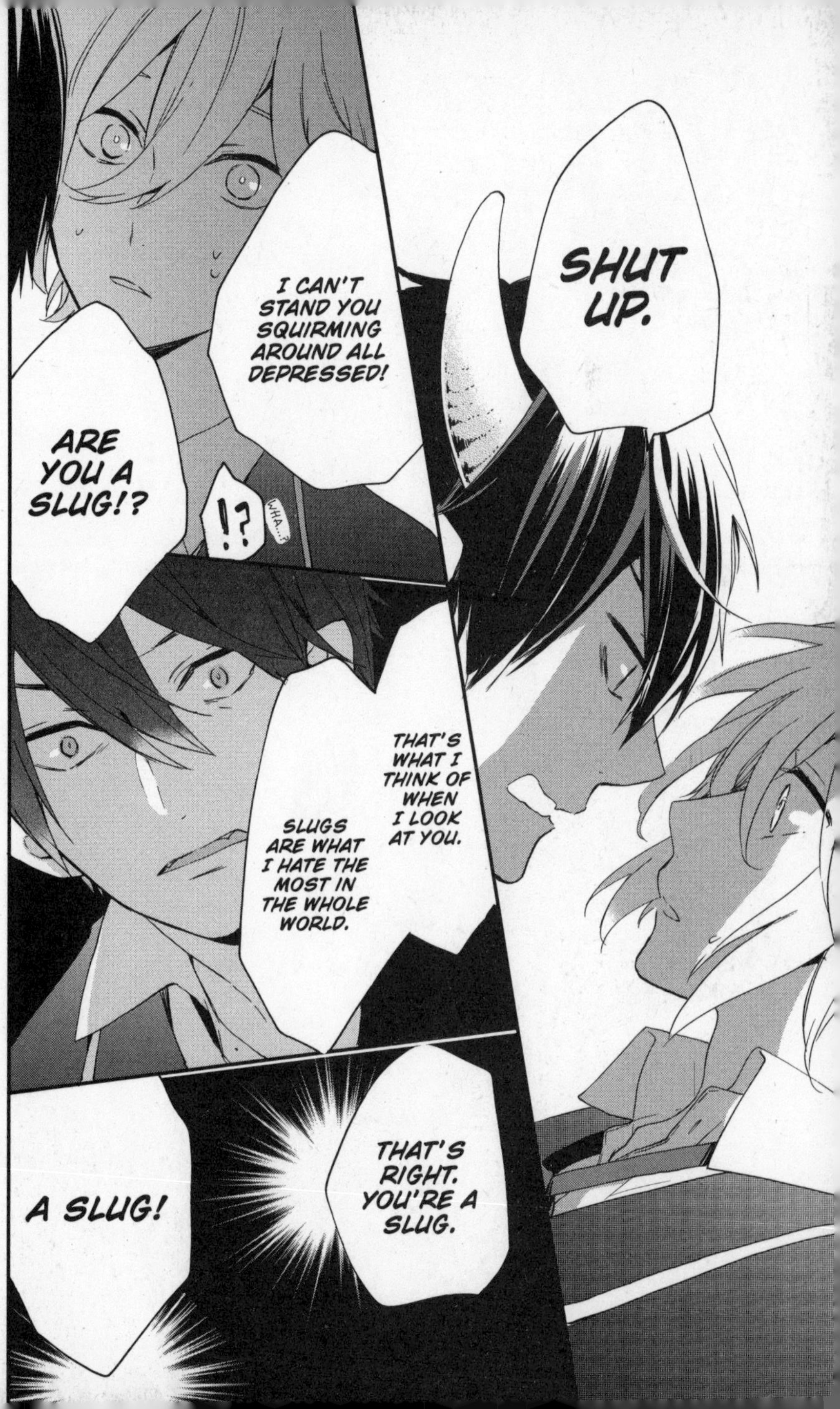
SHUT UP.
I CAN'T STAND YOU SQUIRMING AROUND ALL DEPRESSED!
ARE YOU A SLUG!?
!?
WHA...!?
THAT'S WHAT I THINK OF WHEN I LOOK AT YOU.
SLUGS ARE WHAT I HATE THE MOST IN THE WHOLE WORLD.
THAT'S RIGHT. YOU'RE A SLUG.
A SLUG!

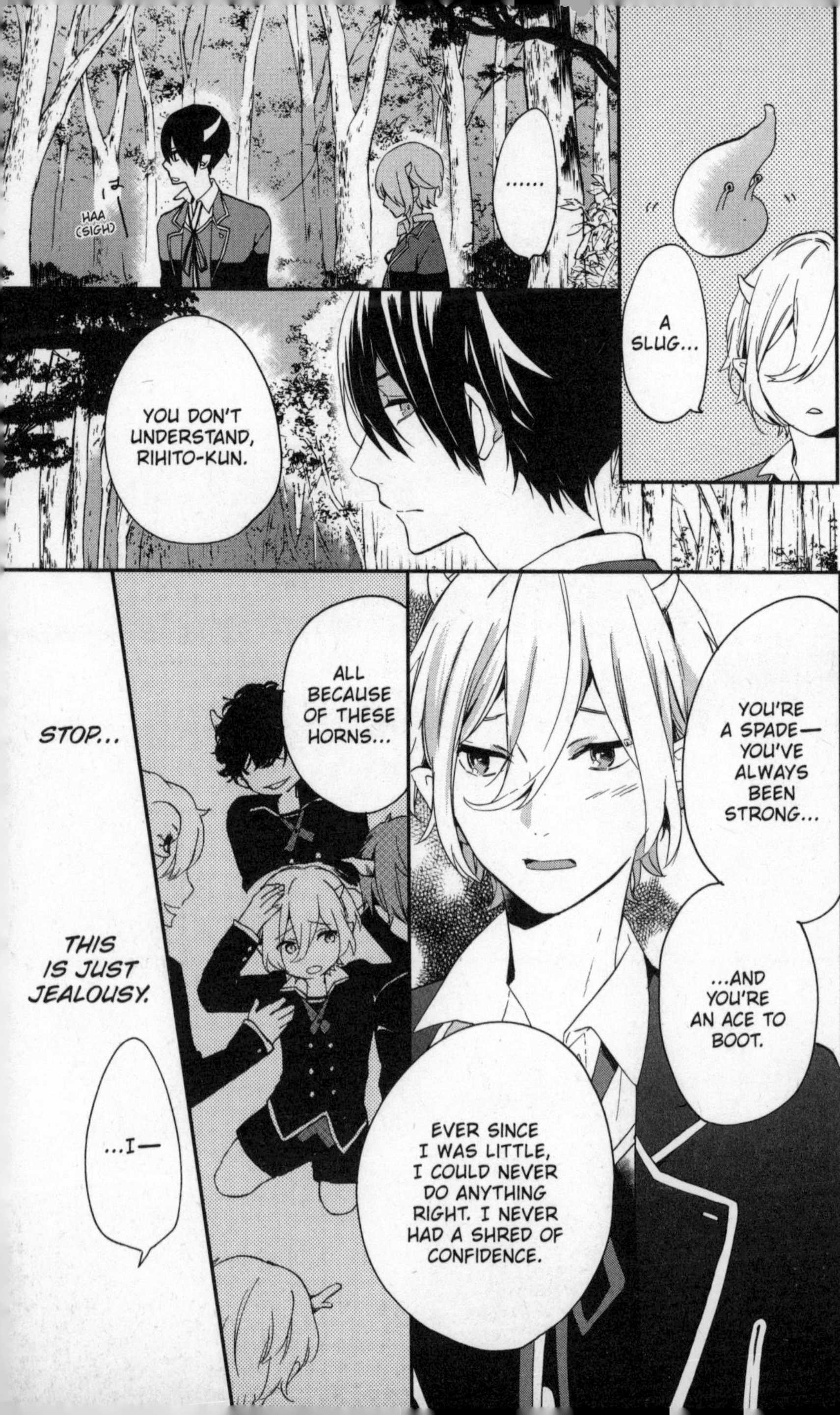
A SLUG...
HAA (SIGH)
......
YOU DON'T UNDERSTAND, RIHITO-KUN.
YOU'RE A SPADE—YOU'VE ALWAYS BEEN STRONG...
...AND YOU'RE AN ACE TO BOOT.
EVER SINCE I WAS LITTLE, I COULD NEVER DO ANYTHING RIGHT. I NEVER HAD A SHRED OF CONFIDENCE.
ALL BECAUSE OF THESE HORNS...
STOP...
THIS IS JUST JEALOUSY.
...I—

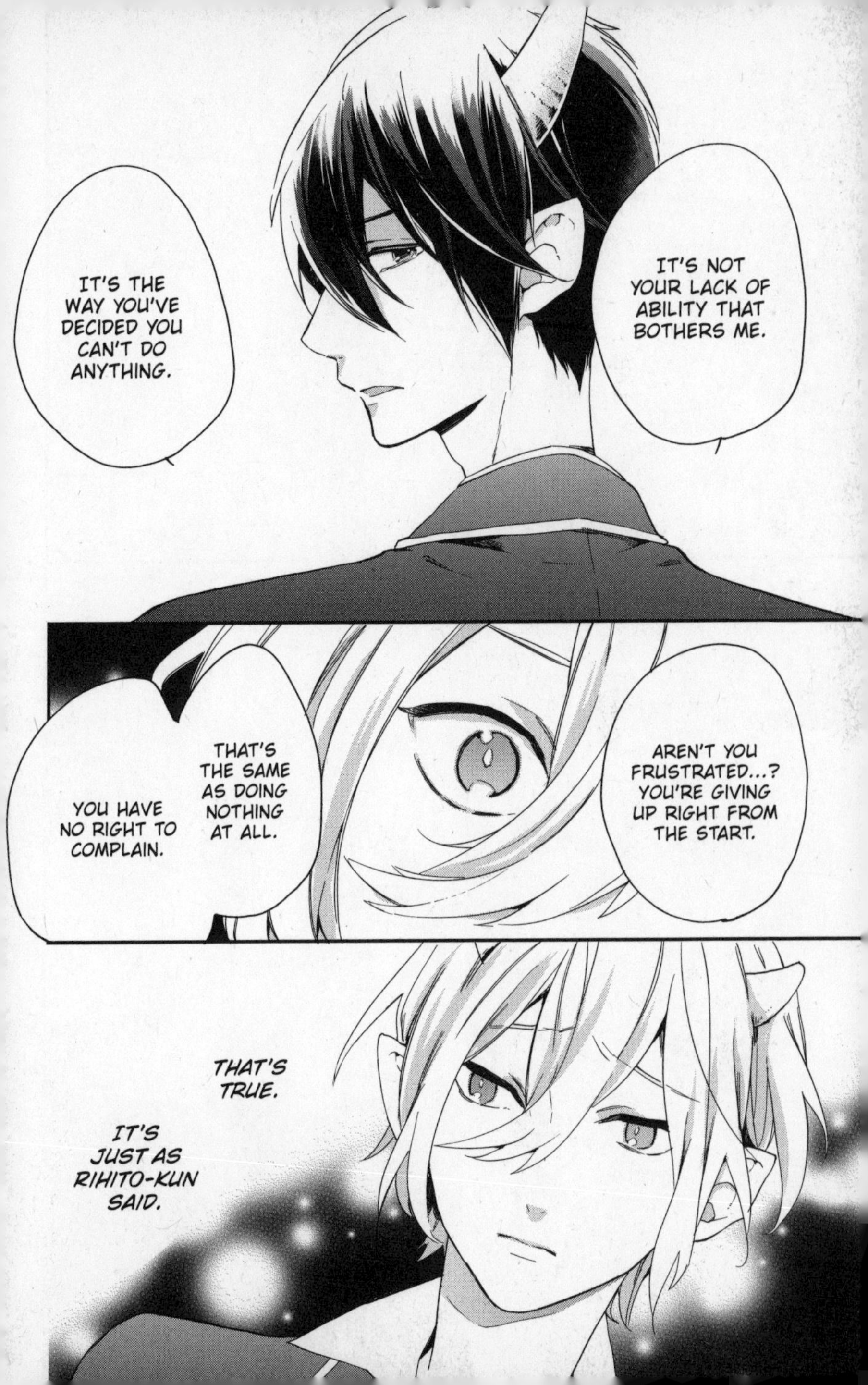
IT'S NOT YOUR LACK OF ABILITY THAT BOTHERS ME.
IT'S THE WAY YOU'VE DECIDED YOU CAN'T DO ANYTHING.
AREN'T YOU FRUSTRATED...? YOU'RE GIVING UP RIGHT FROM THE START.
THAT'S THE SAME AS DOING NOTHING AT ALL.
YOU HAVE NO RIGHT TO COMPLAIN.
THAT'S TRUE.
IT'S JUST AS RIHITO-KUN SAID.

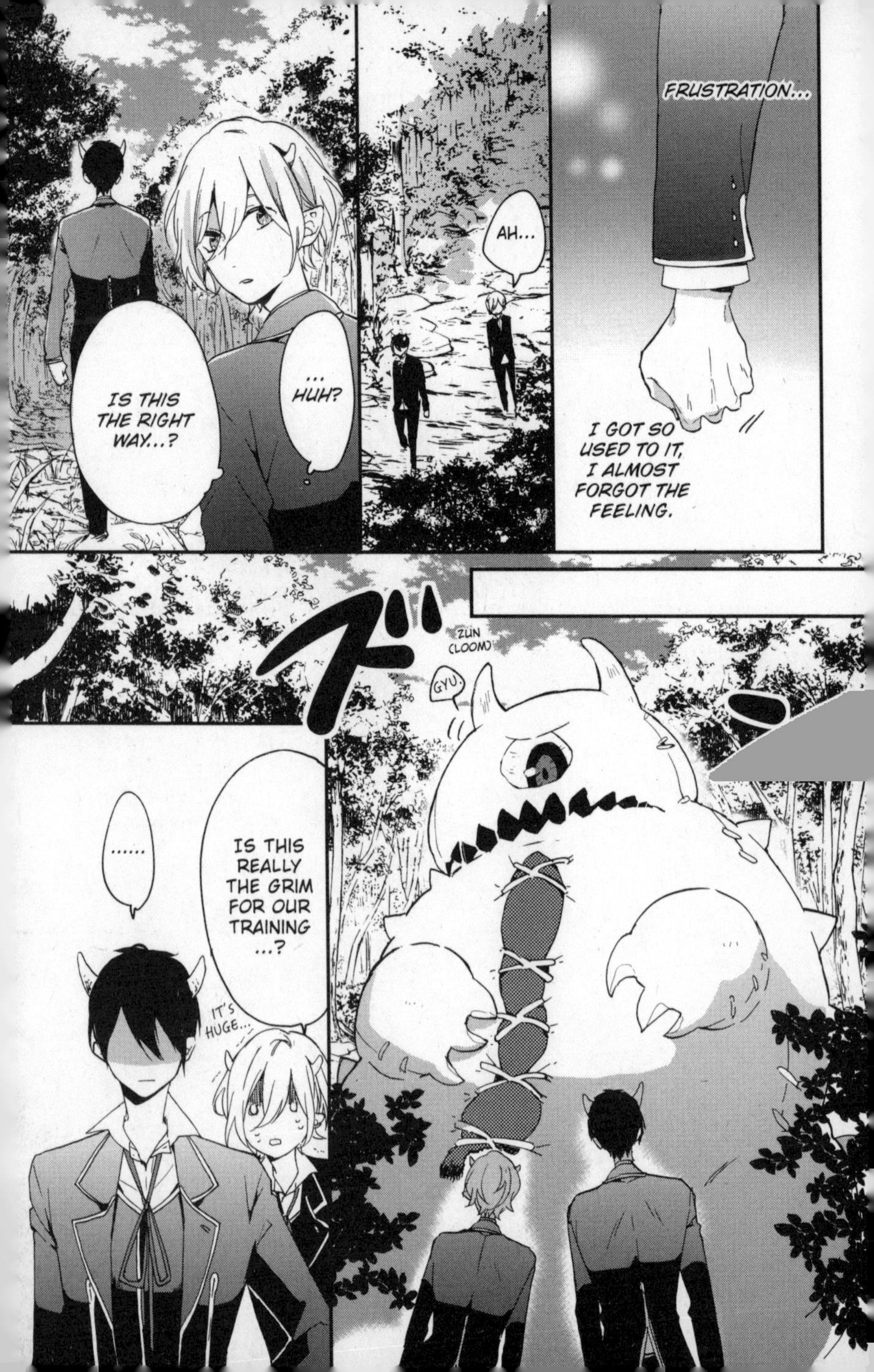
FRUSTRATION...
I GOT SO USED TO IT, I ALMOST FORGOT THE FEELING.
AH...
... HUH?
IS THIS THE RIGHT WAY...?
ZUN (LOOM)
ズ
GYU.
IS THIS REALLY THE GRIM FOR OUR TRAINING ...?
......
IT'S HUGE...

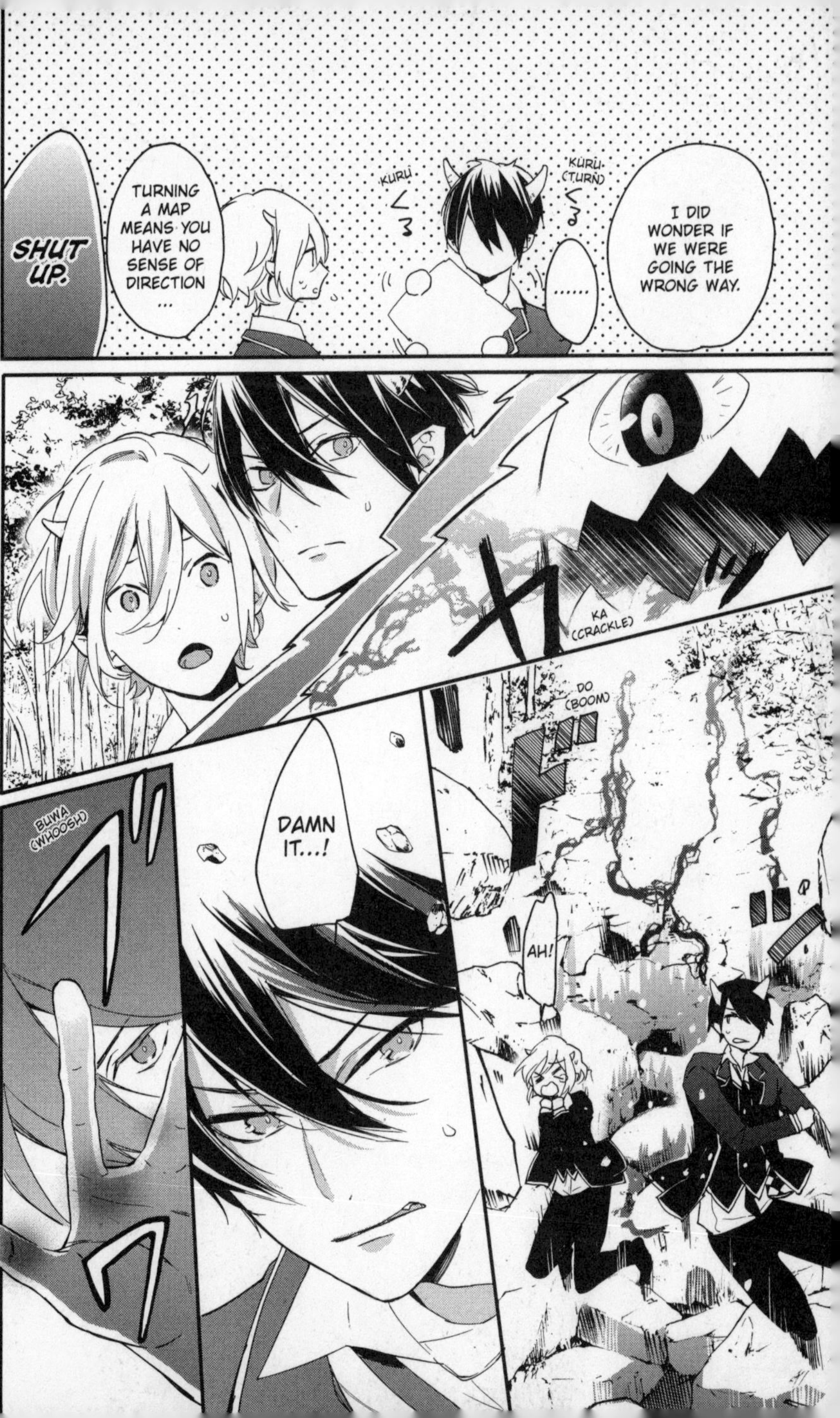
I DID WONDER IF WE WERE GOING THE WRONG WAY.
KURU (TURN)
......
KURU
TURNING A MAP MEANS YOU HAVE NO SENSE OF DIRECTION ...
SHUT UP.
KA (CRACKLE)
DO (BOOM)
AH!
DAMN IT...!
BUWA (WHOOSH)

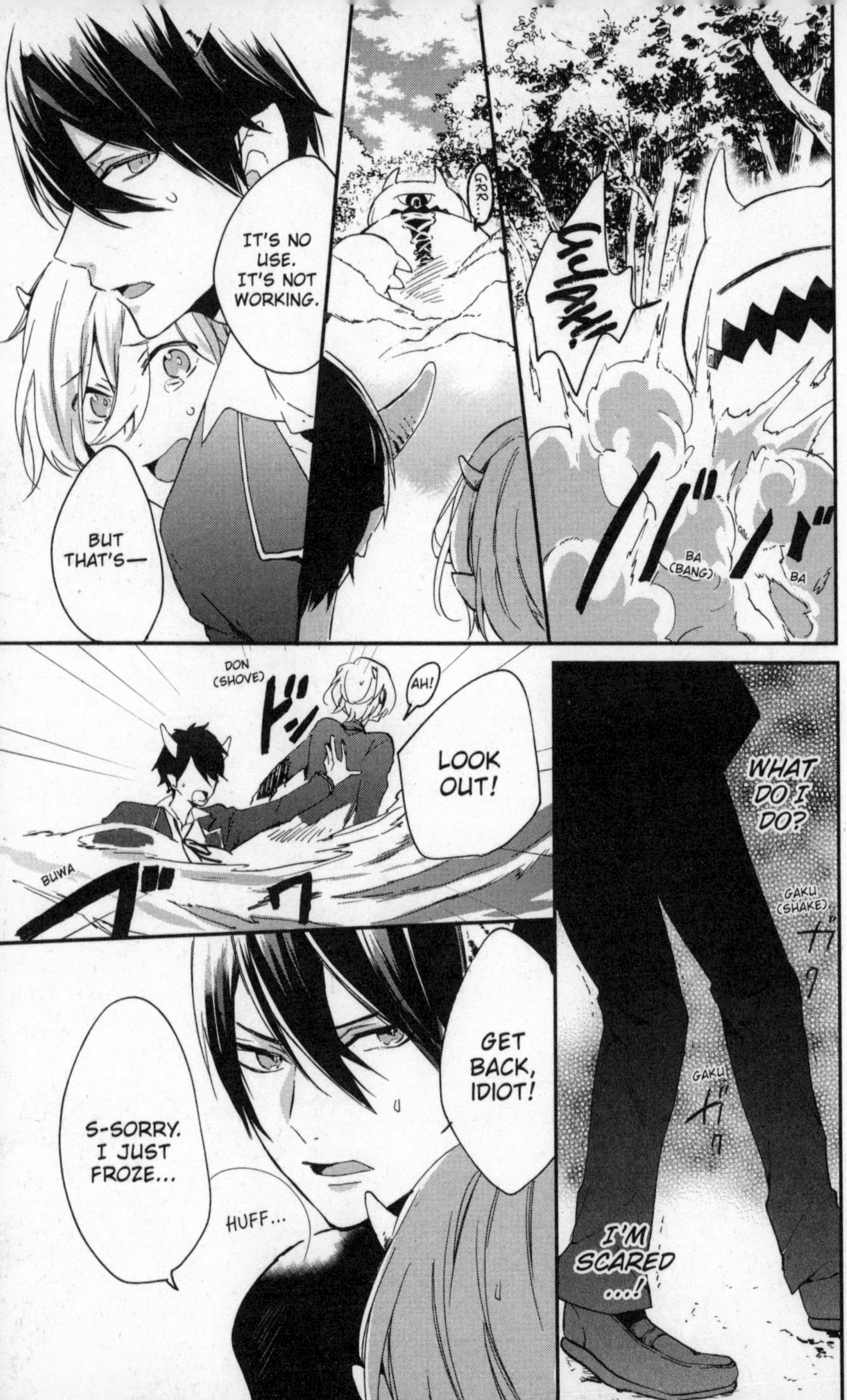
WHAM!
BA (BANG)
BA
GRR...
IT'S NO USE. IT'S NOT WORKING.
BUT THAT'S—
WHAT DO I DO?
GAKU (SHAKE)
GAKU
I'M SCARED...!
DON (SHOVE)
AH!
LOOK OUT!
BUWA
GET BACK, IDIOT!
S-SORRY. I JUST FROZE...
HUFF...

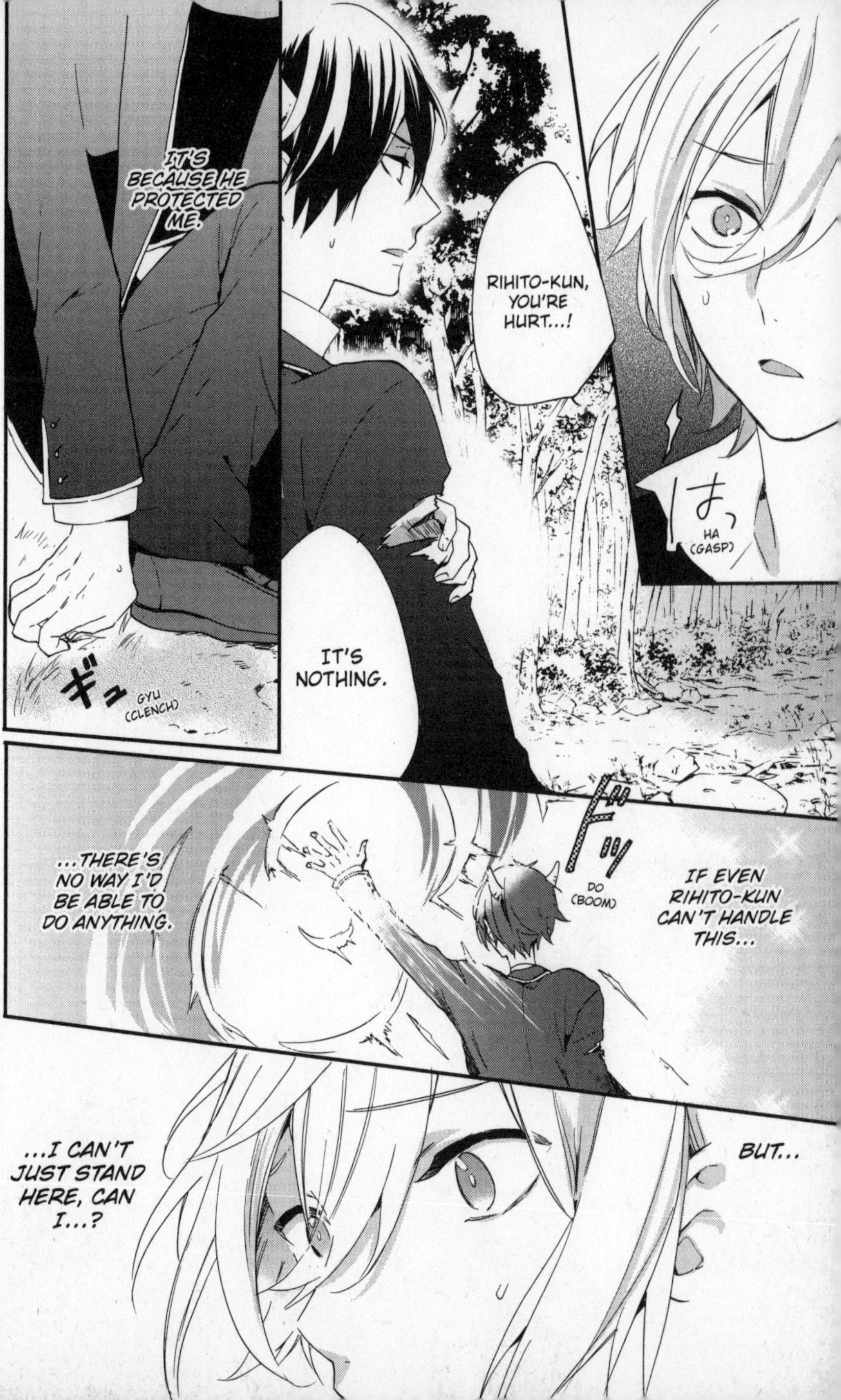
RIHITO-KUN, YOU'RE HURT...!
はっ
HA (GASP)
IT'S NOTHING.
IT'S BECAUSE HE PROTECTED ME.
ギュ
GYU (CLENCH)
IF EVEN RIHITO-KUN CAN'T HANDLE THIS...
ドッ
DO (BOOM)
...THERE'S NO WAY I'D BE ABLE TO DO ANYTHING.
BUT...
...I CAN'T JUST STAND HERE, CAN I...?

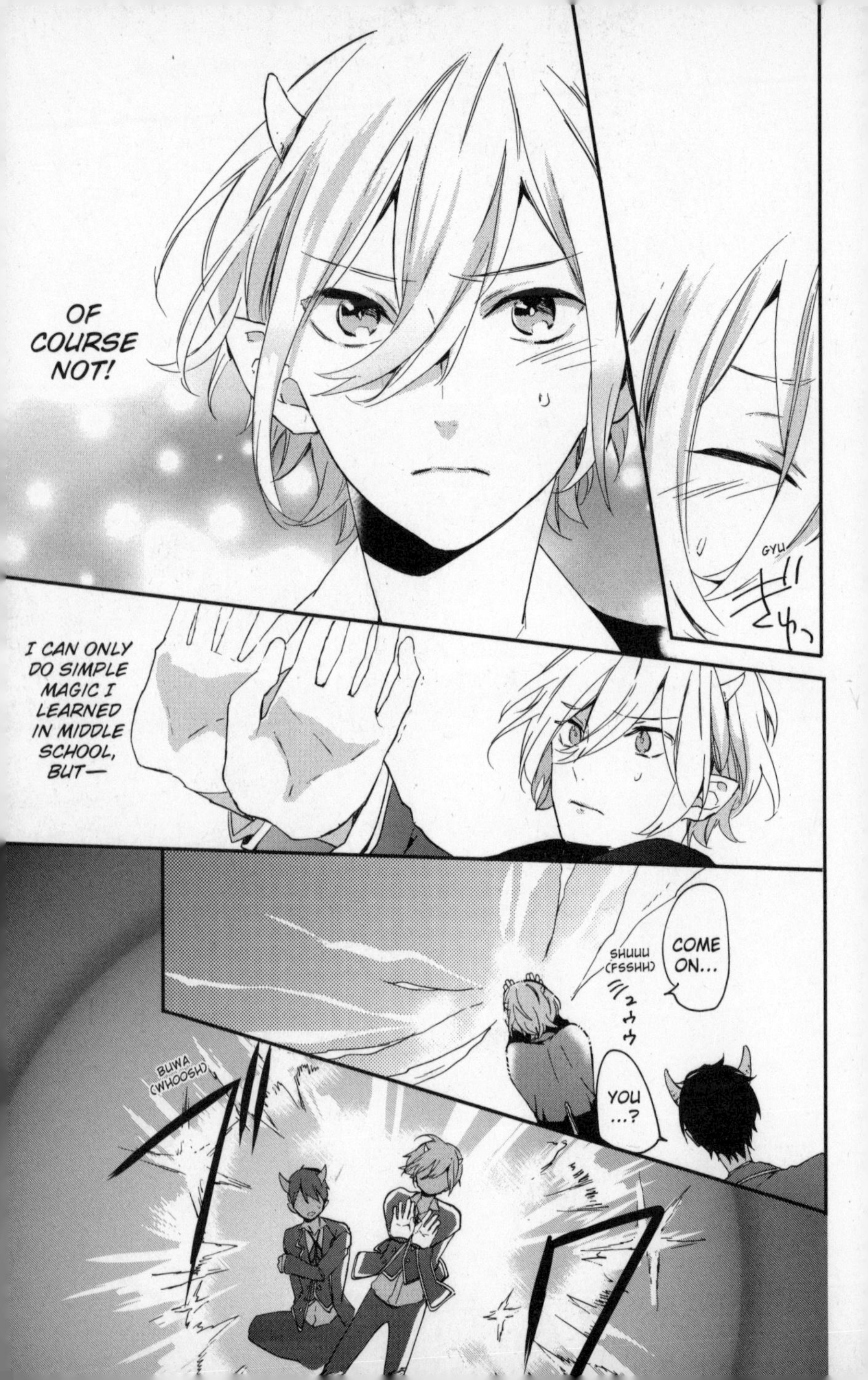
GYU
ぎゅっ
OF COURSE NOT!
I CAN ONLY DO SIMPLE MAGIC I LEARNED IN MIDDLE SCHOOL, BUT—
COME ON...
SHUUU (FSSHH)
シュウウ
YOU ...?
BUWA (WHOOSH)

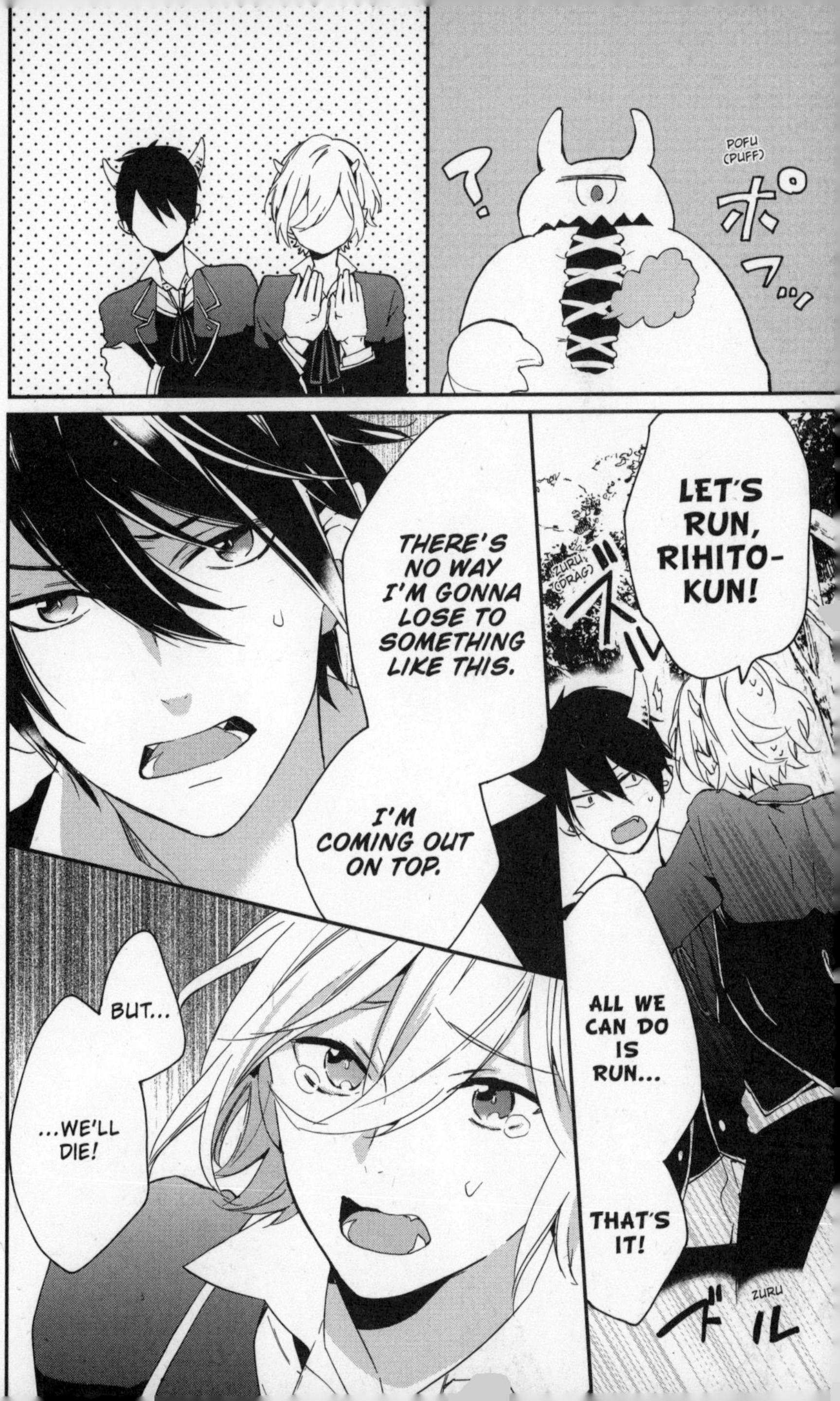
POFU (PUFF)
LET'S RUN, RIHITO-KUN!
ZURU (DRAG)
THERE'S NO WAY I'M GONNA LOSE TO SOMETHING LIKE THIS.
I'M COMING OUT ON TOP.
ALL WE CAN DO IS RUN...
THAT'S IT!
ZURU
BUT...
...WE'LL DIE!

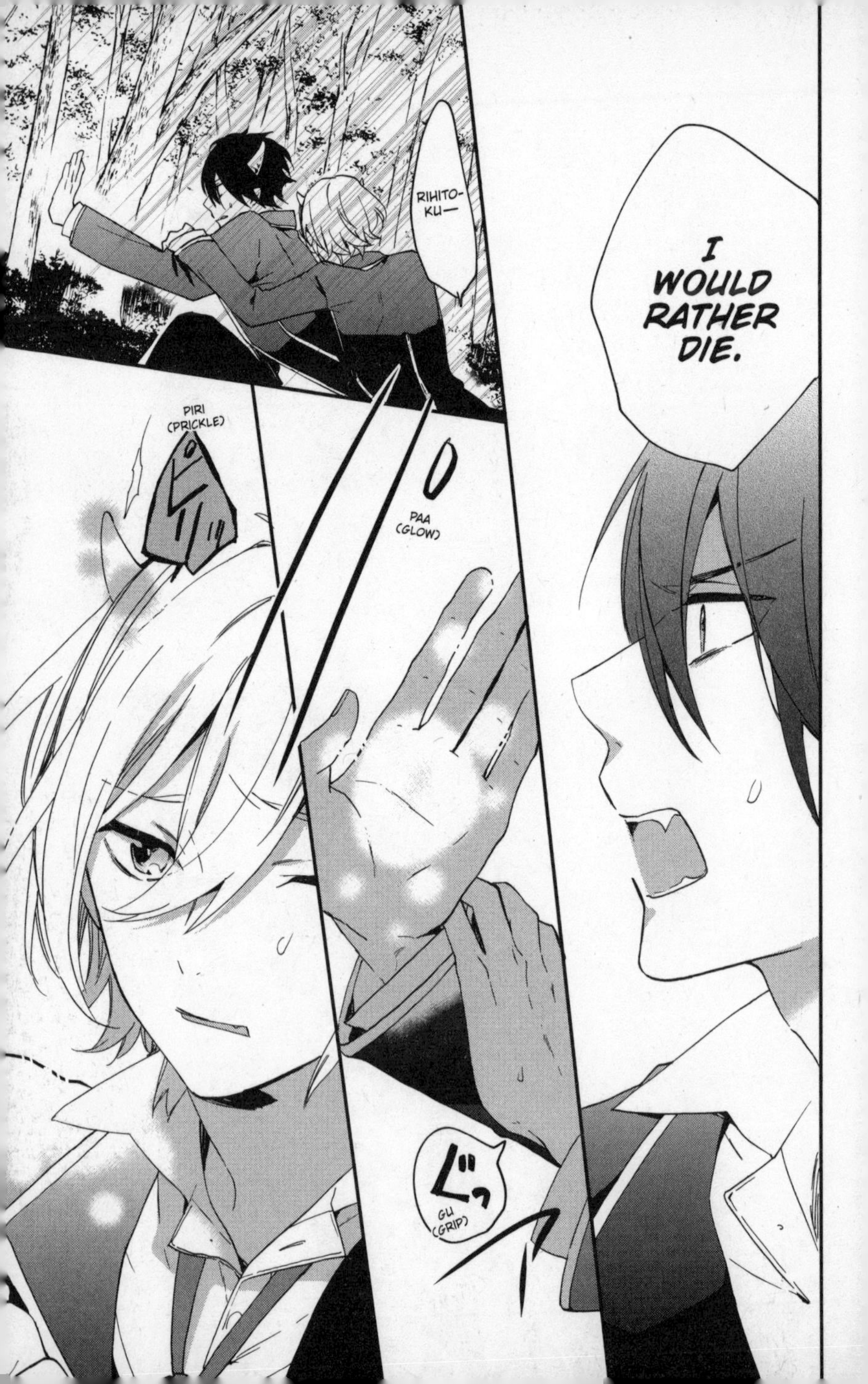
I WOULD RATHER DIE.
RIHITO-KU—
PAA (GLOW)
ぐっ
GU (GRIP)
PIRI (PRICKLE)

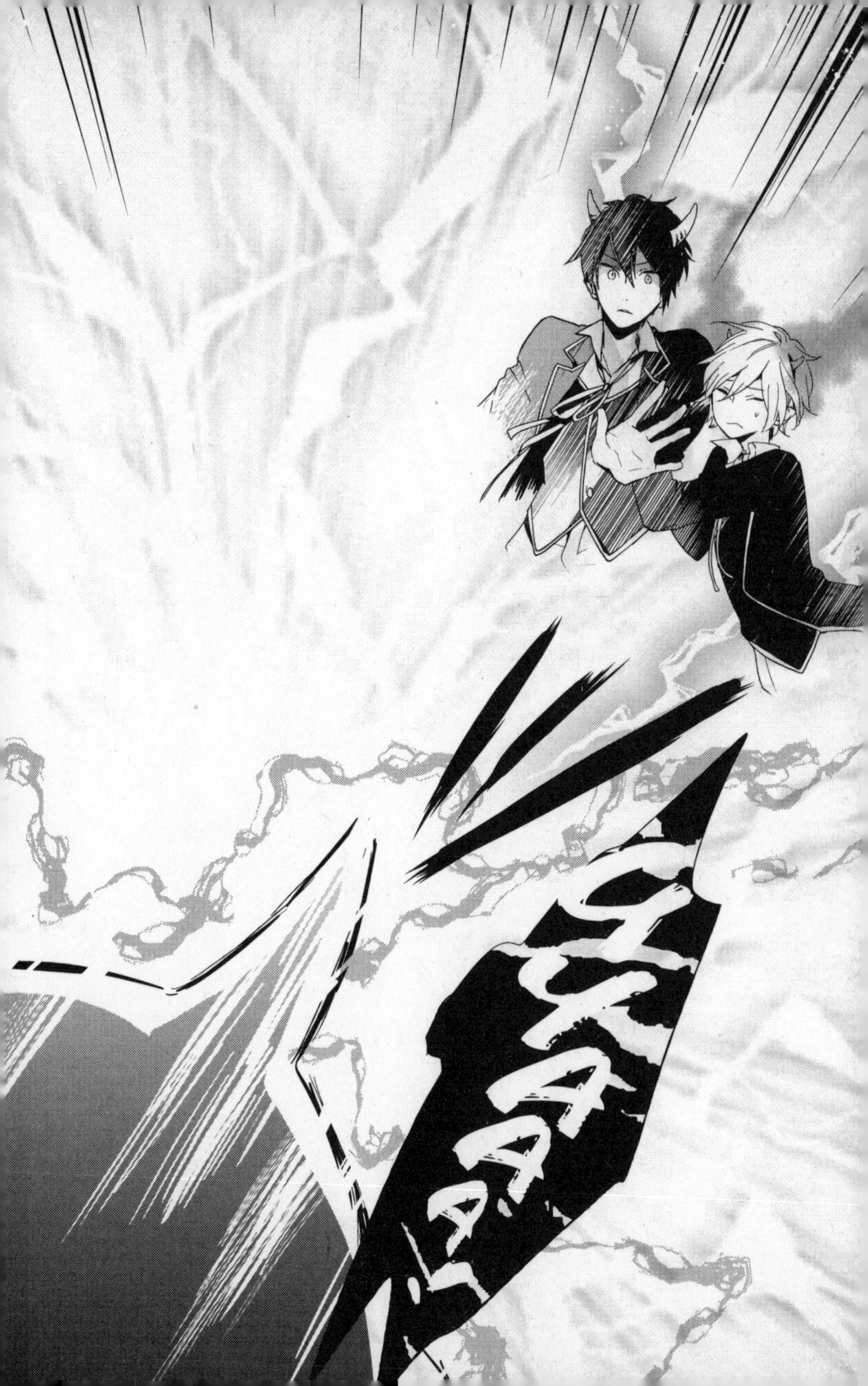

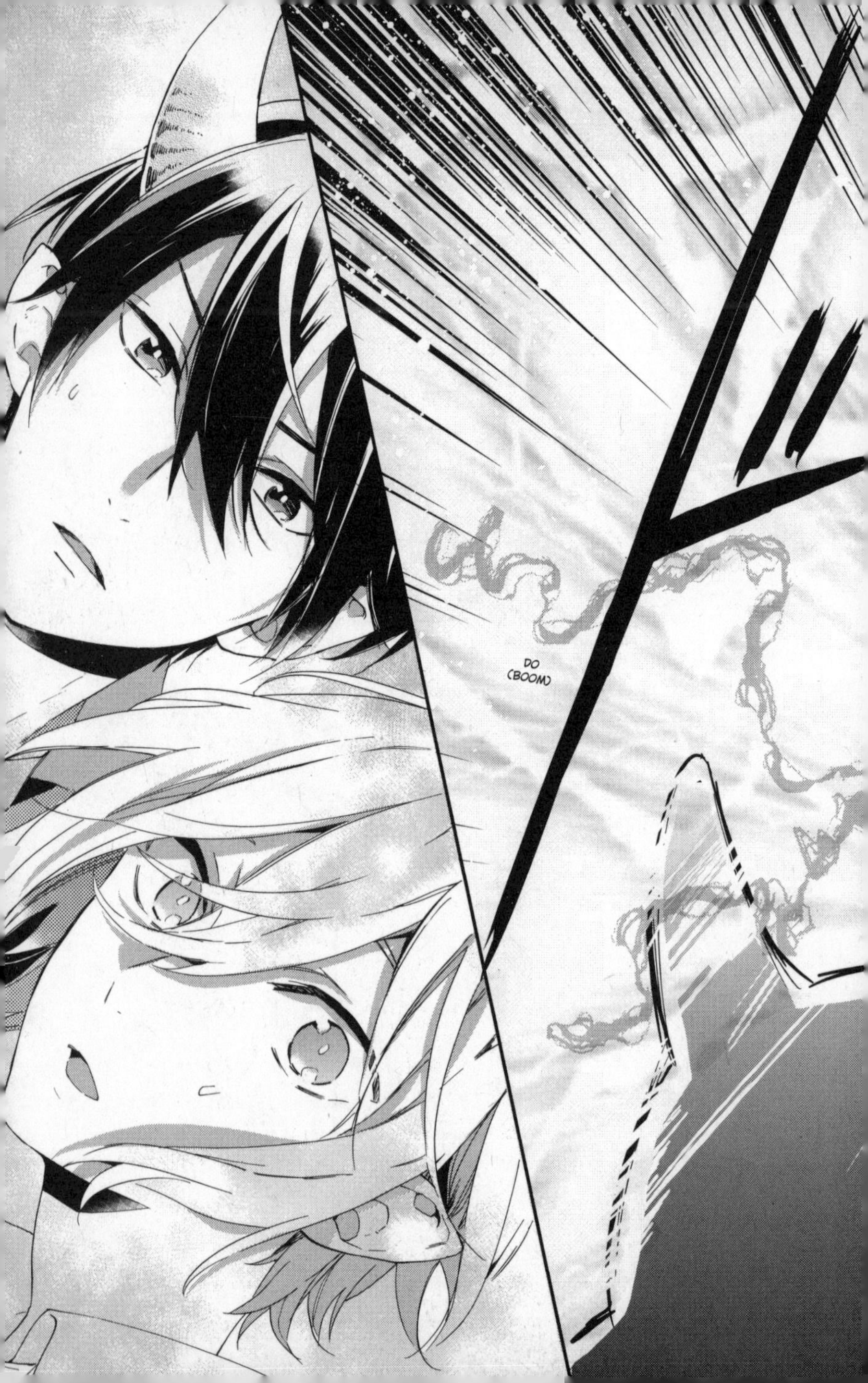
DO
(BOOM)

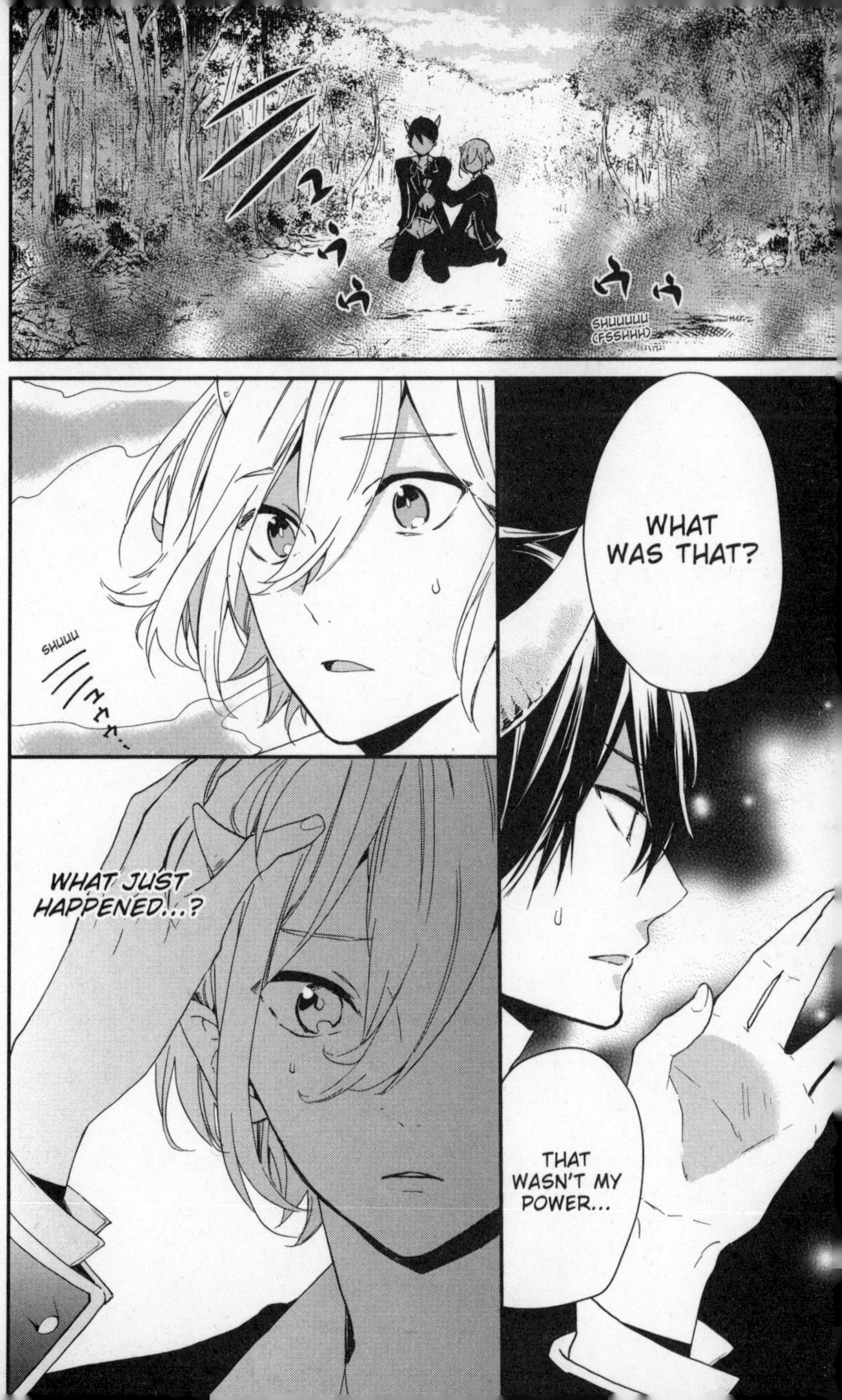
SHUUUUU (FSSHHH)
WHAT WAS THAT?
THAT WASN'T MY POWER...
SHUUU
WHAT JUST HAPPENED...?

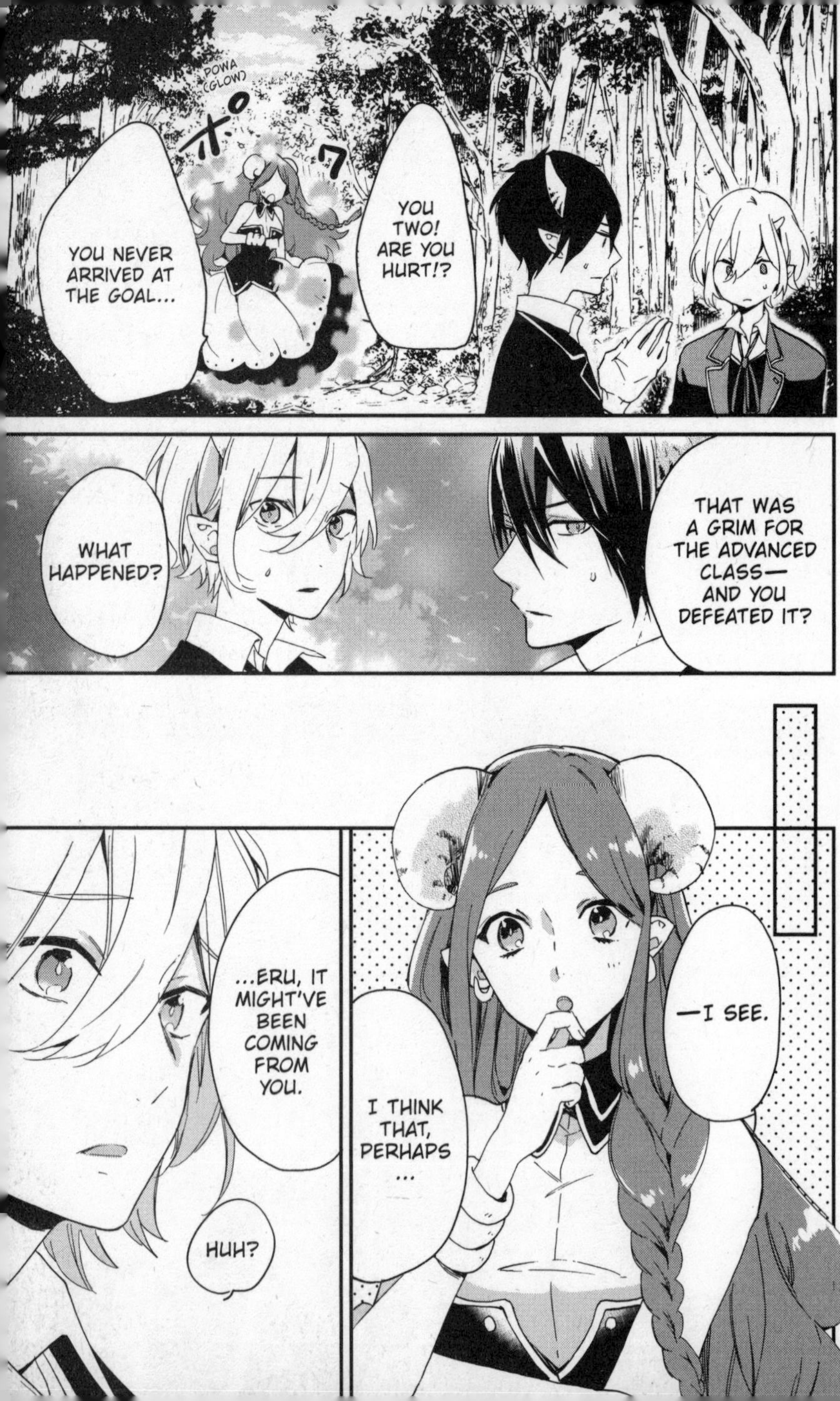
YOU TWO! ARE YOU HURT!?
POWA (GLOW)
YOU NEVER ARRIVED AT THE GOAL...
THAT WAS A GRIM FOR THE ADVANCED CLASS—AND YOU DEFEATED IT?
WHAT HAPPENED?
—I SEE.
I THINK THAT, PERHAPS...
...ERU, IT MIGHT'VE BEEN COMING FROM YOU.
HUH?

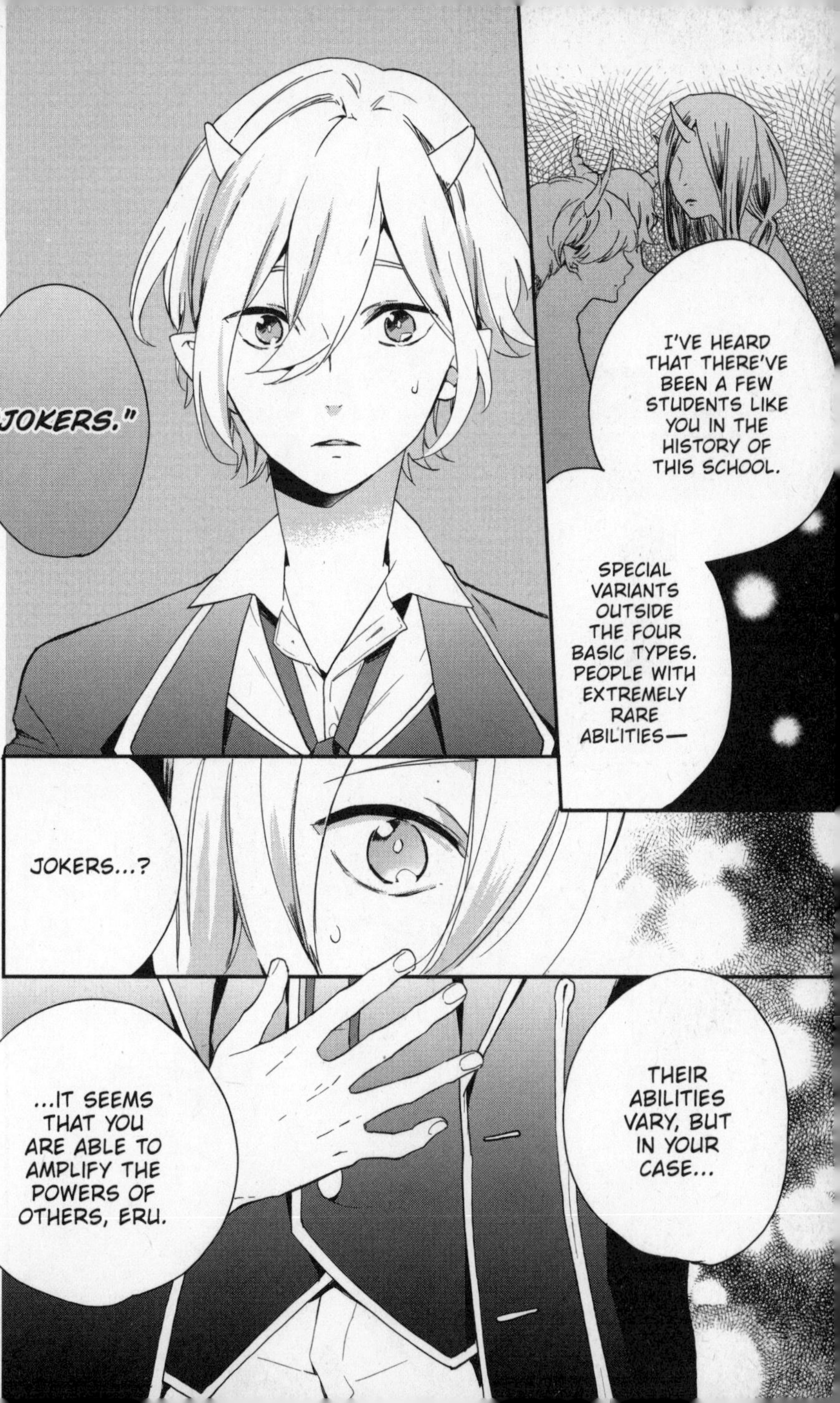
I'VE HEARD THAT THERE'VE BEEN A FEW STUDENTS LIKE YOU IN THE HISTORY OF THIS SCHOOL.
SPECIAL VARIANTS OUTSIDE THE FOUR BASIC TYPES. PEOPLE WITH EXTREMELY RARE ABILITIES—
"JOKERS."
JOKERS...?
THEIR ABILITIES VARY, BUT IN YOUR CASE...
...IT SEEMS THAT YOU ARE ABLE TO AMPLIFY THE POWERS OF OTHERS, ERU.

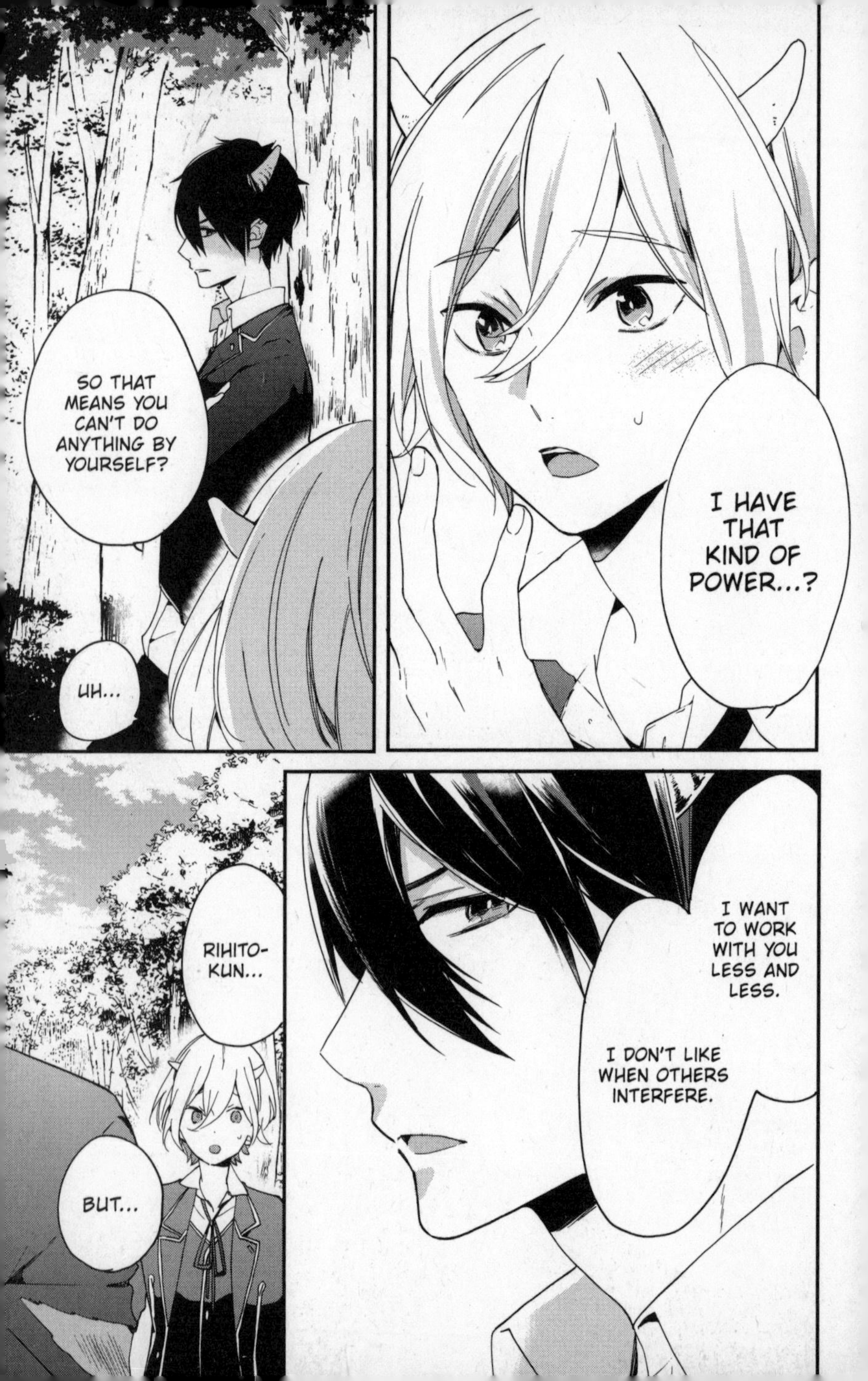
I HAVE THAT KIND OF POWER...?
SO THAT MEANS YOU CAN'T DO ANYTHING BY YOURSELF?
UH...
I WANT TO WORK WITH YOU LESS AND LESS.
I DON'T LIKE WHEN OTHERS INTERFERE.
RIHITO-KUN...
BUT...

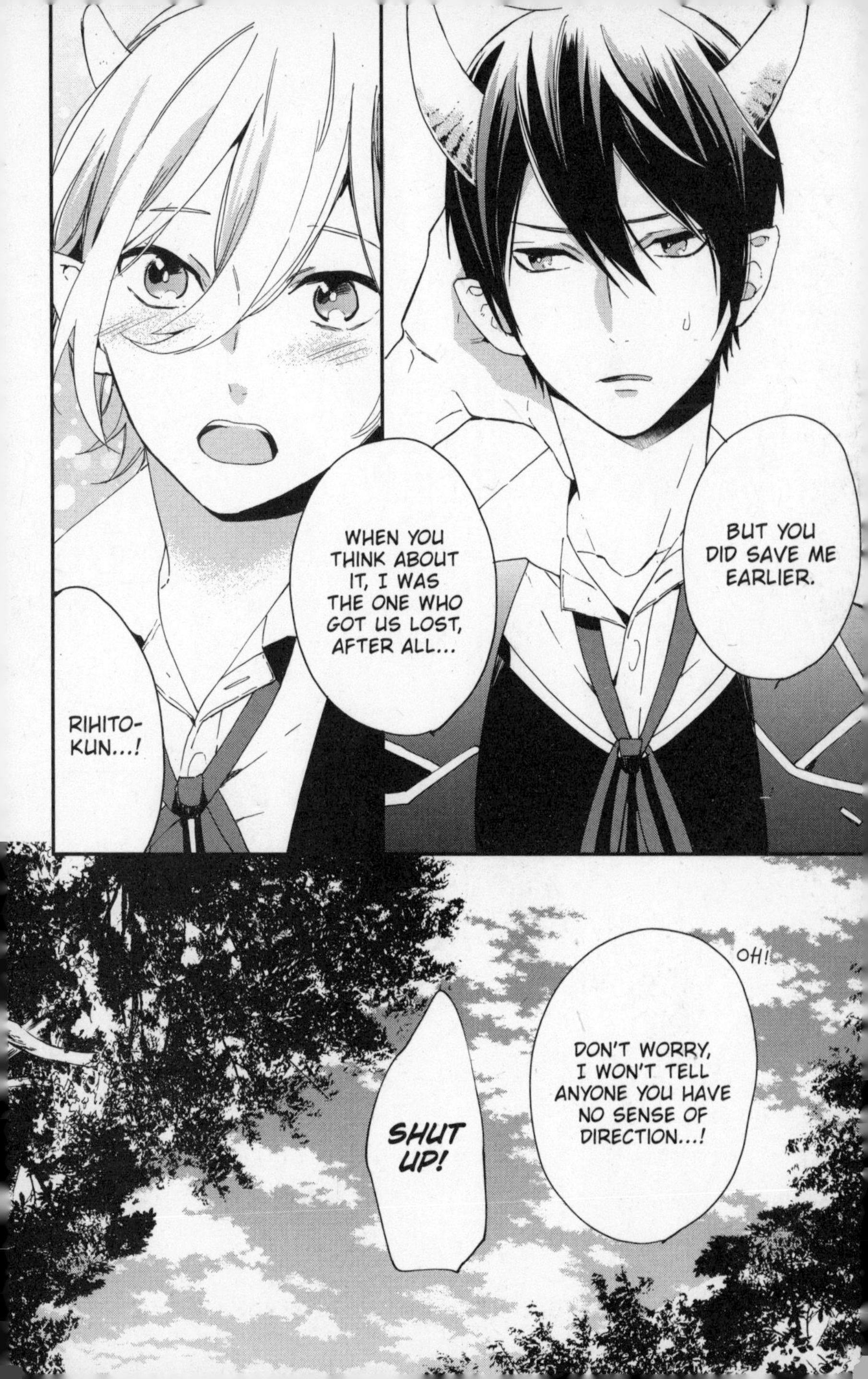
BUT YOU DID SAVE ME EARLIER.
WHEN YOU THINK ABOUT IT, I WAS THE ONE WHO GOT US LOST, AFTER ALL...
RIHITO-KUN...!
OH!
DON'T WORRY, I WON'T TELL ANYONE YOU HAVE NO SENSE OF DIRECTION...!
SHUT UP!

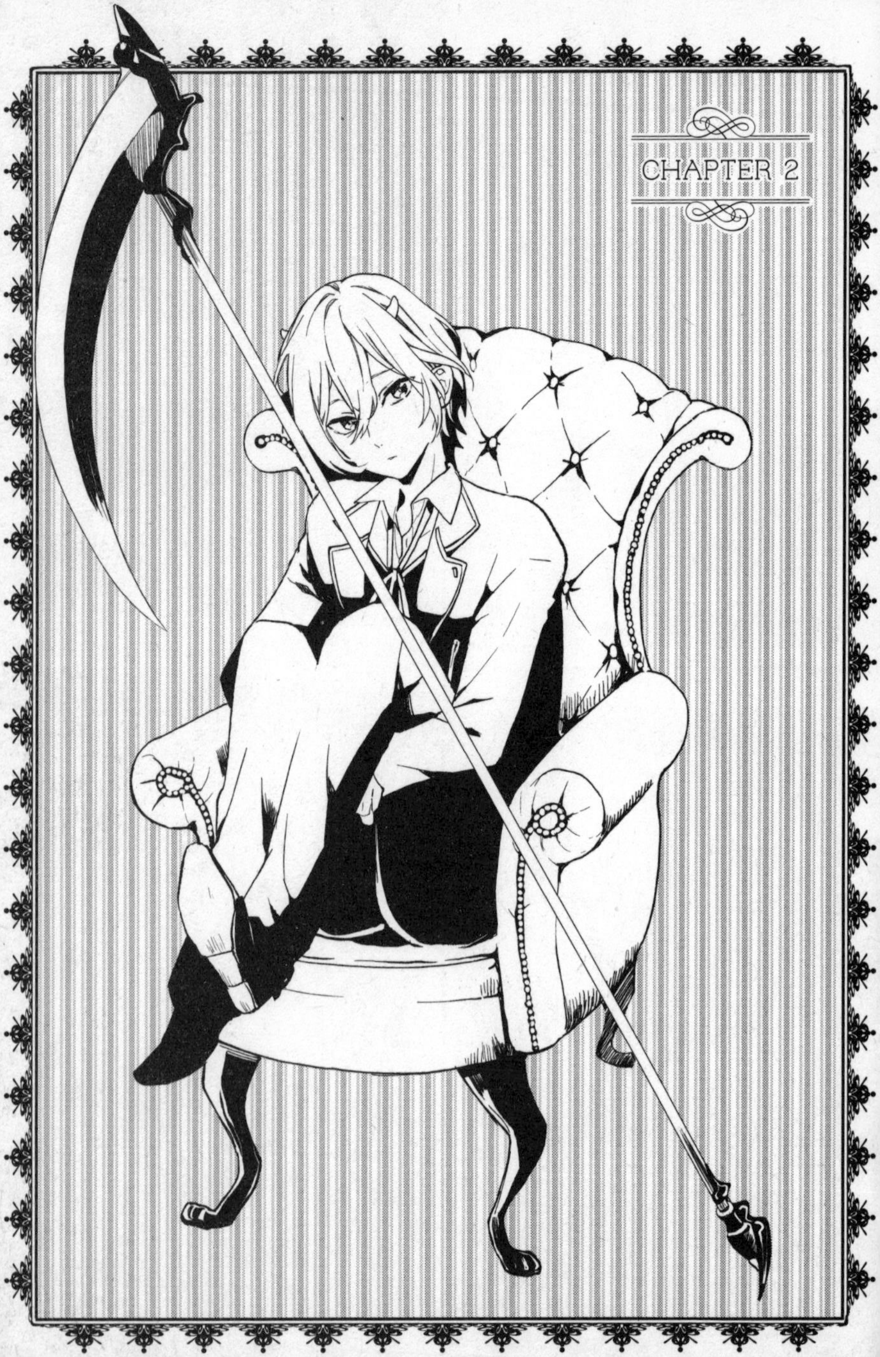
CHAPTER 2

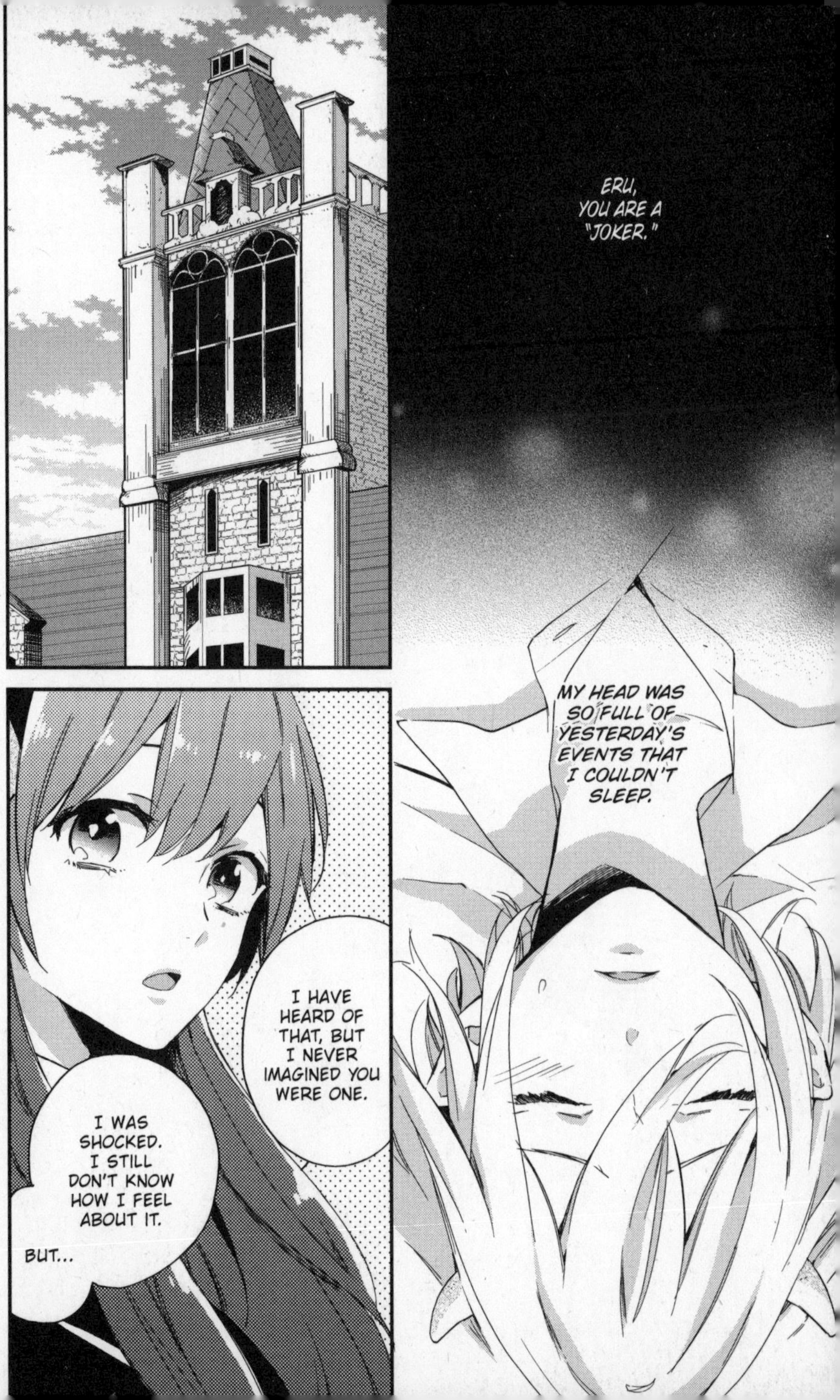
ERU, YOU ARE A "JOKER."
MY HEAD WAS SO FULL OF YESTERDAY'S EVENTS THAT I COULDN'T SLEEP.
I HAVE HEARD OF THAT, BUT I NEVER IMAGINED YOU WERE ONE.
I WAS SHOCKED. I STILL DON'T KNOW HOW I FEEL ABOUT IT.
BUT...

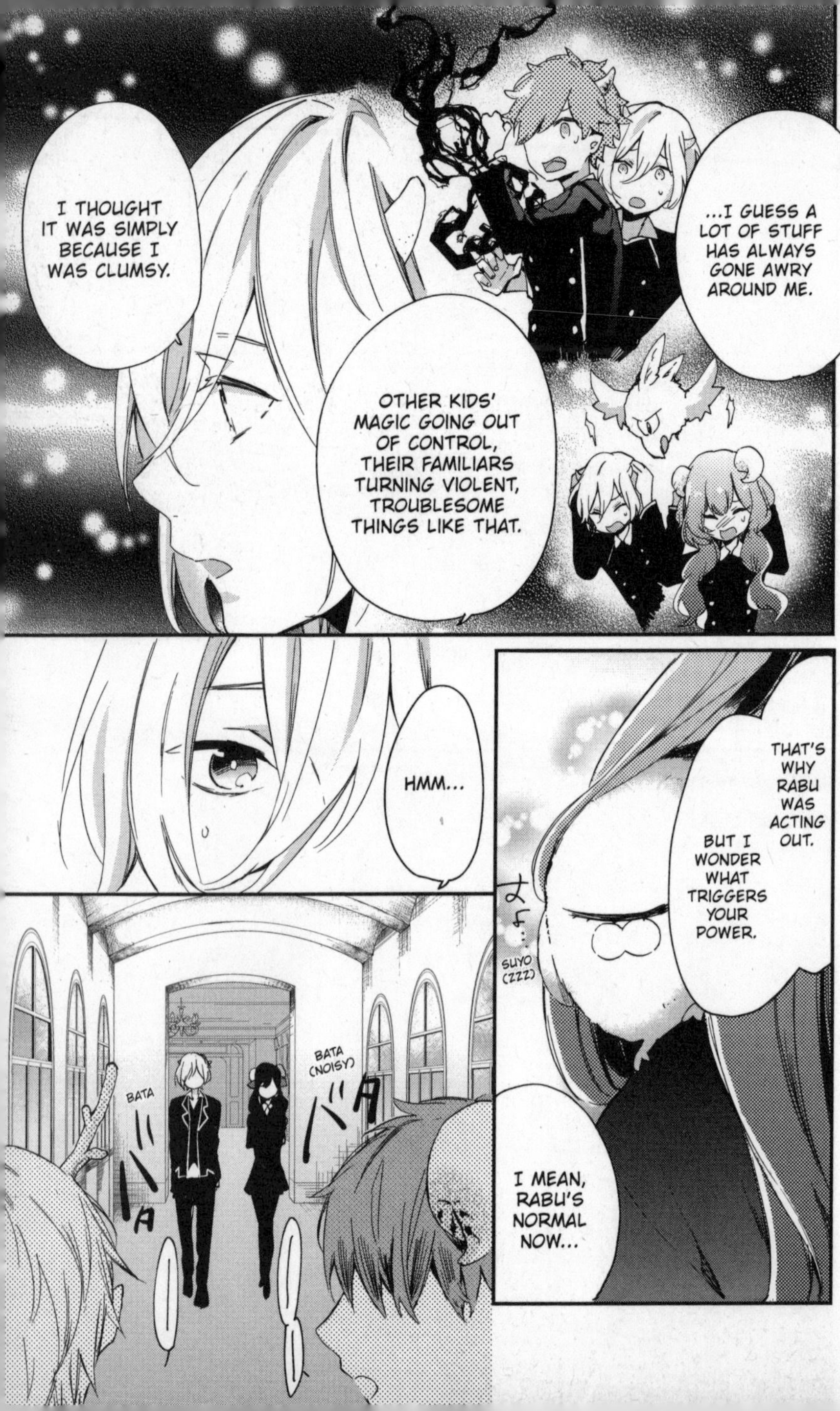
...I GUESS A LOT OF STUFF HAS ALWAYS GONE AWRY AROUND ME.
I THOUGHT IT WAS SIMPLY BECAUSE I WAS CLUMSY.
OTHER KIDS' MAGIC GOING OUT OF CONTROL, THEIR FAMILIARS TURNING VIOLENT, TROUBLESOME THINGS LIKE THAT.
THAT'S WHY RABU WAS ACTING OUT.
BUT I WONDER WHAT TRIGGERS YOUR POWER.
すよ…
SUYO (ZZZ)
I MEAN, RABU'S NORMAL NOW...
HMM...
BATA (NOISY)
バタ
BATA
バタ

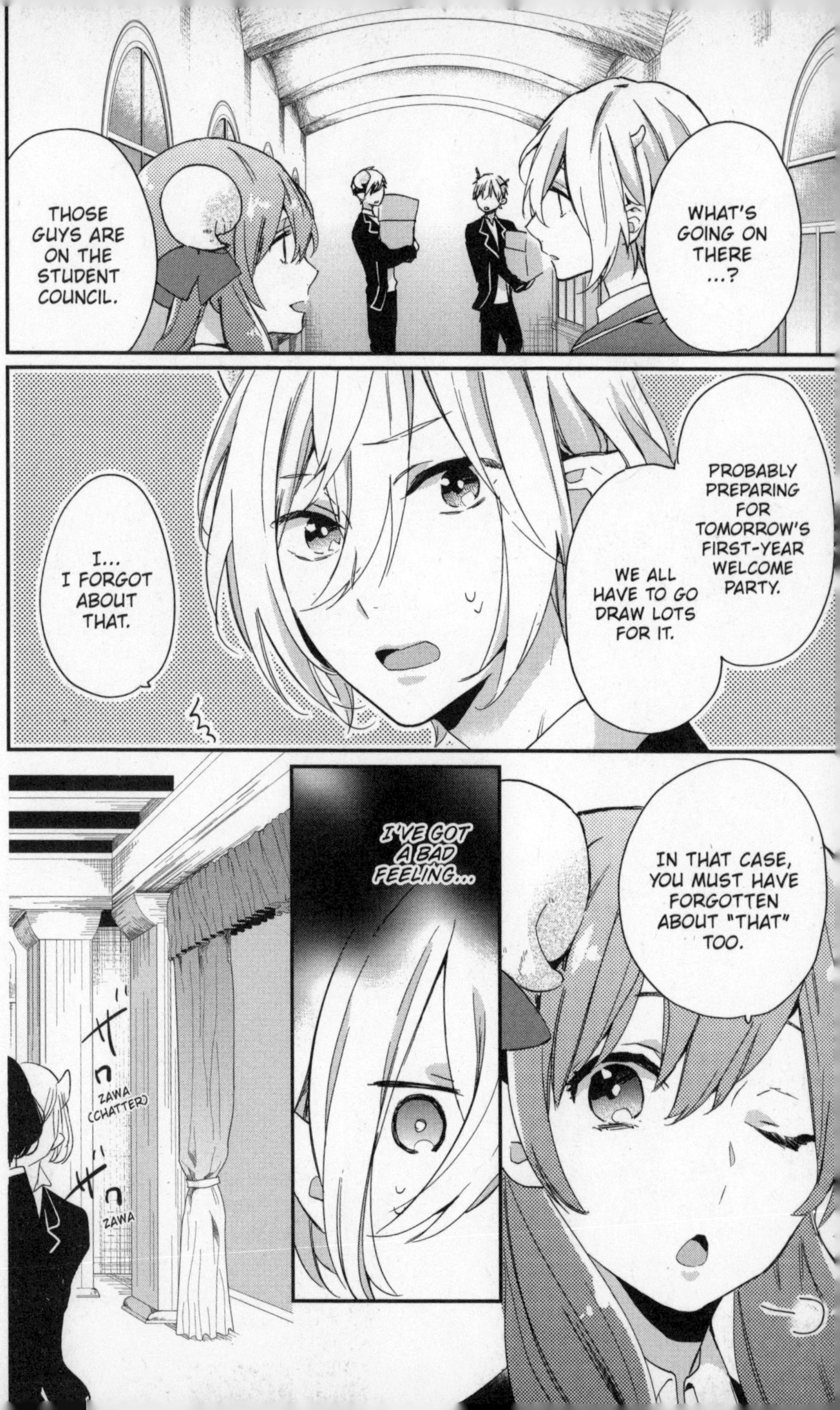
WHAT'S GOING ON THERE ...?
THOSE GUYS ARE ON THE STUDENT COUNCIL.
PROBABLY PREPARING FOR TOMORROW'S FIRST-YEAR WELCOME PARTY.
WE ALL HAVE TO GO DRAW LOTS FOR IT.
I... I FORGOT ABOUT THAT.
IN THAT CASE, YOU MUST HAVE FORGOTTEN ABOUT "THAT" TOO.
I'VE GOT A BAD FEELING...
ZAWA (CHATTER)
ZAWA

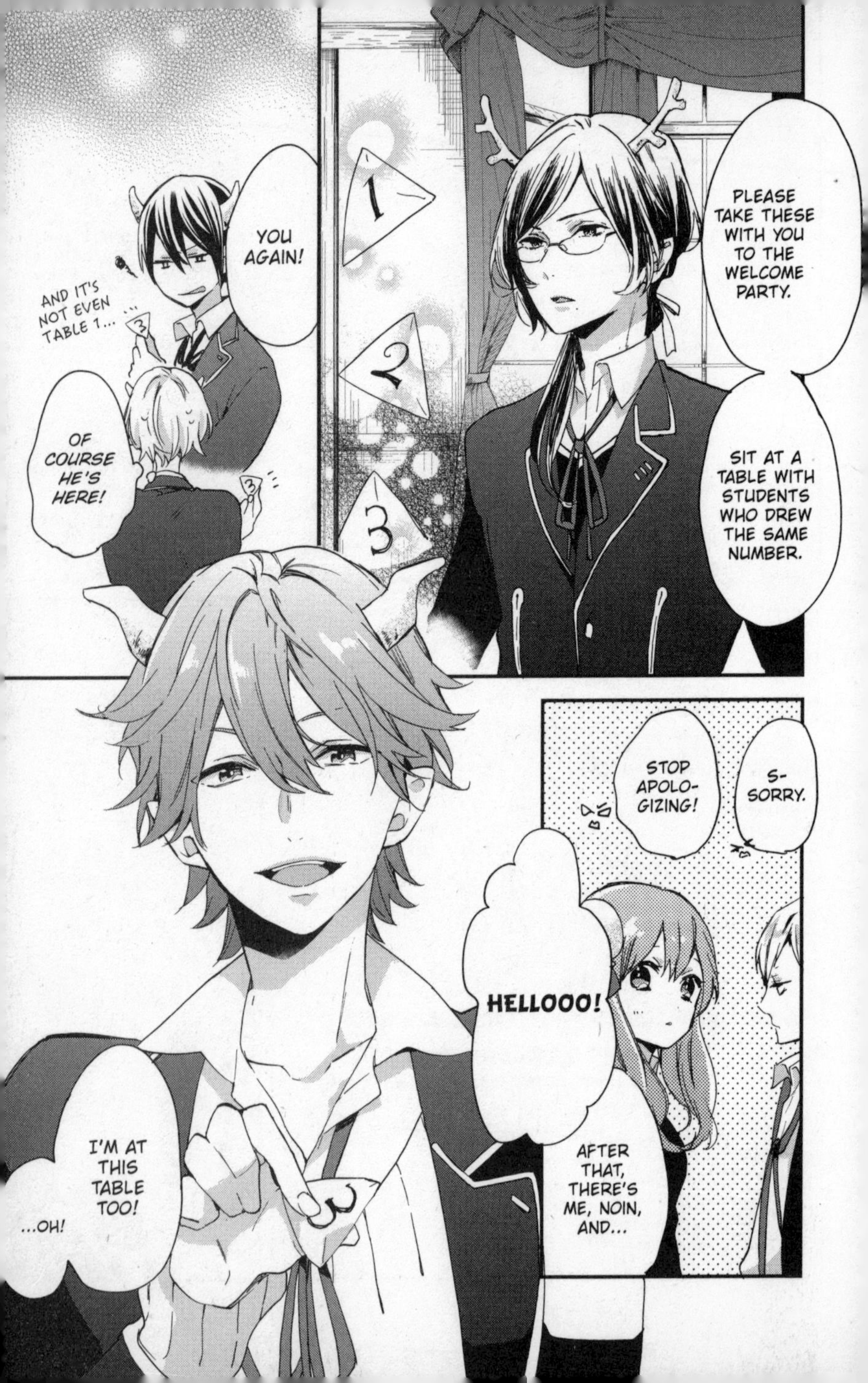
PLEASE TAKE THESE WITH YOU TO THE WELCOME PARTY.
SIT AT A TABLE WITH STUDENTS WHO DREW THE SAME NUMBER.
1
2
3
YOU AGAIN!
AND IT'S NOT EVEN TABLE 1...
OF COURSE HE'S HERE!
S-SORRY.
STOP APOLOGIZING!
AFTER THAT, THERE'S ME, NOIN, AND...
HELLOOO!
I'M AT THIS TABLE TOO!
...OH!

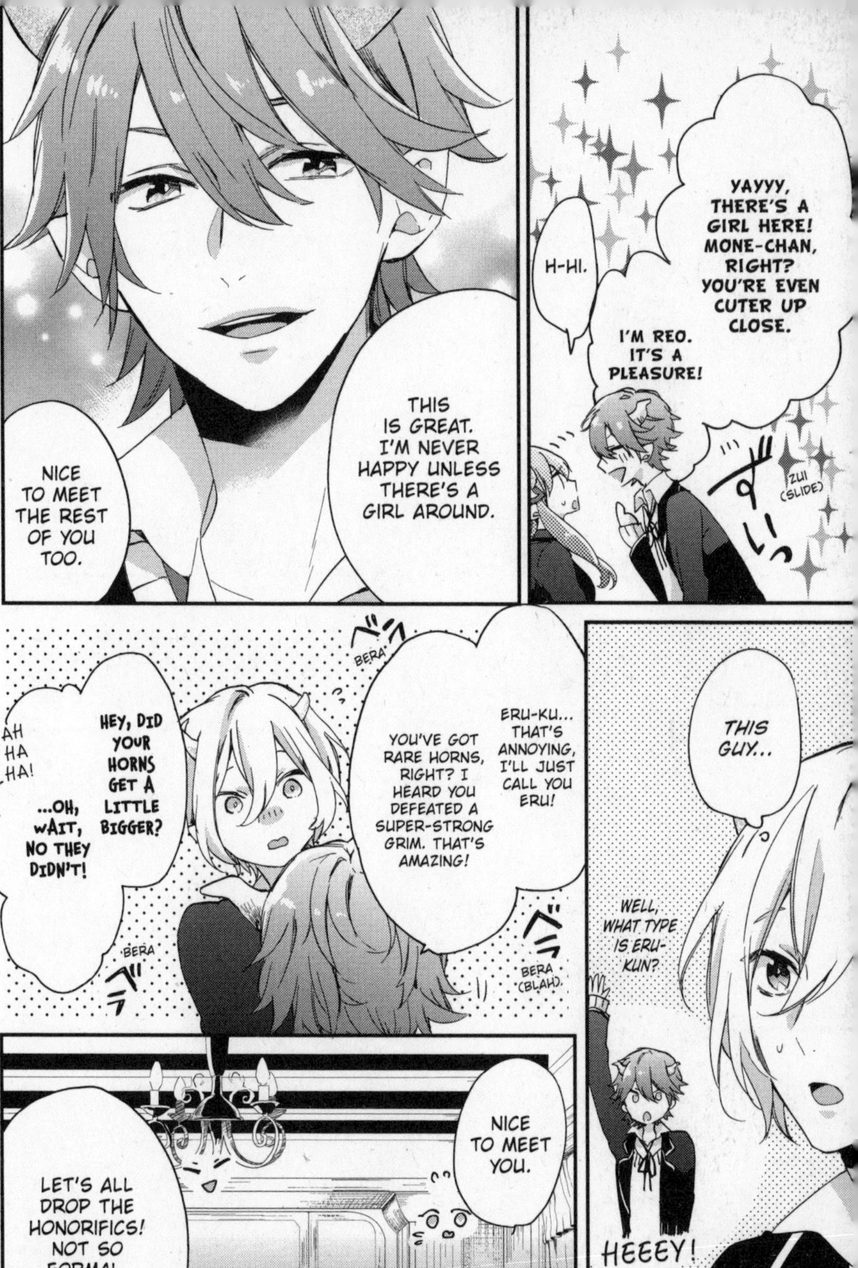
YAYYY, THERE'S A GIRL HERE! MONE-CHAN, RIGHT? YOU'RE EVEN CUTER UP CLOSE.
H-HI.
I'M REO. IT'S A PLEASURE!
ZUI (SLIDE)
THIS IS GREAT. I'M NEVER HAPPY UNLESS THERE'S A GIRL AROUND.
NICE TO MEET THE REST OF YOU TOO.
THIS GUY...
WELL, WHAT TYPE IS ERU-KUN?
HEEEY!
BERA
ERU-KU... THAT'S ANNOYING, I'LL JUST CALL YOU ERU!
YOU'VE GOT RARE HORNS, RIGHT? I HEARD YOU DEFEATED A SUPER-STRONG GRIM. THAT'S AMAZING!
BERA (BLAH)
HEY, DID YOUR HORNS GET A LITTLE BIGGER?
...OH, WAIT, NO THEY DIDN'T!
AH HA HA!
BERA
NICE TO MEET YOU.
LET'S ALL DROP THE HONORIFICS! NOT SO FORMAL.

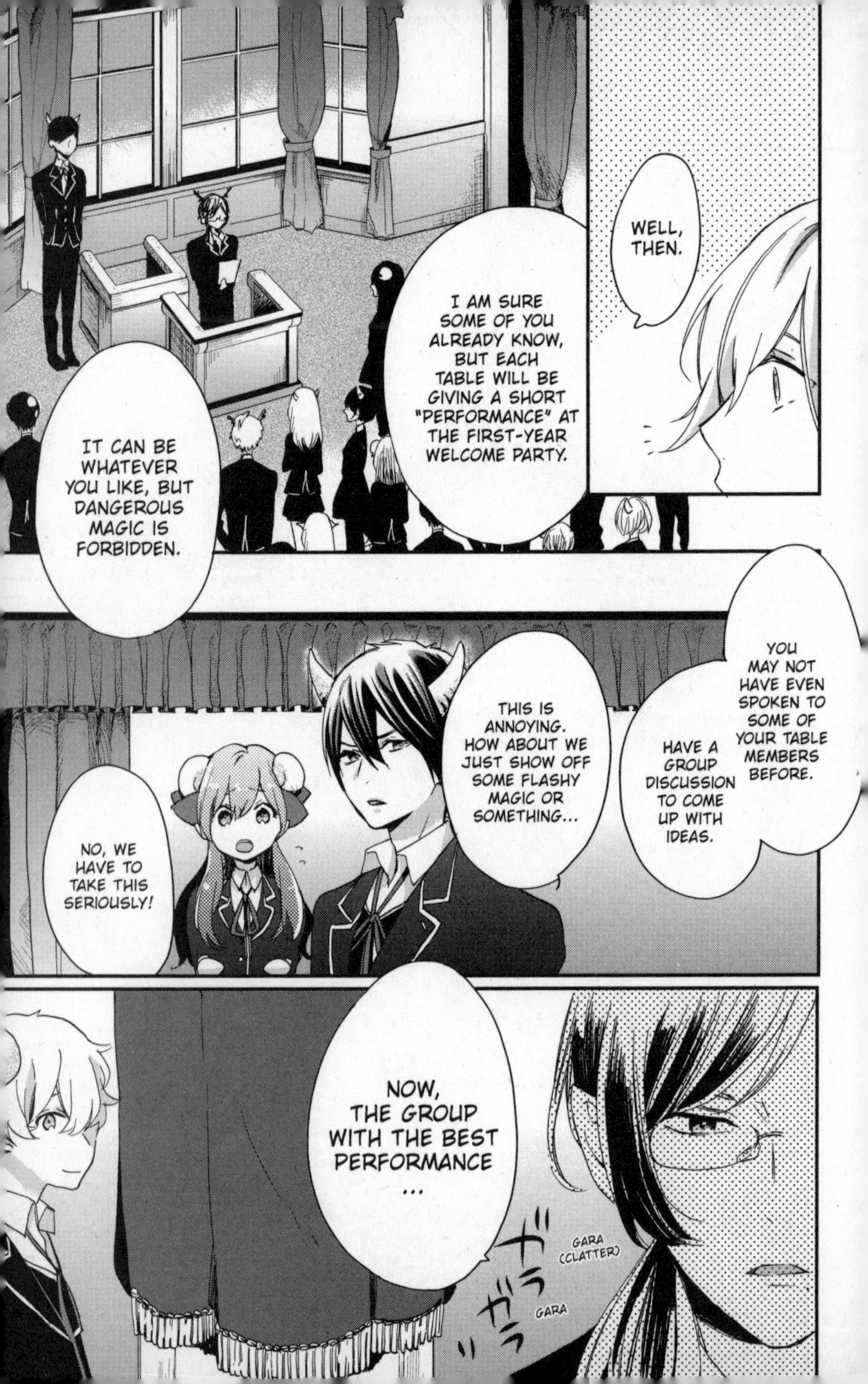
WELL, THEN.
I AM SURE SOME OF YOU ALREADY KNOW, BUT EACH TABLE WILL BE GIVING A SHORT "PERFORMANCE" AT THE FIRST-YEAR WELCOME PARTY.
IT CAN BE WHATEVER YOU LIKE, BUT DANGEROUS MAGIC IS FORBIDDEN.
YOU MAY NOT HAVE EVEN SPOKEN TO SOME OF YOUR TABLE MEMBERS BEFORE.
HAVE A GROUP DISCUSSION TO COME UP WITH IDEAS.
THIS IS ANNOYING. HOW ABOUT WE JUST SHOW OFF SOME FLASHY MAGIC OR SOMETHING...
NO, WE HAVE TO TAKE THIS SERIOUSLY!
NOW, THE GROUP WITH THE BEST PERFORMANCE ...
GARA (CLATTER)
GARA

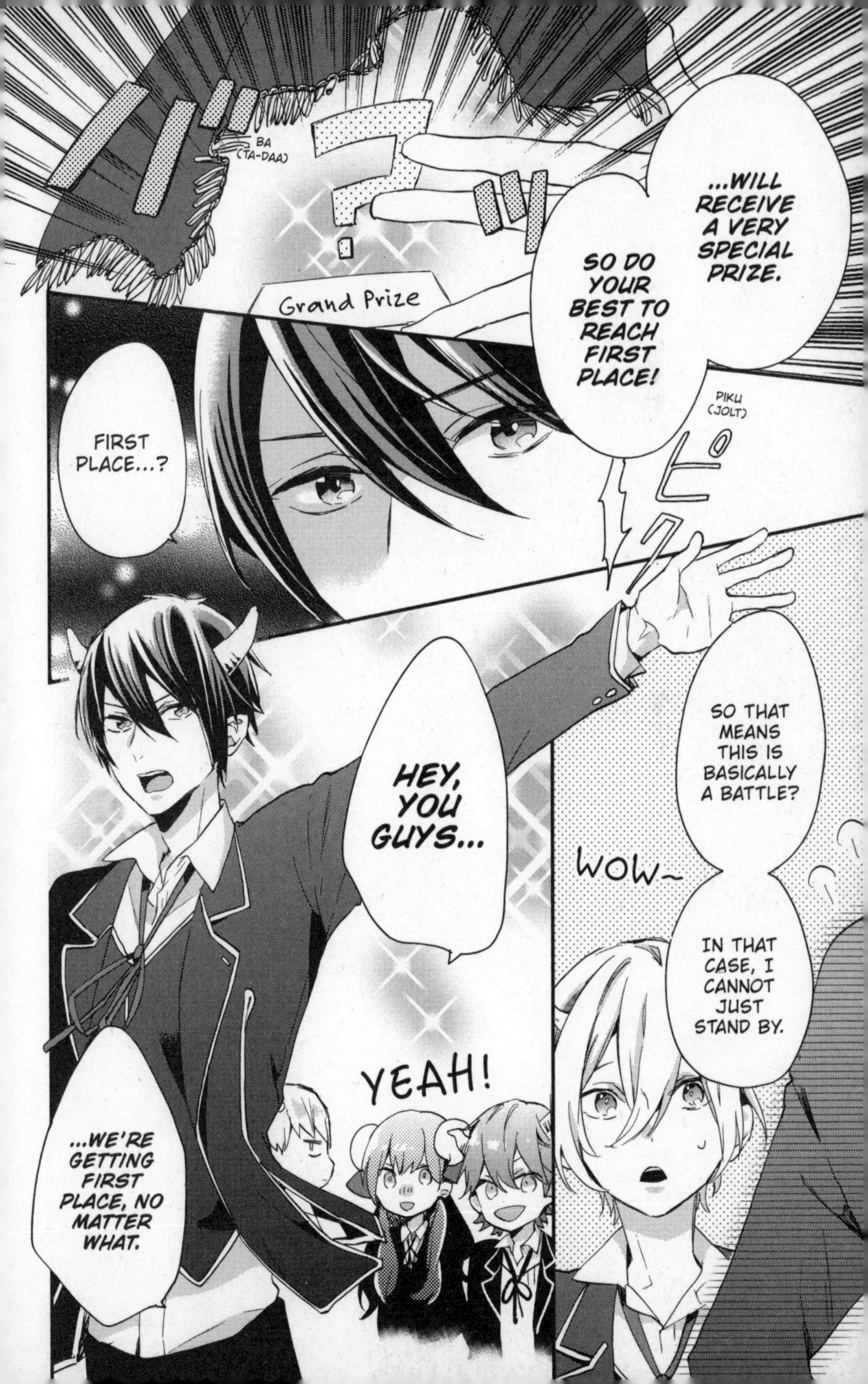
...WILL RECEIVE A VERY SPECIAL PRIZE.
SO DO YOUR BEST TO REACH FIRST PLACE!
BA (TA-DAA)
Grand Prize
PIKU (JOLT)
FIRST PLACE...?
SO THAT MEANS THIS IS BASICALLY A BATTLE?
WOW~
IN THAT CASE, I CANNOT JUST STAND BY.
HEY, YOU GUYS...
...WE'RE GETTING FIRST PLACE, NO MATTER WHAT.
YEAH!

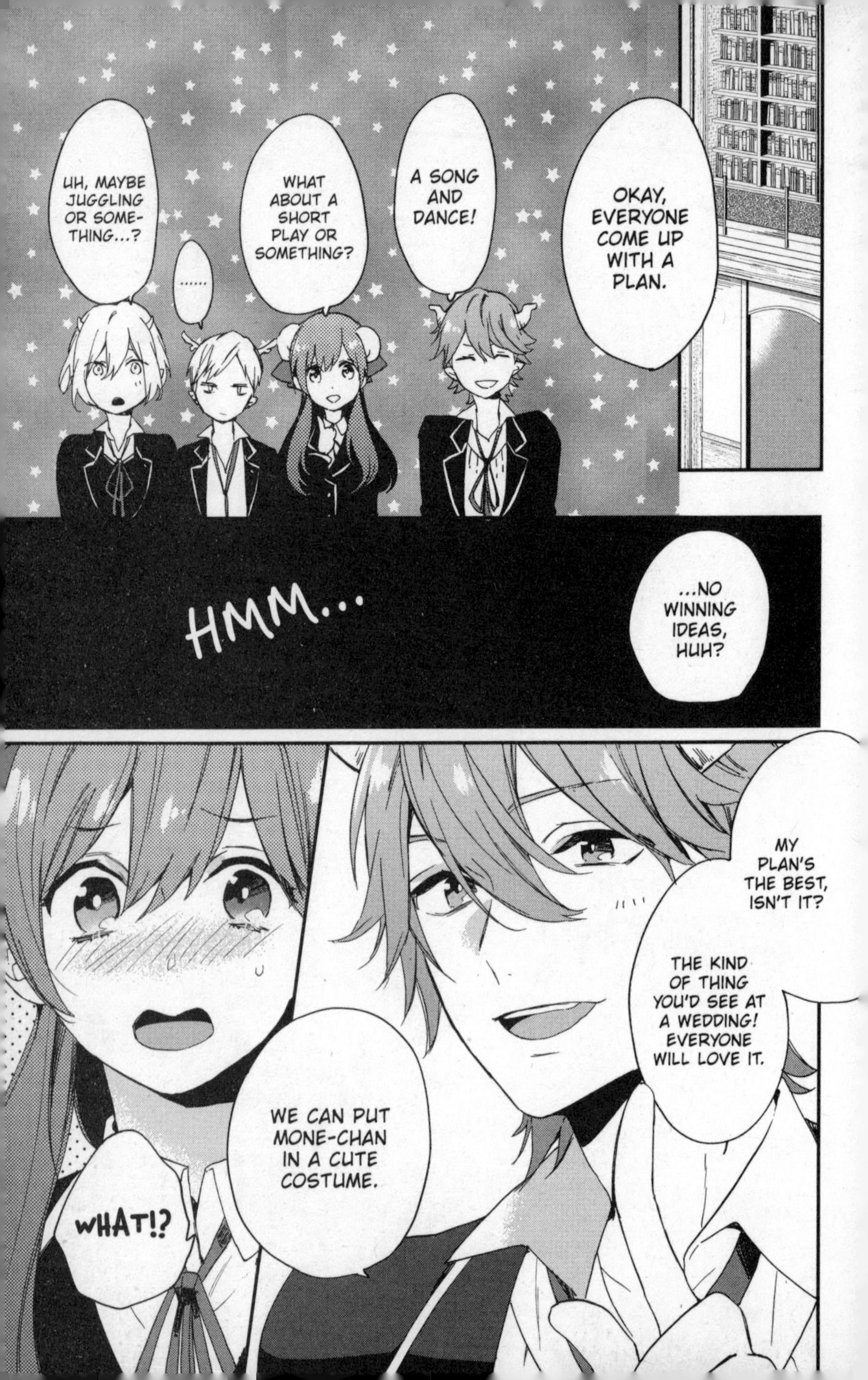
OKAY, EVERYONE COME UP WITH A PLAN.
A SONG AND DANCE!
WHAT ABOUT A SHORT PLAY OR SOMETHING?
......
UH, MAYBE JUGGLING OR SOME-THING...?
...NO WINNING IDEAS, HUH?
HMM...
MY PLAN'S THE BEST, ISN'T IT?
THE KIND OF THING YOU'D SEE AT A WEDDING! EVERYONE WILL LOVE IT.
WE CAN PUT MONE-CHAN IN A CUTE COSTUME.
WHAT!?

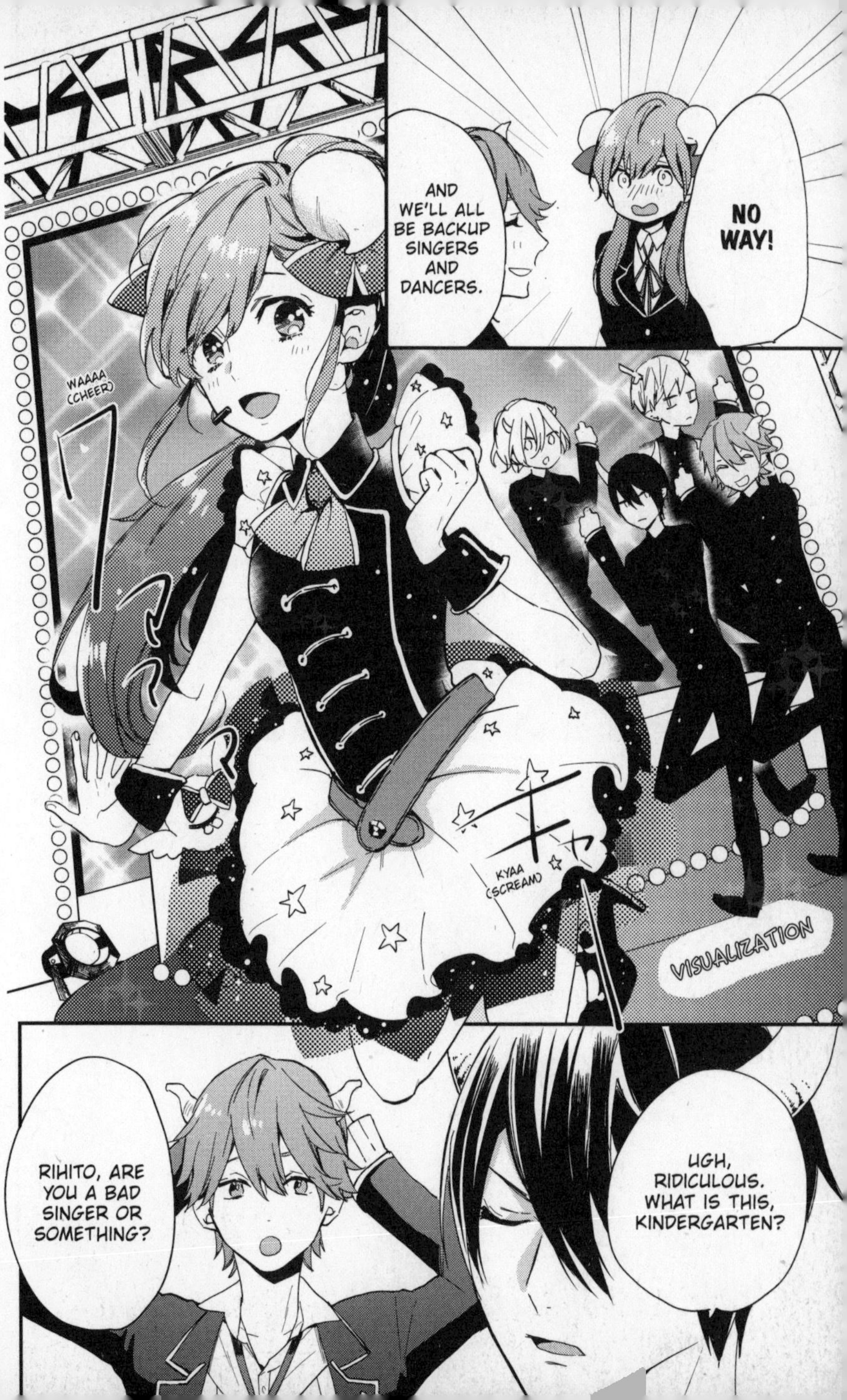
AND WE'LL ALL BE BACKUP SINGERS AND DANCERS.
NO WAY!
WAAAA (CHEER)
KYAA (SCREAM)
VISUALIZATION
UGH, RIDICULOUS. WHAT IS THIS, KINDERGARTEN?
RIHITO, ARE YOU A BAD SINGER OR SOMETHING?

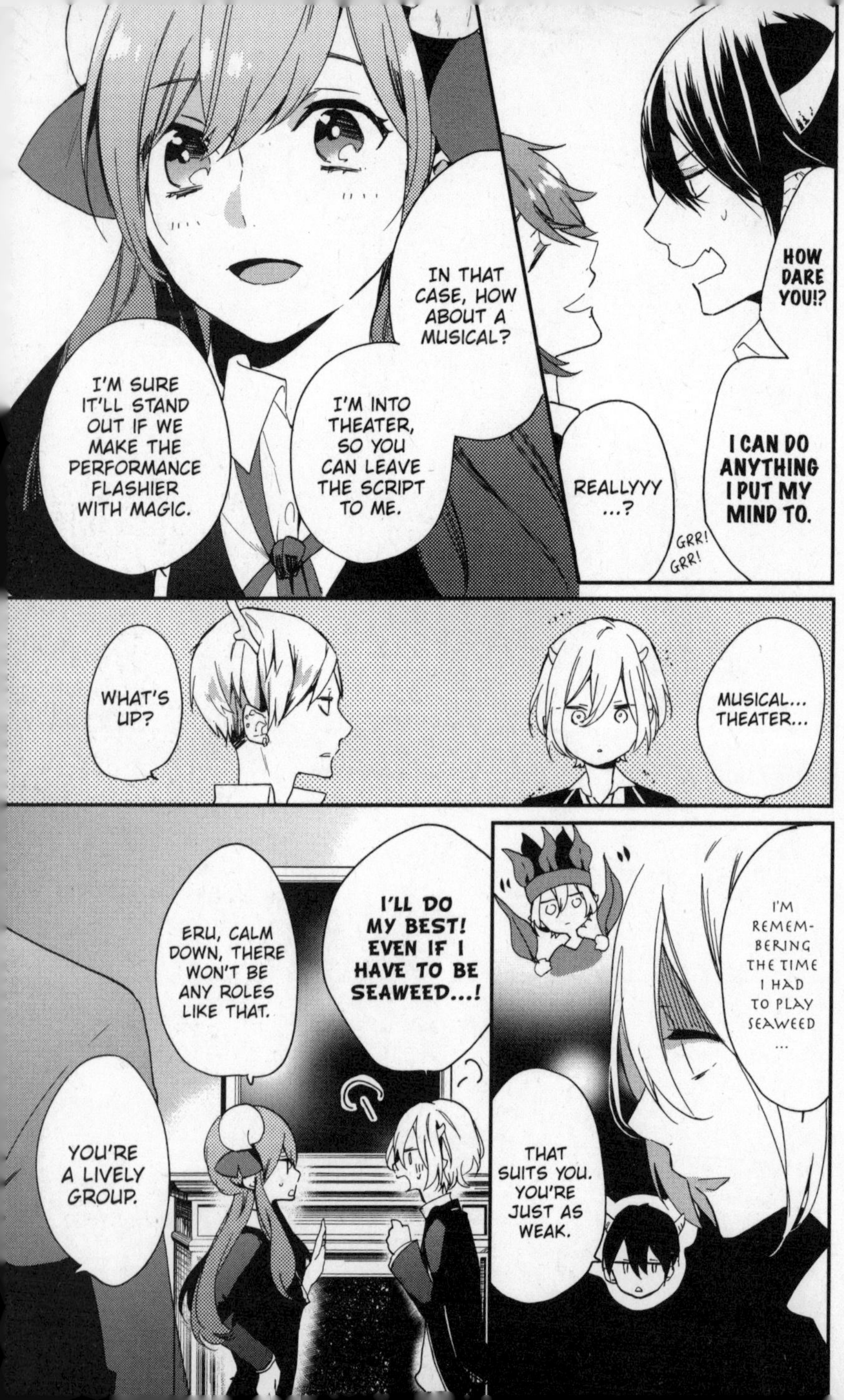
HOW DARE YOU!?
I CAN DO ANYTHING I PUT MY MIND TO.
GRR! GRR!
REALLYYY ...?
IN THAT CASE, HOW ABOUT A MUSICAL?
I'M INTO THEATER, SO YOU CAN LEAVE THE SCRIPT TO ME.
I'M SURE IT'LL STAND OUT IF WE MAKE THE PERFORMANCE FLASHIER WITH MAGIC.
MUSICAL... THEATER...
WHAT'S UP?
I'M REMEM-BERING THE TIME I HAD TO PLAY SEAWEED ...
THAT SUITS YOU. YOU'RE JUST AS WEAK.
I'LL DO MY BEST! EVEN IF I HAVE TO BE SEAWEED...!
ERU, CALM DOWN, THERE WON'T BE ANY ROLES LIKE THAT.
YOU'RE A LIVELY GROUP.

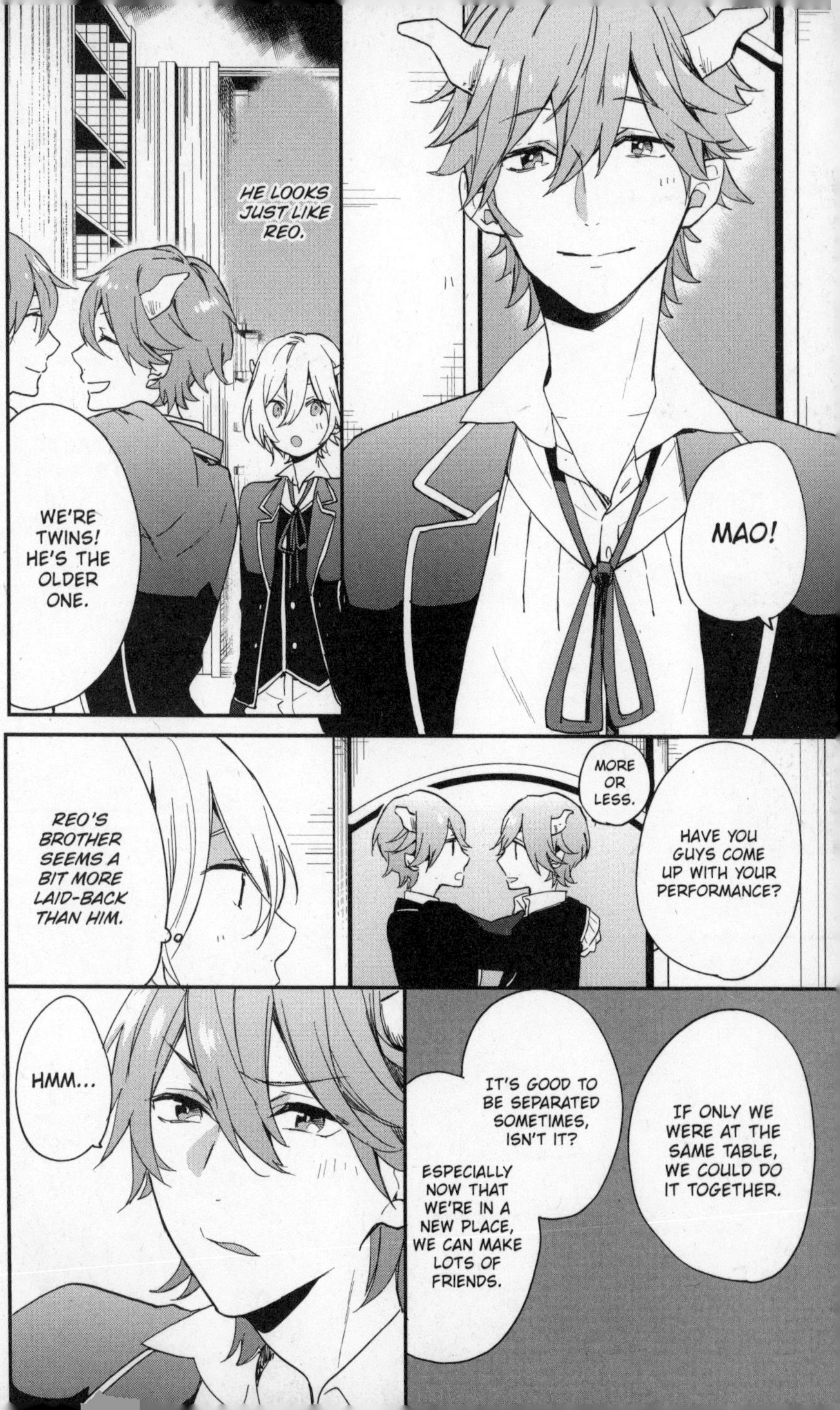
MAO!
HE LOOKS JUST LIKE REO.
WE'RE TWINS! HE'S THE OLDER ONE.
HAVE YOU GUYS COME UP WITH YOUR PERFORMANCE?
MORE OR LESS.
REO'S BROTHER SEEMS A BIT MORE LAID-BACK THAN HIM.
IF ONLY WE WERE AT THE SAME TABLE, WE COULD DO IT TOGETHER.
IT'S GOOD TO BE SEPARATED SOMETIMES, ISN'T IT?
ESPECIALLY NOW THAT WE'RE IN A NEW PLACE, WE CAN MAKE LOTS OF FRIENDS.
HMM...

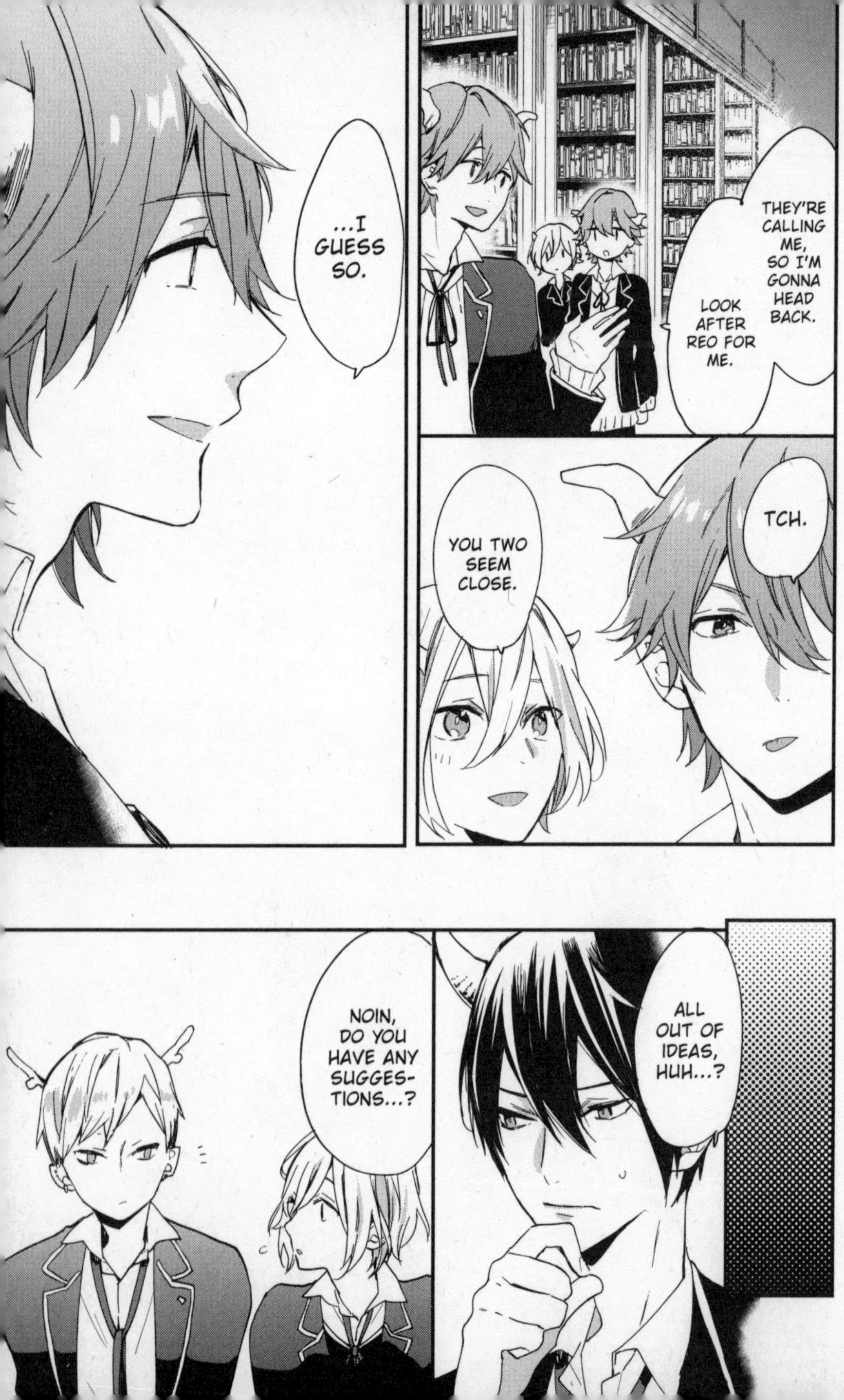
THEY'RE CALLING ME, SO I'M GONNA HEAD BACK.
LOOK AFTER REO FOR ME.
TCH.
YOU TWO SEEM CLOSE.
...I GUESS SO.
ALL OUT OF IDEAS, HUH...?
NOIN, DO YOU HAVE ANY SUGGES-TIONS...?

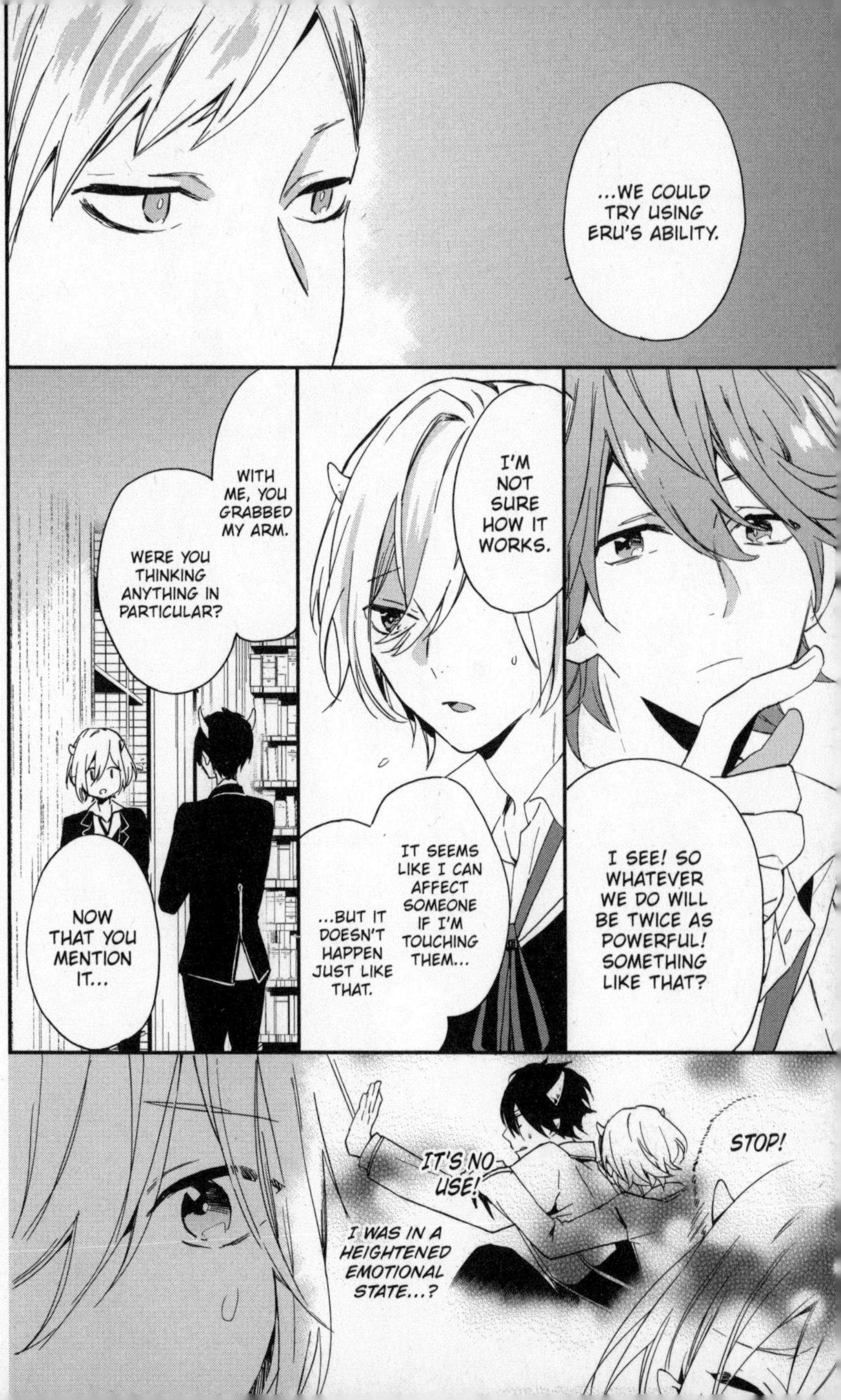
...WE COULD TRY USING ERU'S ABILITY.
I SEE! SO WHATEVER WE DO WILL BE TWICE AS POWERFUL! SOMETHING LIKE THAT?
I'M NOT SURE HOW IT WORKS.
IT SEEMS LIKE I CAN AFFECT SOMEONE IF I'M TOUCHING THEM...
...BUT IT DOESN'T HAPPEN JUST LIKE THAT.
WITH ME, YOU GRABBED MY ARM.
WERE YOU THINKING ANYTHING IN PARTICULAR?
NOW THAT YOU MENTION IT...
STOP!
IT'S NO USE!
I WAS IN A HEIGHTENED EMOTIONAL STATE...?

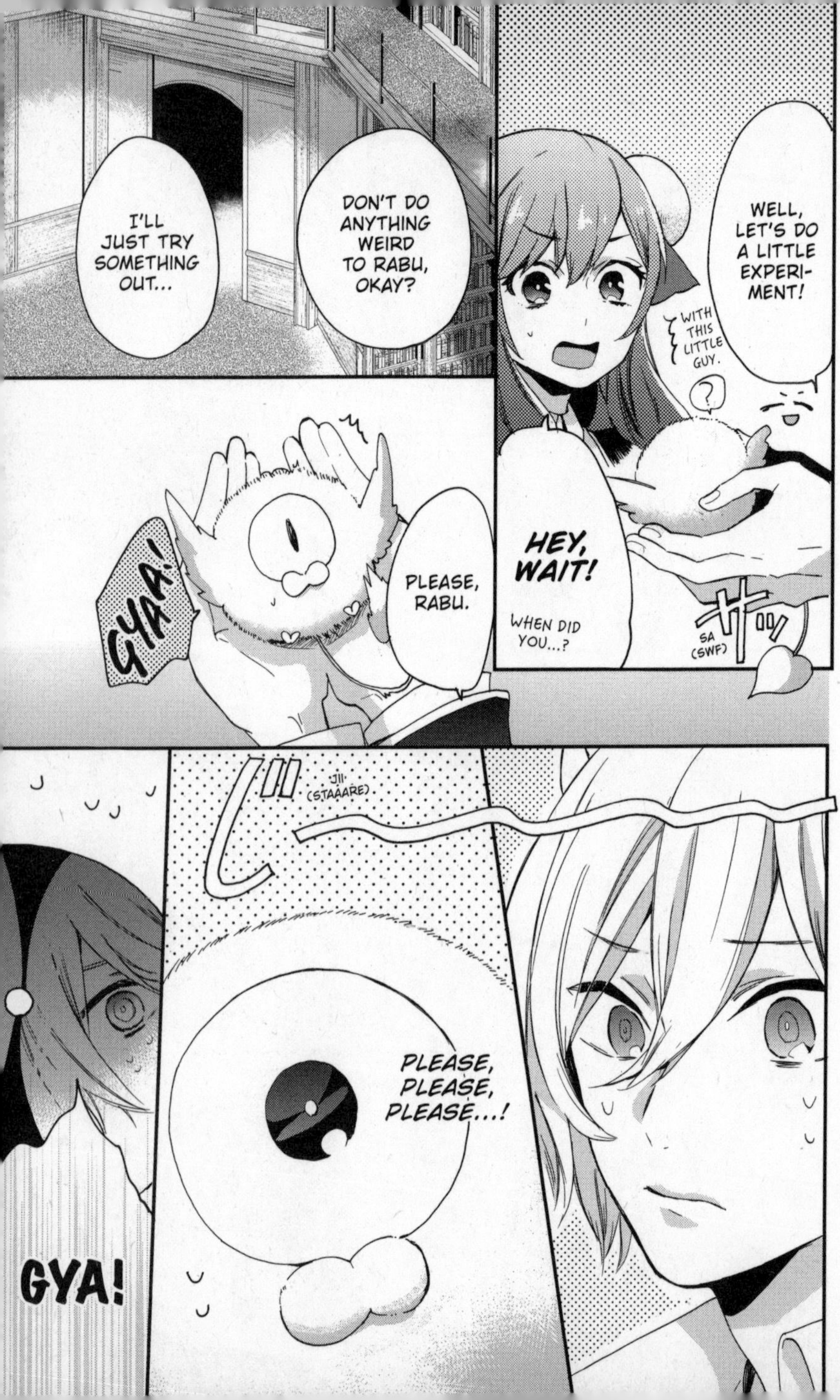
WELL, LET'S DO A LITTLE EXPERIMENT!
WITH THIS LITTLE GUY.
?
HEY, WAIT!
WHEN DID YOU...?
SA (SWF)
DON'T DO ANYTHING WEIRD TO RABU, OKAY?
I'LL JUST TRY SOMETHING OUT...
PLEASE, RABU.
GYA!
JII (STAAARE)
PLEASE, PLEASE, PLEASE...!
GYA!

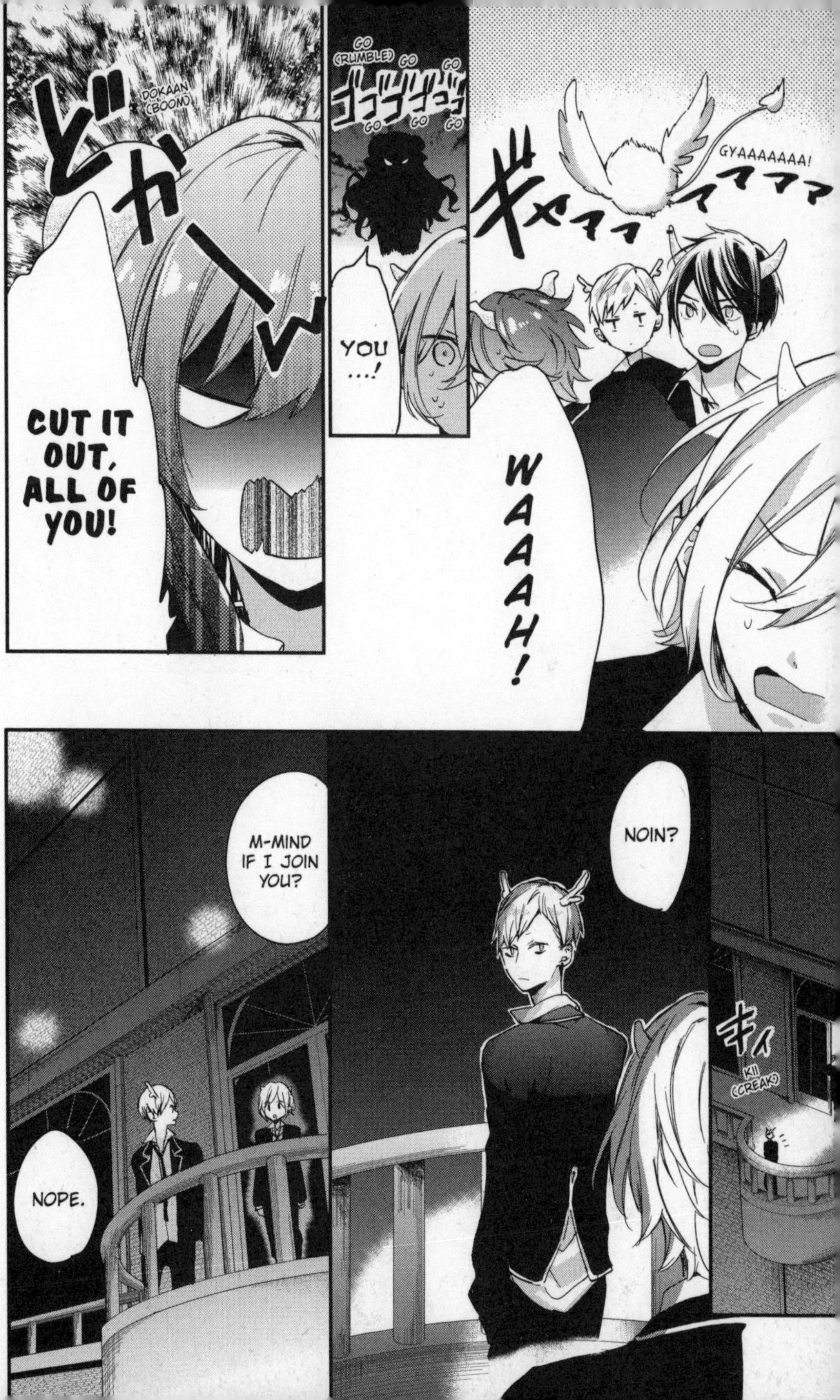
GYAAAAAAA!
WAAAAH!
GO (RUMBLE) GO GO
GO GO GO
YOU...!
DOKAAN (BOOM)
CUT IT OUT, ALL OF YOU!
KII (CREAK)
NOIN?
M-MIND IF I JOIN YOU?
NOPE.

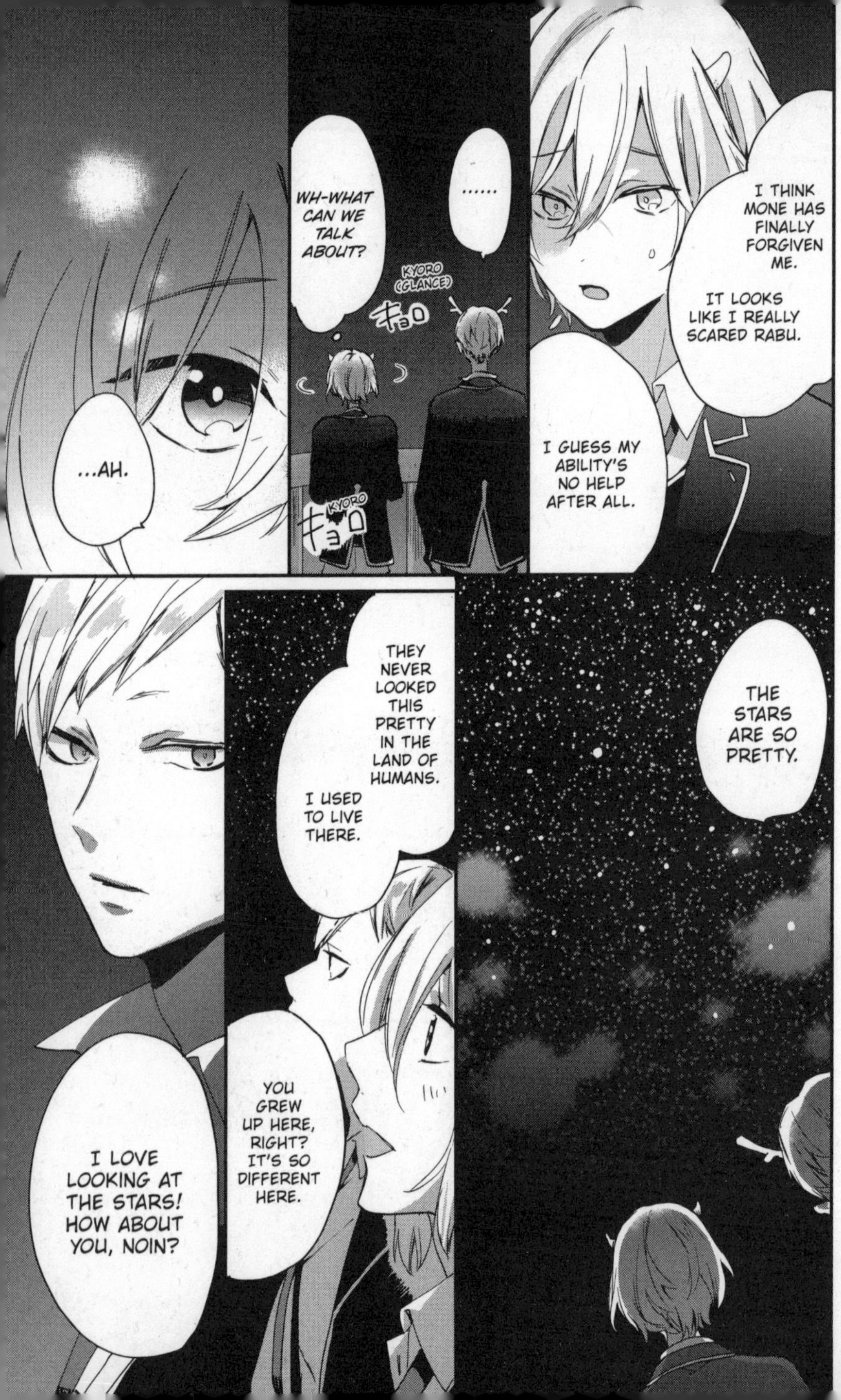
I THINK MONE HAS FINALLY FORGIVEN ME.
IT LOOKS LIKE I REALLY SCARED RABU.
I GUESS MY ABILITY'S NO HELP AFTER ALL.
......
WH-WHAT CAN WE TALK ABOUT?
KYORO (GLANCE)
KYORO
...AH.
THE STARS ARE SO PRETTY.
THEY NEVER LOOKED THIS PRETTY IN THE LAND OF HUMANS.
I USED TO LIVE THERE.
YOU GREW UP HERE, RIGHT? IT'S SO DIFFERENT HERE.
I LOVE LOOKING AT THE STARS! HOW ABOUT YOU, NOIN?

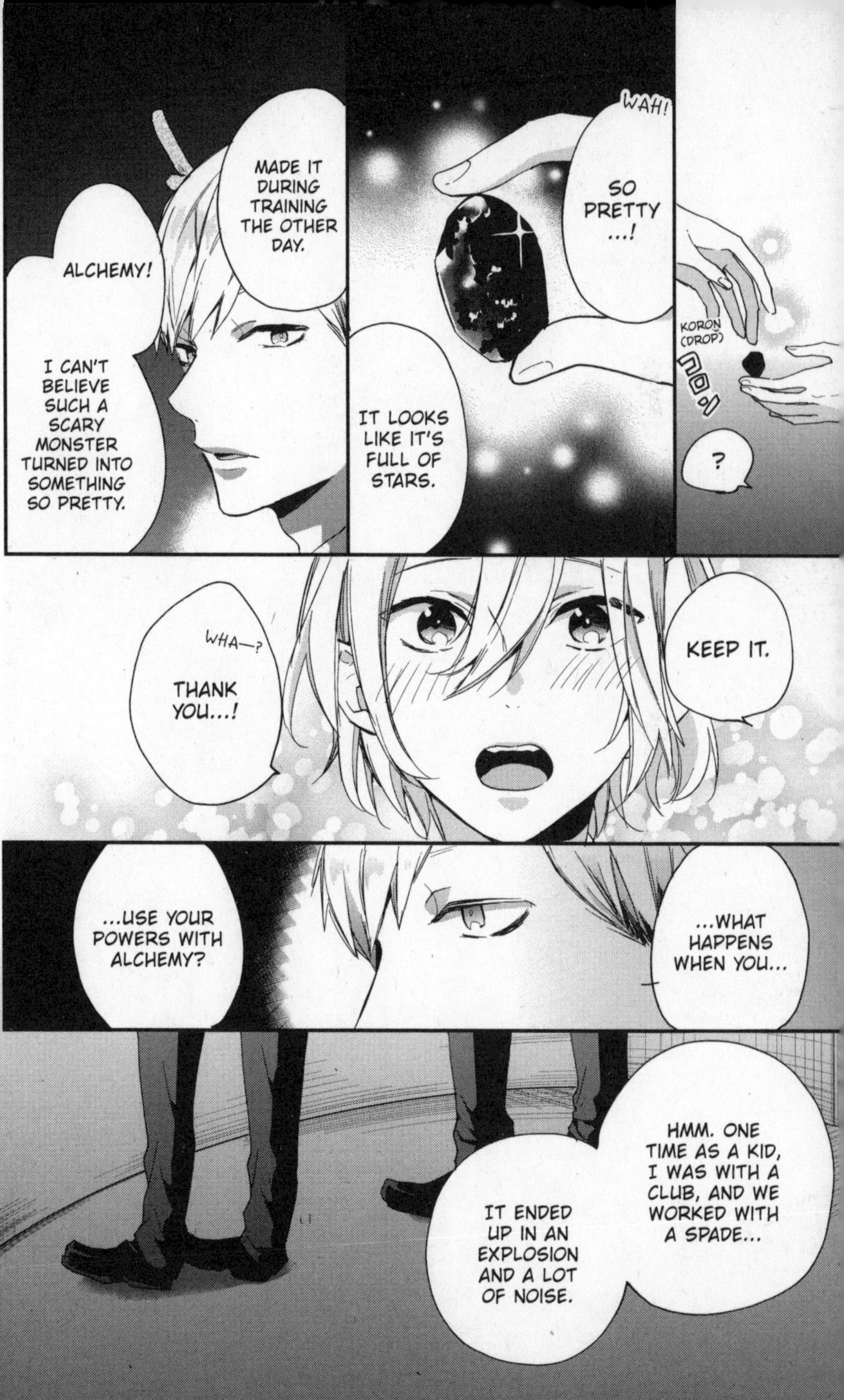
KORON (DROP)
?
WAH!
SO PRETTY ...!
IT LOOKS LIKE IT'S FULL OF STARS.
MADE IT DURING TRAINING THE OTHER DAY.
ALCHEMY!
I CAN'T BELIEVE SUCH A SCARY MONSTER TURNED INTO SOMETHING SO PRETTY.
KEEP IT.
WHA—?
THANK YOU...!
...WHAT HAPPENS WHEN YOU...
...USE YOUR POWERS WITH ALCHEMY?
HMM. ONE TIME AS A KID, I WAS WITH A CLUB, AND WE WORKED WITH A SPADE...
IT ENDED UP IN AN EXPLOSION AND A LOT OF NOISE.

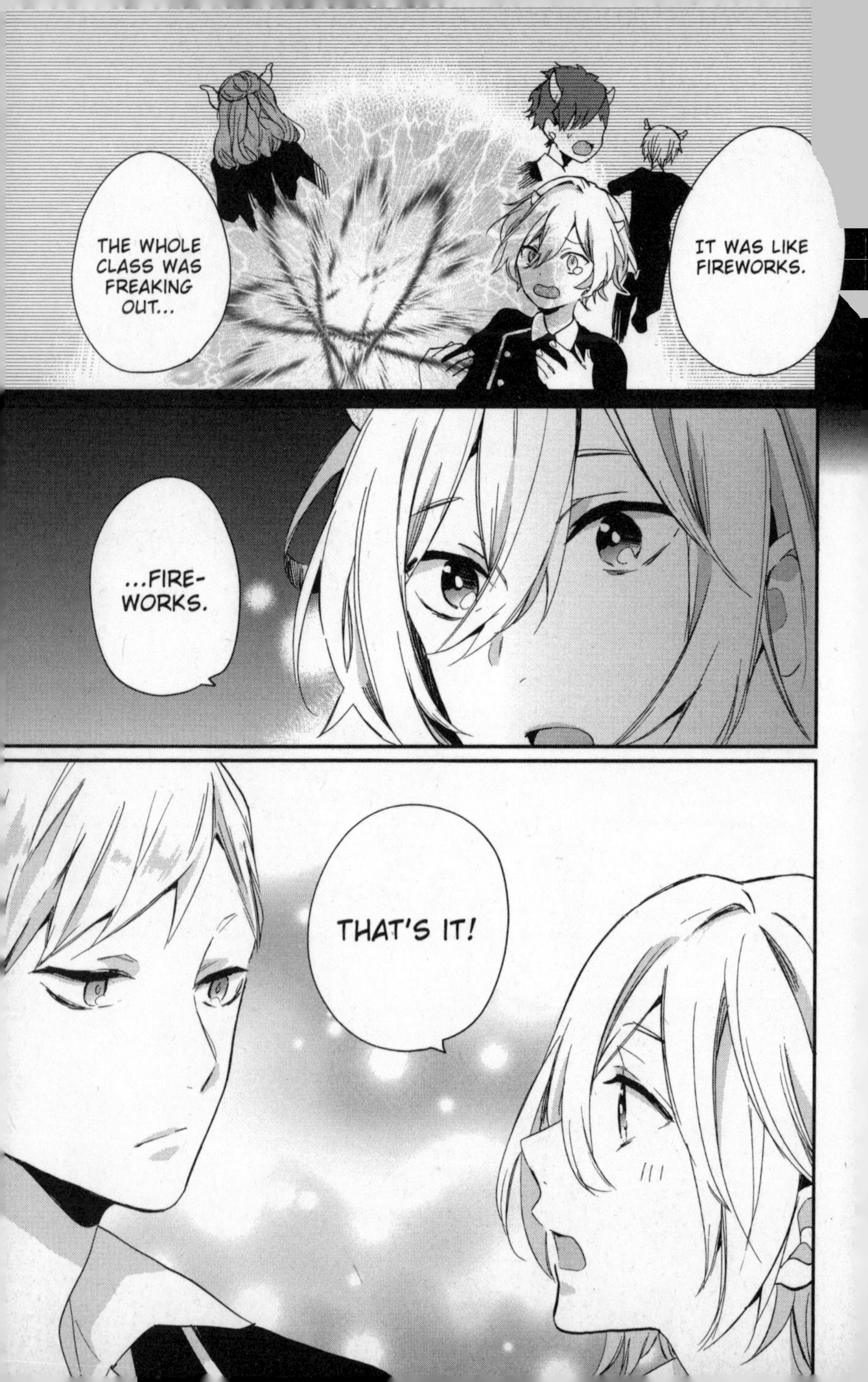
IT WAS LIKE FIREWORKS.
THE WHOLE CLASS WAS FREAKING OUT...
...FIRE-WORKS.
THAT'S IT!

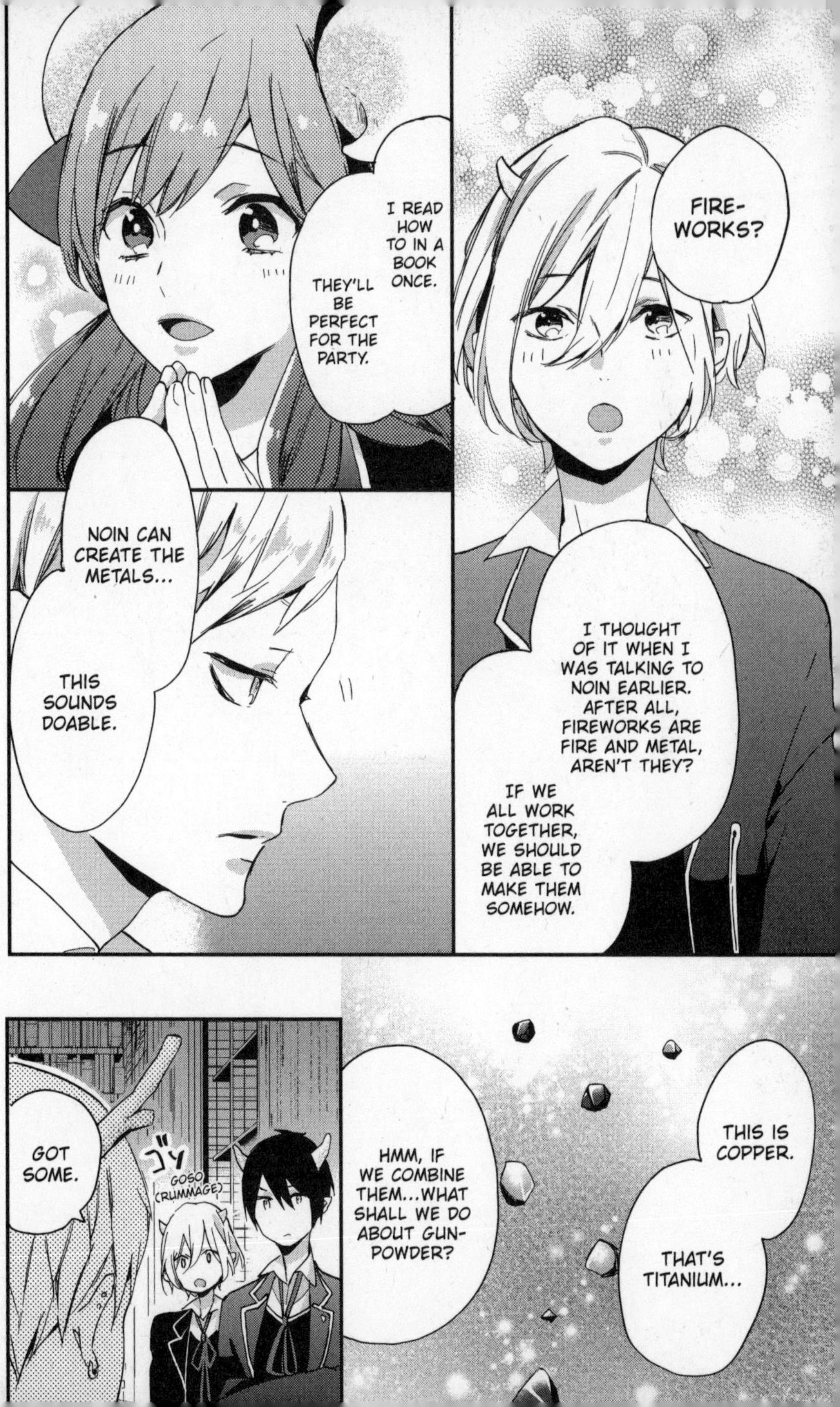
FIRE-WORKS?
I THOUGHT OF IT WHEN I WAS TALKING TO NOIN EARLIER. AFTER ALL, FIREWORKS ARE FIRE AND METAL, AREN'T THEY?
IF WE ALL WORK TOGETHER, WE SHOULD BE ABLE TO MAKE THEM SOMEHOW.
I READ HOW TO IN A BOOK ONCE.
THEY'LL BE PERFECT FOR THE PARTY.
NOIN CAN CREATE THE METALS...
THIS SOUNDS DOABLE.
THIS IS COPPER.
THAT'S TITANIUM...
HMM, IF WE COMBINE THEM...WHAT SHALL WE DO ABOUT GUN-POWDER?
ゴソ
GOSO (RUMMAGE)
GOT SOME.

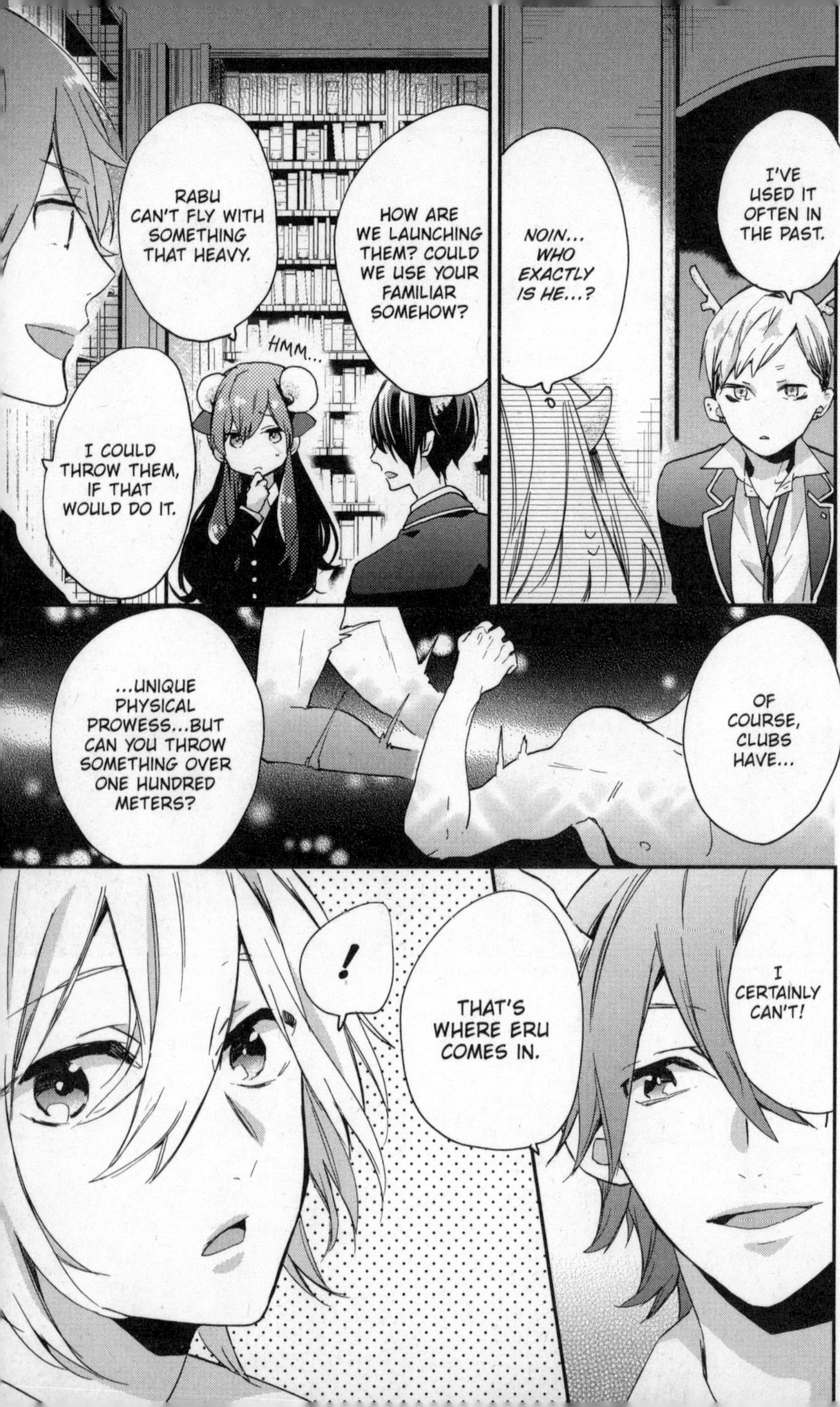
I'VE USED IT OFTEN IN THE PAST.
NOIN... WHO EXACTLY IS HE...?
HOW ARE WE LAUNCHING THEM? COULD WE USE YOUR FAMILIAR SOMEHOW?
HMM...
RABU CAN'T FLY WITH SOMETHING THAT HEAVY.
I COULD THROW THEM, IF THAT WOULD DO IT.
OF COURSE, CLUBS HAVE...
...UNIQUE PHYSICAL PROWESS...BUT CAN YOU THROW SOMETHING OVER ONE HUNDRED METERS?
I CERTAINLY CAN'T!
THAT'S WHERE ERU COMES IN.
!

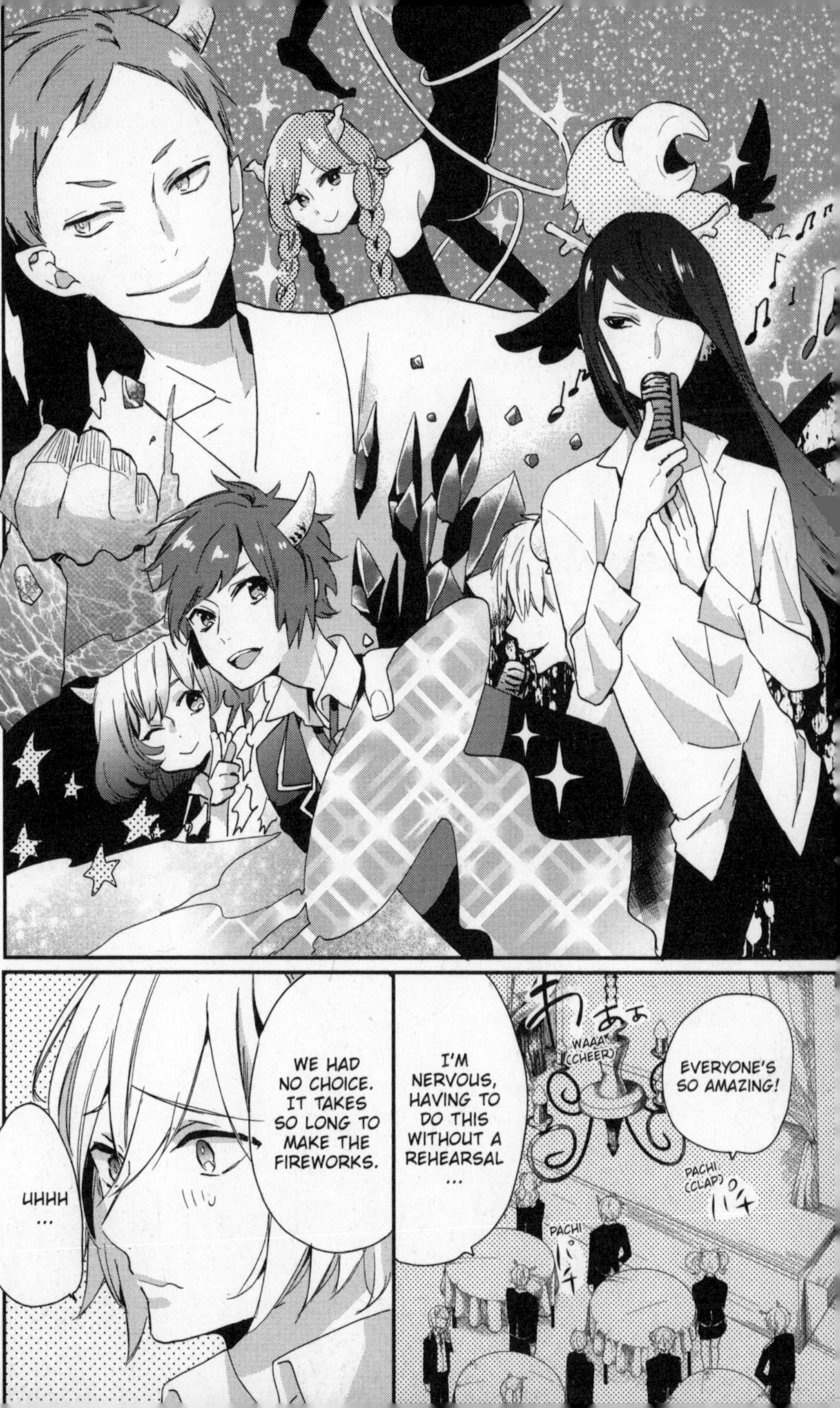
WAAA (CHEER)
EVERYONE'S SO AMAZING!
PACHI (CLAP)
PACHI
I'M NERVOUS, HAVING TO DO THIS WITHOUT A REHEARSAL...
WE HAD NO CHOICE. IT TAKES SO LONG TO MAKE THE FIREWORKS.
UHHH...

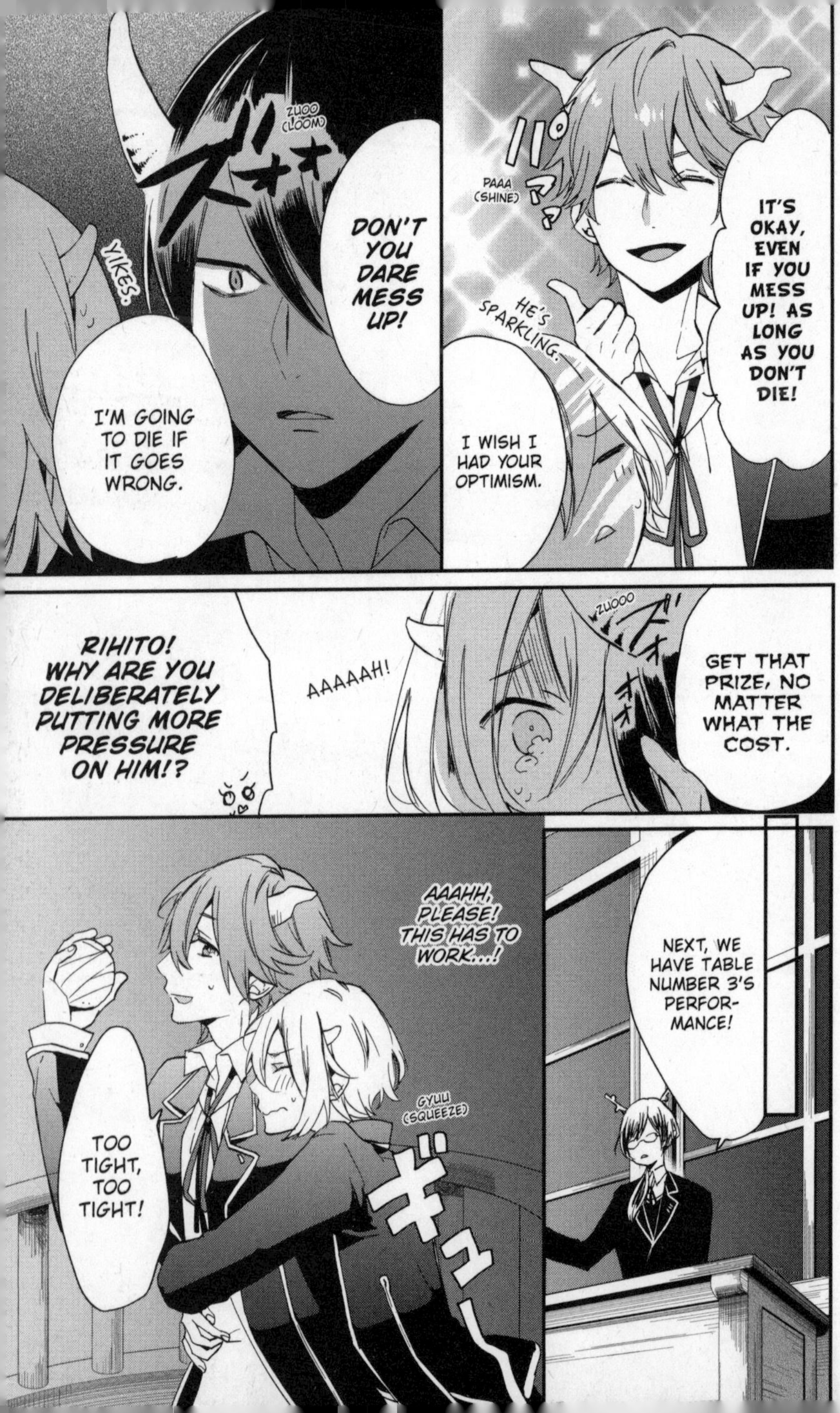
IT'S OKAY, EVEN IF YOU MESS UP! AS LONG AS YOU DON'T DIE!
PAAA (SHINE)
HE'S SPARKLING.
I WISH I HAD YOUR OPTIMISM.
ZUOO (LOOM)
DON'T YOU DARE MESS UP!
YIKES.
I'M GOING TO DIE IF IT GOES WRONG.
ZUOOO
GET THAT PRIZE, NO MATTER WHAT THE COST.
AAAAAH!
RIHITO! WHY ARE YOU DELIBERATELY PUTTING MORE PRESSURE ON HIM!?
NEXT, WE HAVE TABLE NUMBER 3'S PERFORMANCE!
AAAHH, PLEASE! THIS HAS TO WORK...!
GYUU (SQUEEZE)
TOO TIGHT, TOO TIGHT!

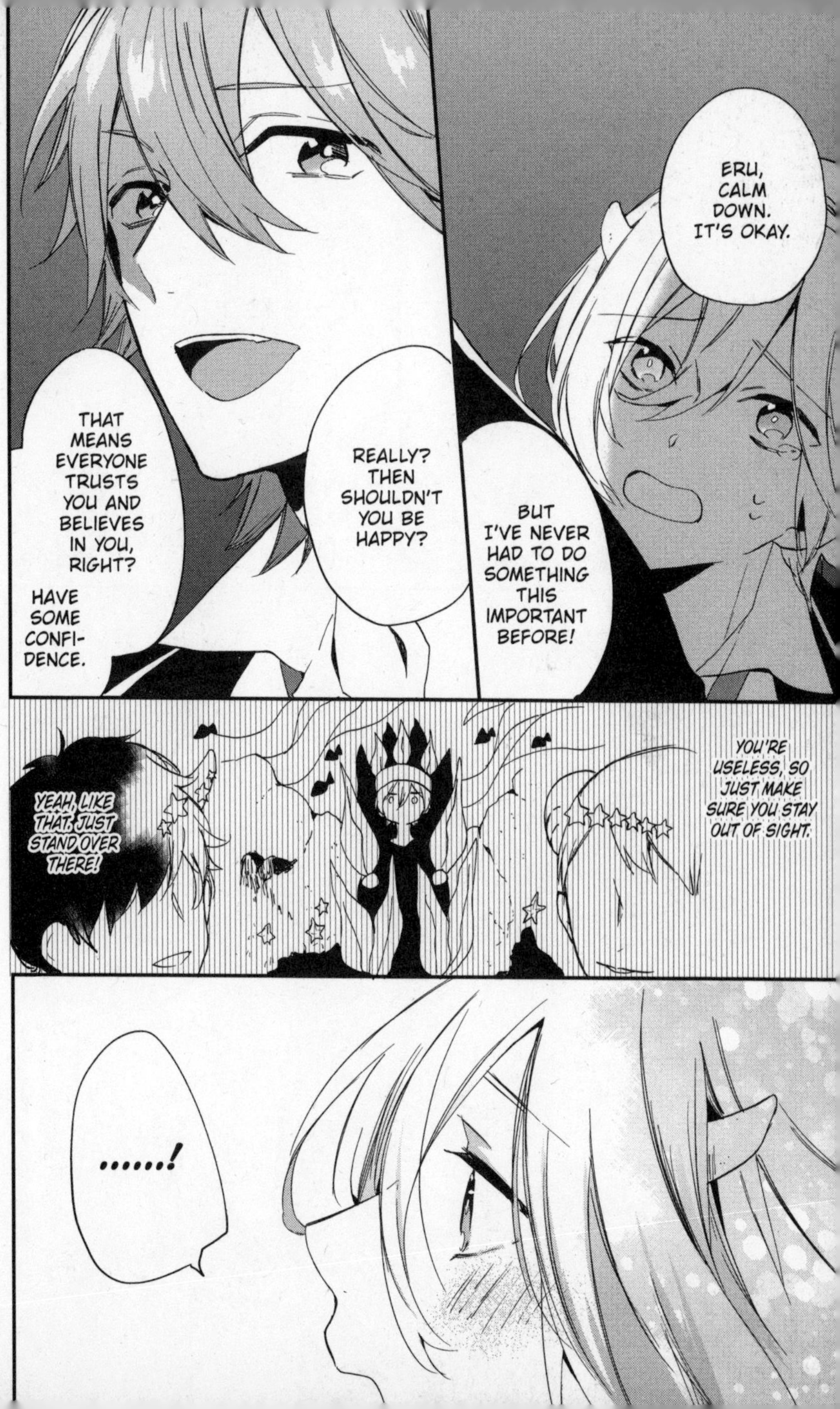
ERU, CALM DOWN. IT'S OKAY.
BUT I'VE NEVER HAD TO DO SOMETHING THIS IMPORTANT BEFORE!
REALLY? THEN SHOULDN'T YOU BE HAPPY?
THAT MEANS EVERYONE TRUSTS YOU AND BELIEVES IN YOU, RIGHT?
HAVE SOME CONFI-DENCE.
YOU'RE USELESS, SO JUST MAKE SURE YOU STAY OUT OF SIGHT.
YEAH, LIKE THAT. JUST STAND OVER THERE!
......!

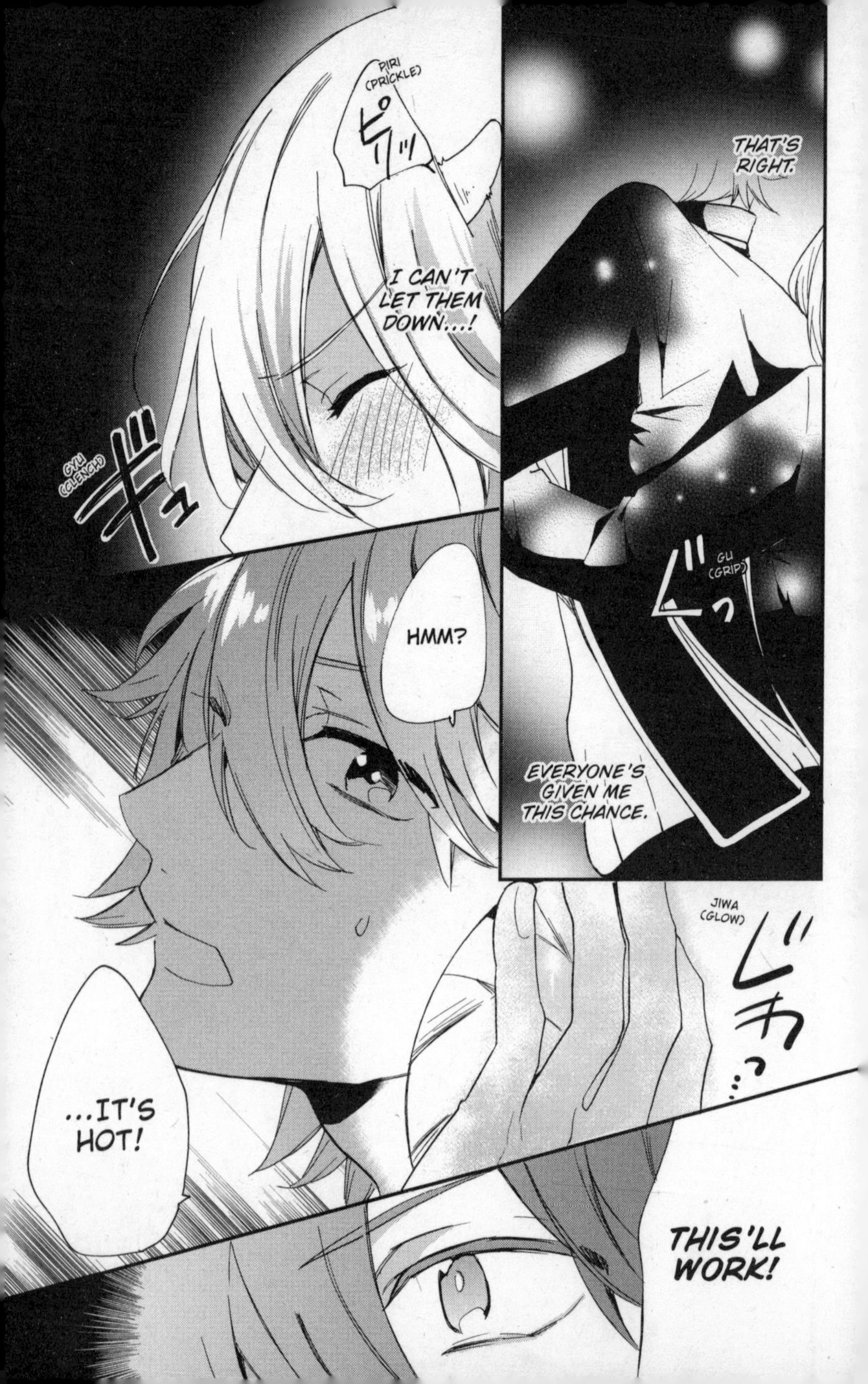
THAT'S RIGHT.
GU (GRIP)
EVERYONE'S GIVEN ME THIS CHANCE.
PIRI (PRICKLE)
I CAN'T LET THEM DOWN...!
GYU (CLENCH)
HMM?
JIWA (GLOW)
...IT'S HOT!
THIS'LL WORK!

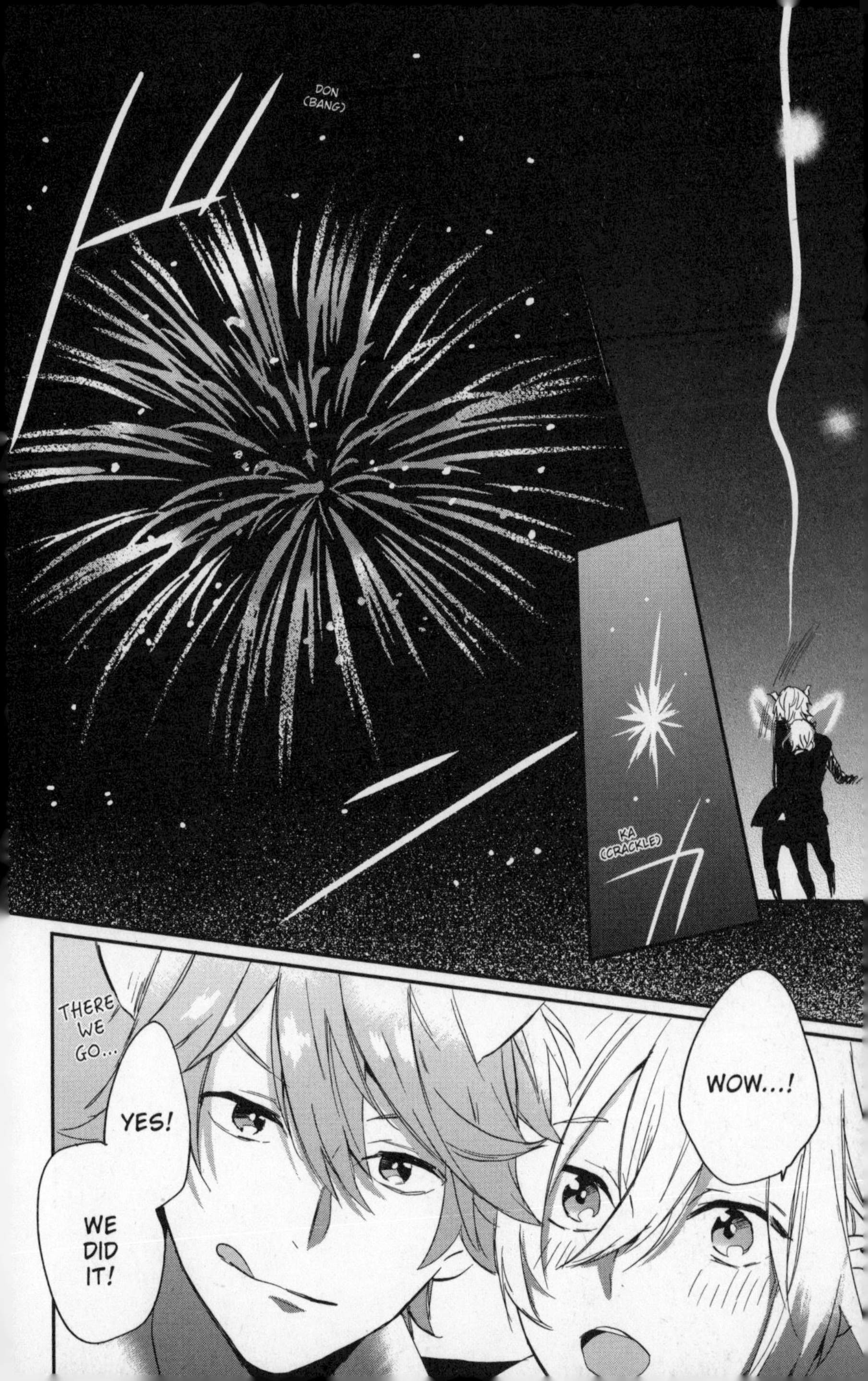
DON (BANG)
KA (CRACKLE)
WOW...!
THERE WE GO...
YES!
WE DID IT!

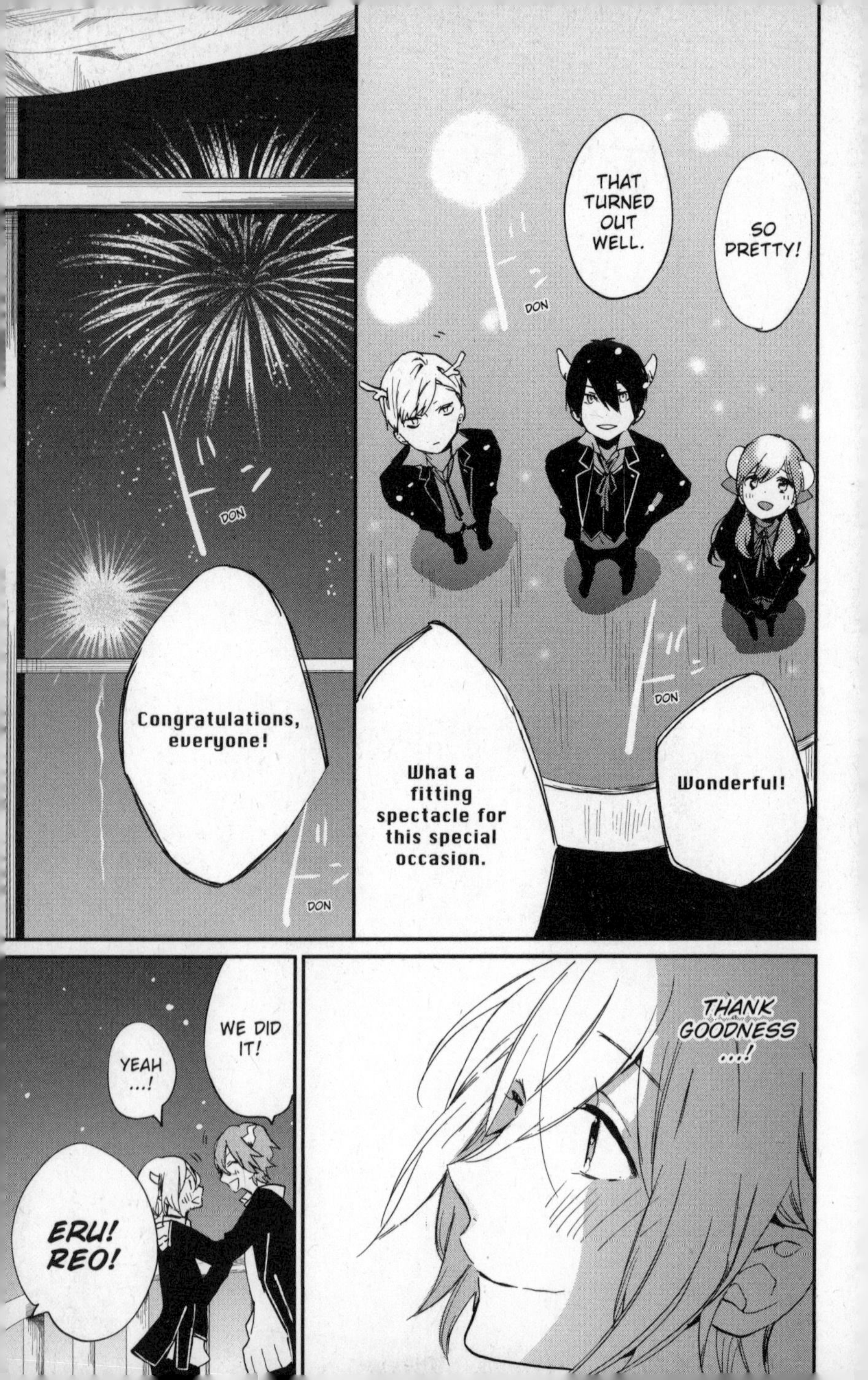
SO PRETTY!
THAT TURNED OUT WELL.
DON
DON
Wonderful!
What a fitting spectacle for this special occasion.
DON
Congratulations, everyone!
DON
THANK GOODNESS ...!
WE DID IT!
YEAH ...!
ERU! REO!

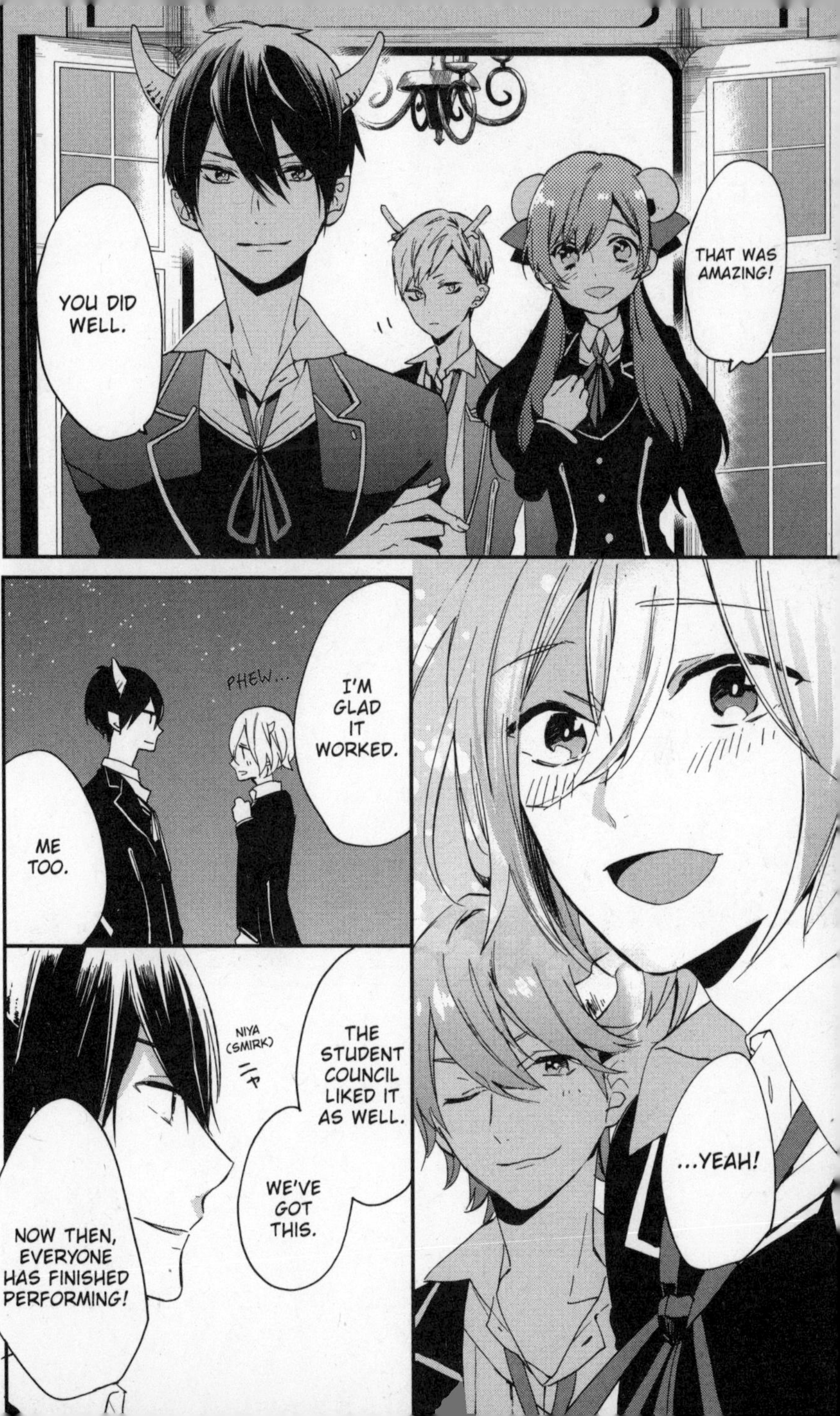
THAT WAS AMAZING!
YOU DID WELL.
...YEAH!
I'M GLAD IT WORKED.
PHEW...
ME TOO.
THE STUDENT COUNCIL LIKED IT AS WELL.
NIYA (SMIRK)
ニヤ
WE'VE GOT THIS.
NOW THEN, EVERYONE HAS FINISHED PERFORMING!

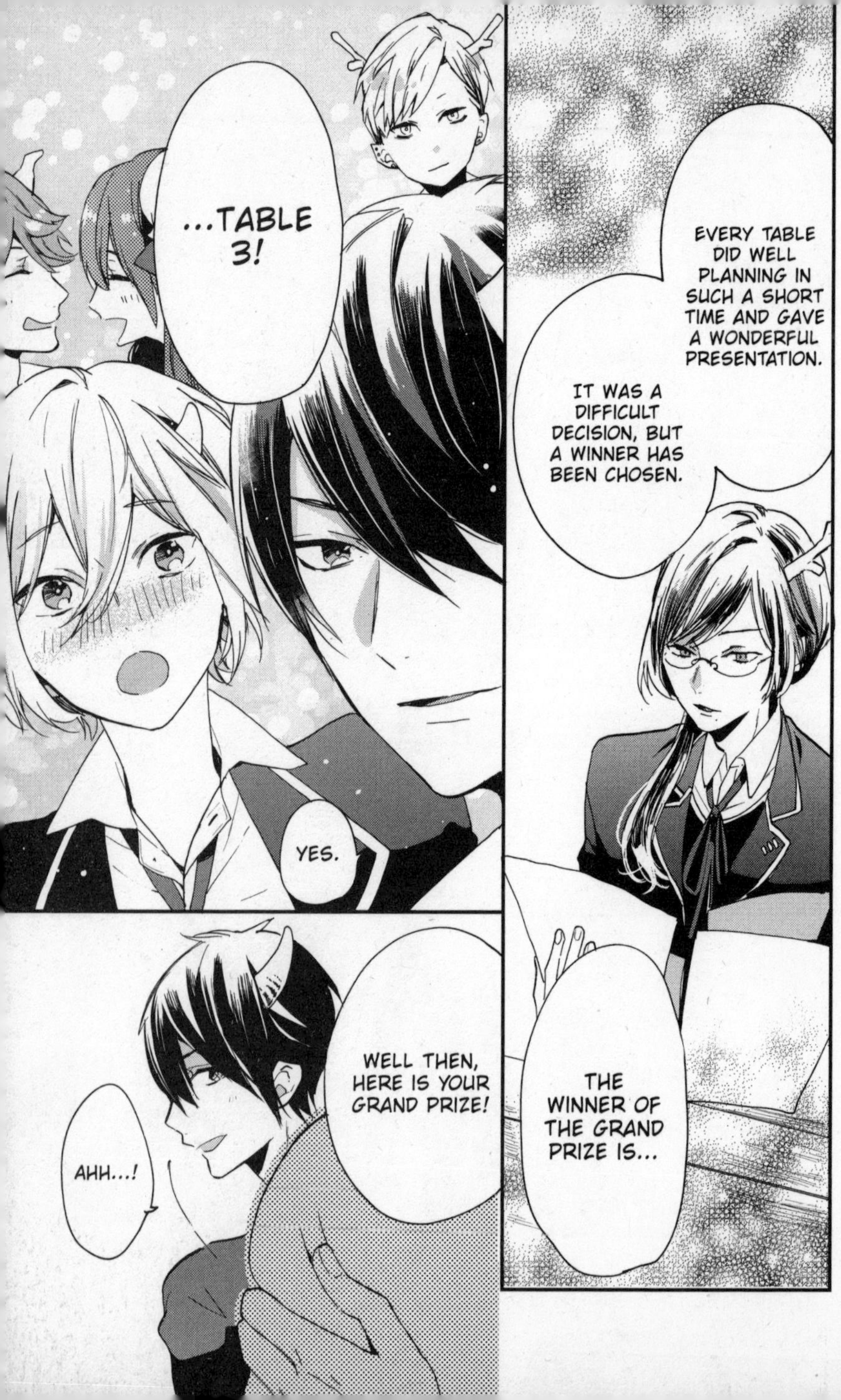
EVERY TABLE DID WELL PLANNING IN SUCH A SHORT TIME AND GAVE A WONDERFUL PRESENTATION.
IT WAS A DIFFICULT DECISION, BUT A WINNER HAS BEEN CHOSEN.
THE WINNER OF THE GRAND PRIZE IS...
...TABLE 3!
YES.
WELL THEN, HERE IS YOUR GRAND PRIZE!
AHH...!

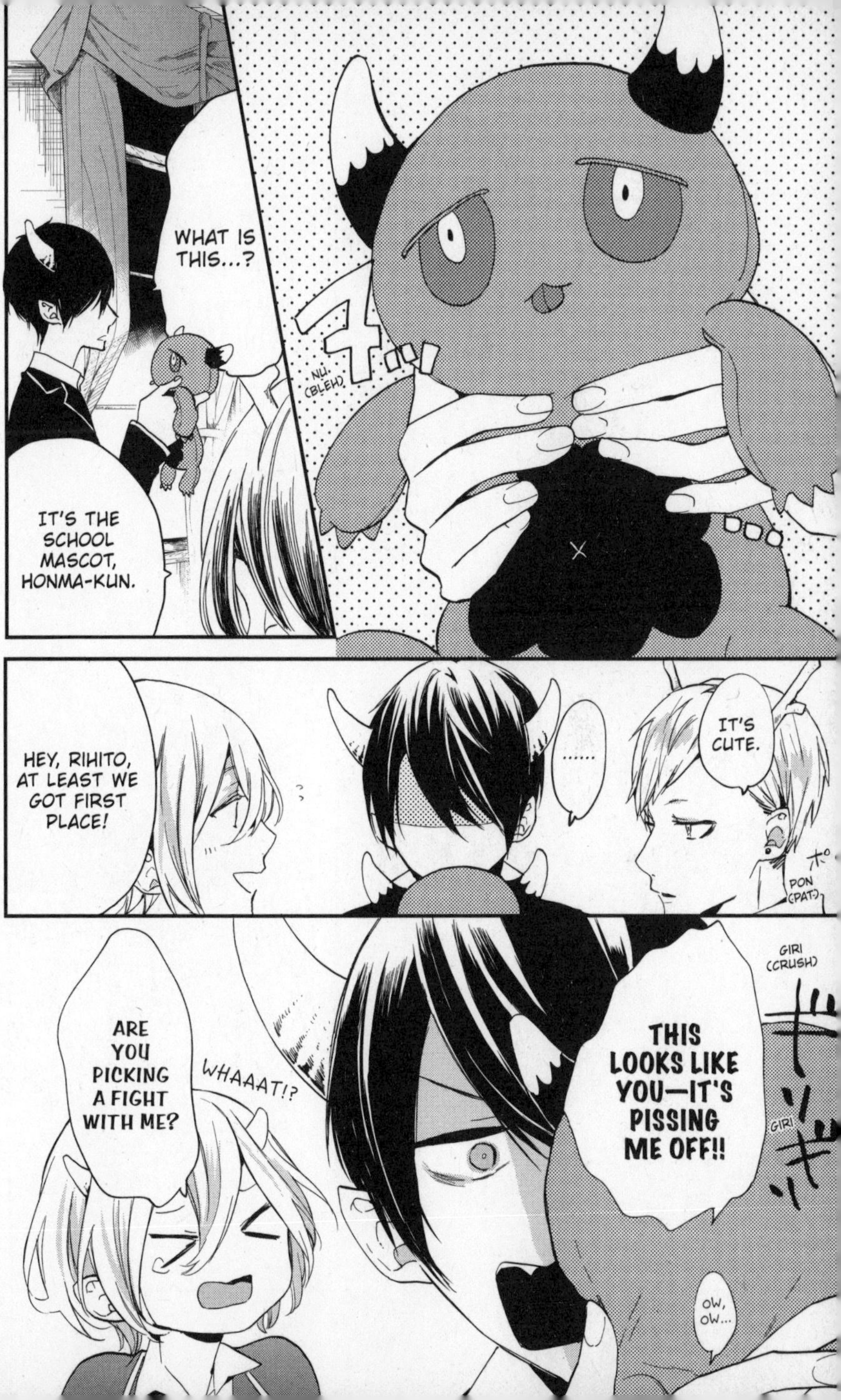
NU. (BLEH)
WHAT IS THIS...?
IT'S THE SCHOOL MASCOT, HONMA-KUN.
IT'S CUTE.
PON (PAT)
......
HEY, RIHITO, AT LEAST WE GOT FIRST PLACE!
GIRI (CRUSH)
THIS LOOKS LIKE YOU—IT'S PISSING ME OFF!!
GIRI
OW, OW...
WHAAAT!?
ARE YOU PICKING A FIGHT WITH ME?

CHAPTER 3

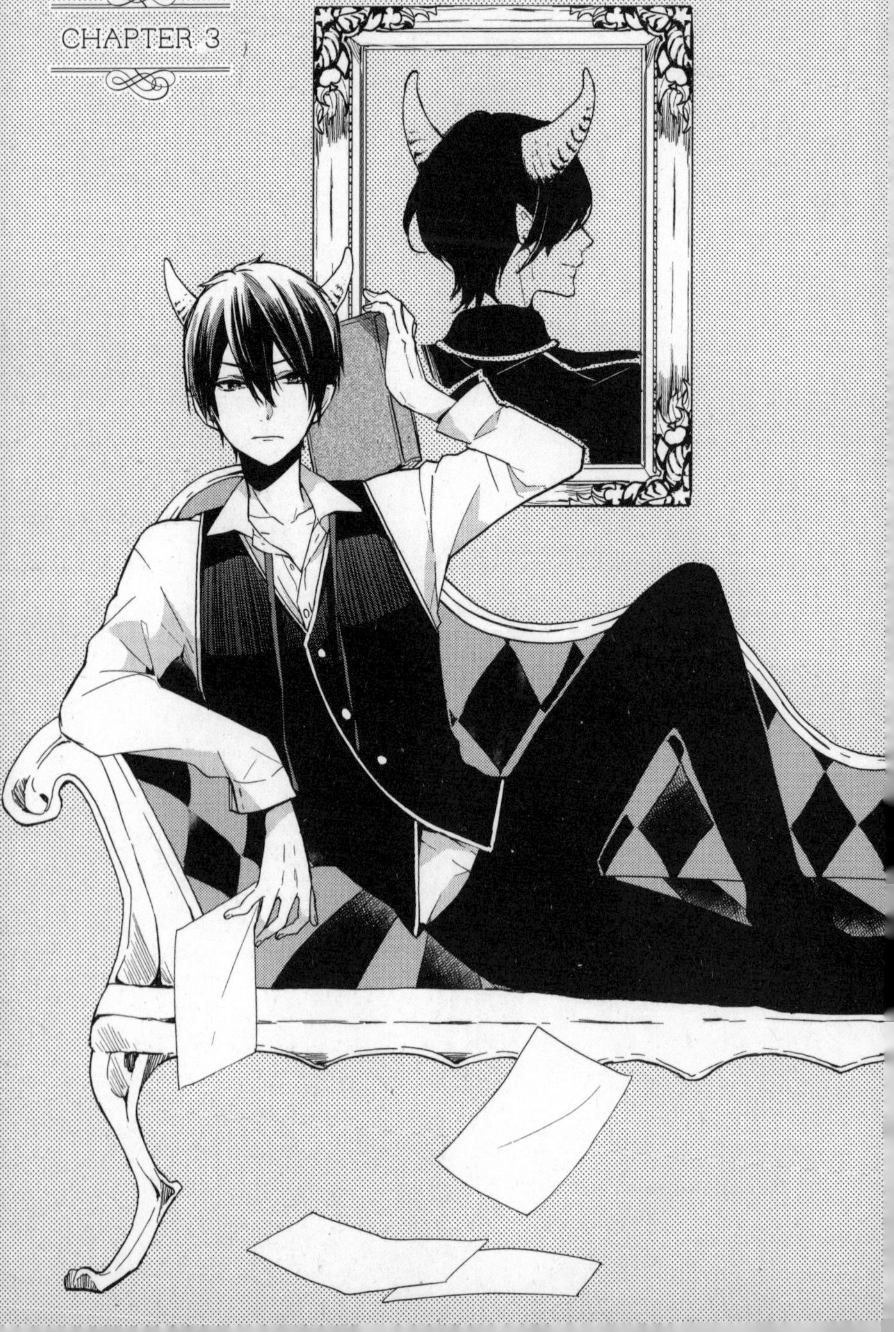

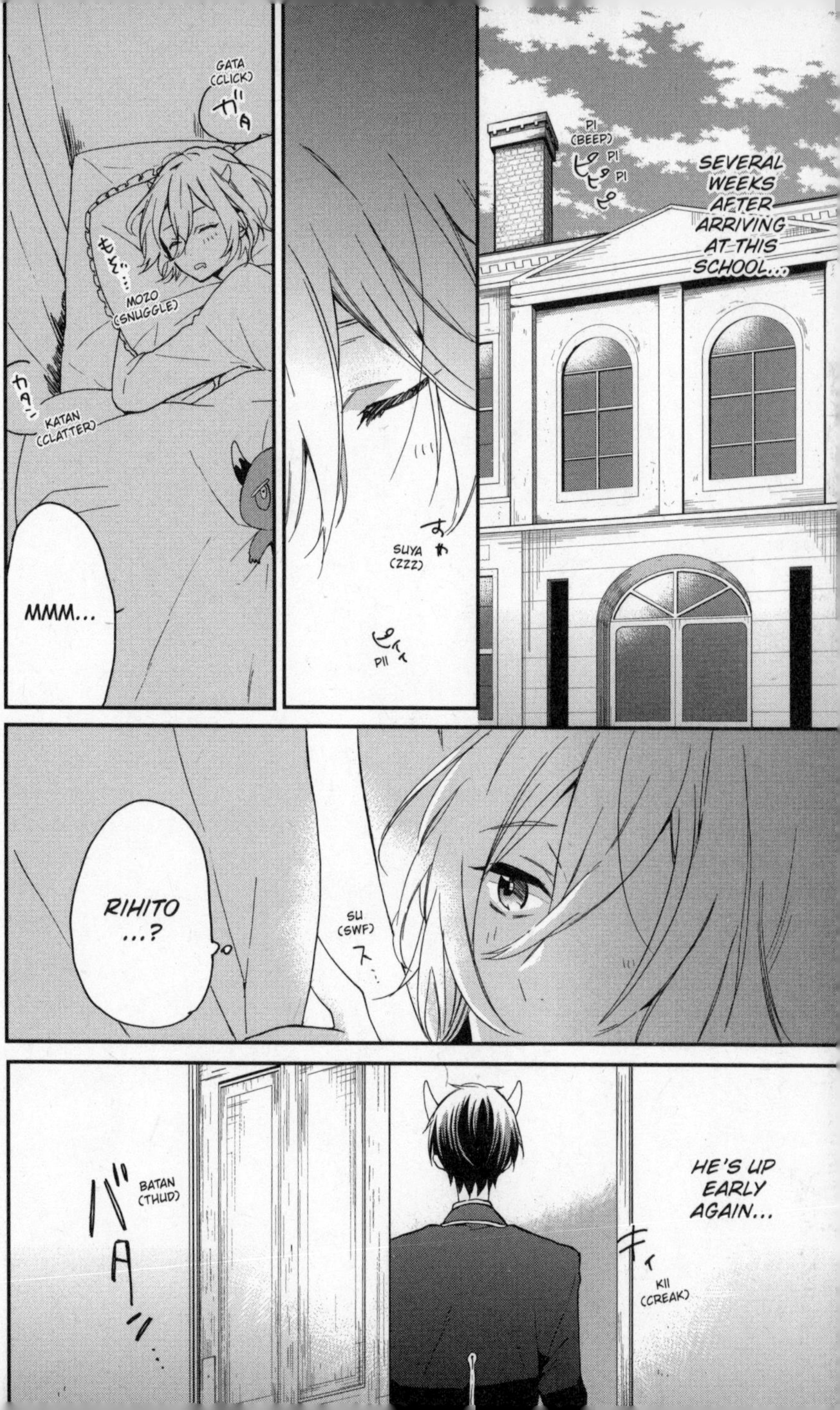
PI (BEEP) PI PI
ピピピ
SEVERAL WEEKS AFTER ARRIVING AT THIS SCHOOL...
すや
SUYA (ZZZ)
ピィ
PII
GATA (CLICK)
ガタ
もぞ…
MOZO (SNUGGLE)
カタン
KATAN (CLATTER)
MMM...
SU (SWF)
ス…
RIHITO ...?
HE'S UP EARLY AGAIN...
ギィ
KII (CREAK)
バタン…
BATAN (THUD)

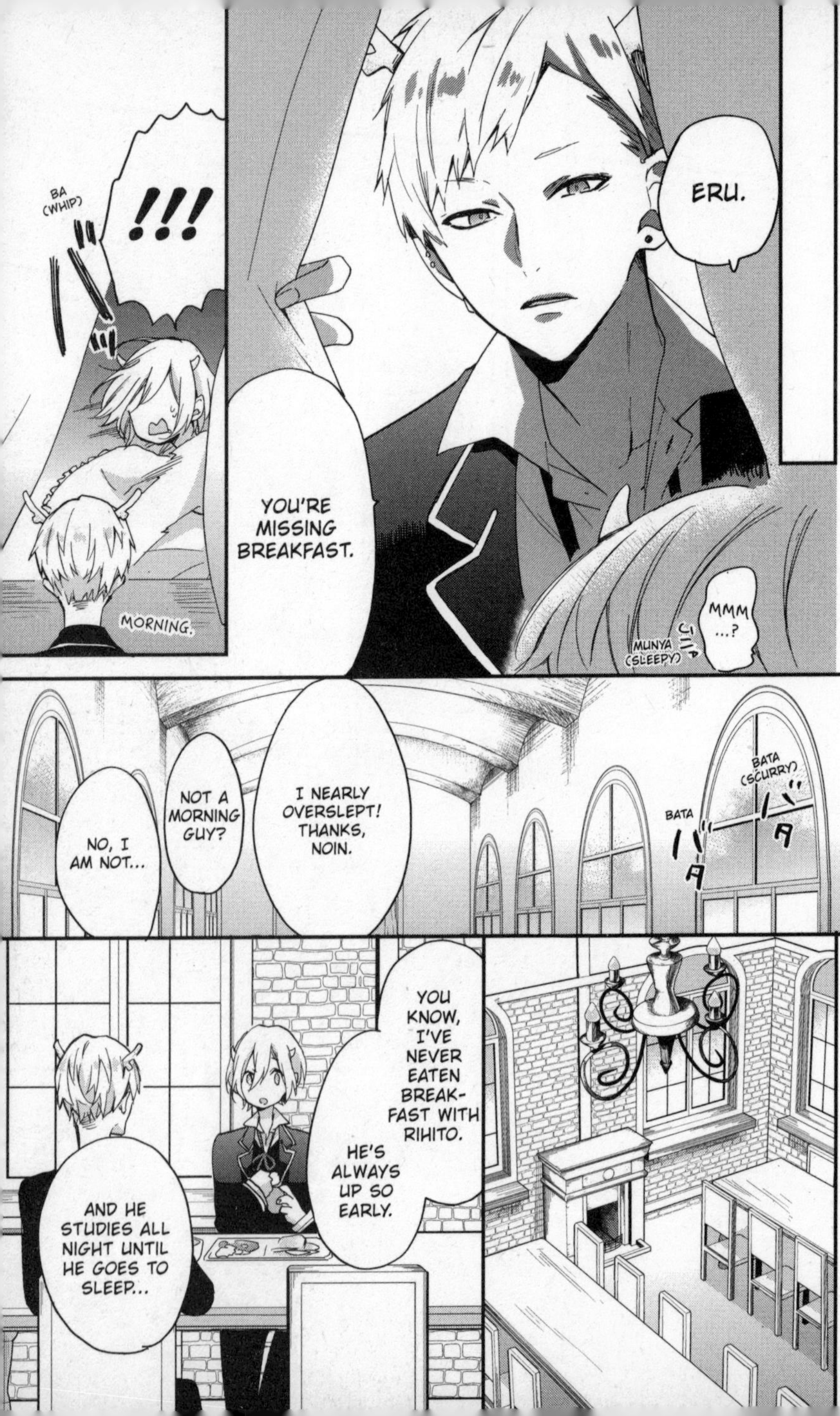
ERU.
YOU'RE MISSING BREAKFAST.
MMM ...?
MUNYA (SLEEPY)
BA (WHIP)
!!!
MORNING.
BATA (SCURRY)
BATA
I NEARLY OVERSLEPT! THANKS, NOIN.
NOT A MORNING GUY?
NO, I AM NOT...
YOU KNOW, I'VE NEVER EATEN BREAK-FAST WITH RIHITO.
HE'S ALWAYS UP SO EARLY.
AND HE STUDIES ALL NIGHT UNTIL HE GOES TO SLEEP...

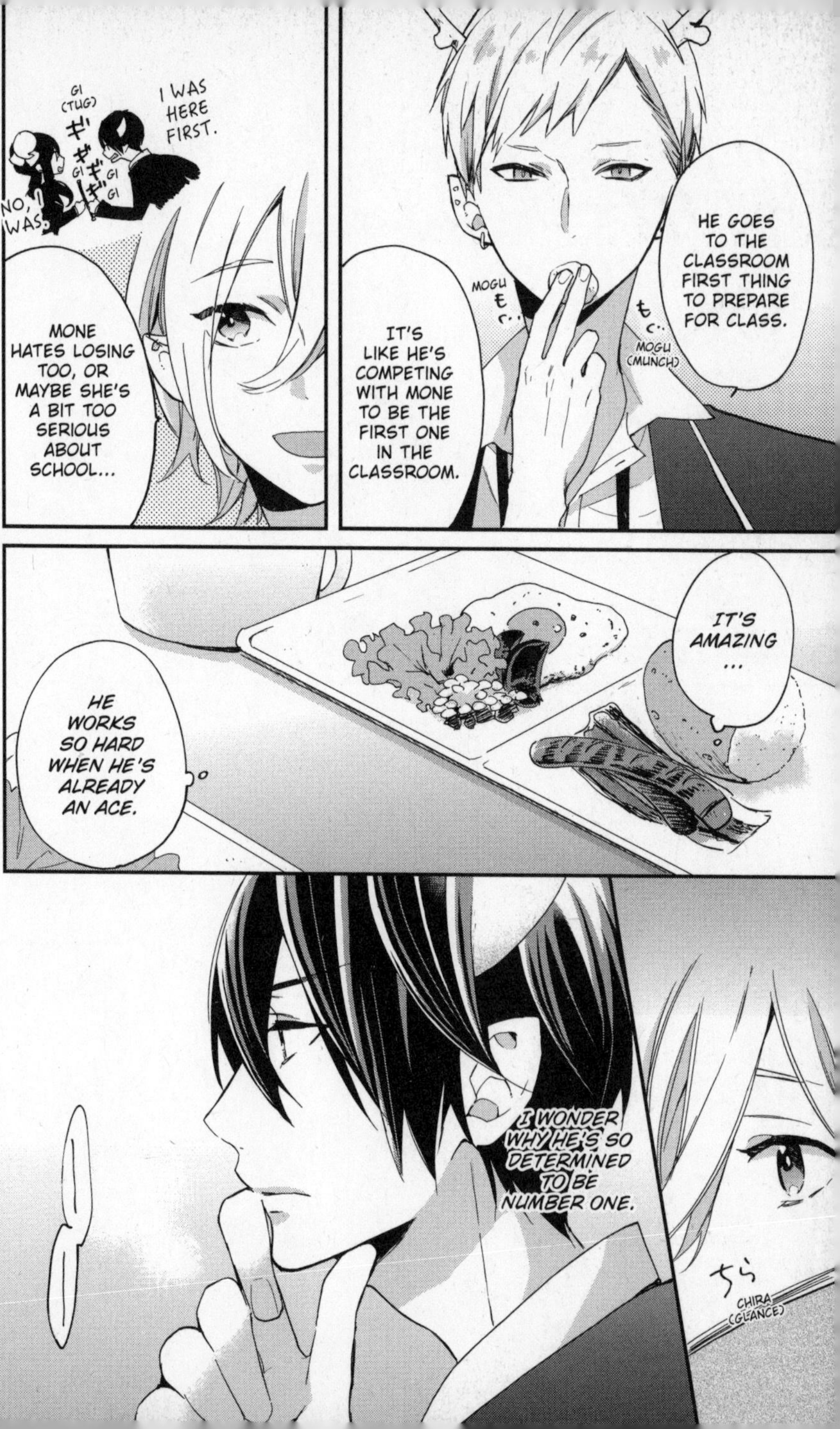

HE GOES TO THE CLASSROOM FIRST THING TO PREPARE FOR CLASS.
MOGU (MUNCH)
IT'S LIKE HE'S COMPETING WITH MONE TO BE THE FIRST ONE IN THE CLASSROOM.
MOGU
I WAS HERE FIRST.
GI (TUG)
GI GI GI
NO, I WAS.
MONE HATES LOSING TOO, OR MAYBE SHE'S A BIT TOO SERIOUS ABOUT SCHOOL...
IT'S AMAZING...
HE WORKS SO HARD WHEN HE'S ALREADY AN ACE.
CHIRA (GLANCE)
I WONDER WHY HE'S SO DETERMINED TO BE NUMBER ONE.

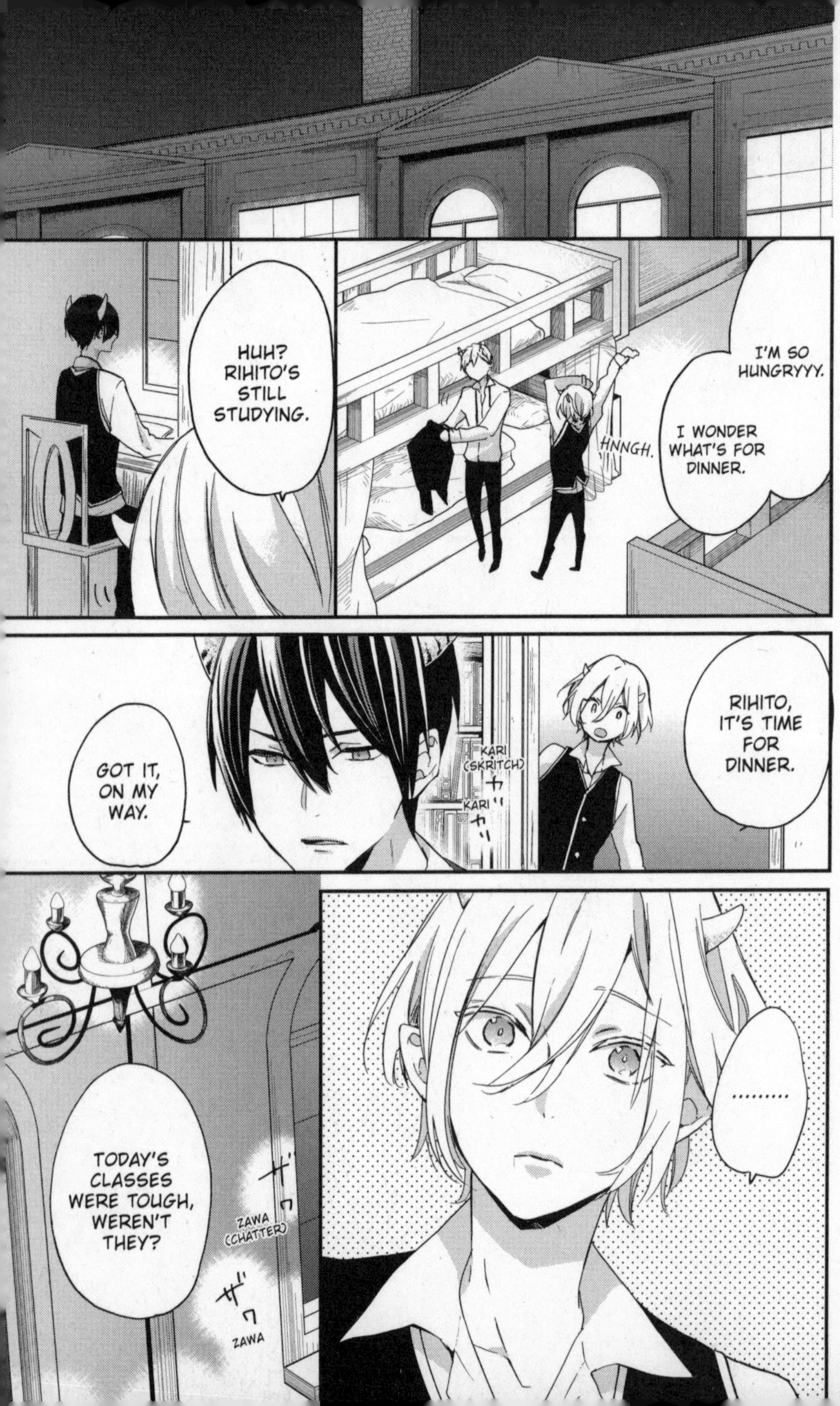
I'M SO HUNGRYYY.
I WONDER WHAT'S FOR DINNER.
HNNGH.
HUH? RIHITO'S STILL STUDYING.
RIHITO, IT'S TIME FOR DINNER.
KARI (SKRITCH)
KARI
GOT IT, ON MY WAY.
....
TODAY'S CLASSES WERE TOUGH, WEREN'T THEY?
ZAWA (CHATTER)
ZAWA

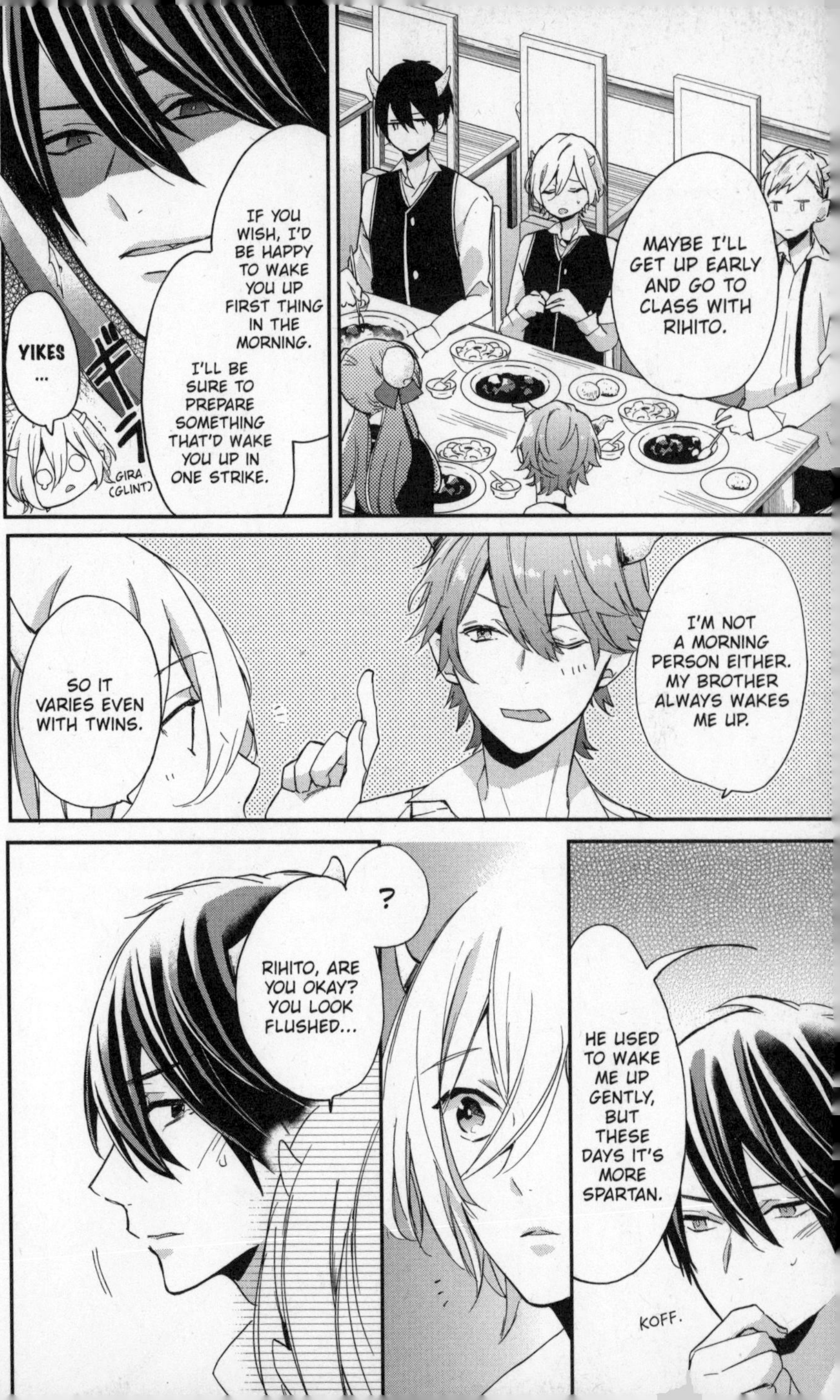
MAYBE I'LL GET UP EARLY AND GO TO CLASS WITH RIHITO.
IF YOU WISH, I'D BE HAPPY TO WAKE YOU UP FIRST THING IN THE MORNING.
I'LL BE SURE TO PREPARE SOMETHING THAT'D WAKE YOU UP IN ONE STRIKE.
YIKES ...
GIRA (GLINT)
I'M NOT A MORNING PERSON EITHER. MY BROTHER ALWAYS WAKES ME UP.
SO IT VARIES EVEN WITH TWINS.
HE USED TO WAKE ME UP GENTLY, BUT THESE DAYS IT'S MORE SPARTAN.
KOFF.
?
RIHITO, ARE YOU OKAY? YOU LOOK FLUSHED...

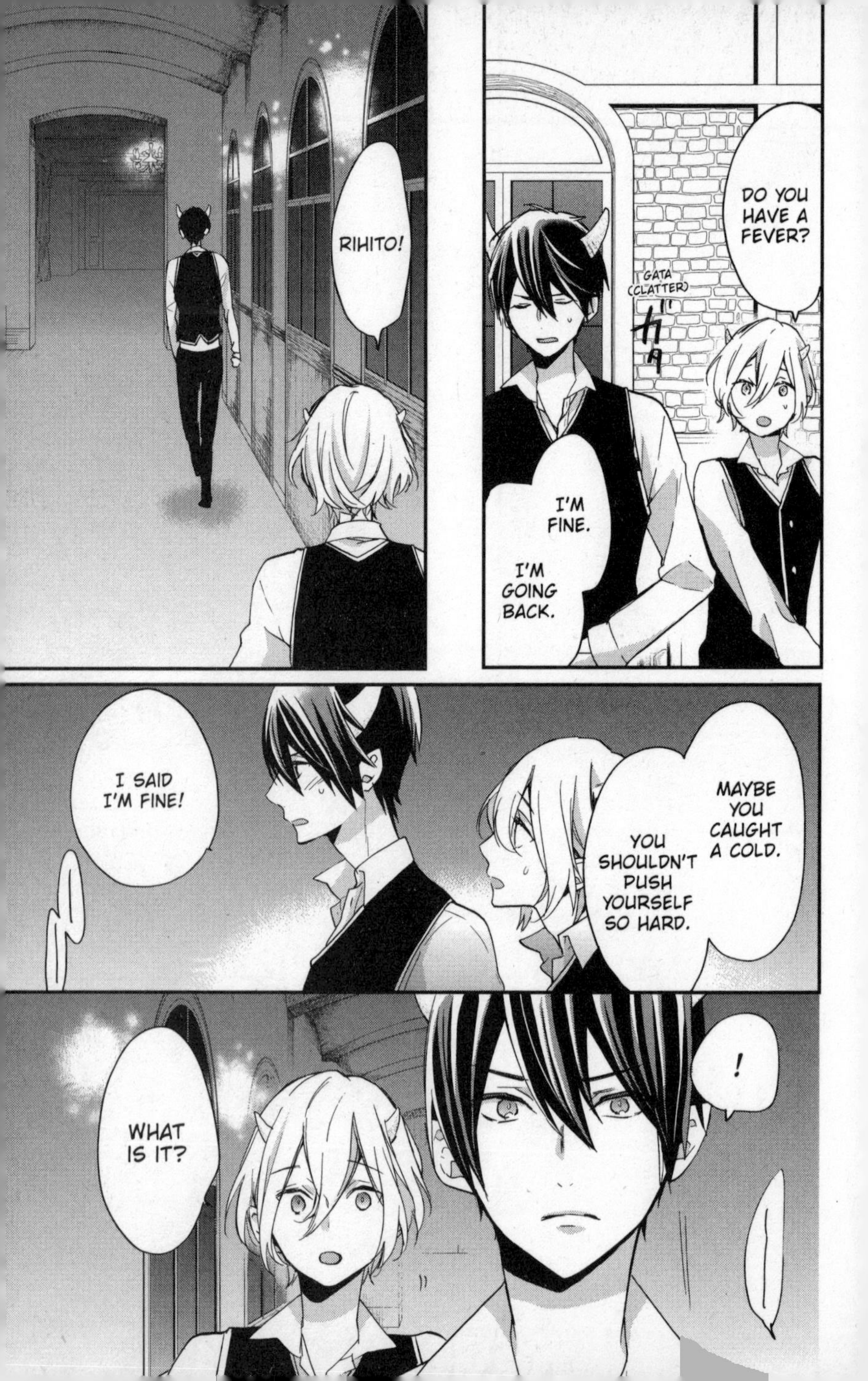
DO YOU HAVE A FEVER?
GATA (CLATTER)
I'M FINE.
I'M GOING BACK.
RIHITO!
MAYBE YOU CAUGHT A COLD.
YOU SHOULDN'T PUSH YOURSELF SO HARD.
I SAID I'M FINE!
!
WHAT IS IT?

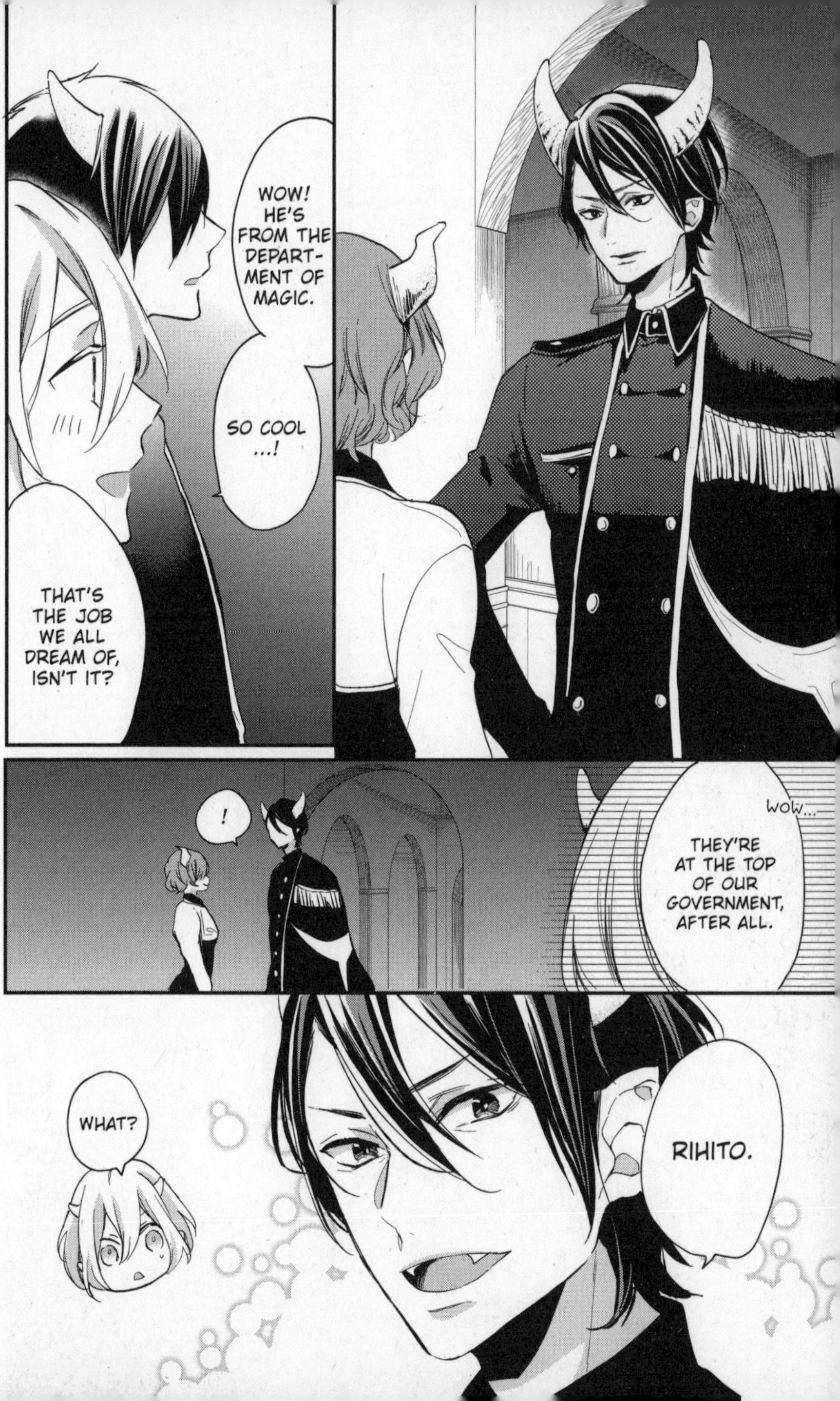
WOW! HE'S FROM THE DEPART-MENT OF MAGIC.
SO COOL ...!
THAT'S THE JOB WE ALL DREAM OF, ISN'T IT?
WOW...
THEY'RE AT THE TOP OF OUR GOVERNMENT, AFTER ALL.
!
RIHITO.
WHAT?

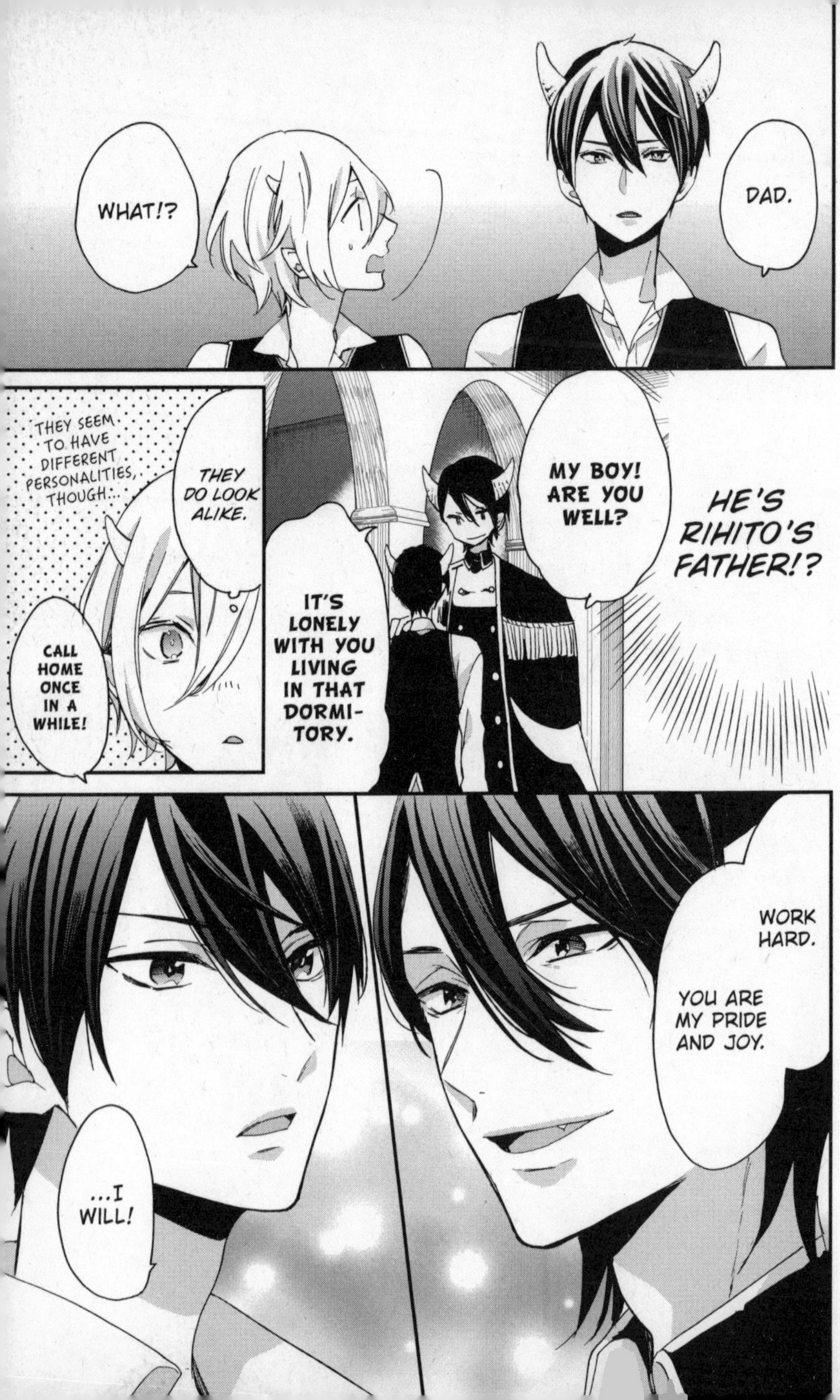
DAD.
WHAT!?
HE'S RIHITO'S FATHER!?
MY BOY! ARE YOU WELL?
IT'S LONELY WITH YOU LIVING IN THAT DORMITORY.
THEY DO LOOK ALIKE.
THEY SEEM TO HAVE DIFFERENT PERSONALITIES, THOUGH...
CALL HOME ONCE IN A WHILE!
WORK HARD.
YOU ARE MY PRIDE AND JOY.
...I WILL!

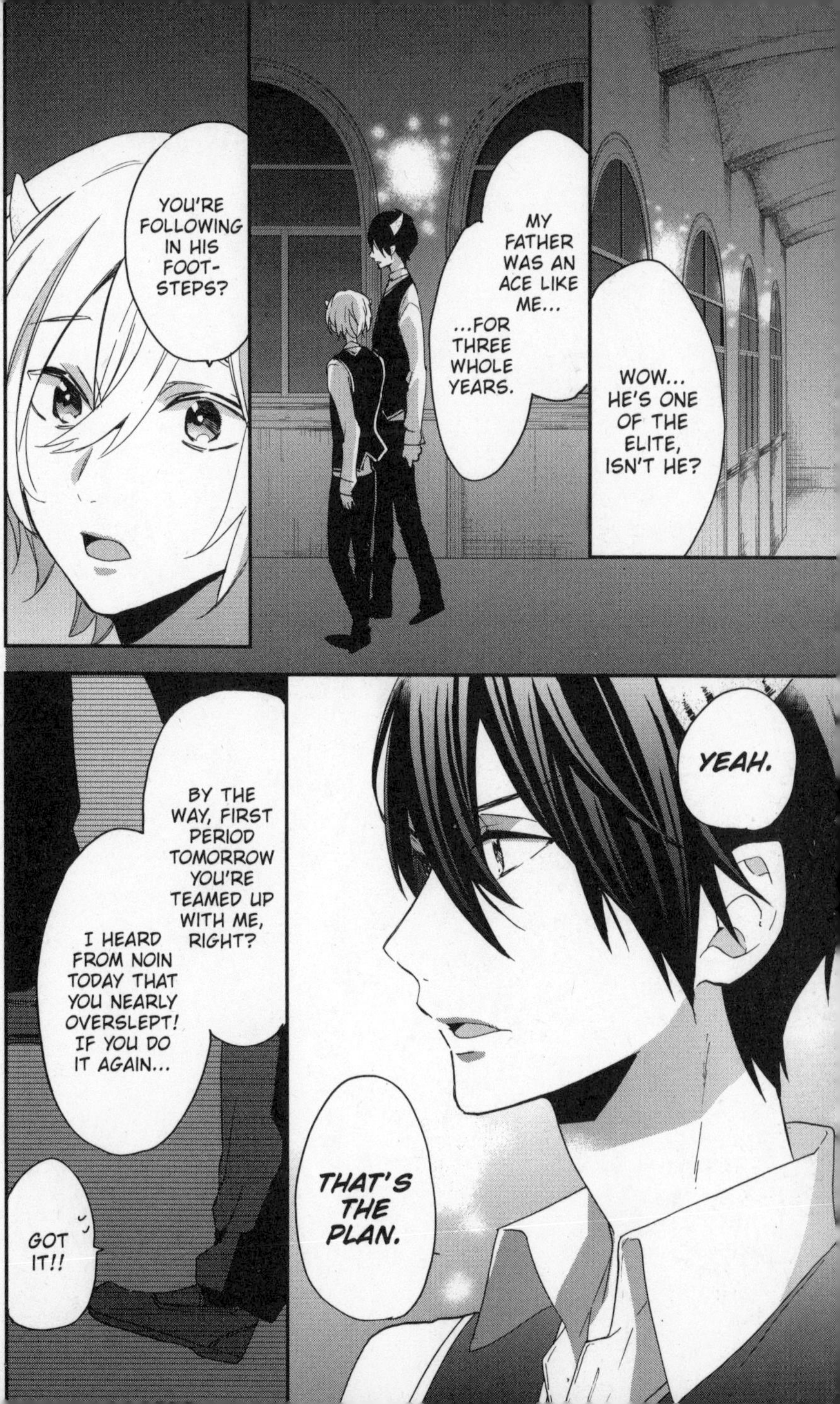
WOW... HE'S ONE OF THE ELITE, ISN'T HE?
MY FATHER WAS AN ACE LIKE ME...
...FOR THREE WHOLE YEARS.
YOU'RE FOLLOWING IN HIS FOOT-STEPS?
YEAH.
THAT'S THE PLAN.
BY THE WAY, FIRST PERIOD TOMORROW YOU'RE TEAMED UP WITH ME, RIGHT?
I HEARD FROM NOIN TODAY THAT YOU NEARLY OVERSLEPT! IF YOU DO IT AGAIN...
GOT IT!!

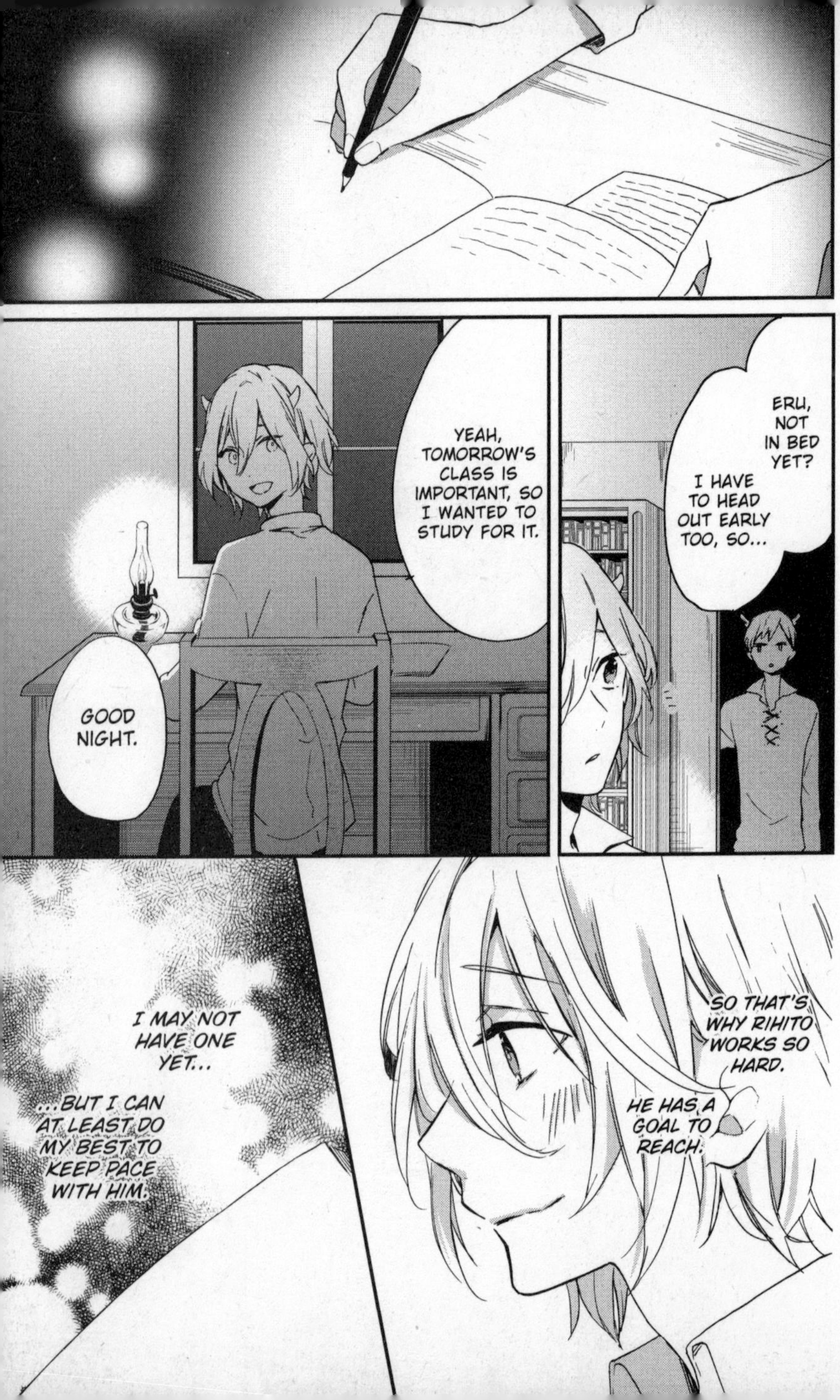
ERU, NOT IN BED YET?
I HAVE TO HEAD OUT EARLY TOO, SO...
YEAH, TOMORROW'S CLASS IS IMPORTANT, SO I WANTED TO STUDY FOR IT.
GOOD NIGHT.
SO THAT'S WHY RIHITO WORKS SO HARD.
HE HAS A GOAL TO REACH.
I MAY NOT HAVE ONE YET...
...BUT I CAN AT LEAST DO MY BEST TO KEEP PACE WITH HIM.

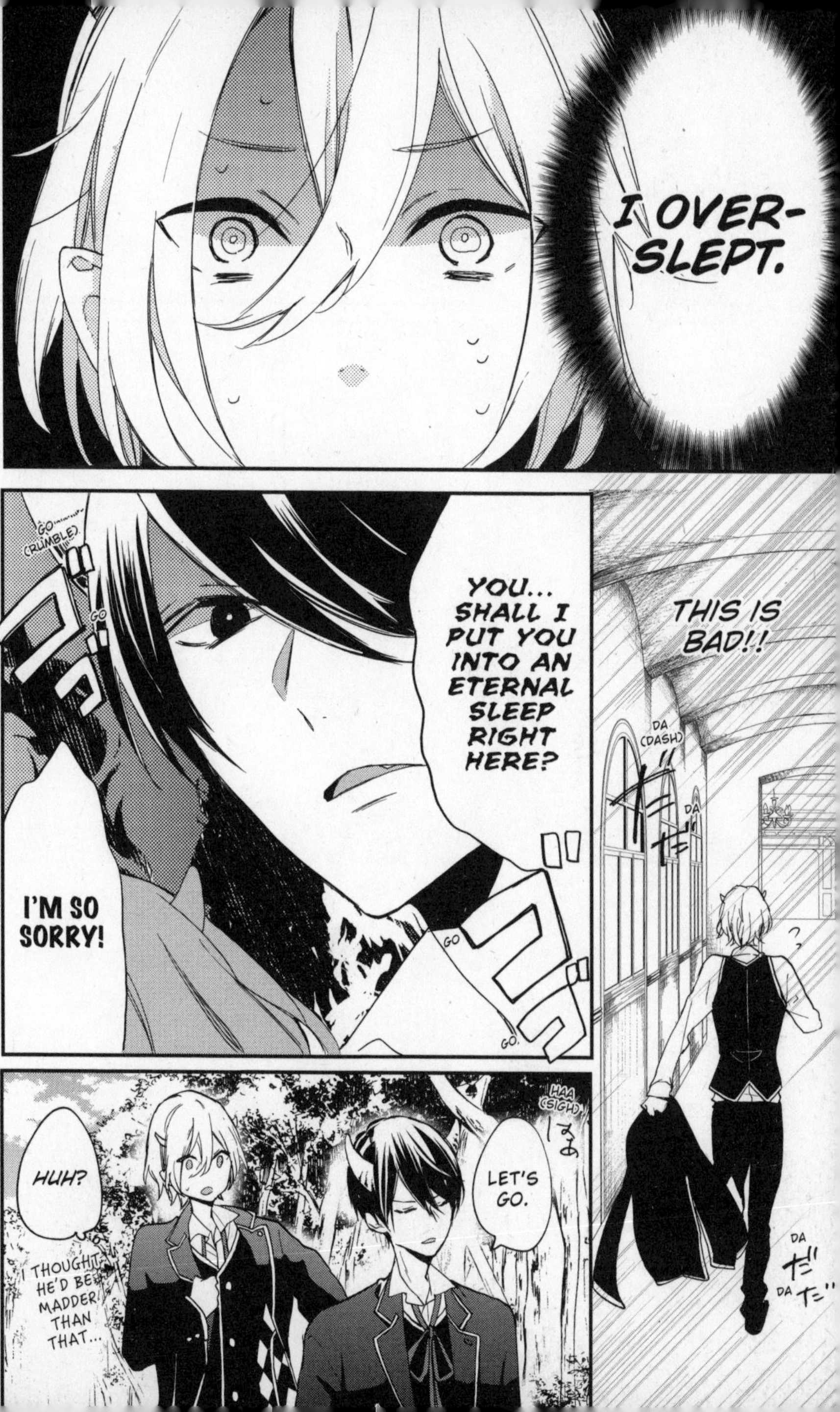
I OVER-SLEPT.
THIS IS BAD!!
DA (DASH)
DA
DA
DA
GO (RUMBLE)
GO
YOU... SHALL I PUT YOU INTO AN ETERNAL SLEEP RIGHT HERE?
I'M SO SORRY!
GO
GO
HAA (SIGH)
LET'S GO.
HUH?
I THOUGHT HE'D BE MADDER THAN THAT...

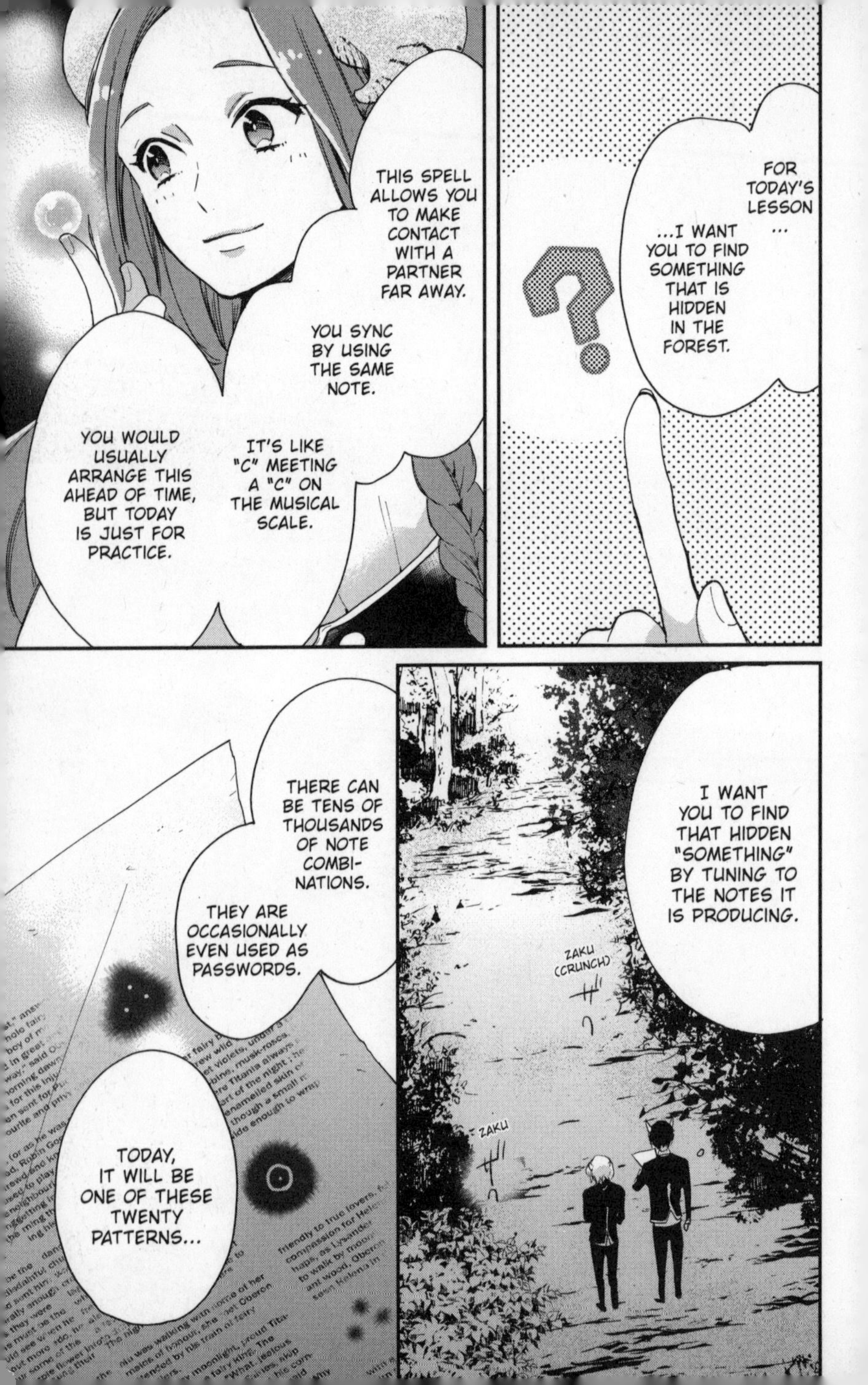
FOR TODAY'S LESSON ...
...I WANT YOU TO FIND SOMETHING THAT IS HIDDEN IN THE FOREST.
THIS SPELL ALLOWS YOU TO MAKE CONTACT WITH A PARTNER FAR AWAY.
YOU SYNC BY USING THE SAME NOTE.
IT'S LIKE "C" MEETING A "C" ON THE MUSICAL SCALE.
YOU WOULD USUALLY ARRANGE THIS AHEAD OF TIME, BUT TODAY IS JUST FOR PRACTICE.
I WANT YOU TO FIND THAT HIDDEN "SOMETHING" BY TUNING TO THE NOTES IT IS PRODUCING.
ZAKU (CRUNCH)
ZAKU
THERE CAN BE TENS OF THOUSANDS OF NOTE COMBI-NATIONS.
THEY ARE OCCASIONALLY EVEN USED AS PASSWORDS.
TODAY, IT WILL BE ONE OF THESE TWENTY PATTERNS...

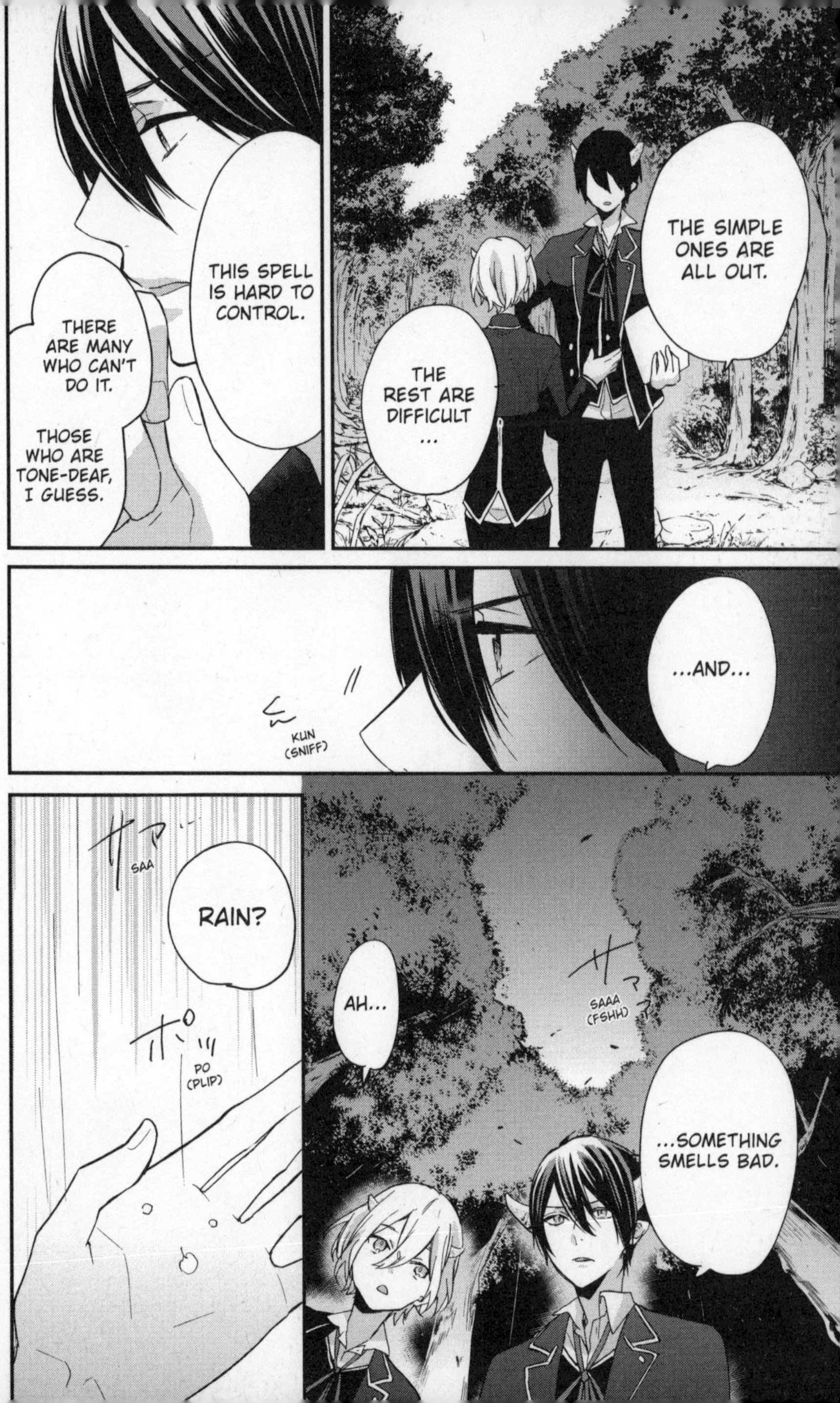
THE SIMPLE ONES ARE ALL OUT.
THE REST ARE DIFFICULT ...
THIS SPELL IS HARD TO CONTROL.
THERE ARE MANY WHO CAN'T DO IT.
THOSE WHO ARE TONE-DEAF, I GUESS.
...AND...
KUN (SNIFF)
SAAA (FSHH)
...SOMETHING SMELLS BAD.
AH...
SAA
RAIN?
PO (PLIP)

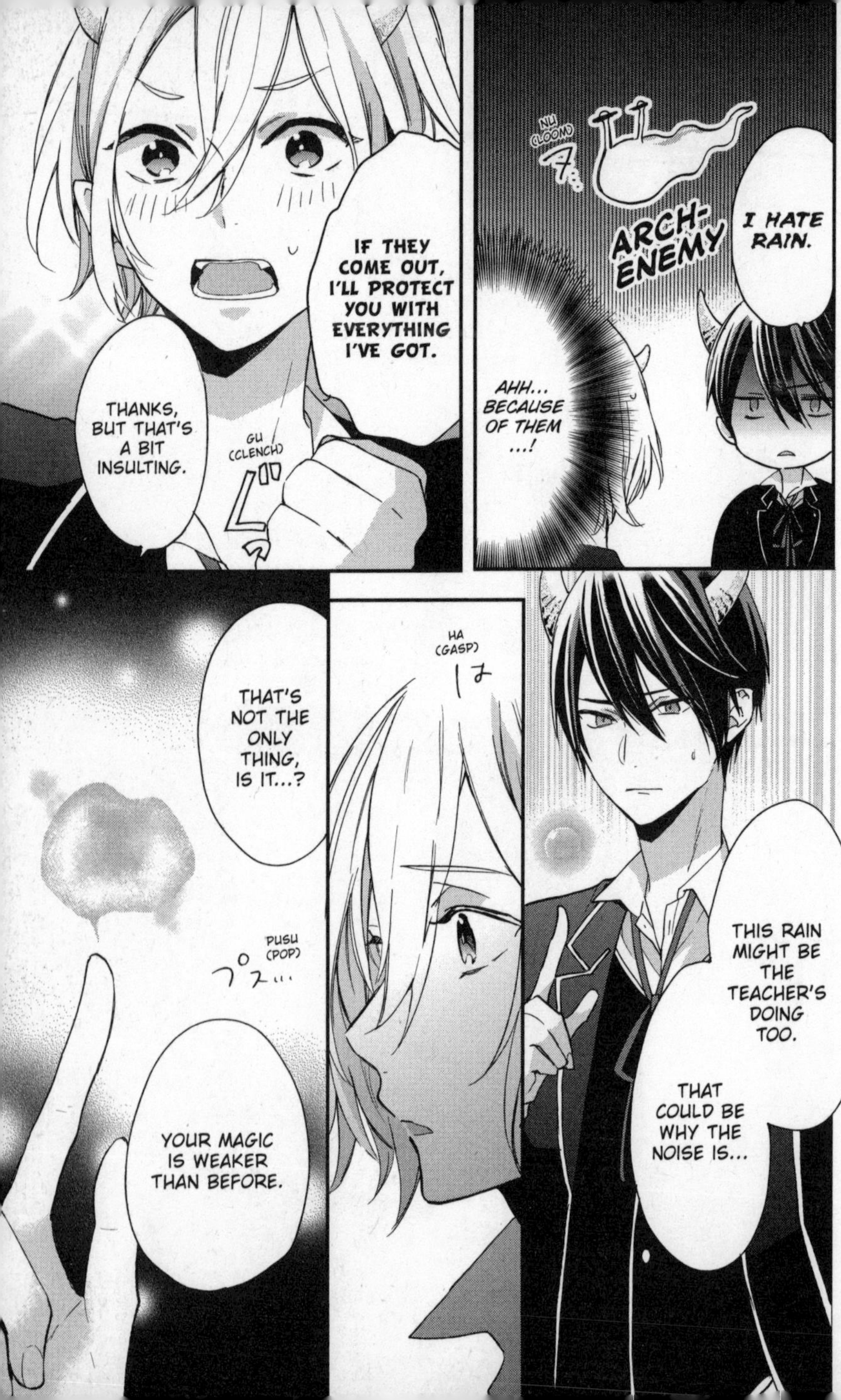
I HATE RAIN.
NU (LOOM)
ARCH-ENEMY
AHH... BECAUSE OF THEM ...!
IF THEY COME OUT, I'LL PROTECT YOU WITH EVERYTHING I'VE GOT.
GU (CLENCH)
THANKS, BUT THAT'S A BIT INSULTING.
THIS RAIN MIGHT BE THE TEACHER'S DOING TOO.
THAT COULD BE WHY THE NOISE IS...
HA (GASP)
THAT'S NOT THE ONLY THING, IS IT...?
PUSU (POP)
YOUR MAGIC IS WEAKER THAN BEFORE.

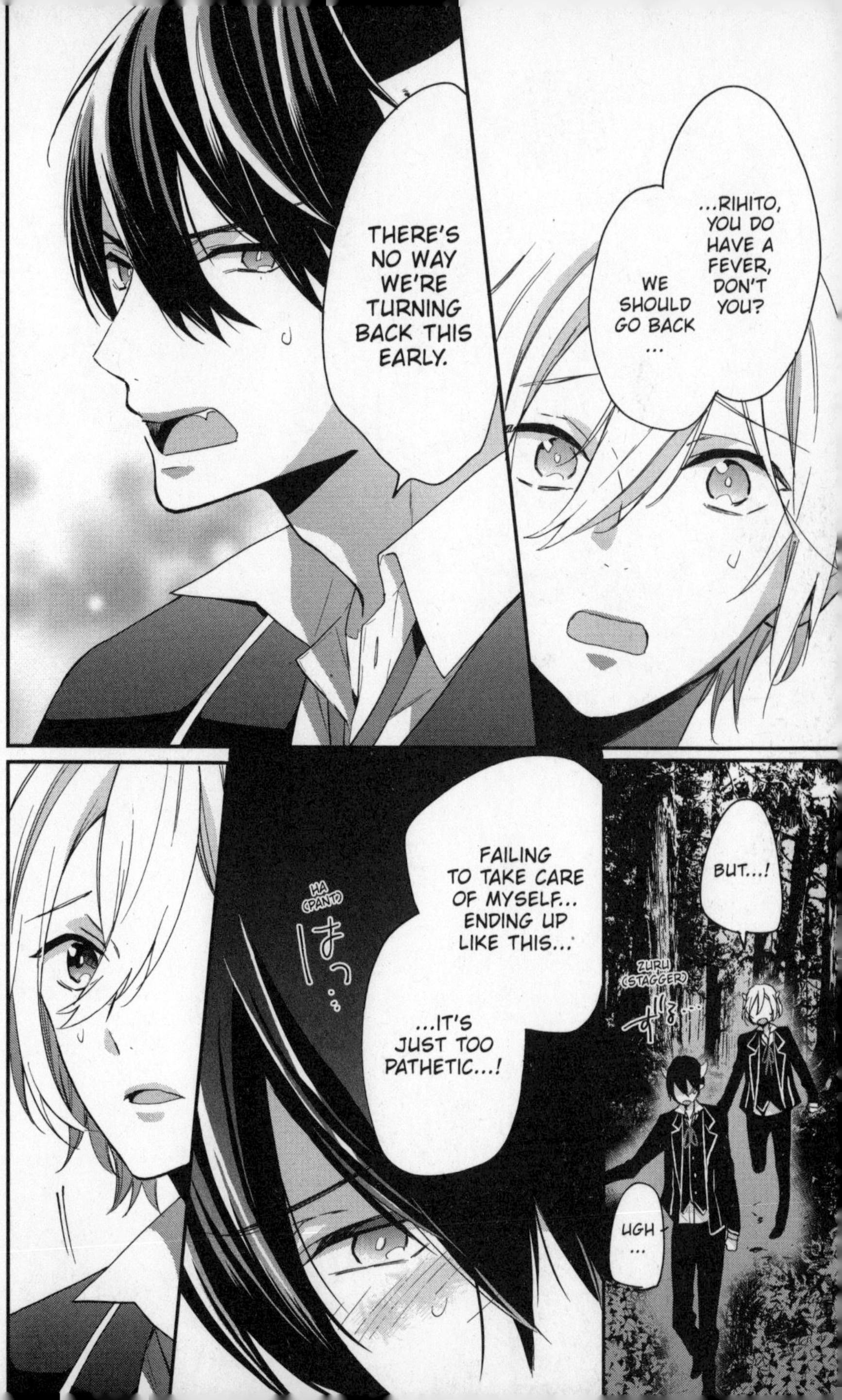
...RIHITO, YOU DO HAVE A FEVER, DON'T YOU?
WE SHOULD GO BACK...
THERE'S NO WAY WE'RE TURNING BACK THIS EARLY.
BUT...!
ZURU (STAGGER)
UGH...
HA (PANT)
FAILING TO TAKE CARE OF MYSELF... ENDING UP LIKE THIS...
...IT'S JUST TOO PATHETIC...!

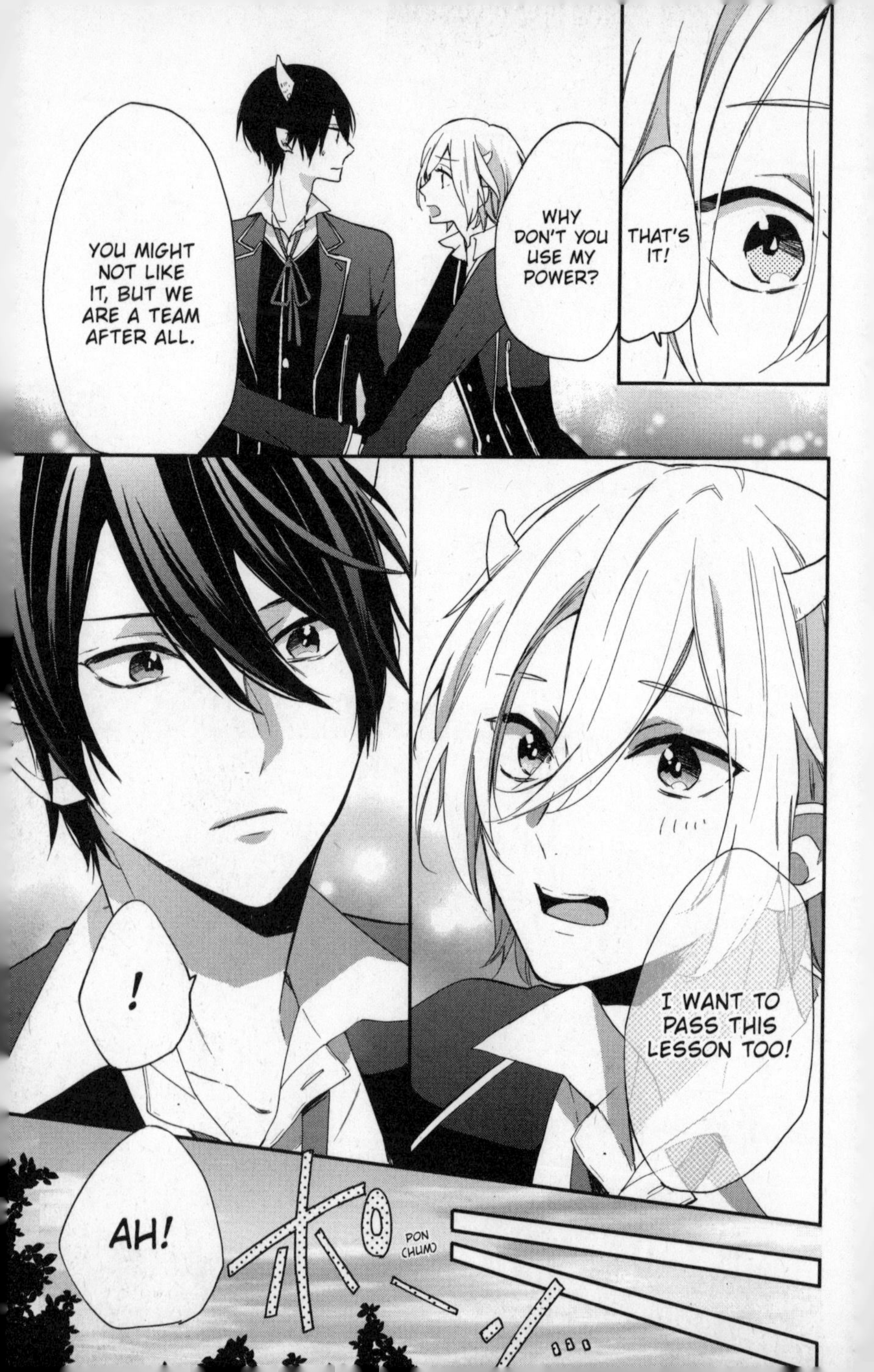
THAT'S IT!
WHY DON'T YOU USE MY POWER?
YOU MIGHT NOT LIKE IT, BUT WE ARE A TEAM AFTER ALL.
I WANT TO PASS THIS LESSON TOO!
!
PON (HUM)
AH!

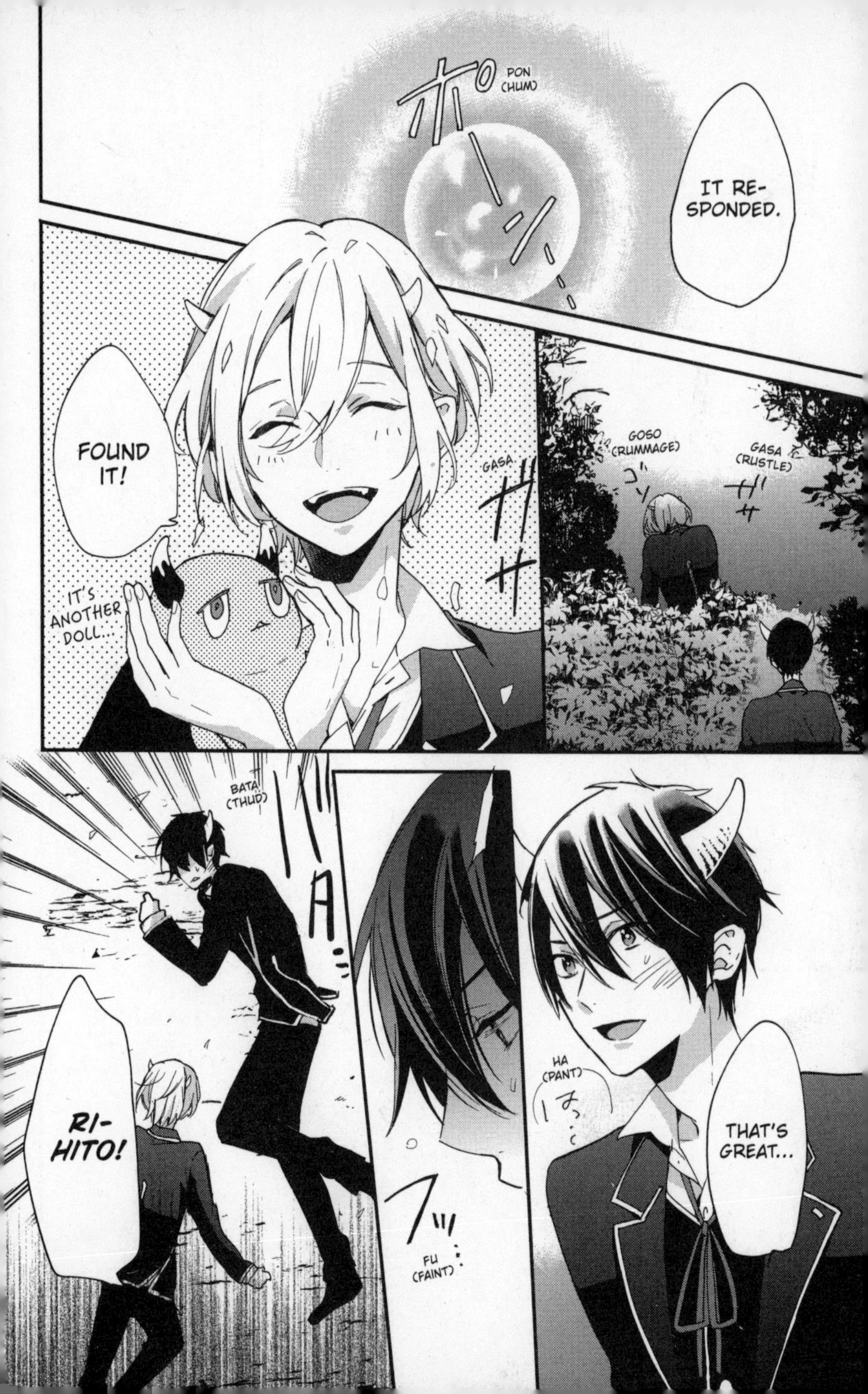
PON (HUM)
IT RE-SPONDED.
GOSO (RUMMAGE)
GASA (RUSTLE)
FOUND IT!
GASA
IT'S ANOTHER DOLL...
HA (PANT)
THAT'S GREAT...
FU (FAINT)
BATA (THUD)
RI-HITO!

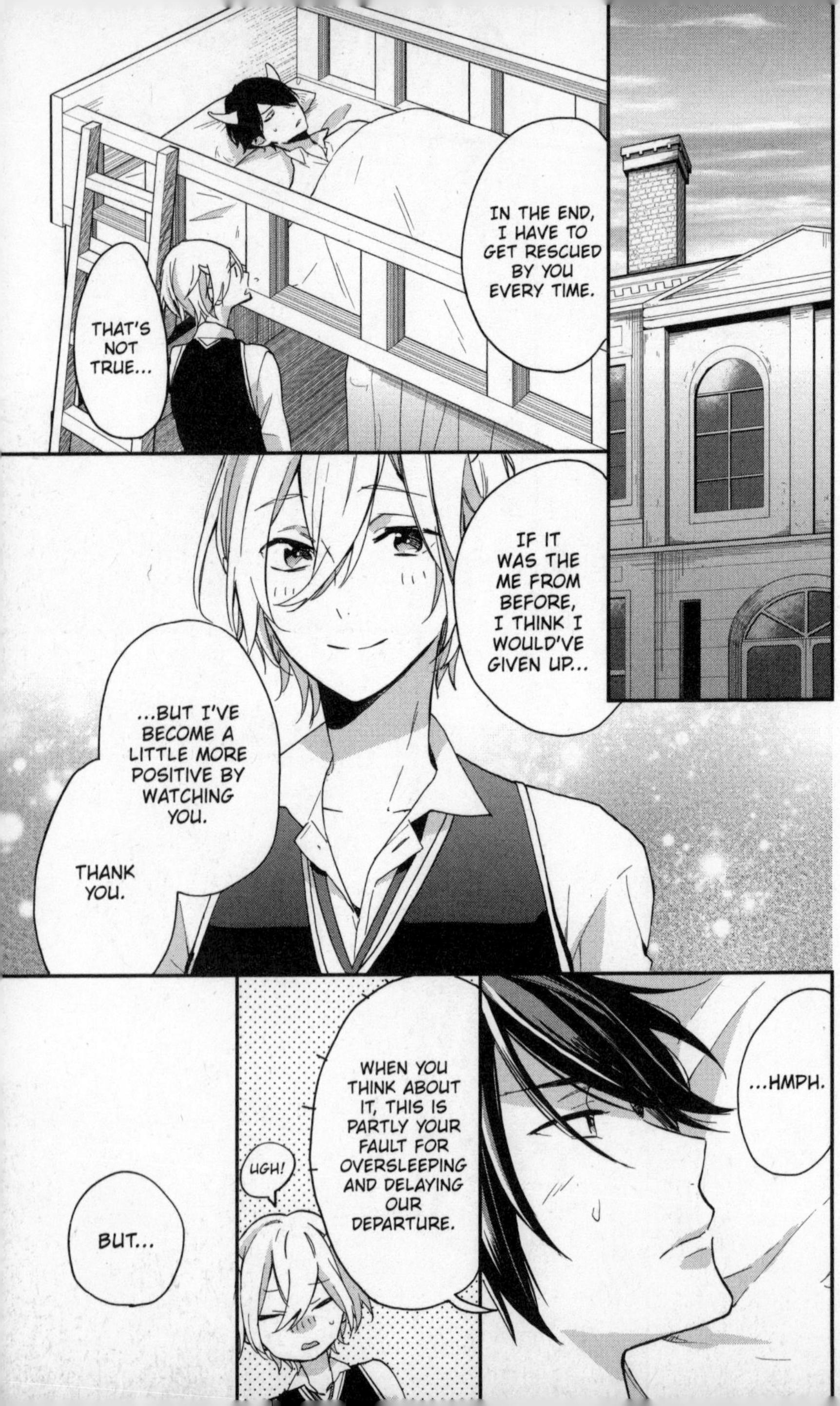
IN THE END, I HAVE TO GET RESCUED BY YOU EVERY TIME.
THAT'S NOT TRUE...
IF IT WAS THE ME FROM BEFORE, I THINK I WOULD'VE GIVEN UP...
...BUT I'VE BECOME A LITTLE MORE POSITIVE BY WATCHING YOU.
THANK YOU.
...HMPH.
WHEN YOU THINK ABOUT IT, THIS IS PARTLY YOUR FAULT FOR OVERSLEEPING AND DELAYING OUR DEPARTURE.
UGH!
BUT...

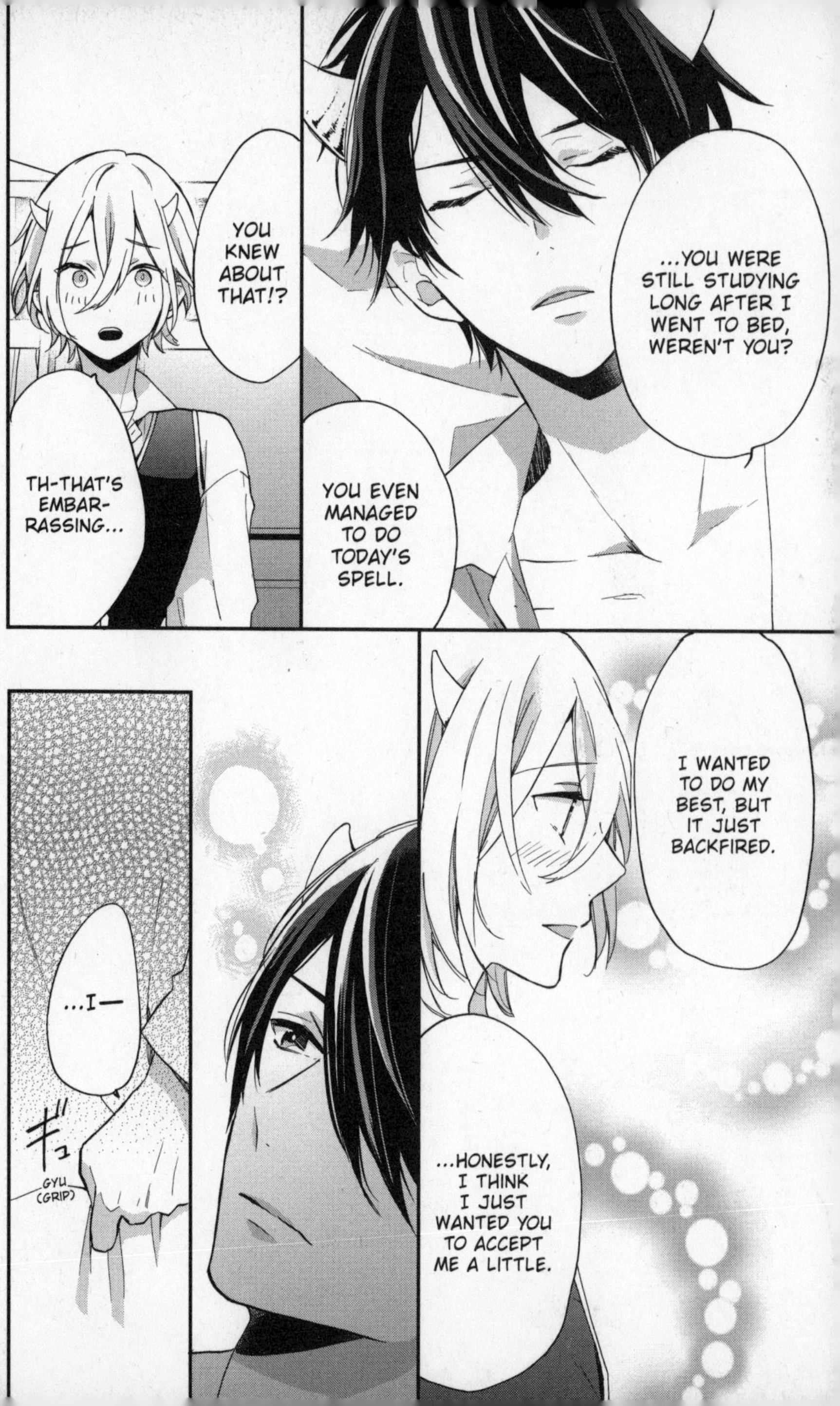
...YOU WERE STILL STUDYING LONG AFTER I WENT TO BED, WEREN'T YOU?
YOU EVEN MANAGED TO DO TODAY'S SPELL.
YOU KNEW ABOUT THAT!?
TH-THAT'S EMBAR-RASSING...
I WANTED TO DO MY BEST, BUT IT JUST BACKFIRED.
...HONESTLY, I THINK I JUST WANTED YOU TO ACCEPT ME A LITTLE.
...I—
ギュ
GYU (GRIP)

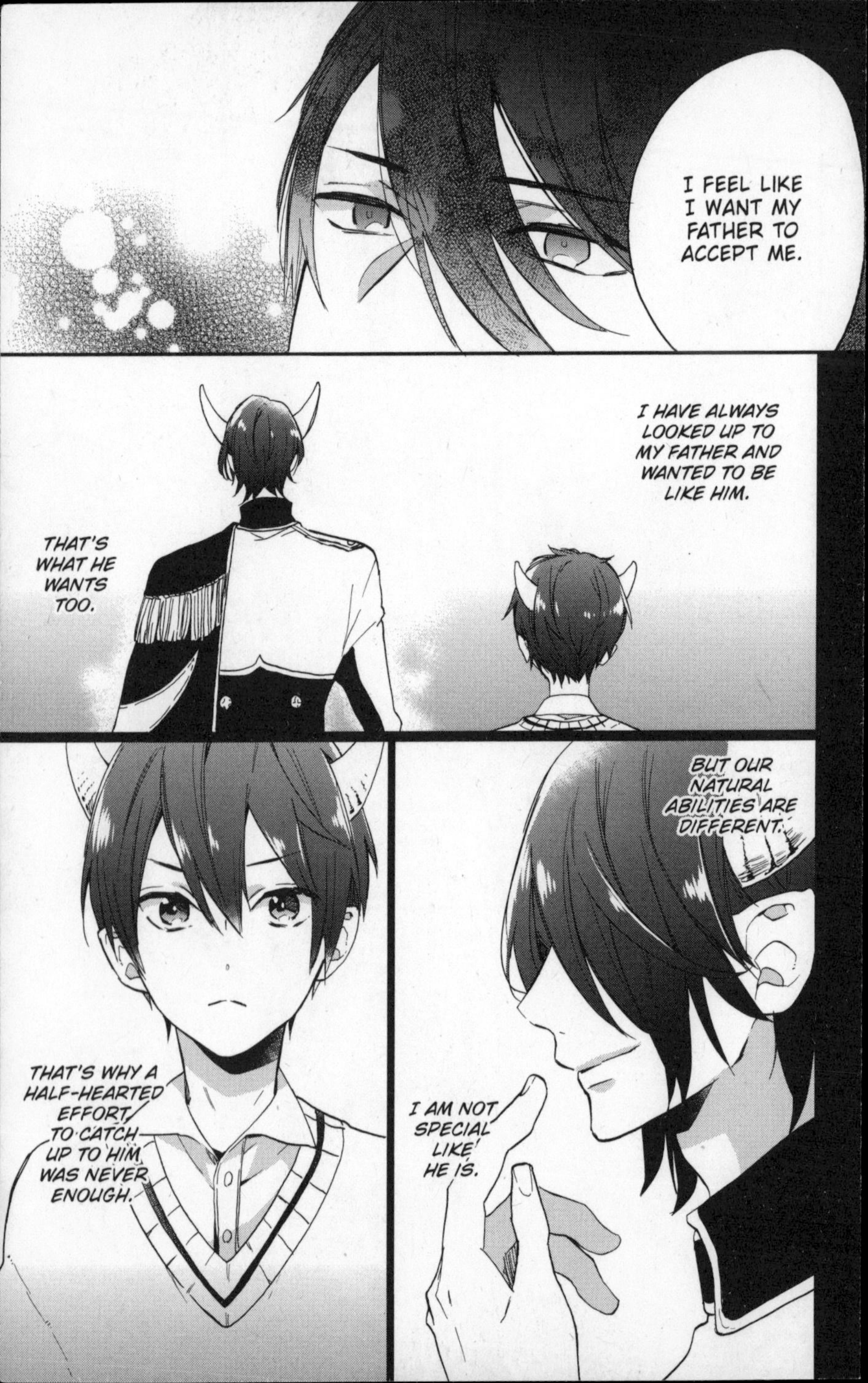
I FEEL LIKE I WANT MY FATHER TO ACCEPT ME.
I HAVE ALWAYS LOOKED UP TO MY FATHER AND WANTED TO BE LIKE HIM.
THAT'S WHAT HE WANTS TOO.
BUT OUR NATURAL ABILITIES ARE DIFFERENT.
I AM NOT SPECIAL LIKE HE IS.
THAT'S WHY A HALF-HEARTED EFFORT TO CATCH UP TO HIM WAS NEVER ENOUGH.

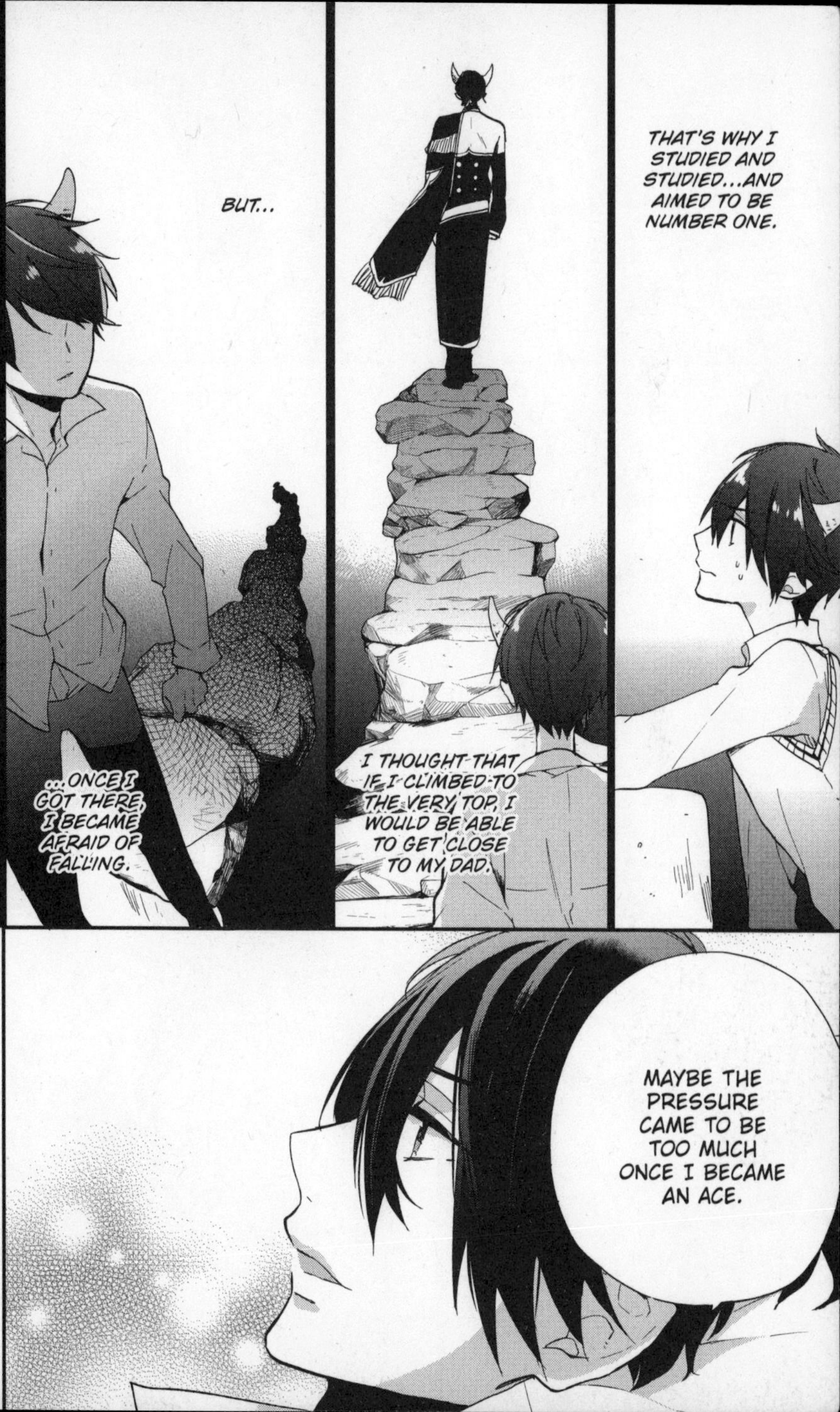
THAT'S WHY I STUDIED AND STUDIED...AND AIMED TO BE NUMBER ONE.
I THOUGHT THAT IF I CLIMBED TO THE VERY TOP, I WOULD BE ABLE TO GET CLOSE TO MY DAD.
BUT...
...ONCE I GOT THERE, I BECAME AFRAID OF FALLING.
MAYBE THE PRESSURE CAME TO BE TOO MUCH ONCE I BECAME AN ACE.

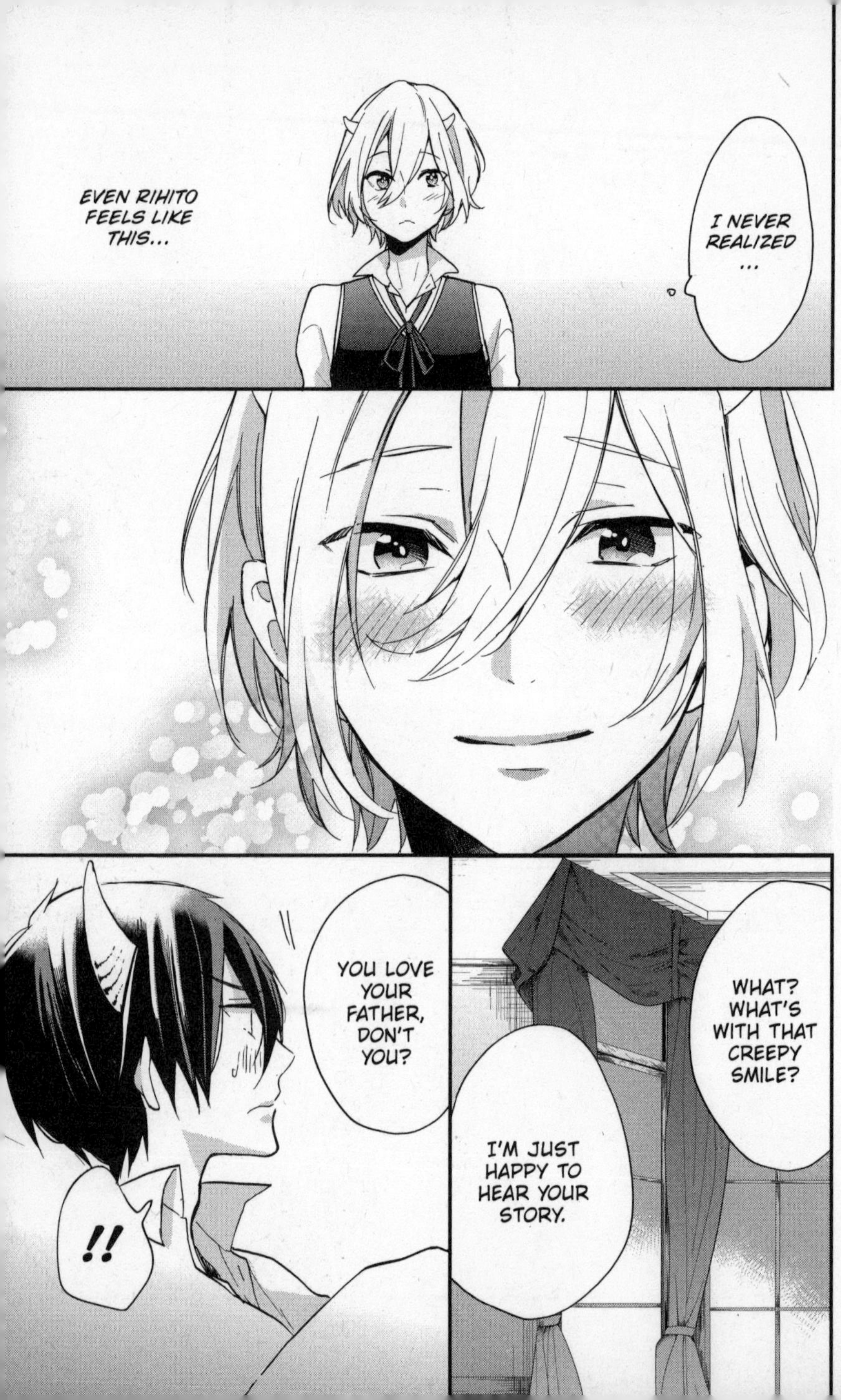
I NEVER REALIZED...
EVEN RIHITO FEELS LIKE THIS...
WHAT? WHAT'S WITH THAT CREEPY SMILE?
I'M JUST HAPPY TO HEAR YOUR STORY.
YOU LOVE YOUR FATHER, DON'T YOU?
!!

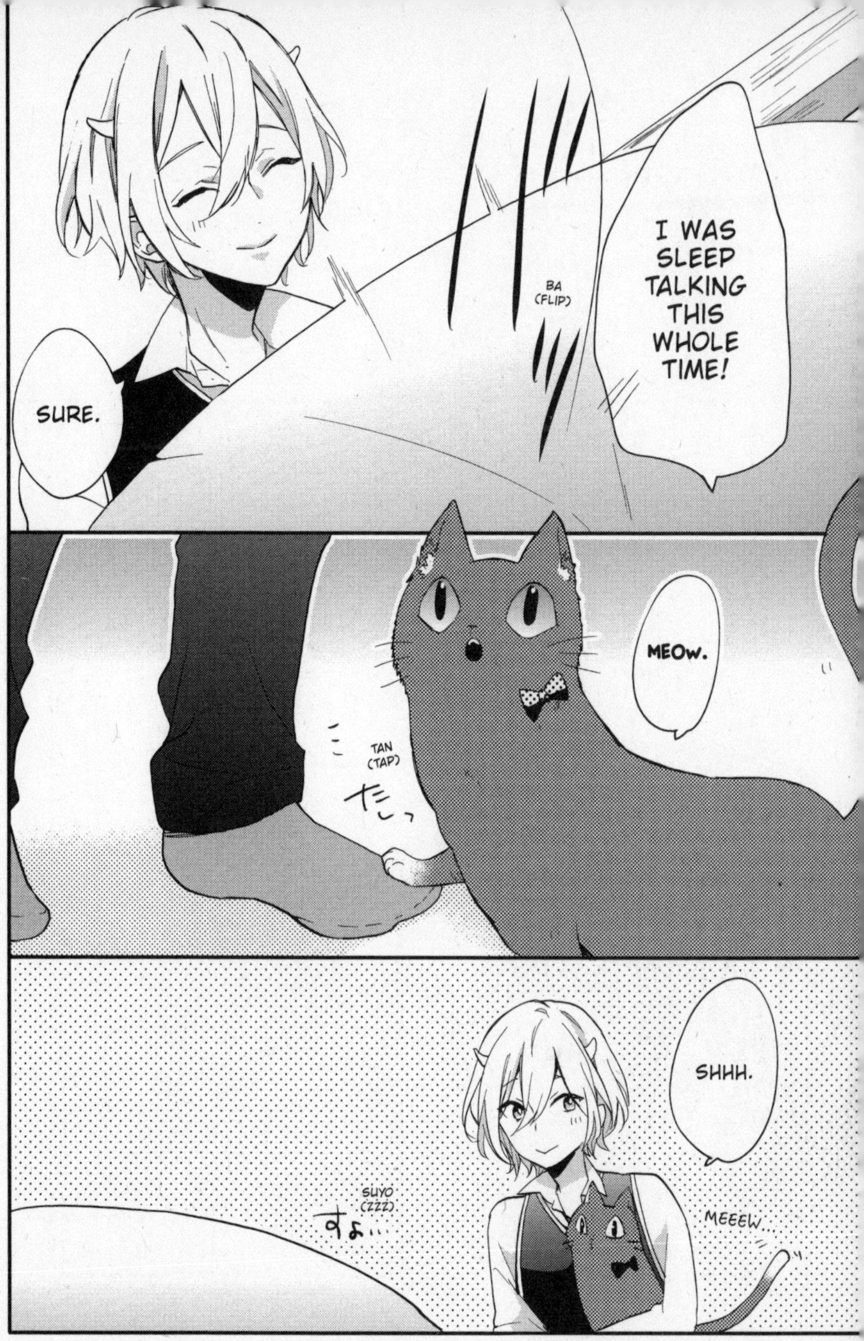
I WAS SLEEP TALKING THIS WHOLE TIME!
BA (FLIP)
SURE.
MEOW.
TAN (TAP)
たしっ
SHHH.
MEEEW...
SUYO (ZZZ)
すよ…

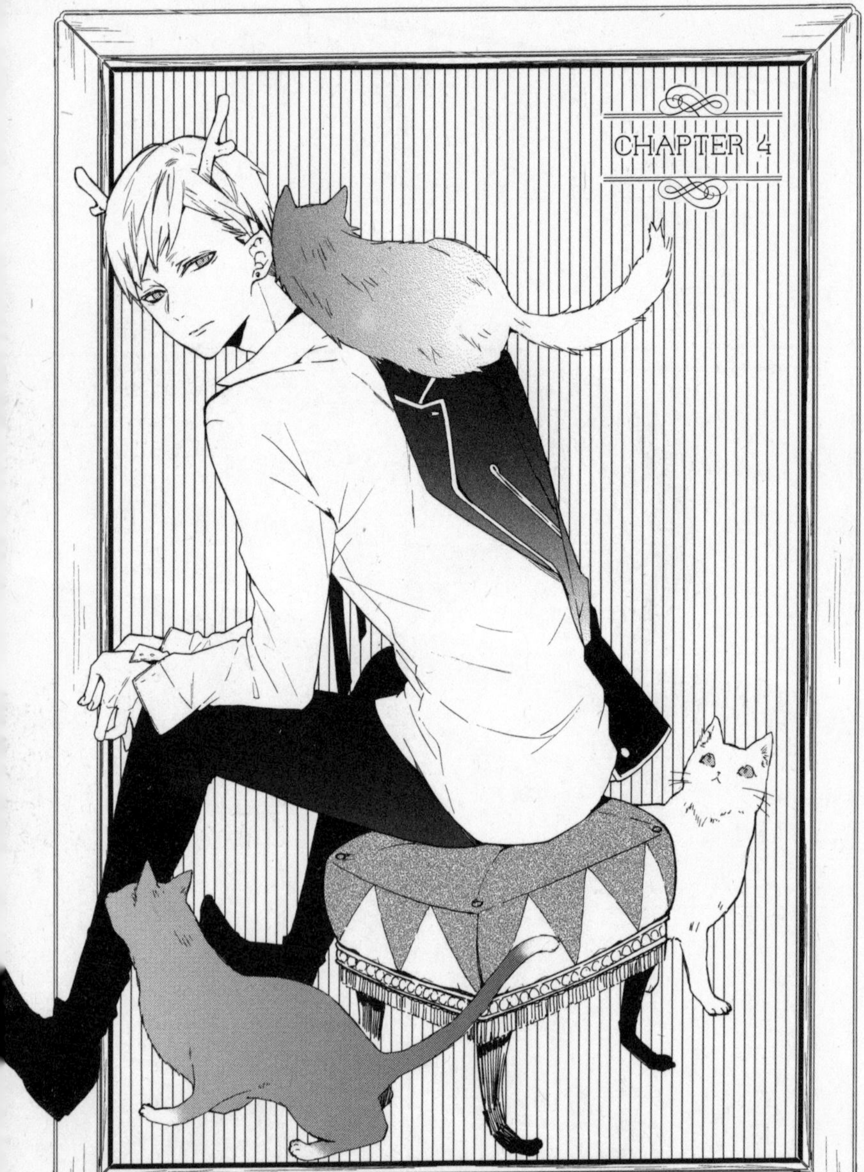
CHAPTER 4

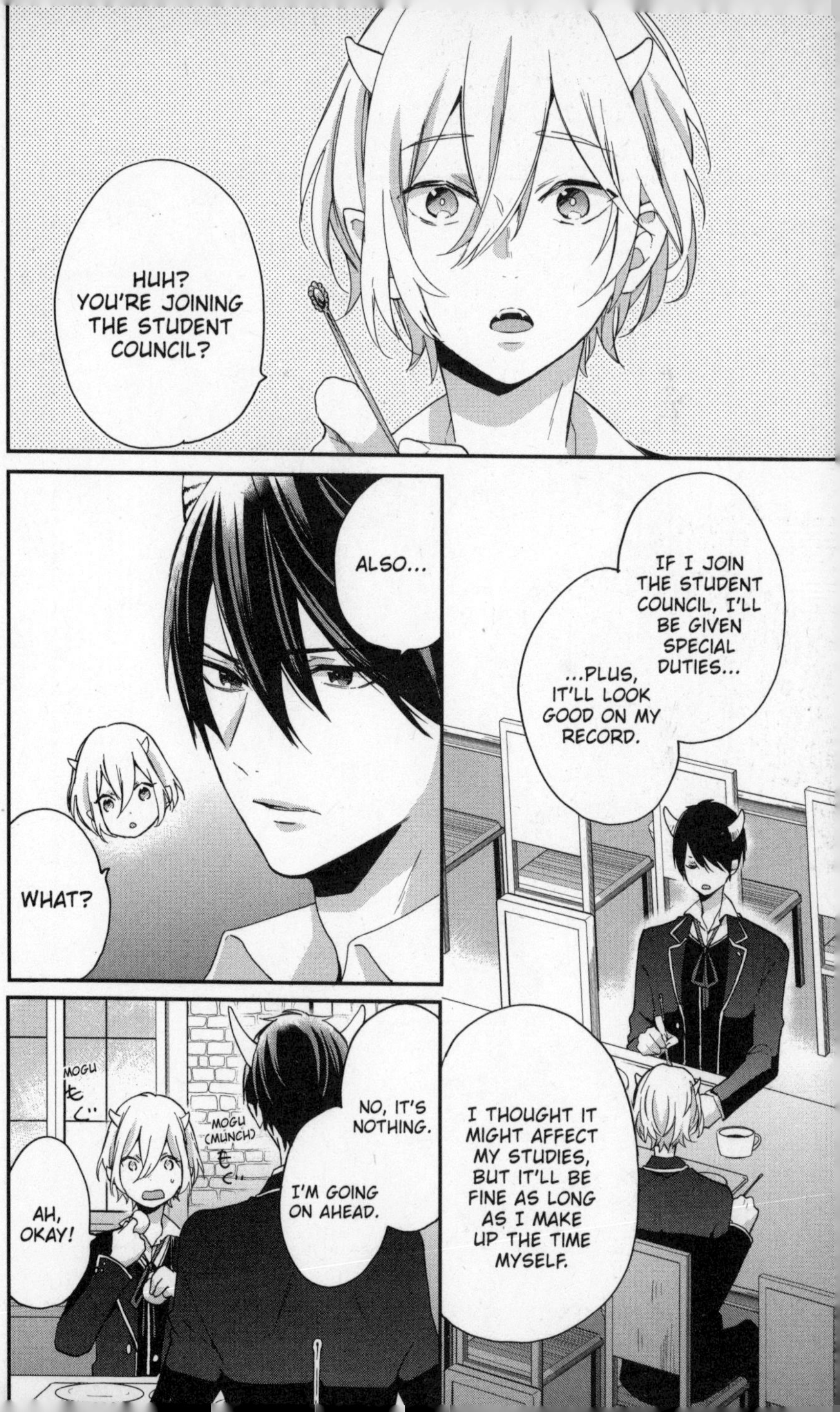
HUH? YOU'RE JOINING THE STUDENT COUNCIL?
IF I JOIN THE STUDENT COUNCIL, I'LL BE GIVEN SPECIAL DUTIES...
...PLUS, IT'LL LOOK GOOD ON MY RECORD.
I THOUGHT IT MIGHT AFFECT MY STUDIES, BUT IT'LL BE FINE AS LONG AS I MAKE UP THE TIME MYSELF.
ALSO...
WHAT?
NO, IT'S NOTHING.
I'M GOING ON AHEAD.
MOGU (MUNCH)
もぐ
MOGU
もぐ
AH, OKAY!

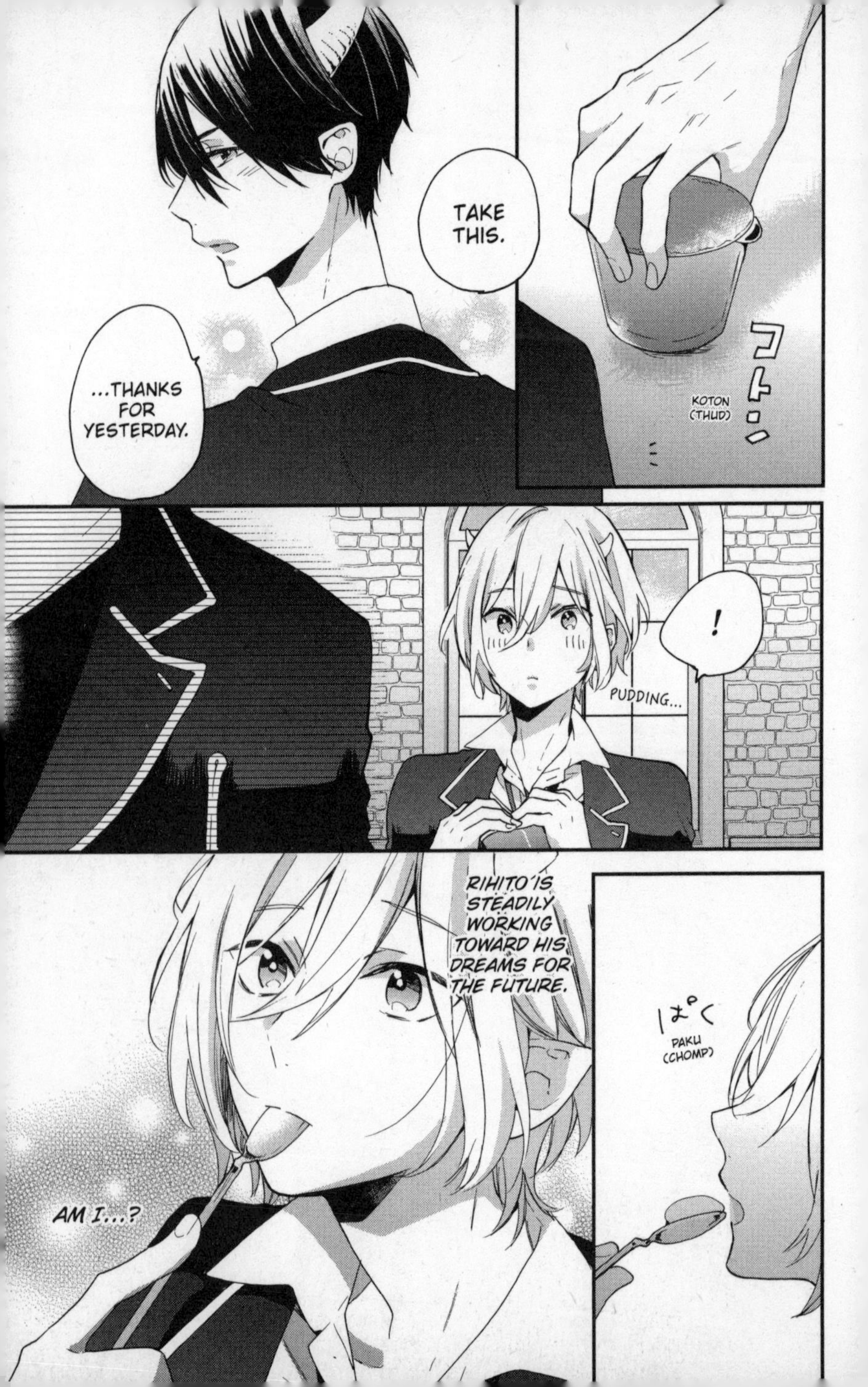
コト…
KOTON (THUD)
TAKE THIS.
...THANKS FOR YESTERDAY.
!
PUDDING...
ぱく
PAKU (CHOMP)
RIHITO IS STEADILY WORKING TOWARD HIS DREAMS FOR THE FUTURE.
AM I...?

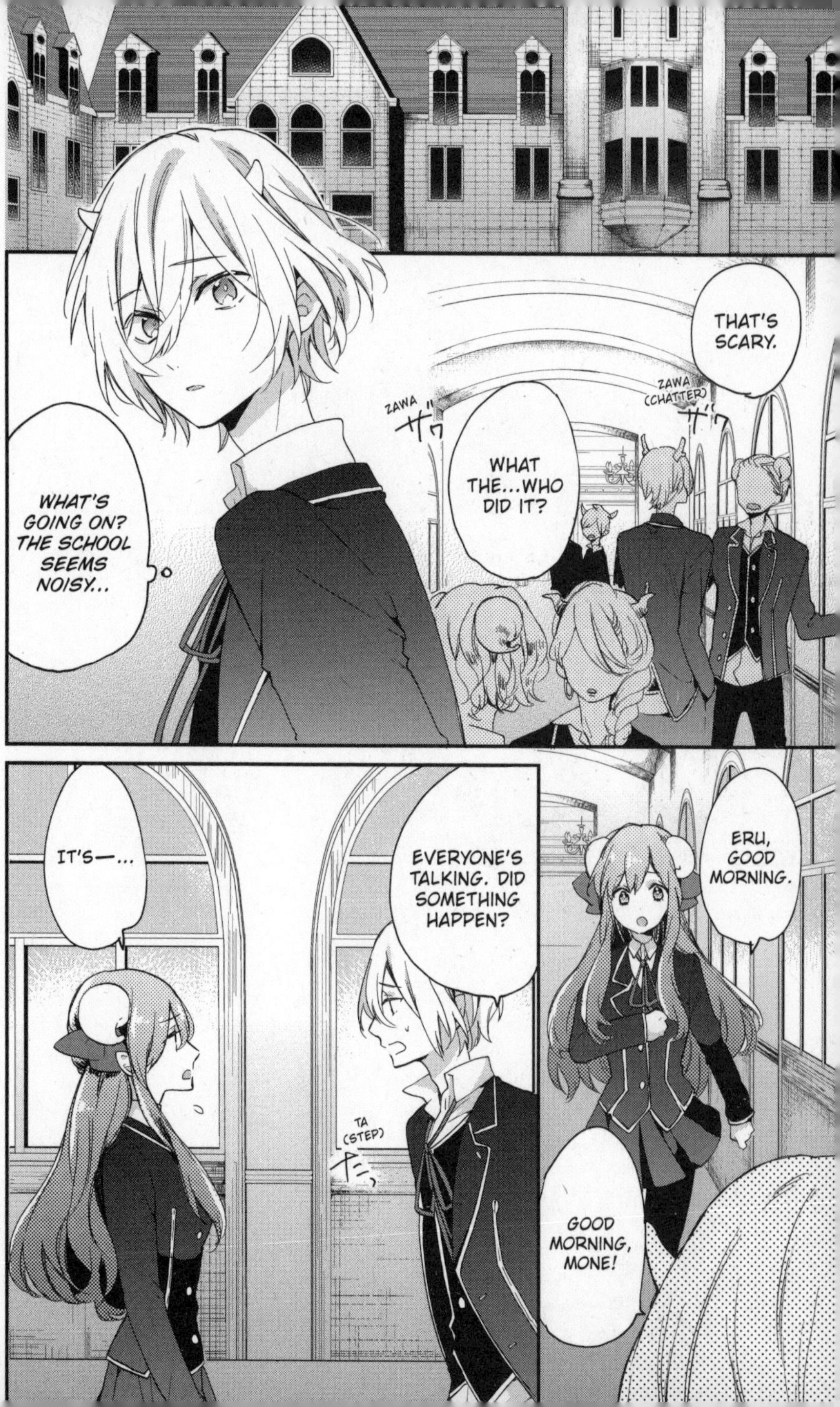
THAT'S SCARY.
ZAWA (CHATTER)
WHAT THE...WHO DID IT?
ZAWA
WHAT'S GOING ON? THE SCHOOL SEEMS NOISY...
ERU, GOOD MORNING.
GOOD MORNING, MONE!
TA (STEP)
EVERYONE'S TALKING. DID SOMETHING HAPPEN?
IT'S—...

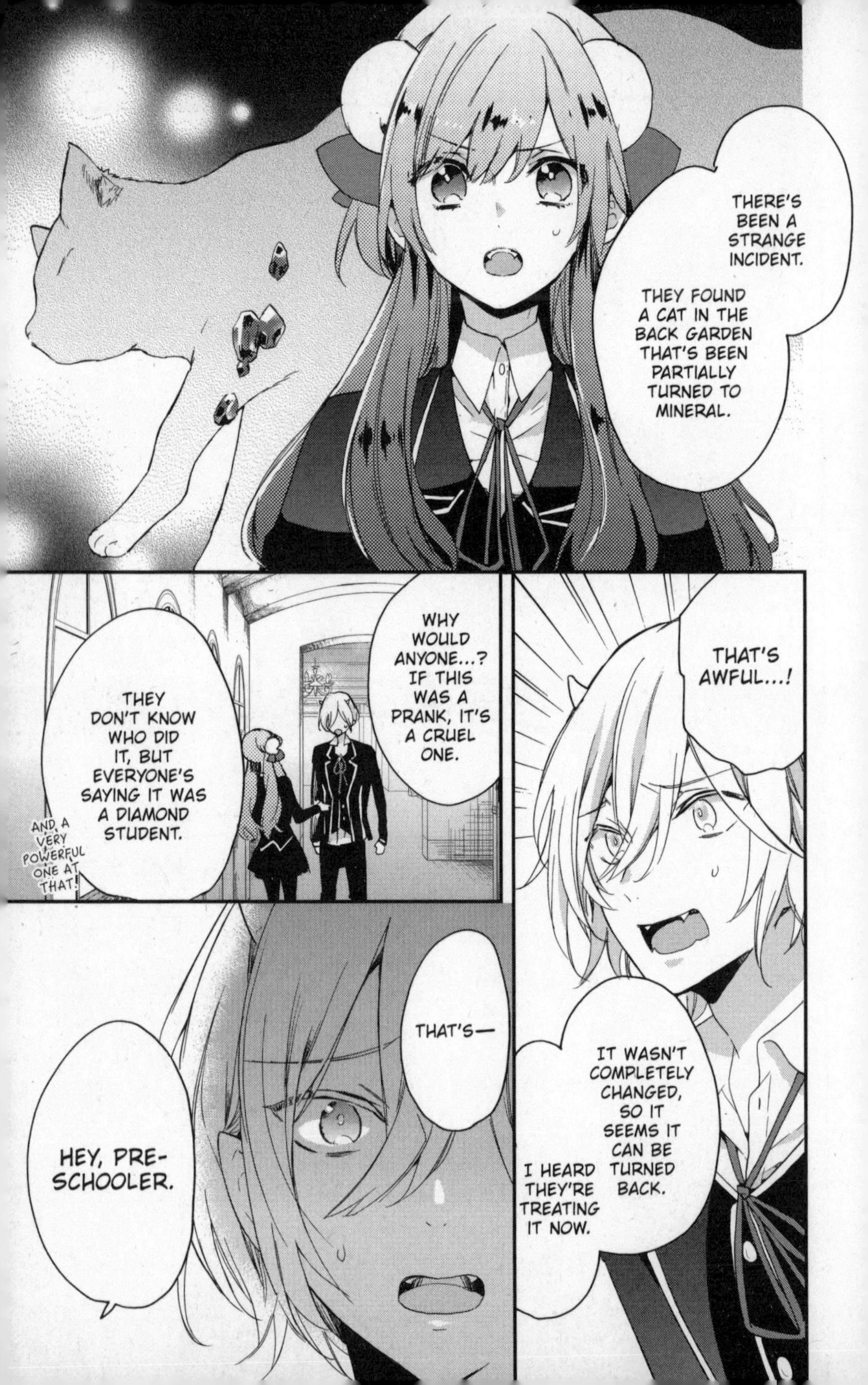
THERE'S BEEN A STRANGE INCIDENT.
THEY FOUND A CAT IN THE BACK GARDEN THAT'S BEEN PARTIALLY TURNED TO MINERAL.
THAT'S AWFUL...!
WHY WOULD ANYONE...? IF THIS WAS A PRANK, IT'S A CRUEL ONE.
THEY DON'T KNOW WHO DID IT, BUT EVERYONE'S SAYING IT WAS A DIAMOND STUDENT.
AND A VERY POWERFUL ONE AT THAT!
IT WASN'T COMPLETELY CHANGED, SO IT SEEMS IT CAN BE TURNED BACK.
I HEARD THEY'RE TREATING IT NOW.
THAT'S—
HEY, PRE-SCHOOLER.

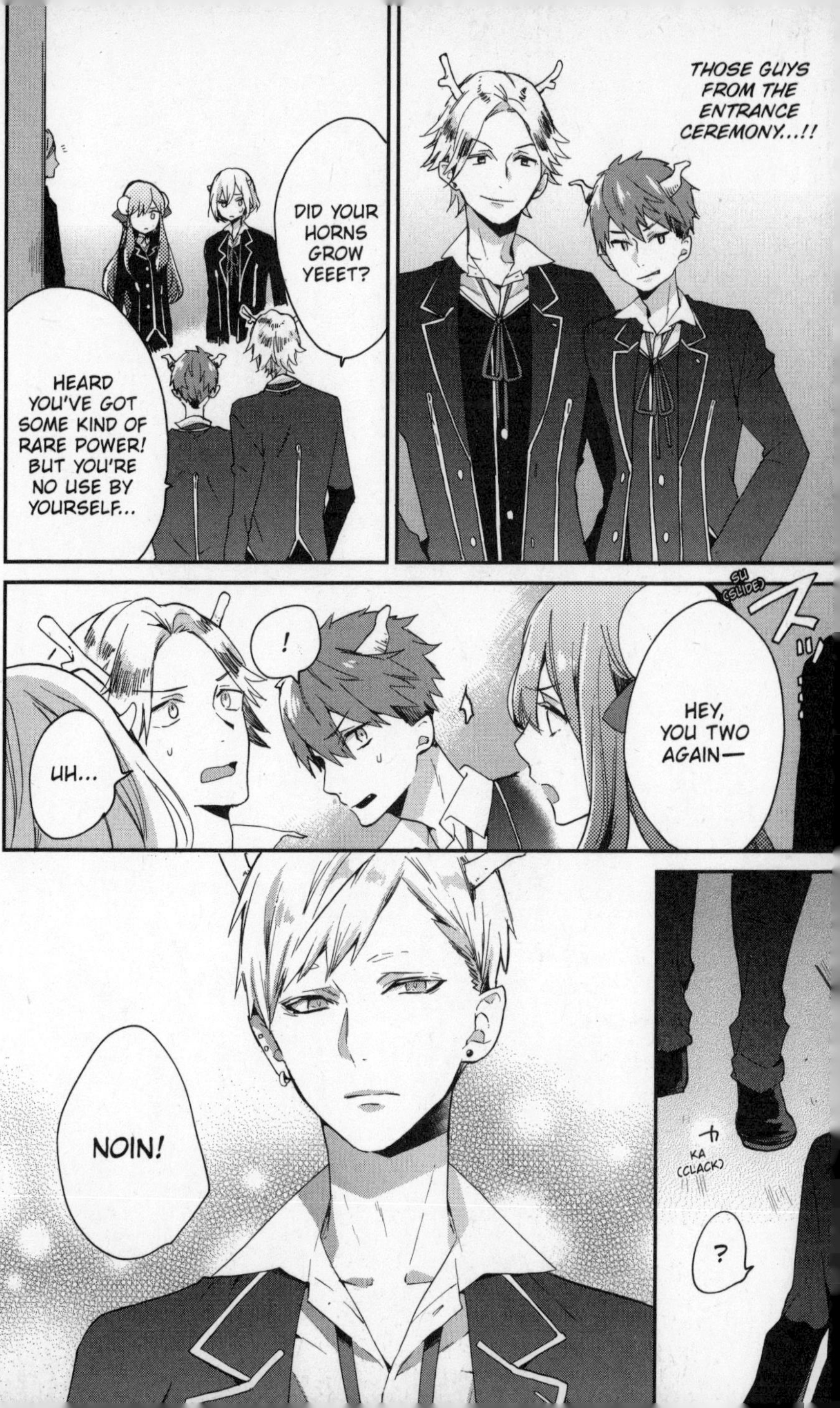
THOSE GUYS FROM THE ENTRANCE CEREMONY...!!
DID YOUR HORNS GROW YEEET?
HEARD YOU'VE GOT SOME KIND OF RARE POWER! BUT YOU'RE NO USE BY YOURSELF...
SU (SLIDE)
HEY, YOU TWO AGAIN—
!
UH...
KA (CLACK)
?
NOIN!

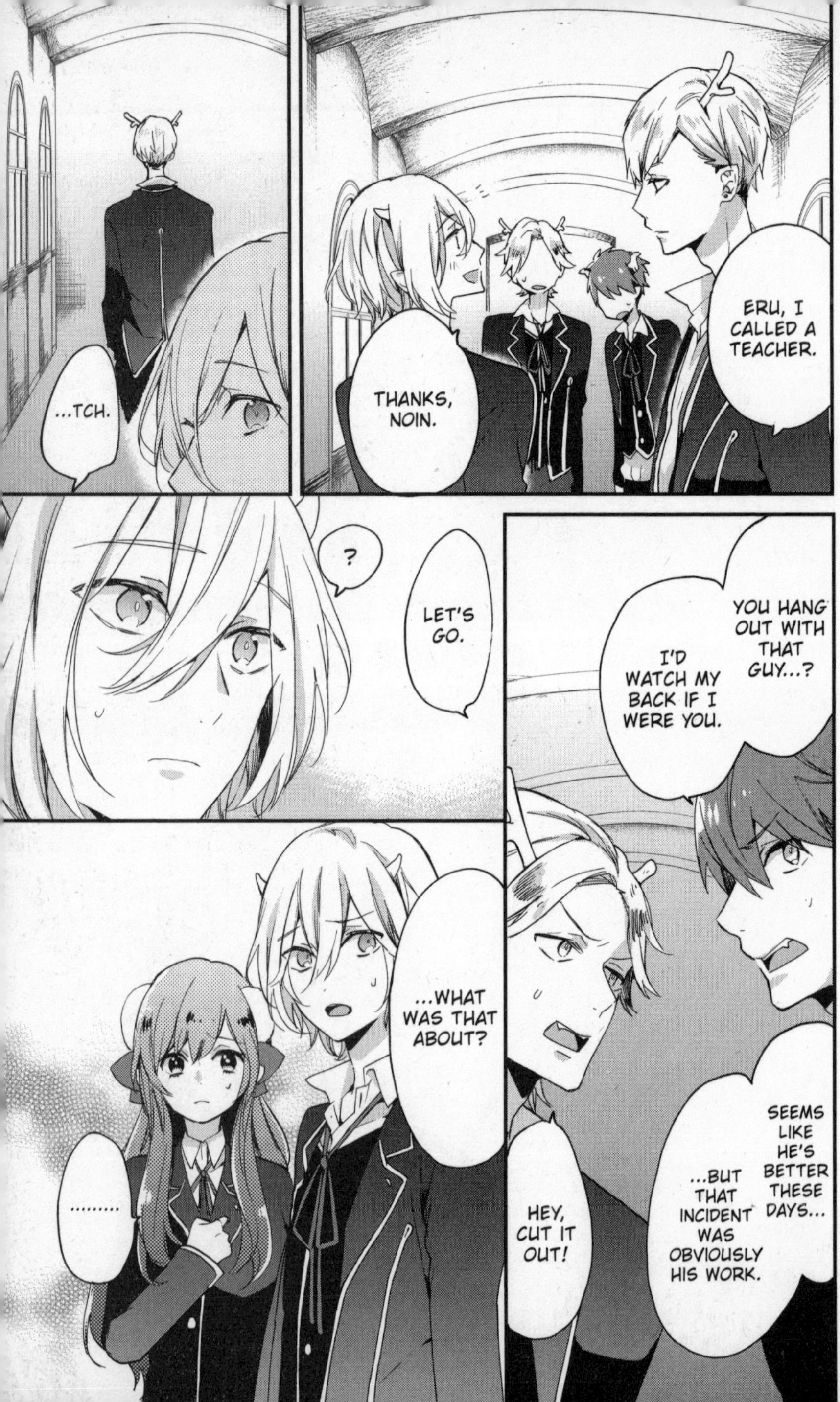
ERU, I CALLED A TEACHER.
THANKS, NOIN.
...TCH.
YOU HANG OUT WITH THAT GUY...?
I'D WATCH MY BACK IF I WERE YOU.
SEEMS LIKE HE'S BETTER THESE DAYS...
...BUT THAT INCIDENT WAS OBVIOUSLY HIS WORK.
HEY, CUT IT OUT!
LET'S GO.
?
...WHAT WAS THAT ABOUT?
....

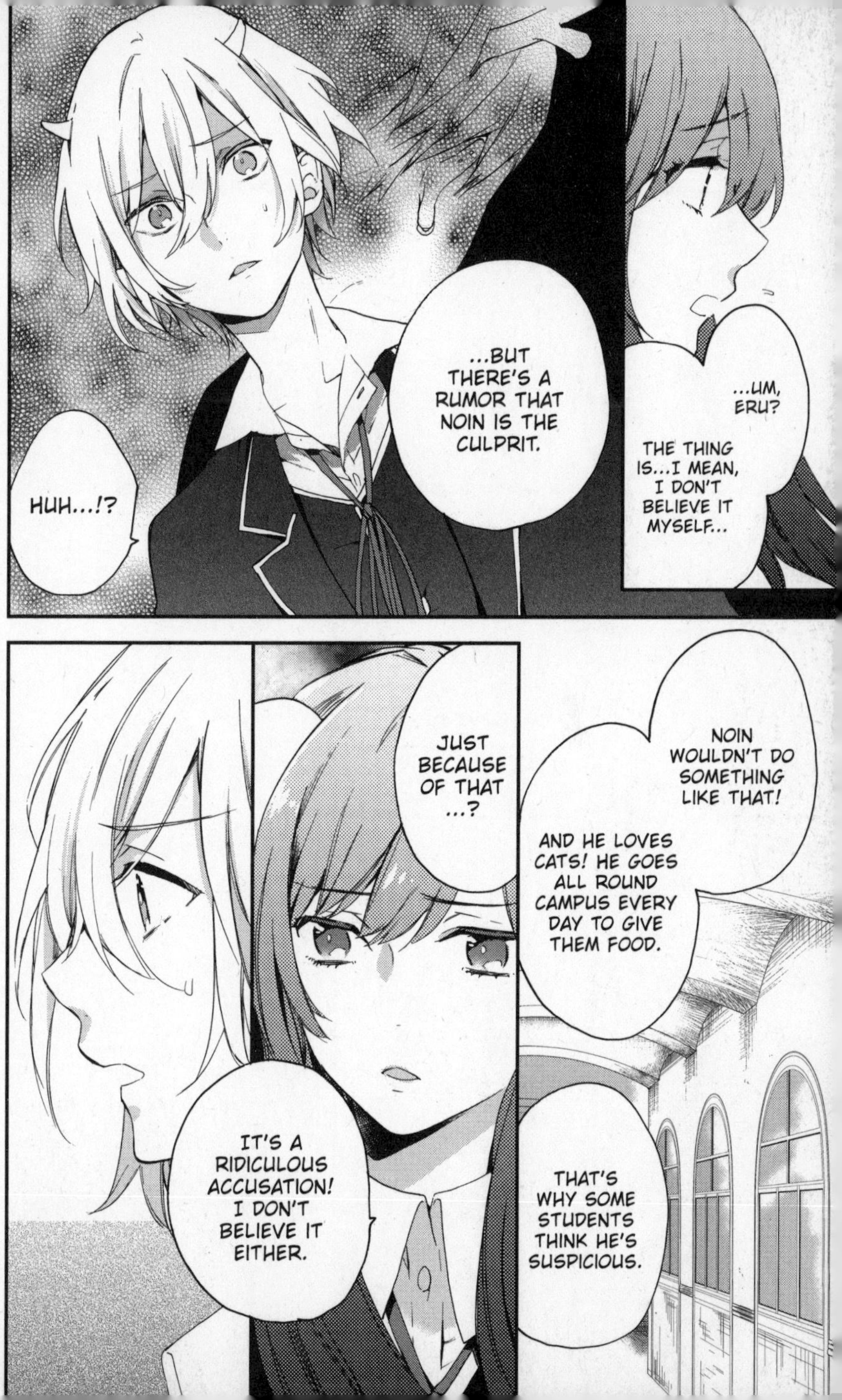
...UM, ERU?
THE THING IS...I MEAN, I DON'T BELIEVE IT MYSELF...
...BUT THERE'S A RUMOR THAT NOIN IS THE CULPRIT.
HUH...!?
NOIN WOULDN'T DO SOMETHING LIKE THAT!
AND HE LOVES CATS! HE GOES ALL ROUND CAMPUS EVERY DAY TO GIVE THEM FOOD.
THAT'S WHY SOME STUDENTS THINK HE'S SUSPICIOUS.
JUST BECAUSE OF THAT ...?
IT'S A RIDICULOUS ACCUSATION! I DON'T BELIEVE IT EITHER.

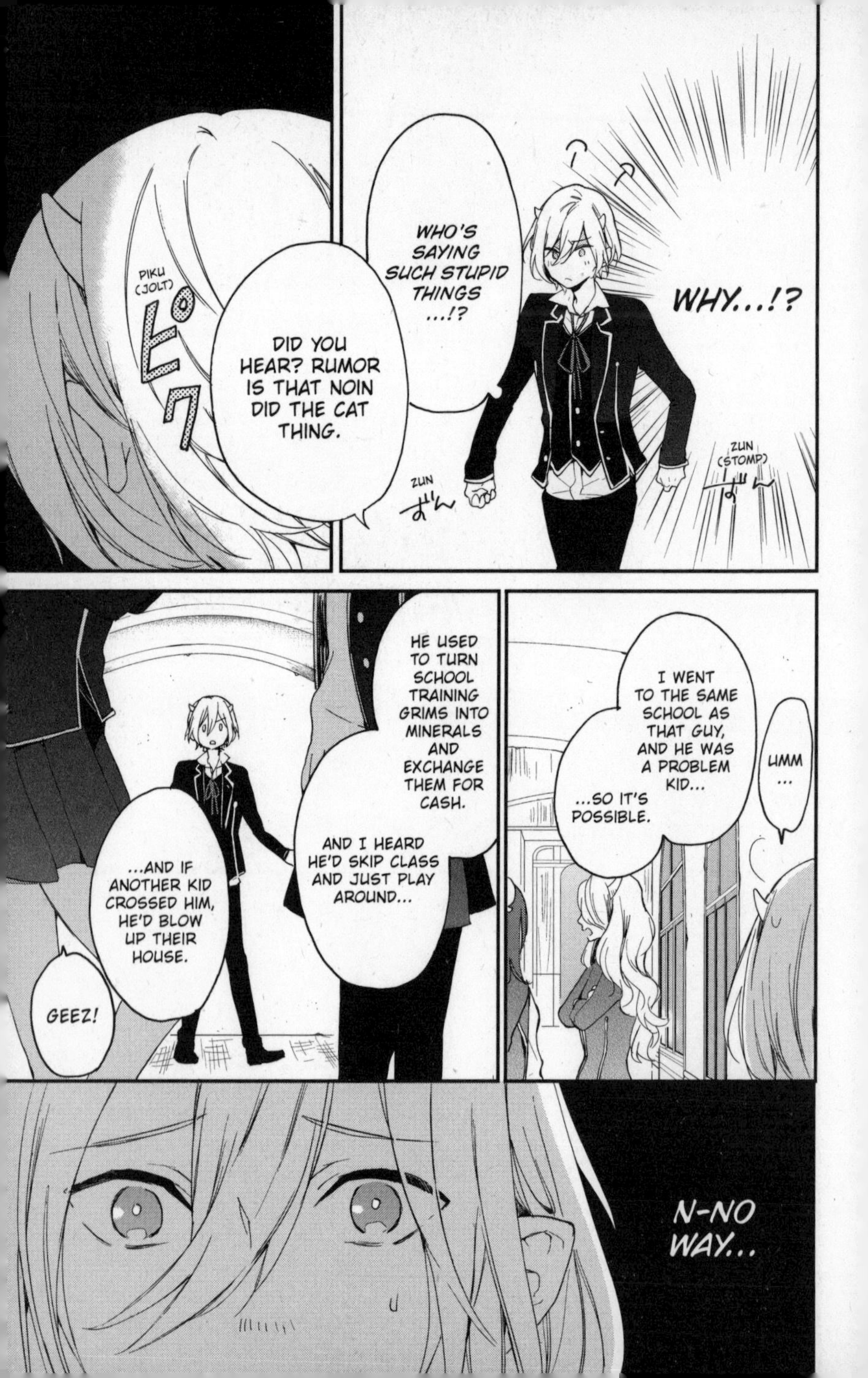
WHY...!?
ZUN (STOMP) ずん
ZUN ずん
WHO'S SAYING SUCH STUPID THINGS ...!?
PIKU (JOLT) ピク
DID YOU HEAR? RUMOR IS THAT NOIN DID THE CAT THING.
UMM ...
I WENT TO THE SAME SCHOOL AS THAT GUY, AND HE WAS A PROBLEM KID...
...SO IT'S POSSIBLE.
HE USED TO TURN SCHOOL TRAINING GRIMS INTO MINERALS AND EXCHANGE THEM FOR CASH.
AND I HEARD HE'D SKIP CLASS AND JUST PLAY AROUND...
...AND IF ANOTHER KID CROSSED HIM, HE'D BLOW UP THEIR HOUSE.
GEEZ!
N-NO WAY...

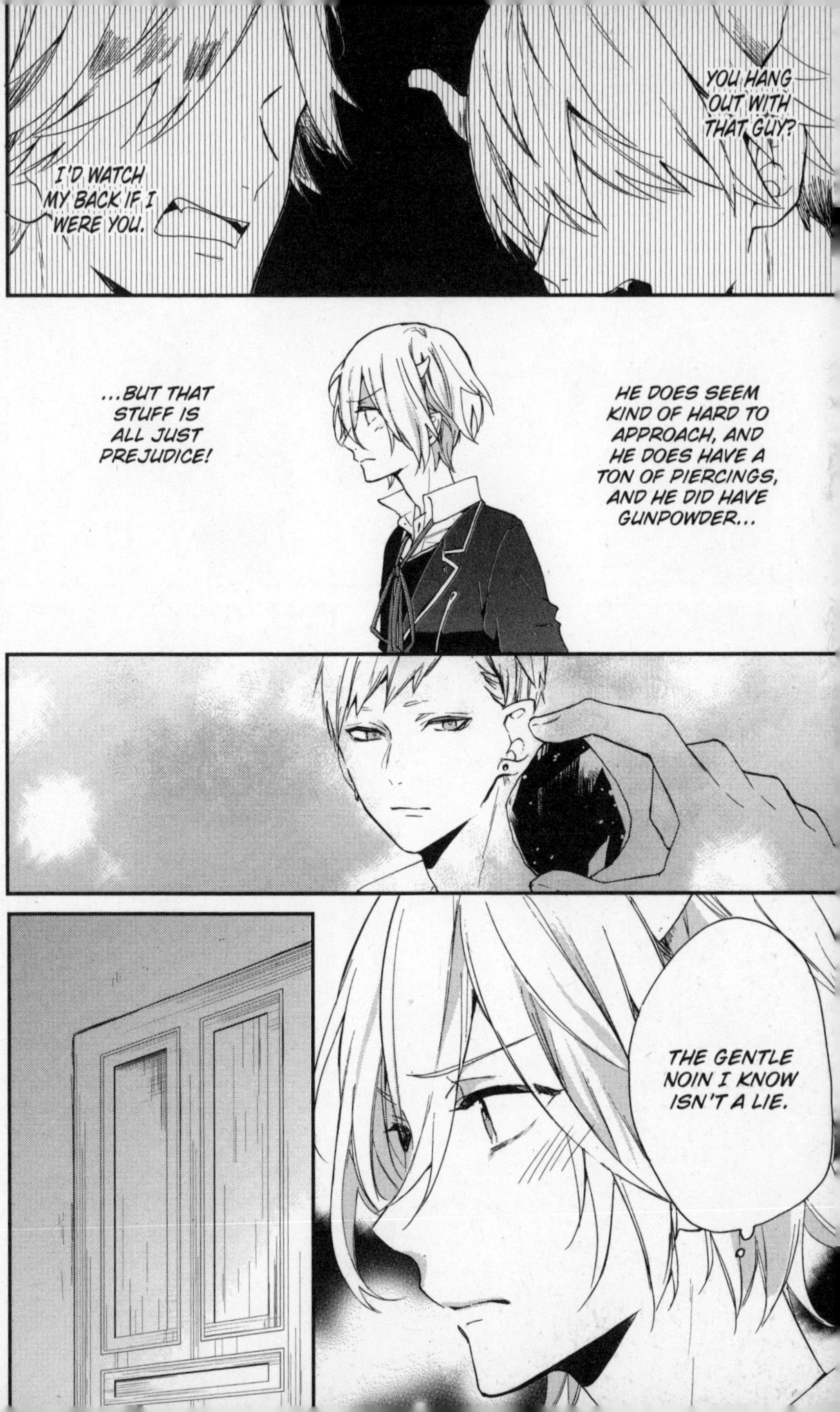
YOU HANG OUT WITH THAT GUY?
I'D WATCH MY BACK IF I WERE YOU.
HE DOES SEEM KIND OF HARD TO APPROACH, AND HE DOES HAVE A TON OF PIERCINGS, AND HE DID HAVE GUNPOWDER...
...BUT THAT STUFF IS ALL JUST PREJUDICE!
THE GENTLE NOIN I KNOW ISN'T A LIE.

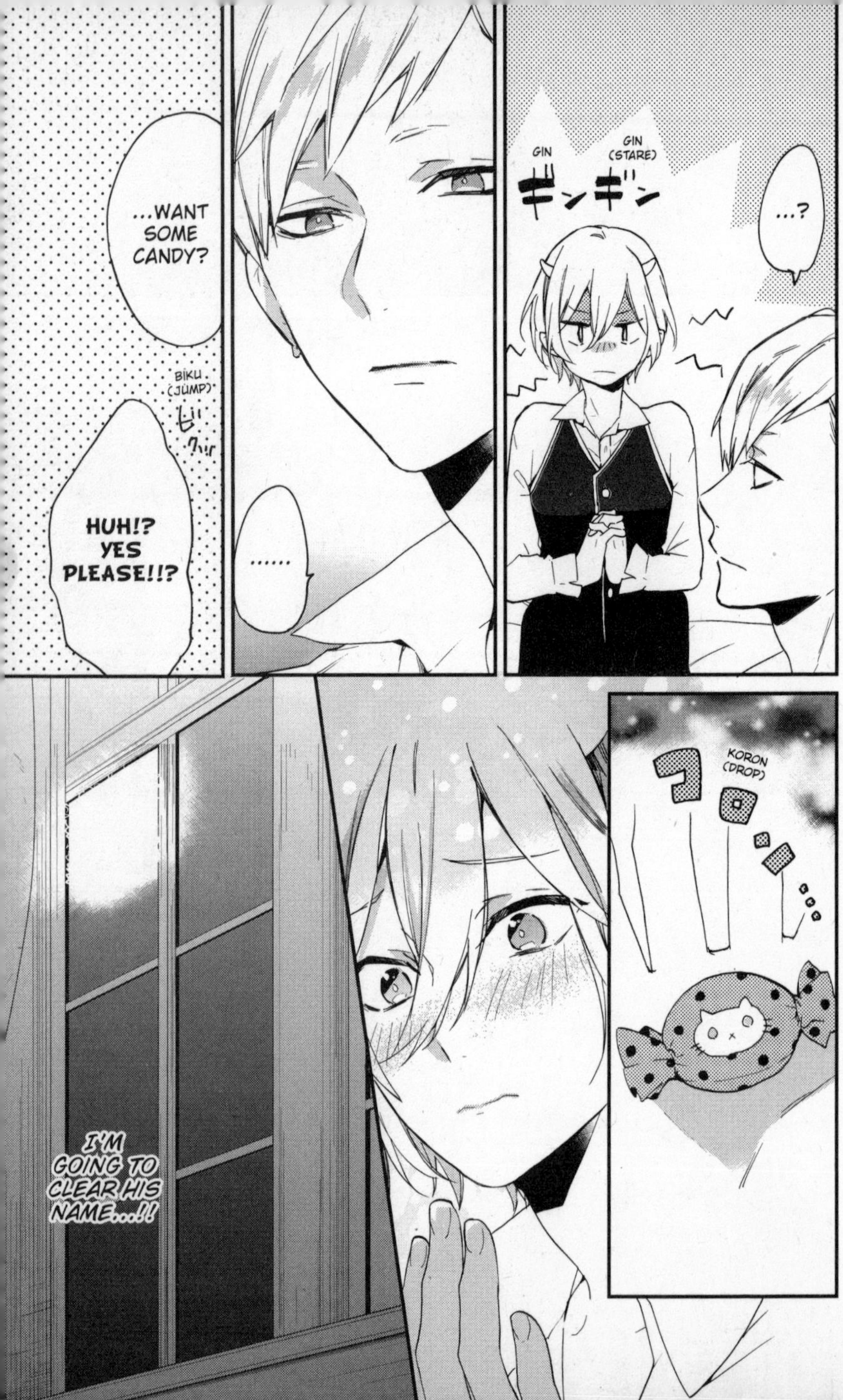
GIN
GIN (STARE)
ギンギン
...?
......
...WANT SOME CANDY?
BIKU (JUMP)
HUH!? YES PLEASE!!?
KORON (DROP)
コロン...
I'M GOING TO CLEAR HIS NAME...!!

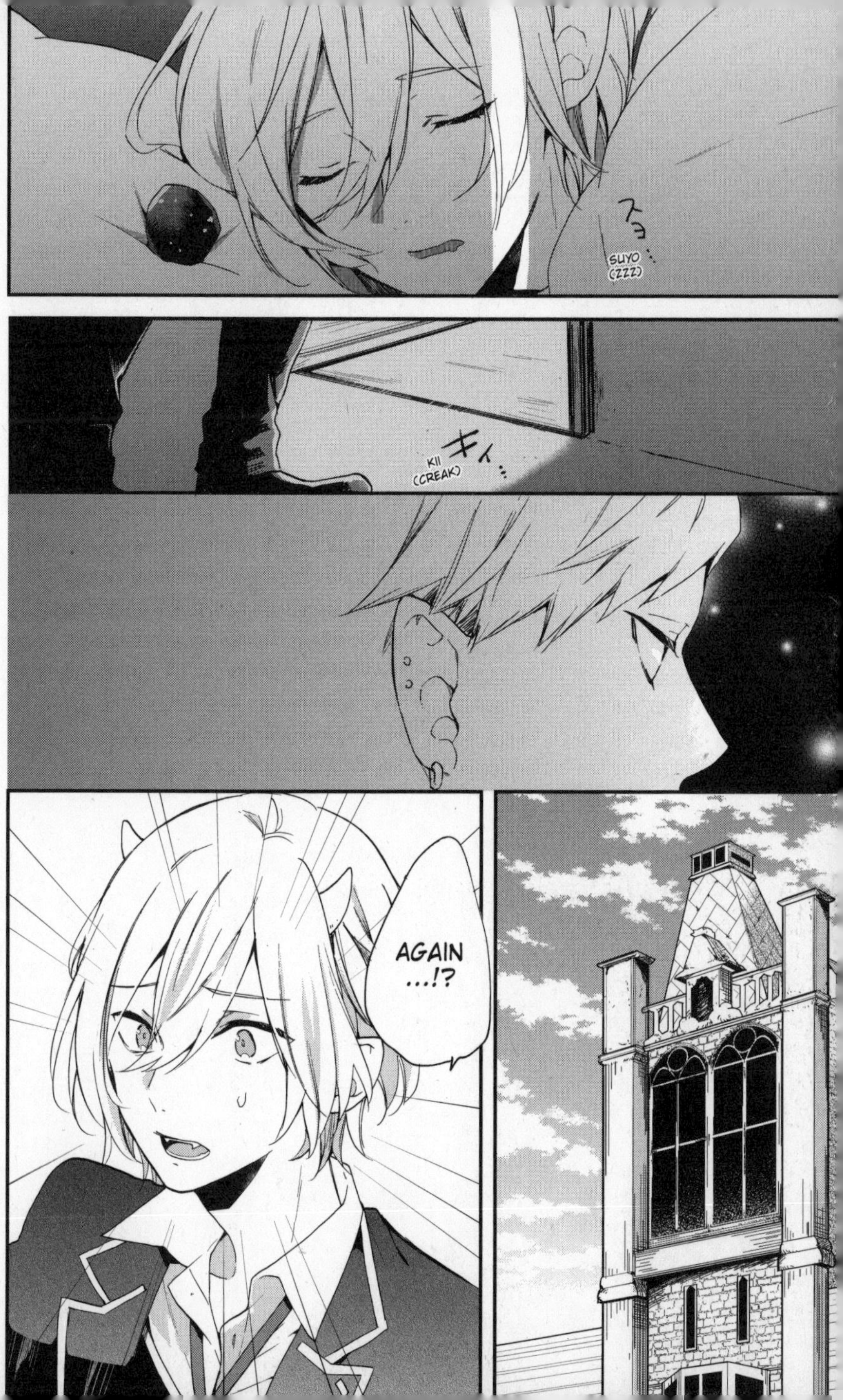
スヨ…
SUYO (ZZZ)
キィ…
KII (CREAK)
AGAIN …!?

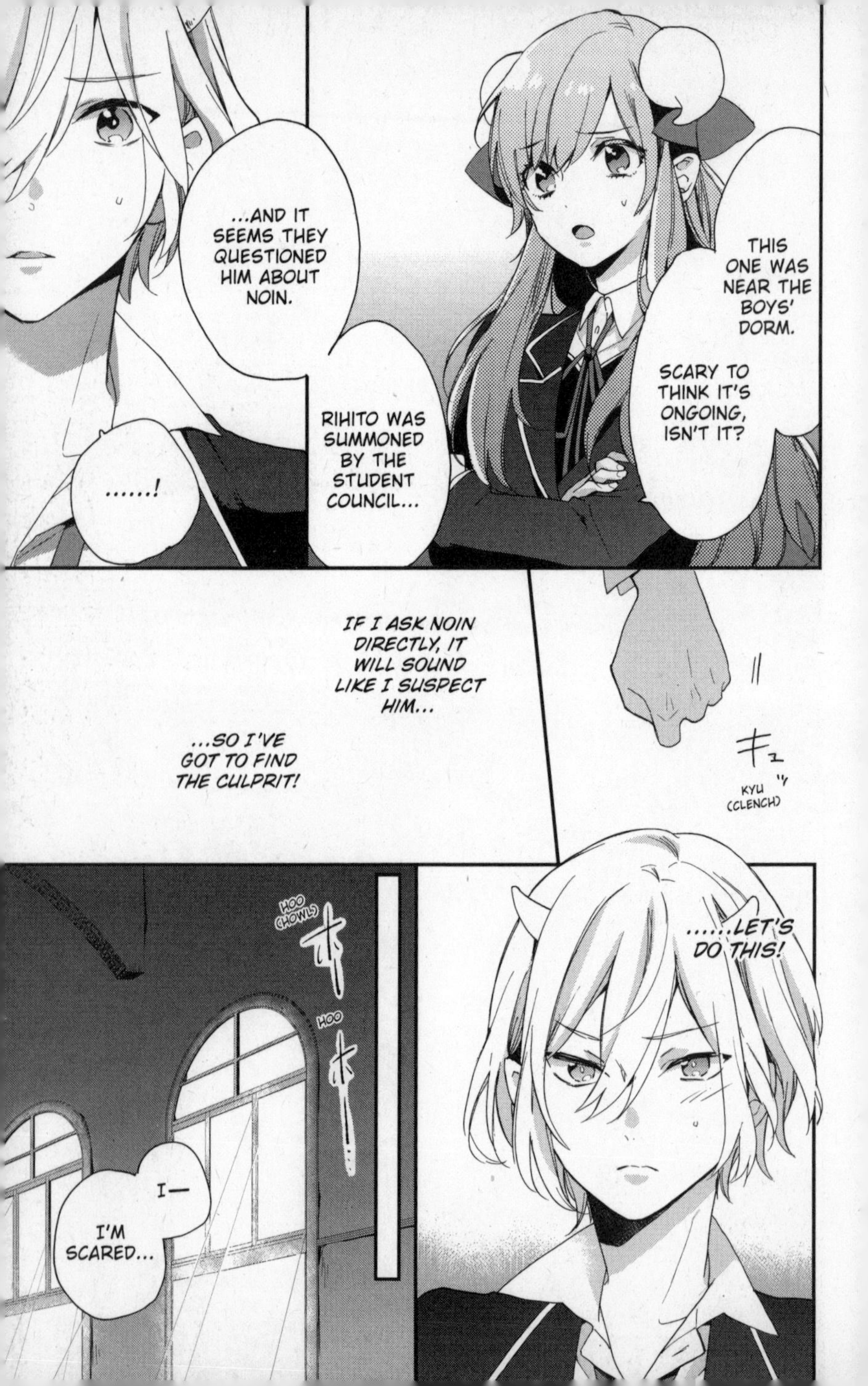
THIS ONE WAS NEAR THE BOYS' DORM.
SCARY TO THINK IT'S ONGOING, ISN'T IT?
RIHITO WAS SUMMONED BY THE STUDENT COUNCIL...
...AND IT SEEMS THEY QUESTIONED HIM ABOUT NOIN.
......!
KYU (CLENCH)
IF I ASK NOIN DIRECTLY, IT WILL SOUND LIKE I SUSPECT HIM...
...SO I'VE GOT TO FIND THE CULPRIT!
......LET'S DO THIS!
HOO (HOWL)
HOO
I— I'M SCARED...

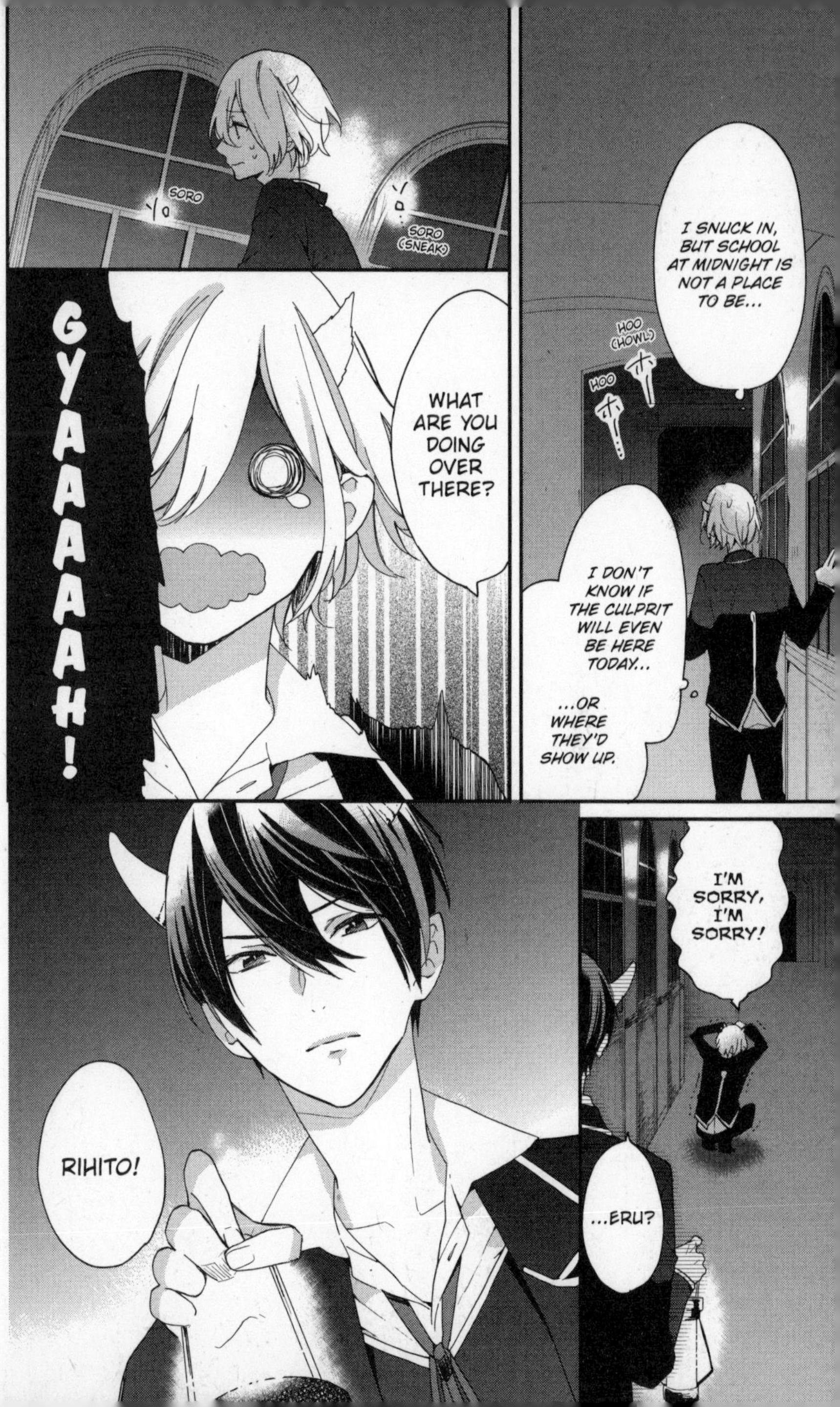
I SNUCK IN, BUT SCHOOL AT MIDNIGHT IS NOT A PLACE TO BE...
HOO (HOWL)
HOO
I DON'T KNOW IF THE CULPRIT WILL EVEN BE HERE TODAY...
...OR WHERE THEY'D SHOW UP.
SORO
SORO (SNEAK)
WHAT ARE YOU DOING OVER THERE?
GYAAAAAAH!
I'M SORRY, I'M SORRY!
...ERU?
RIHITO!

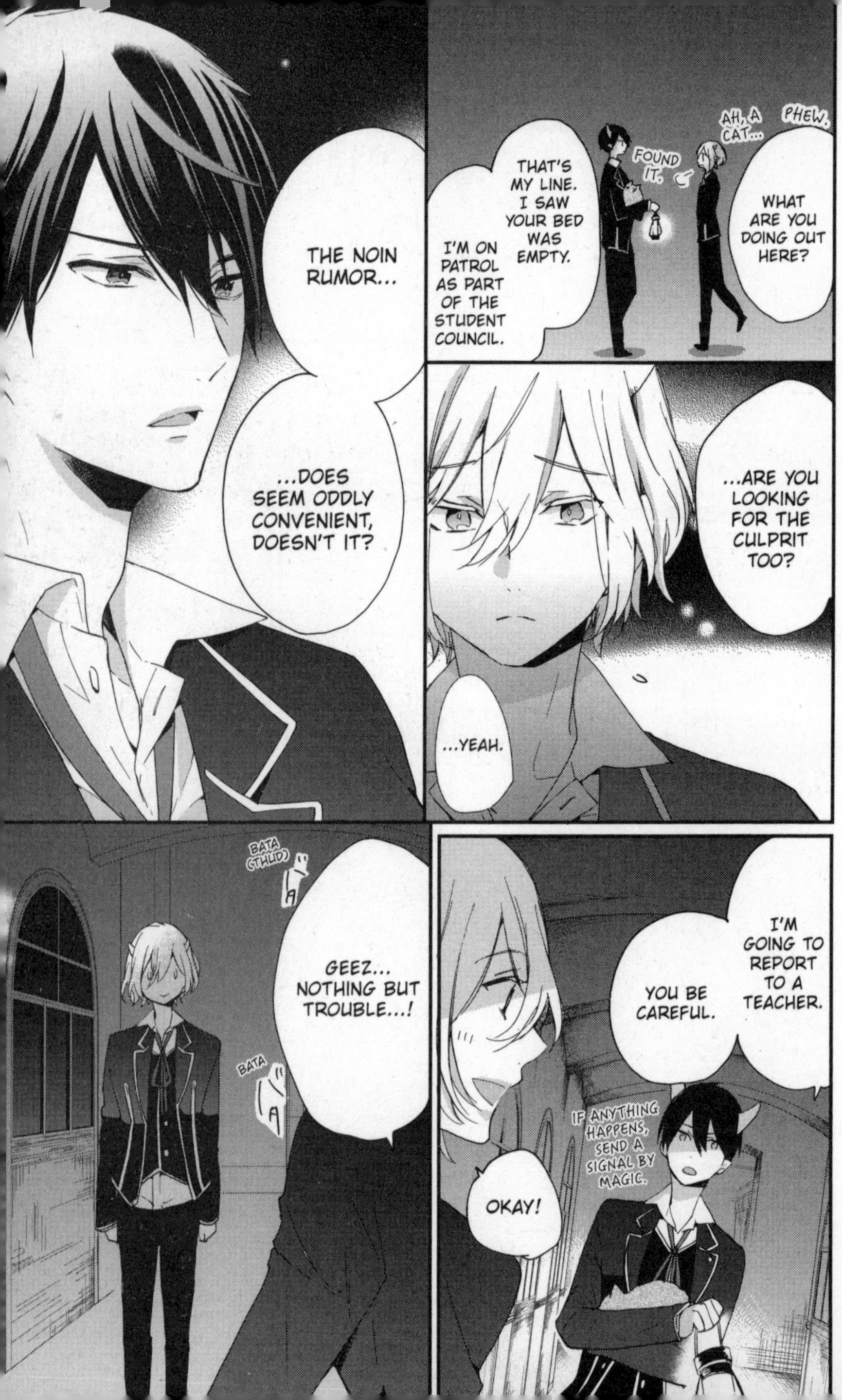
PHEW.
AH, A CAT...
FOUND IT.
WHAT ARE YOU DOING OUT HERE?
THAT'S MY LINE. I SAW YOUR BED WAS EMPTY.
I'M ON PATROL AS PART OF THE STUDENT COUNCIL.
...ARE YOU LOOKING FOR THE CULPRIT TOO?
...YEAH.
THE NOIN RUMOR...
...DOES SEEM ODDLY CONVENIENT, DOESN'T IT?
I'M GOING TO REPORT TO A TEACHER.
YOU BE CAREFUL.
IF ANYTHING HAPPENS, SEND A SIGNAL BY MAGIC.
OKAY!
BATA (THUD)
GEEZ... NOTHING BUT TROUBLE...!
BATA

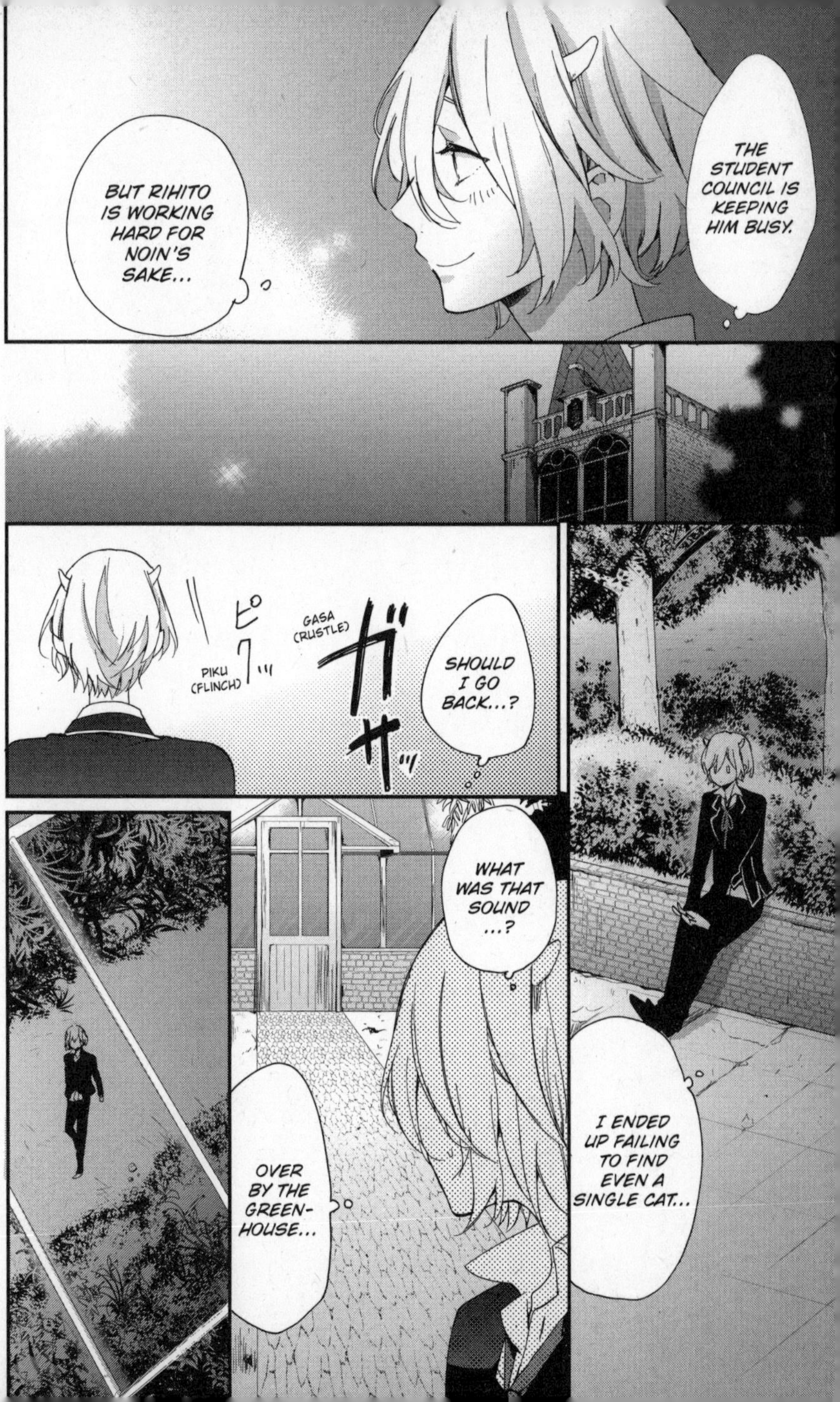
THE STUDENT COUNCIL IS KEEPING HIM BUSY.
BUT RIHITO IS WORKING HARD FOR NOIN'S SAKE...
I ENDED UP FAILING TO FIND EVEN A SINGLE CAT...
SHOULD I GO BACK...?
GASA (RUSTLE)
PIKU (FLINCH)
WHAT WAS THAT SOUND ...?
OVER BY THE GREEN-HOUSE...

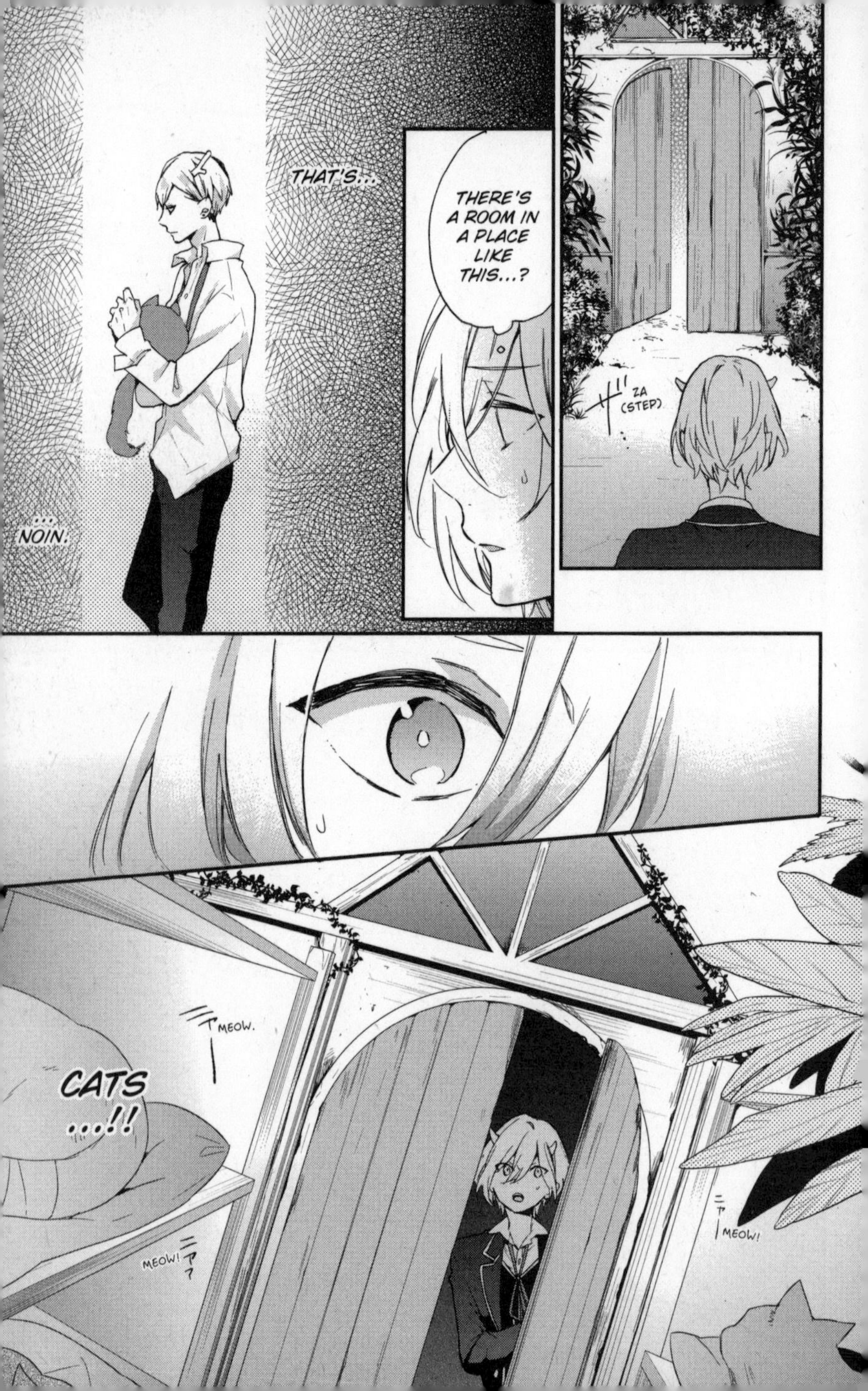
ZA (STEP)
THERE'S A ROOM IN A PLACE LIKE THIS...?
THAT'S...
...NOIN.
MEOW.
CATS...!!
MEOW!
MEOW!

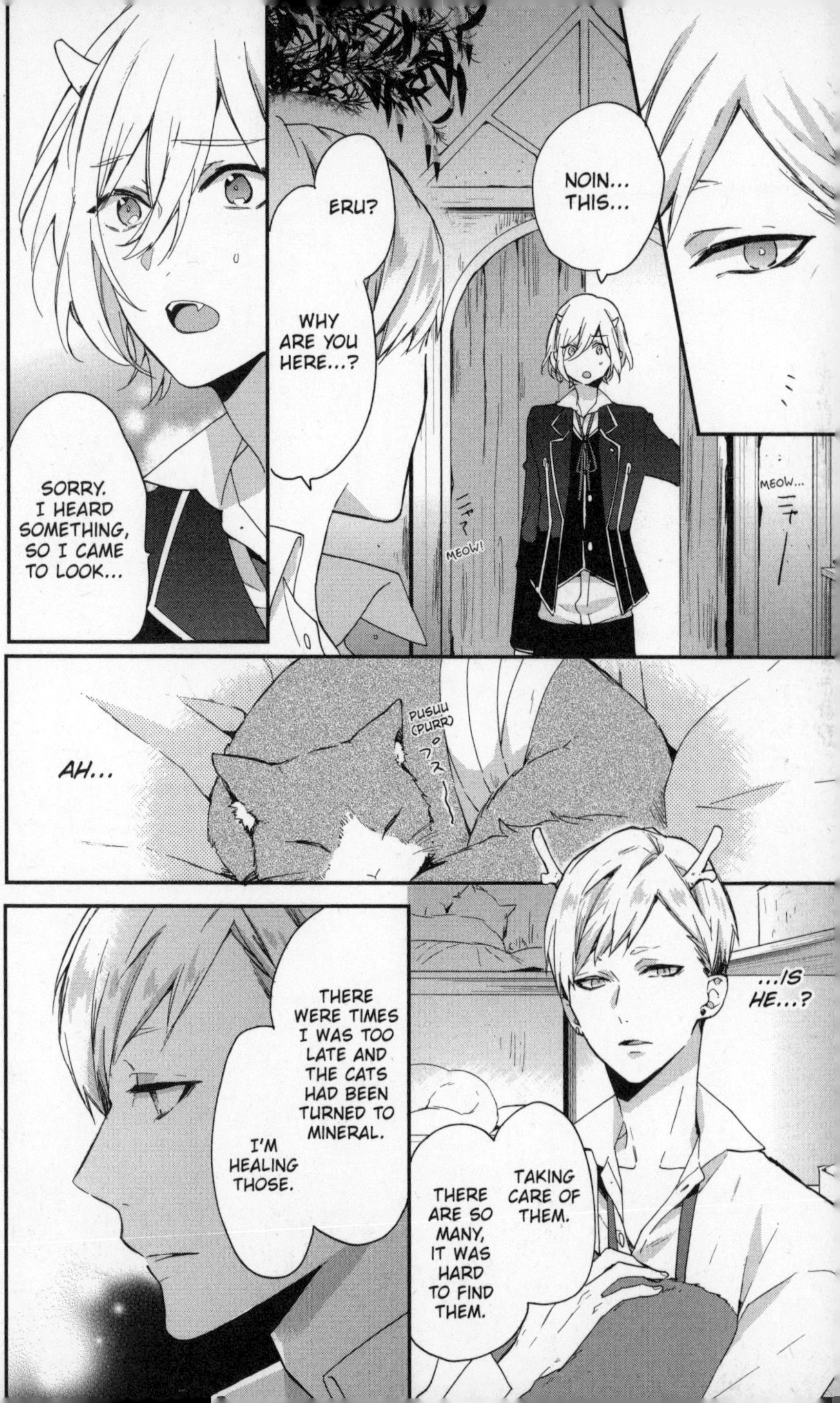
NOIN... THIS...
MEOW...
ニャ
ニャ
MEOW!
ERU?
WHY ARE YOU HERE...?
SORRY. I HEARD SOMETHING, SO I CAME TO LOOK...
PUSUU (PURR)
プスー
AH...
...IS HE...?
TAKING CARE OF THEM.
THERE ARE SO MANY, IT WAS HARD TO FIND THEM.
THERE WERE TIMES I WAS TOO LATE AND THE CATS HAD BEEN TURNED TO MINERAL.
I'M HEALING THOSE.

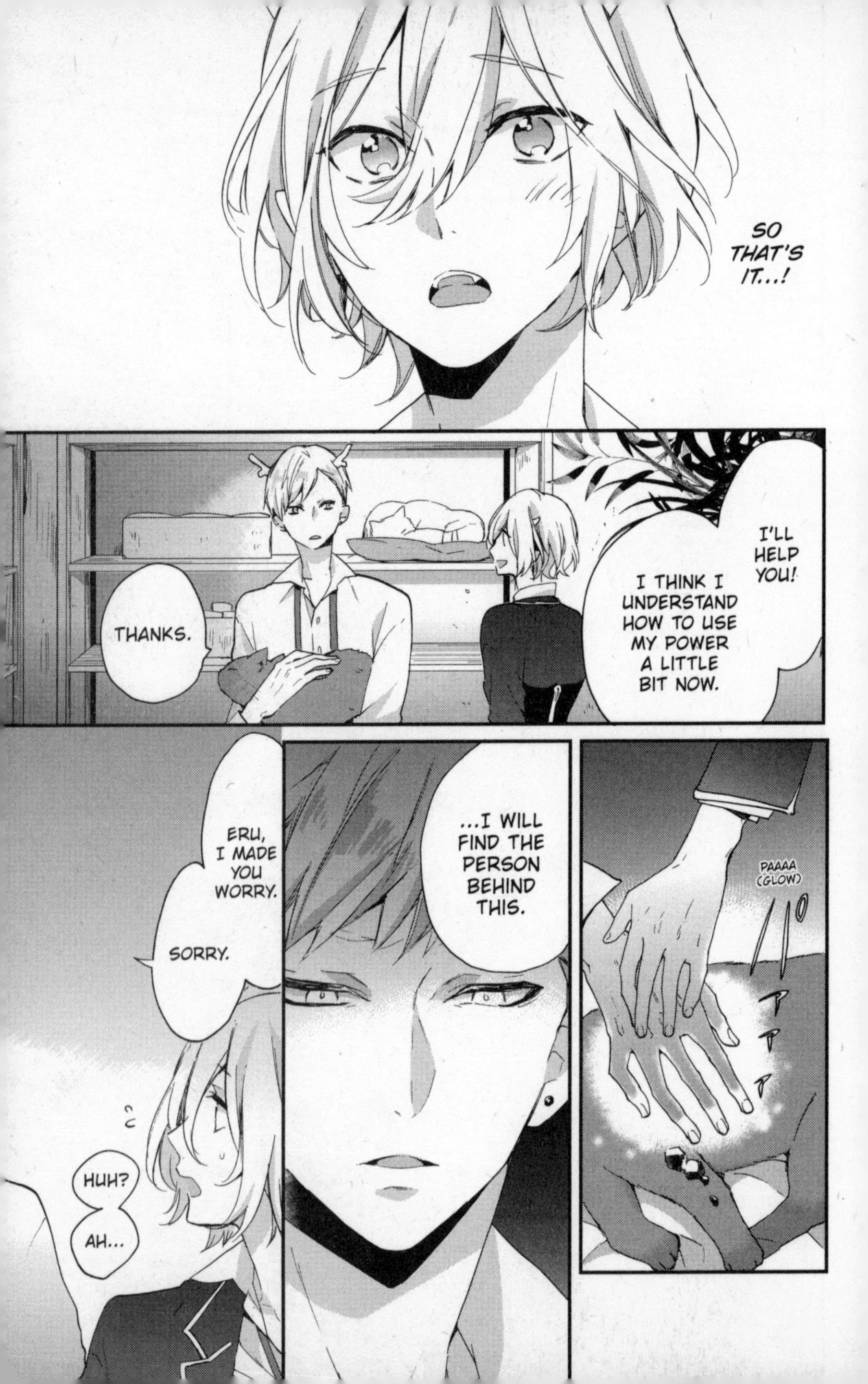
SO THAT'S IT...!
I'LL HELP YOU!
I THINK I UNDERSTAND HOW TO USE MY POWER A LITTLE BIT NOW.
THANKS.
PAAAA (GLOW)
...I WILL FIND THE PERSON BEHIND THIS.
ERU, I MADE YOU WORRY.
SORRY.
HUH?
AH...

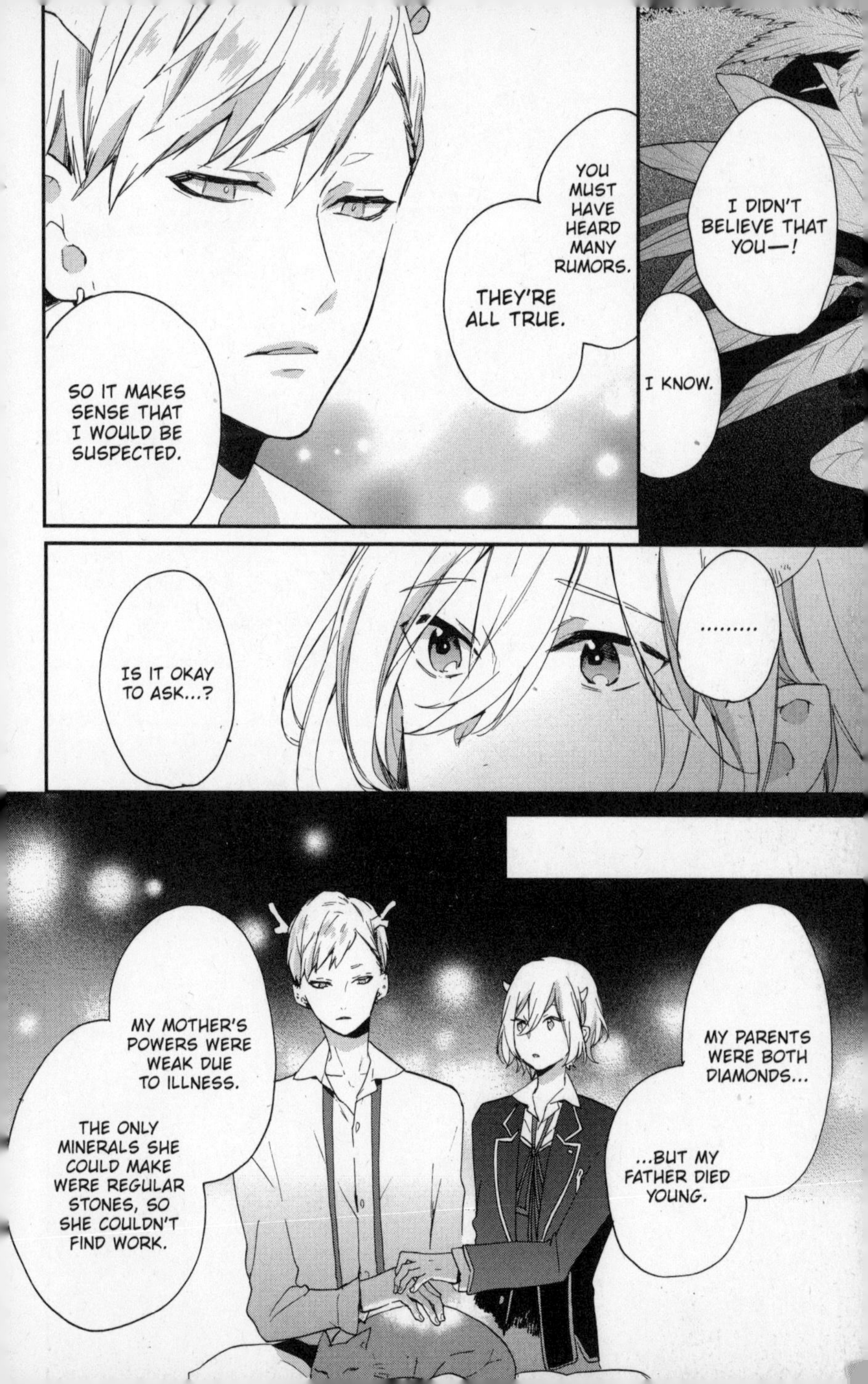
I DIDN'T BELIEVE THAT YOU—!
I KNOW.
YOU MUST HAVE HEARD MANY RUMORS.
THEY'RE ALL TRUE.
SO IT MAKES SENSE THAT I WOULD BE SUSPECTED.
....
IS IT OKAY TO ASK...?
MY PARENTS WERE BOTH DIAMONDS...
...BUT MY FATHER DIED YOUNG.
MY MOTHER'S POWERS WERE WEAK DUE TO ILLNESS.
THE ONLY MINERALS SHE COULD MAKE WERE REGULAR STONES, SO SHE COULDN'T FIND WORK.

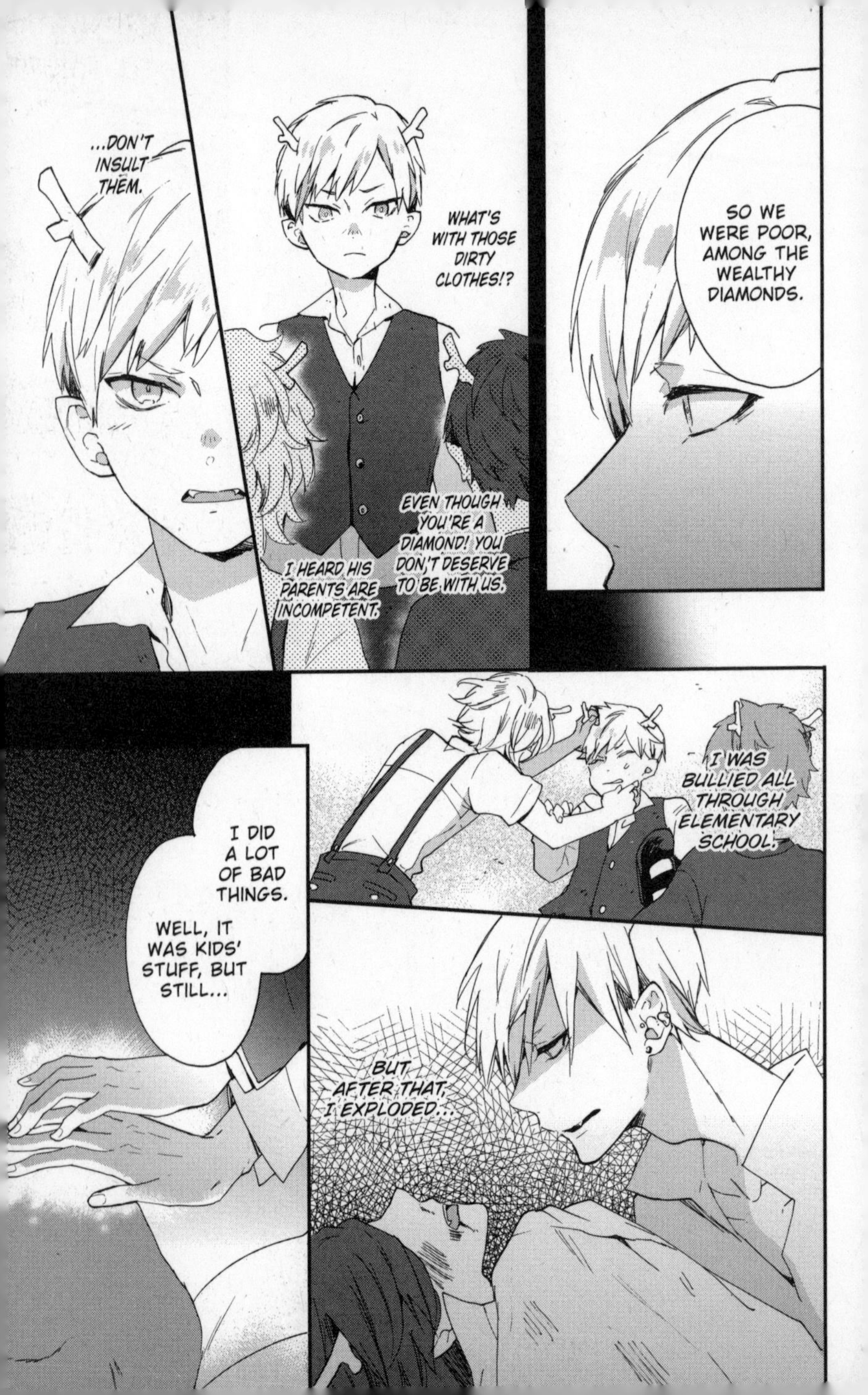
SO WE WERE POOR, AMONG THE WEALTHY DIAMONDS.
WHAT'S WITH THOSE DIRTY CLOTHES!?
EVEN THOUGH YOU'RE A DIAMOND! YOU DON'T DESERVE TO BE WITH US.
I HEARD HIS PARENTS ARE INCOMPETENT.
...DON'T INSULT THEM.
I WAS BULLIED ALL THROUGH ELEMENTARY SCHOOL.
BUT AFTER THAT, I EXPLODED...
I DID A LOT OF BAD THINGS.
WELL, IT WAS KIDS' STUFF, BUT STILL...

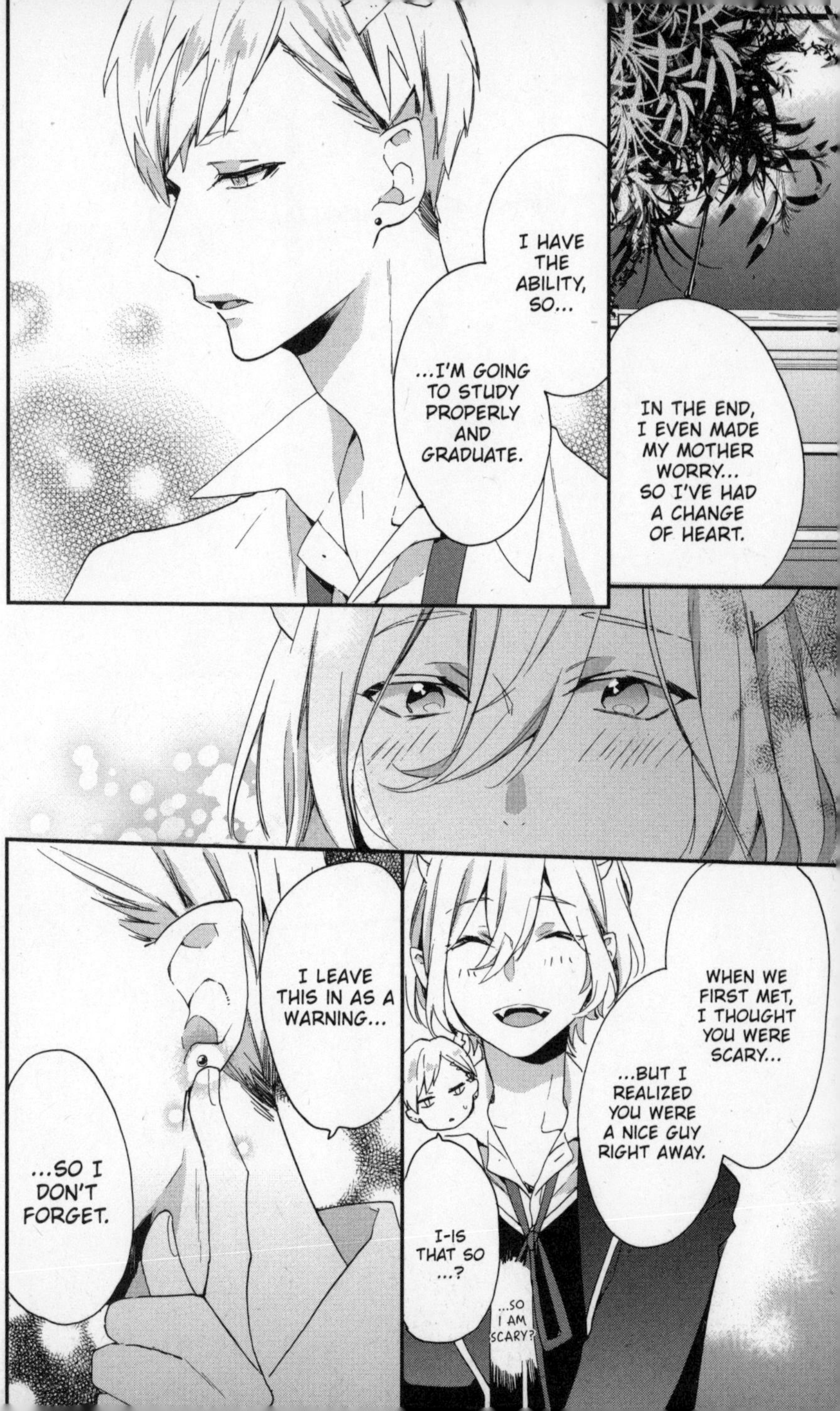
IN THE END, I EVEN MADE MY MOTHER WORRY... SO I'VE HAD A CHANGE OF HEART.
I HAVE THE ABILITY, SO...
...I'M GOING TO STUDY PROPERLY AND GRADUATE.
WHEN WE FIRST MET, I THOUGHT YOU WERE SCARY...
...BUT I REALIZED YOU WERE A NICE GUY RIGHT AWAY.
I-IS THAT SO ...?
...SO I AM SCARY?
I LEAVE THIS IN AS A WARNING...
...SO I DON'T FORGET.

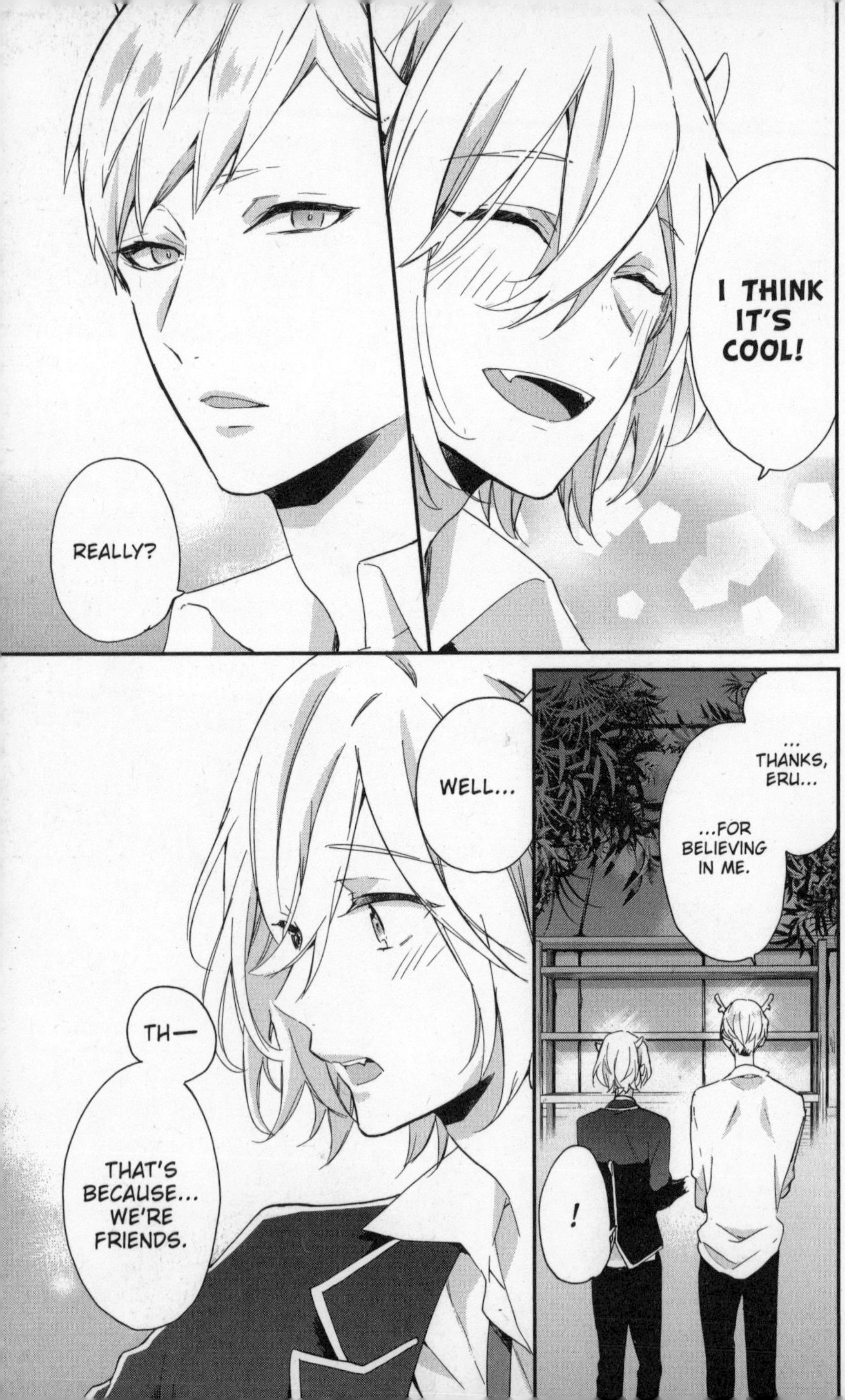
I THINK IT'S COOL!
REALLY?
... THANKS, ERU...
...FOR BELIEVING IN ME.
!
WELL...
TH—
THAT'S BECAUSE... WE'RE FRIENDS.

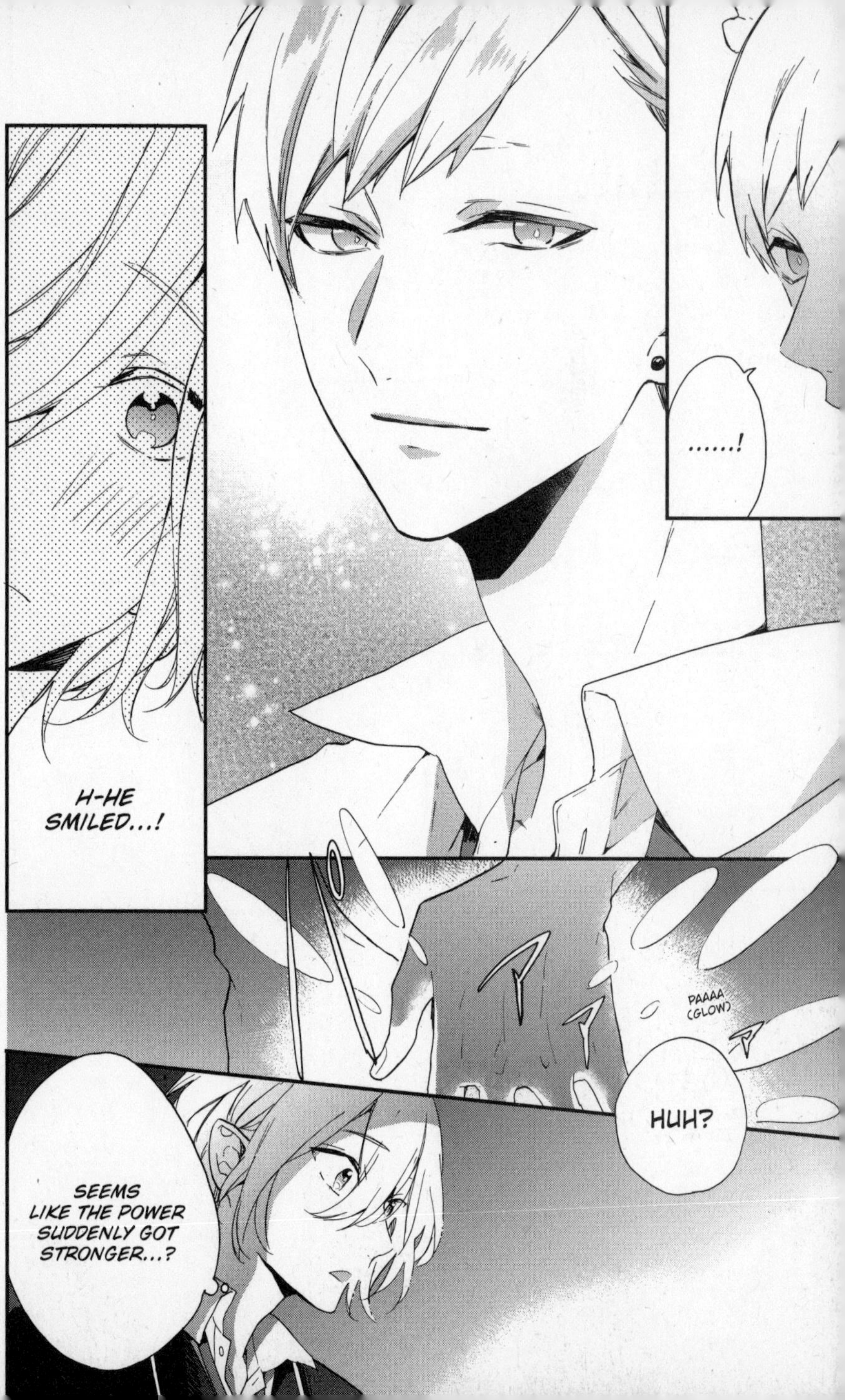
......!
H-HE SMILED...!
PAAAA (GLOW)
HUH?
SEEMS LIKE THE POWER SUDDENLY GOT STRONGER...?

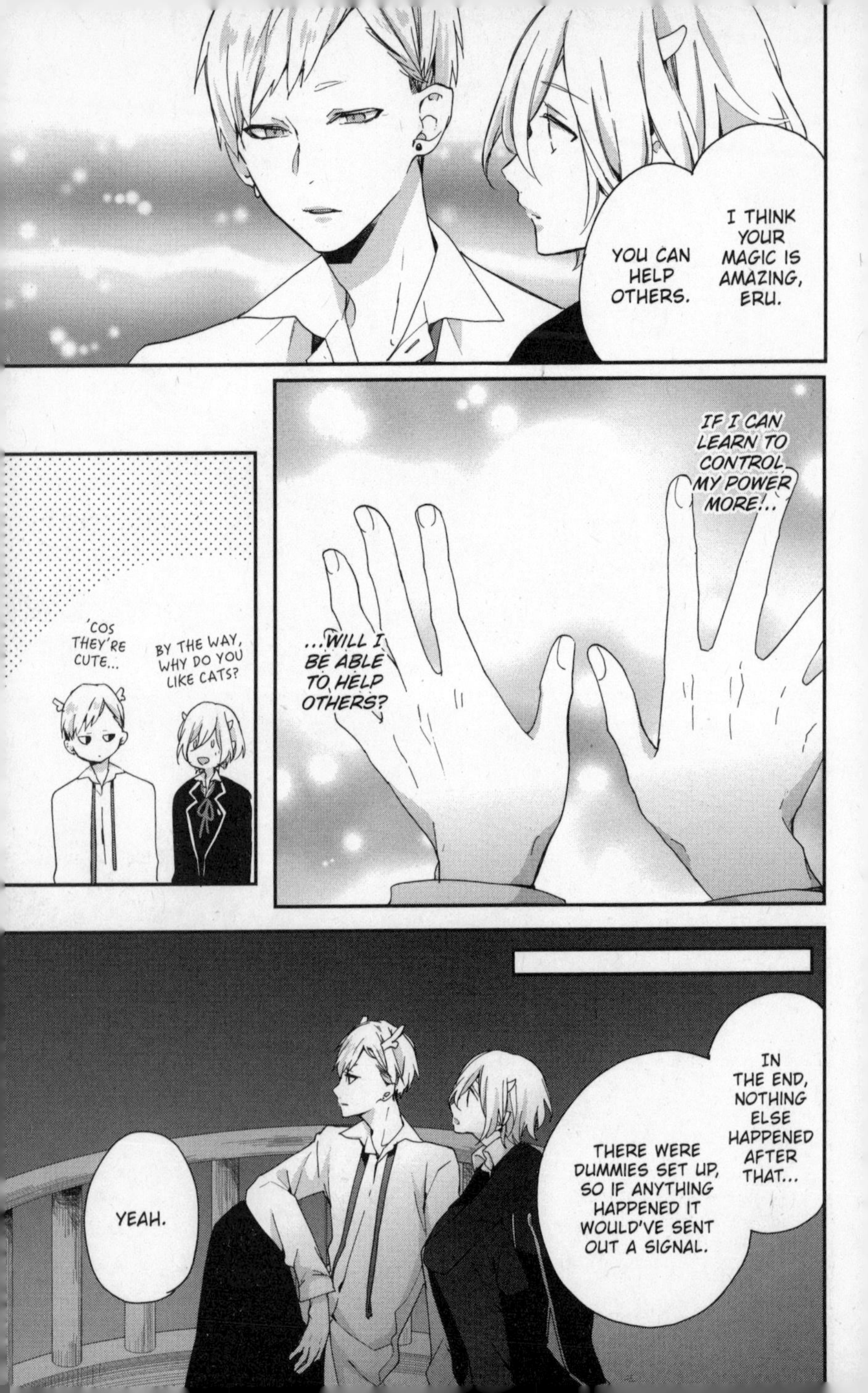

I THINK YOUR MAGIC IS AMAZING, ERU.
YOU CAN HELP OTHERS.
IF I CAN LEARN TO CONTROL MY POWER MORE...
...WILL I BE ABLE TO HELP OTHERS?
BY THE WAY, WHY DO YOU LIKE CATS?
'COS THEY'RE CUTE...
IN THE END, NOTHING ELSE HAPPENED AFTER THAT...
THERE WERE DUMMIES SET UP, SO IF ANYTHING HAPPENED IT WOULD'VE SENT OUT A SIGNAL.
YEAH.

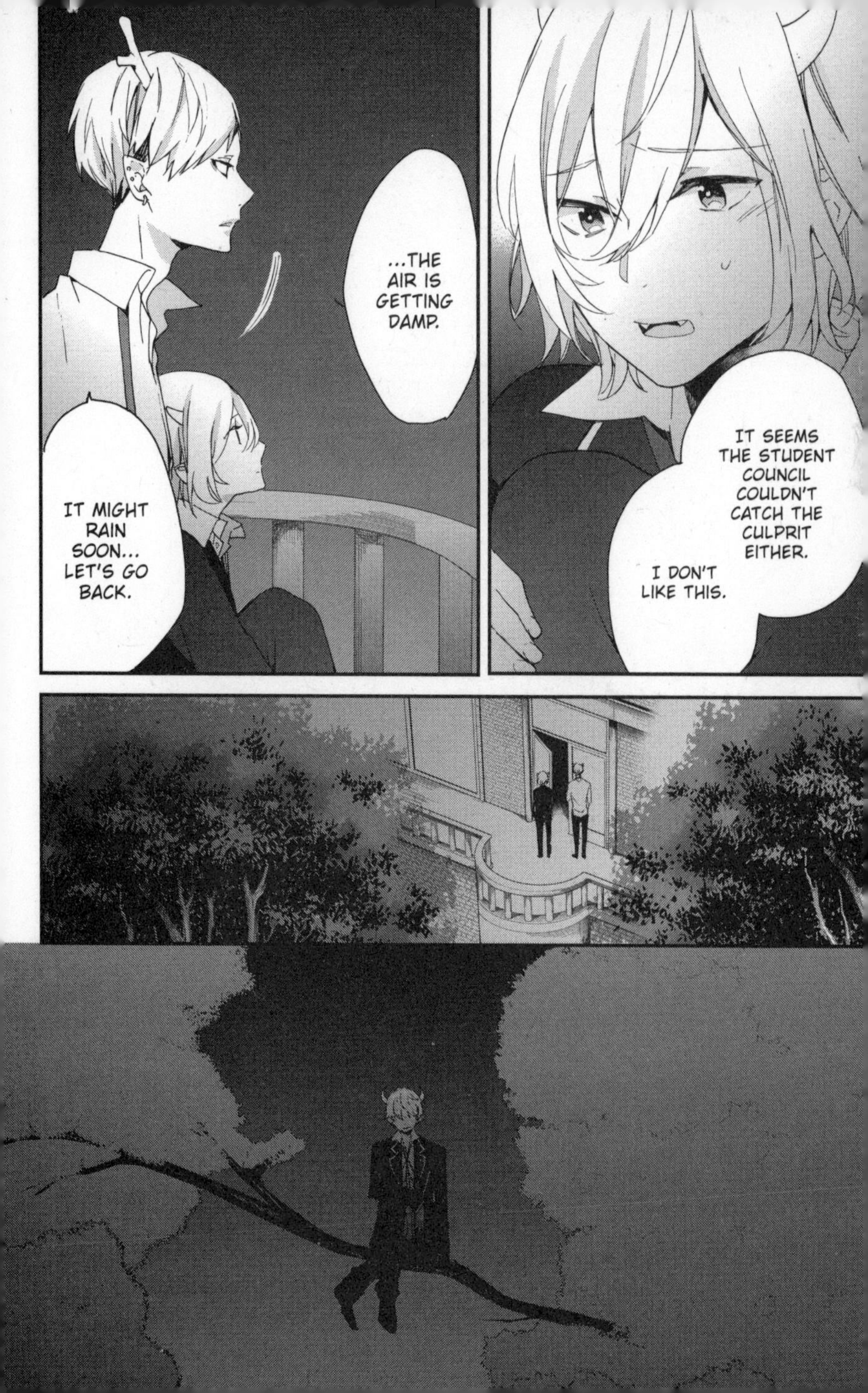
IT SEEMS THE STUDENT COUNCIL COULDN'T CATCH THE CULPRIT EITHER.
I DON'T LIKE THIS.
...THE AIR IS GETTING DAMP.
IT MIGHT RAIN SOON... LET'S GO BACK.

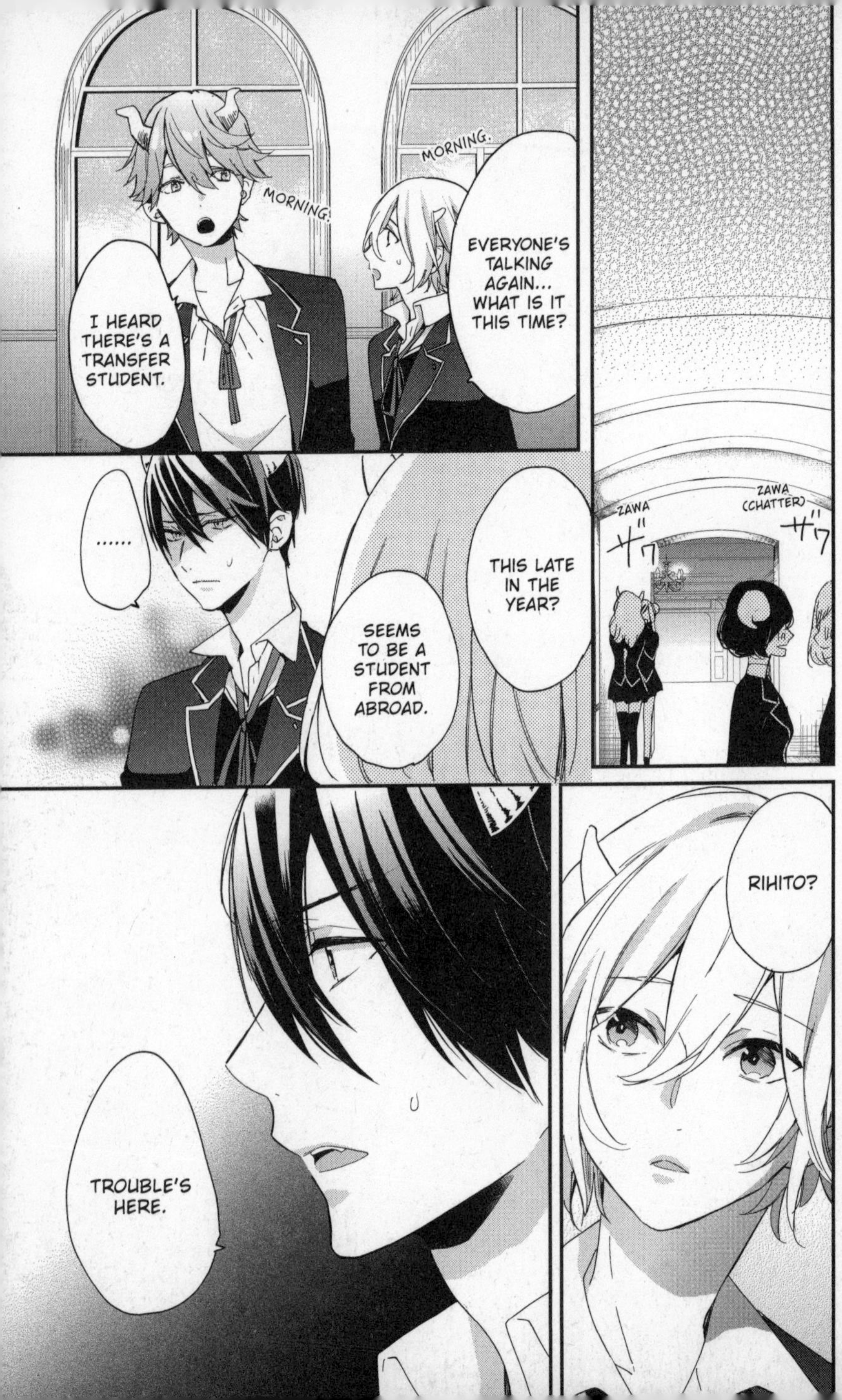
ZAWA (CHATTER)
ザワ
ZAWA
ザワ
EVERYONE'S TALKING AGAIN... WHAT IS IT THIS TIME?
MORNING.
MORNING!
I HEARD THERE'S A TRANSFER STUDENT.
THIS LATE IN THE YEAR?
SEEMS TO BE A STUDENT FROM ABROAD.
......
RIHITO?
TROUBLE'S HERE.

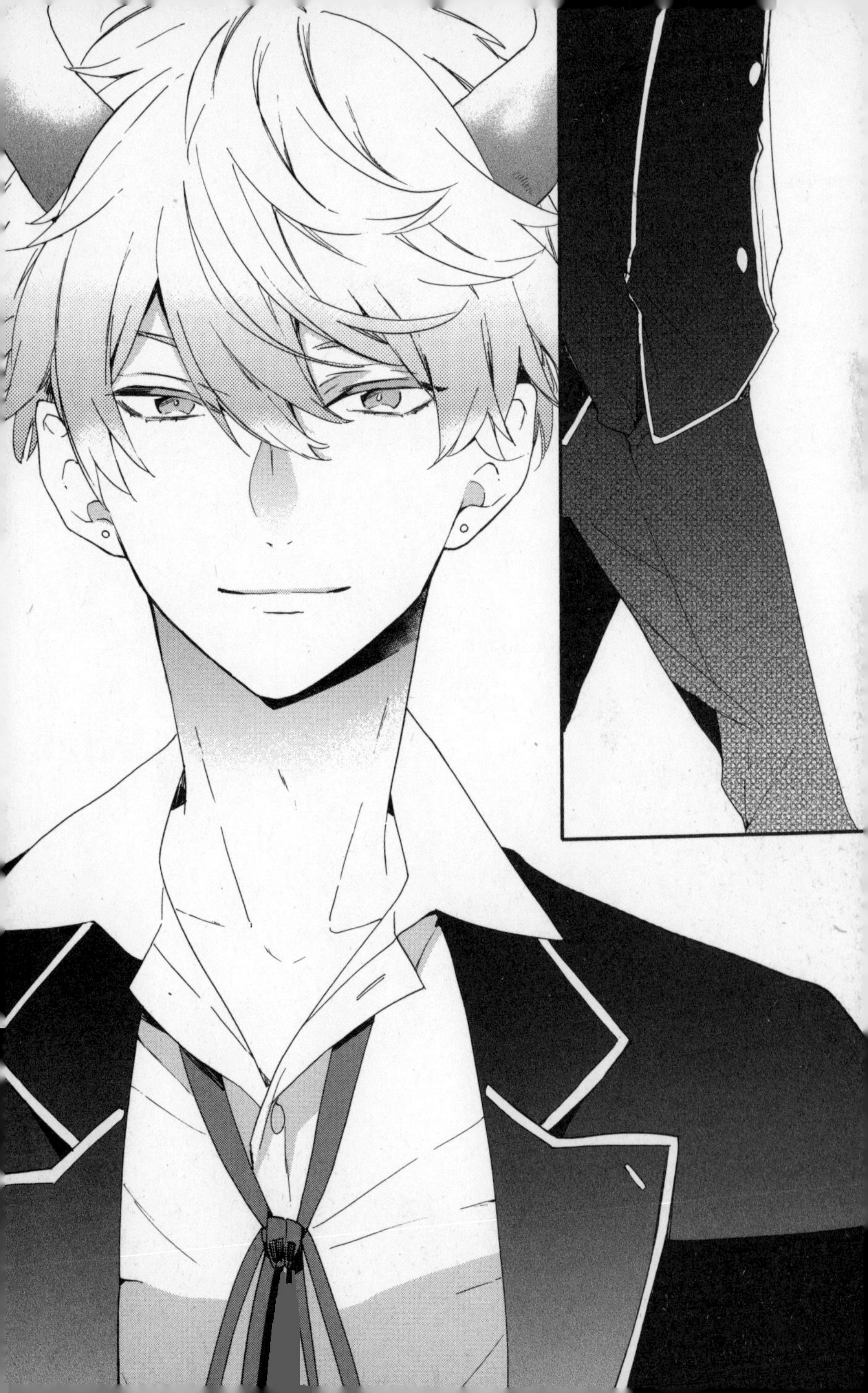

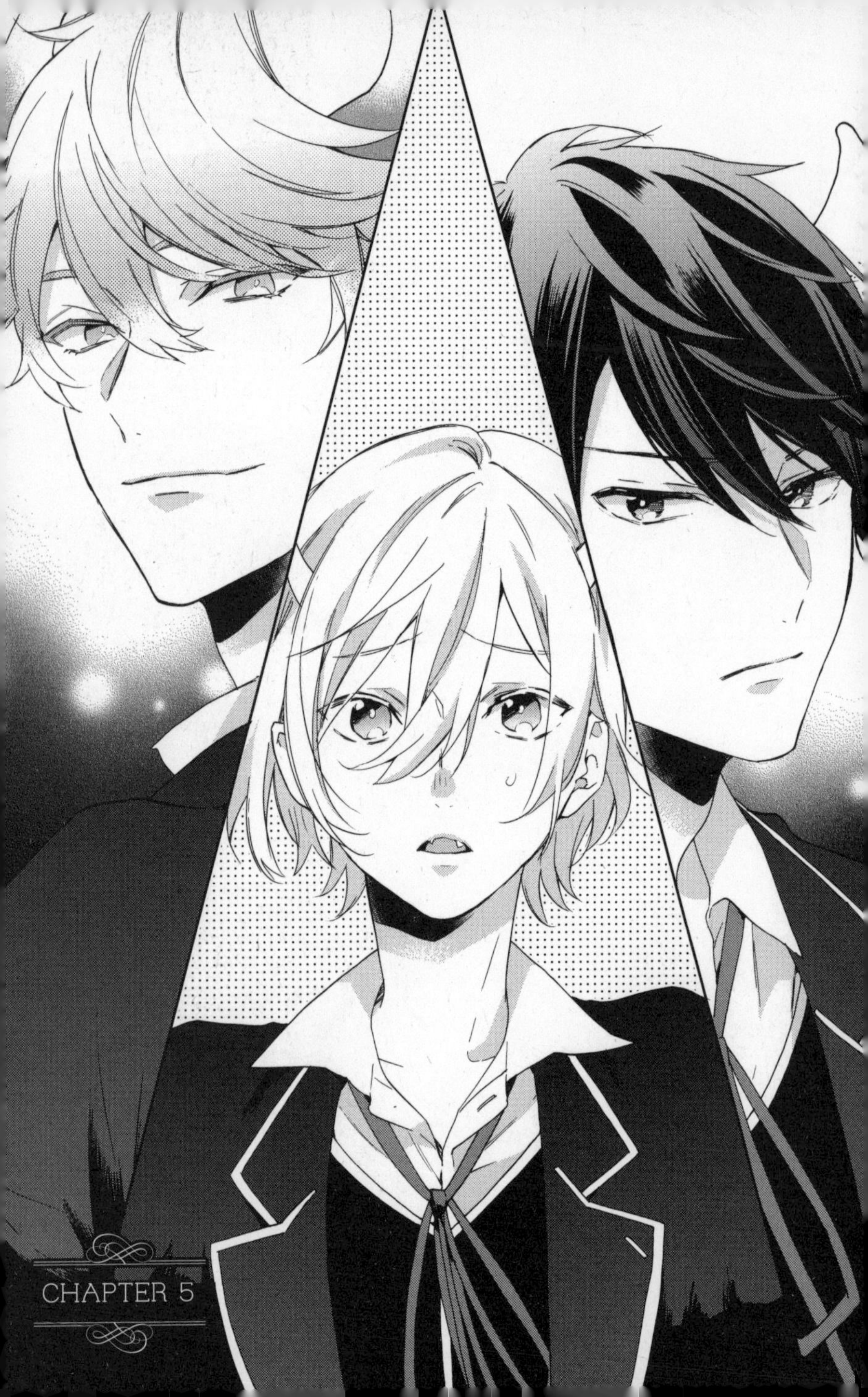
CHAPTER 5

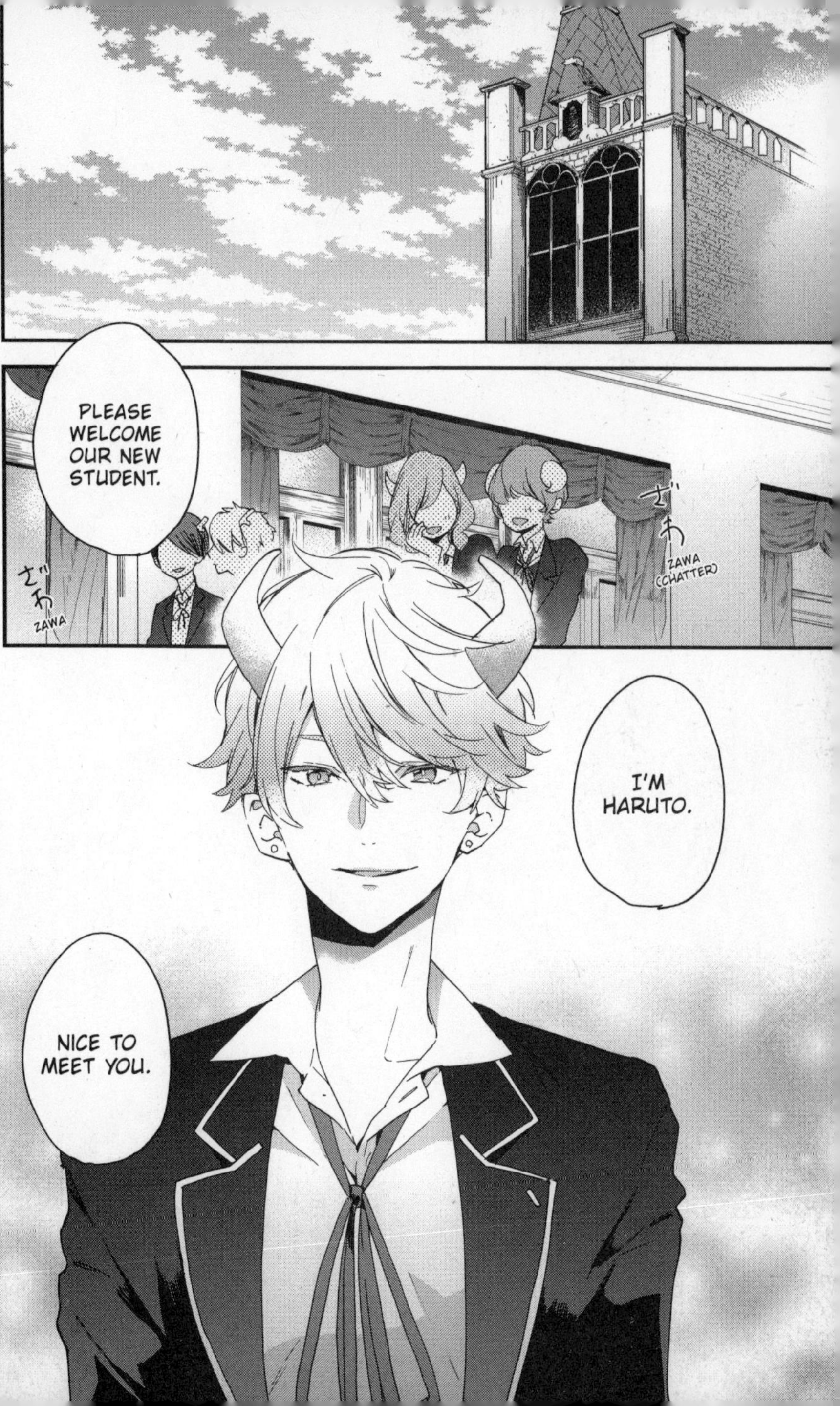
PLEASE WELCOME OUR NEW STUDENT.
ざわ
ZAWA (CHATTER)
ざわ
ZAWA
I'M HARUTO.
NICE TO MEET YOU.

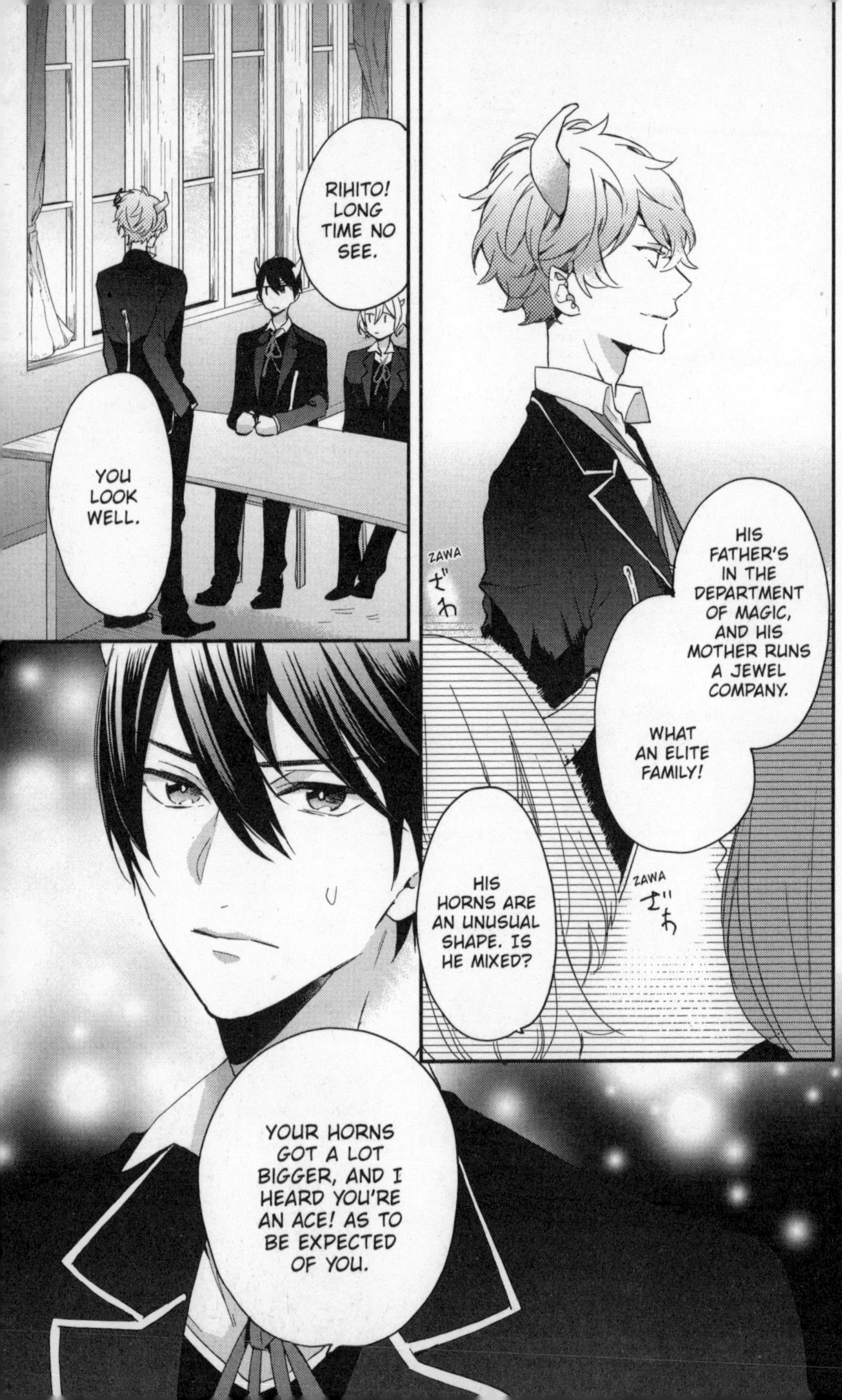

ZAWA
ざわ
HIS FATHER'S IN THE DEPARTMENT OF MAGIC, AND HIS MOTHER RUNS A JEWEL COMPANY.
WHAT AN ELITE FAMILY!
ZAWA
ざわ
HIS HORNS ARE AN UNUSUAL SHAPE. IS HE MIXED?
RIHITO! LONG TIME NO SEE.
YOU LOOK WELL.
YOUR HORNS GOT A LOT BIGGER, AND I HEARD YOU'RE AN ACE! AS TO BE EXPECTED OF YOU.

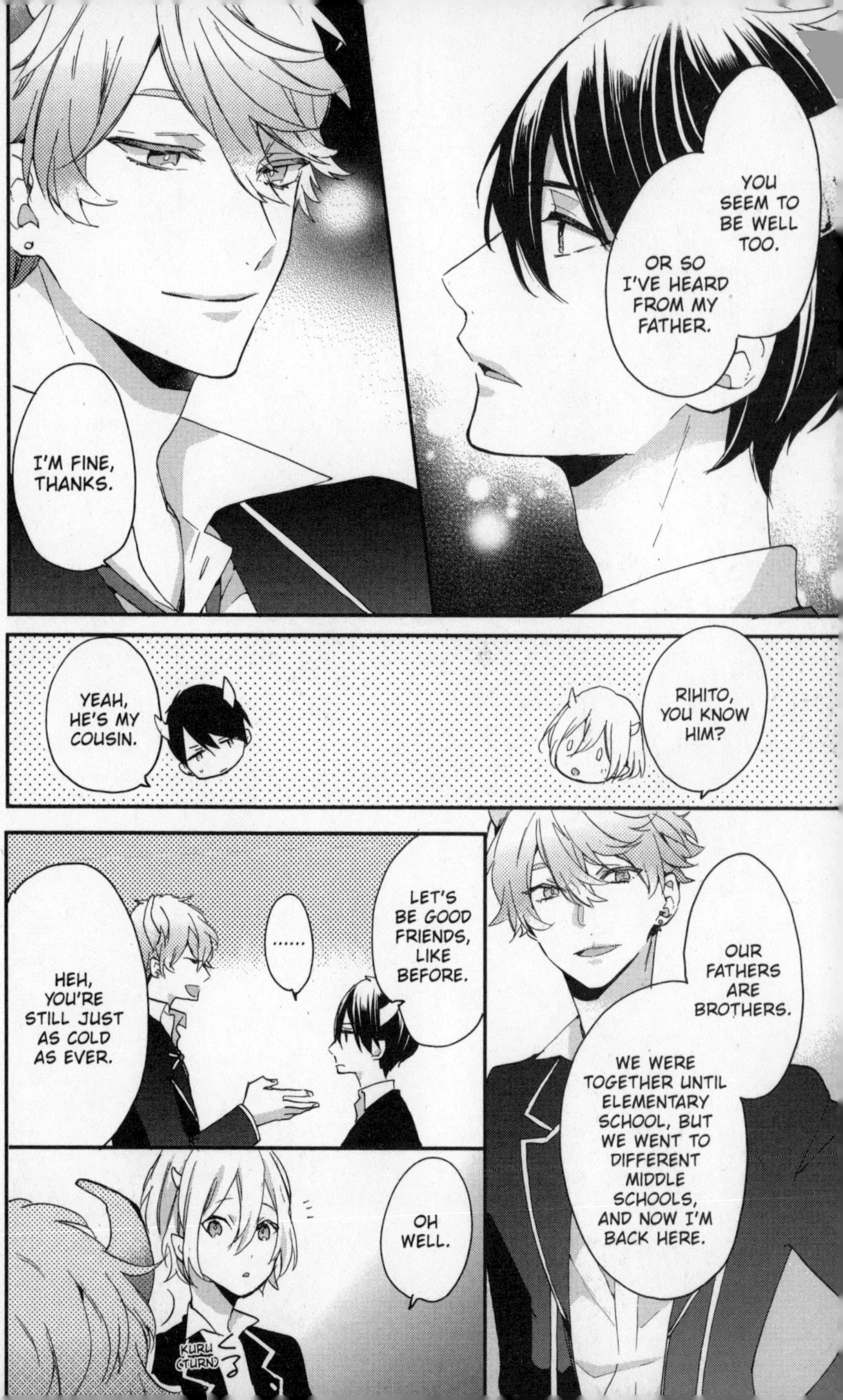
YOU SEEM TO BE WELL TOO.
OR SO I'VE HEARD FROM MY FATHER.
I'M FINE, THANKS.
RIHITO, YOU KNOW HIM?
YEAH, HE'S MY COUSIN.
OUR FATHERS ARE BROTHERS.
WE WERE TOGETHER UNTIL ELEMENTARY SCHOOL, BUT WE WENT TO DIFFERENT MIDDLE SCHOOLS, AND NOW I'M BACK HERE.
LET'S BE GOOD FRIENDS, LIKE BEFORE.
......
HEH, YOU'RE STILL JUST AS COLD AS EVER.
OH WELL.
KURU (TURN)

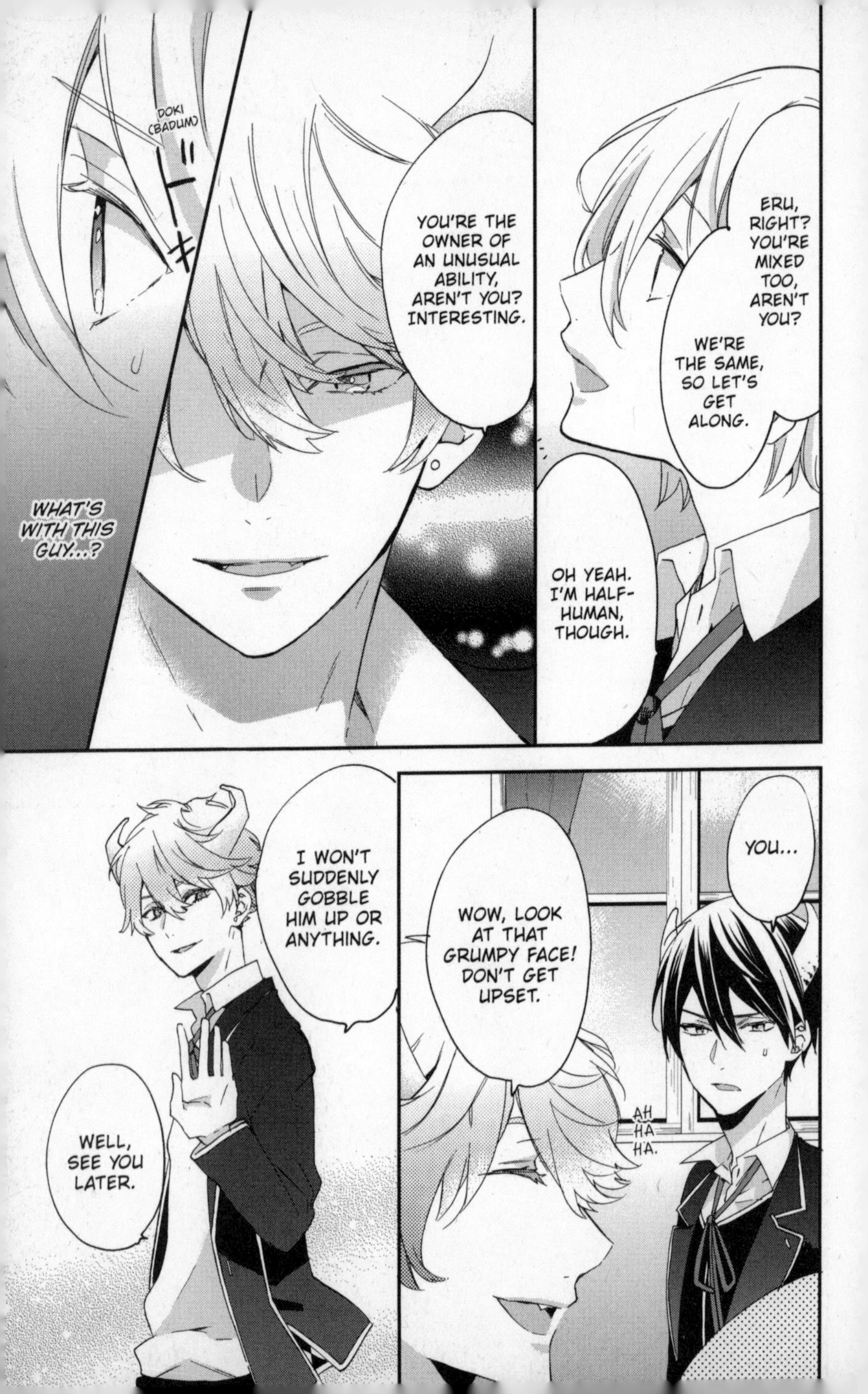
ERU, RIGHT? YOU'RE MIXED TOO, AREN'T YOU?
WE'RE THE SAME, SO LET'S GET ALONG.
OH YEAH. I'M HALF-HUMAN, THOUGH.
YOU'RE THE OWNER OF AN UNUSUAL ABILITY, AREN'T YOU? INTERESTING.
DOKI (BADUM)
WHAT'S WITH THIS GUY...?
YOU...
WOW, LOOK AT THAT GRUMPY FACE! DON'T GET UPSET.
AH HA HA.
I WON'T SUDDENLY GOBBLE HIM UP OR ANYTHING.
WELL, SEE YOU LATER.

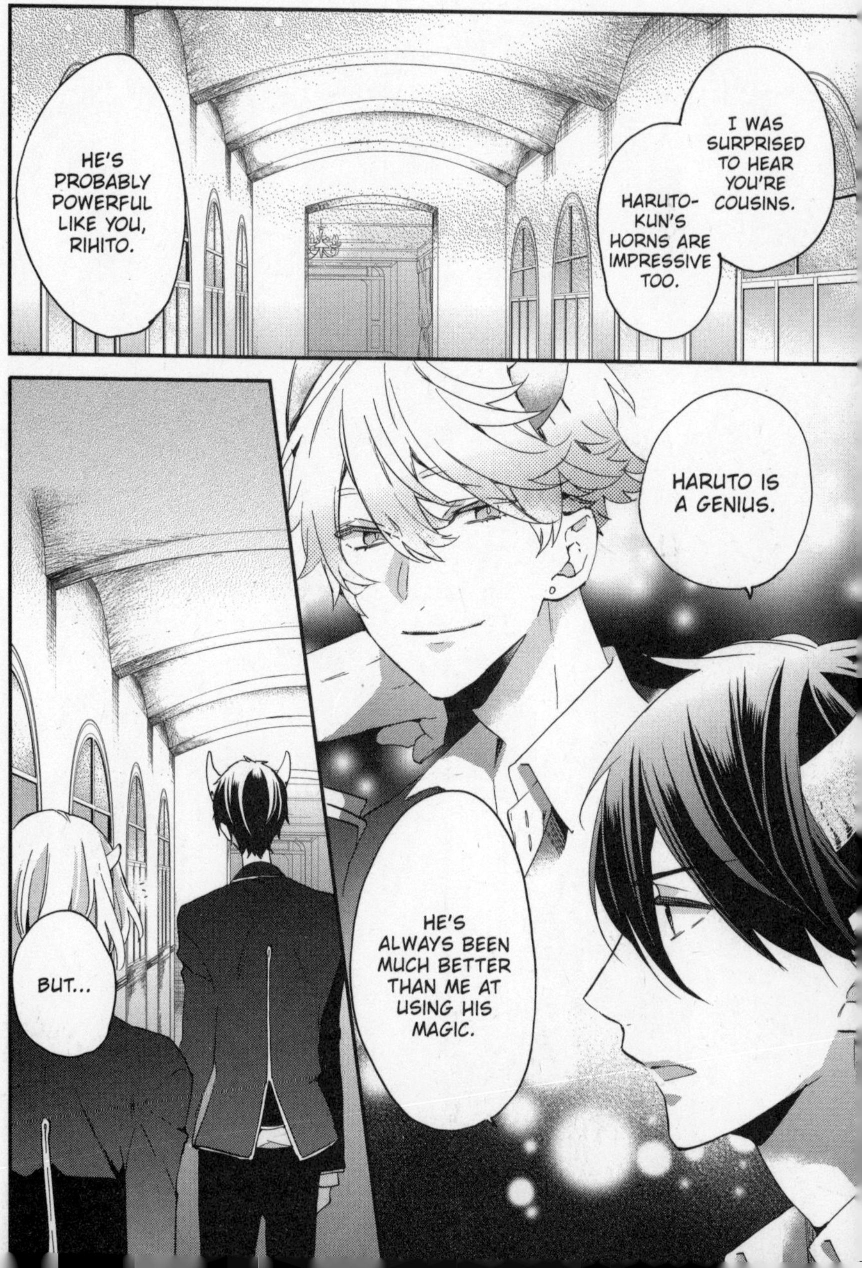
I WAS SURPRISED TO HEAR YOU'RE COUSINS.
HARUTO-KUN'S HORNS ARE IMPRESSIVE TOO.
HE'S PROBABLY POWERFUL LIKE YOU, RIHITO.
HARUTO IS A GENIUS.
HE'S ALWAYS BEEN MUCH BETTER THAN ME AT USING HIS MAGIC.
BUT...

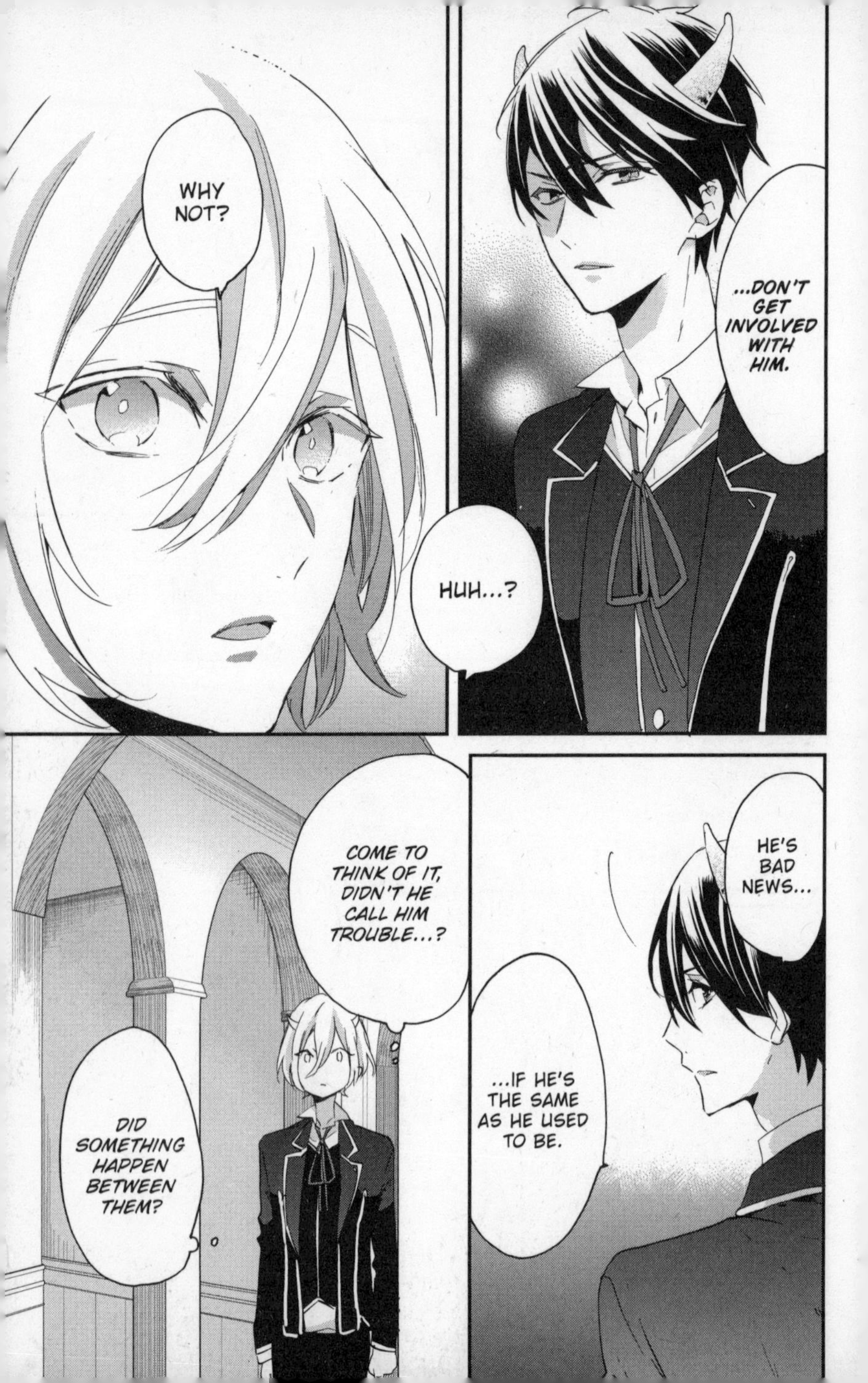
...DON'T GET INVOLVED WITH HIM.
HUH...?
WHY NOT?
HE'S BAD NEWS...
...IF HE'S THE SAME AS HE USED TO BE.
COME TO THINK OF IT, DIDN'T HE CALL HIM TROUBLE...?
DID SOMETHING HAPPEN BETWEEN THEM?

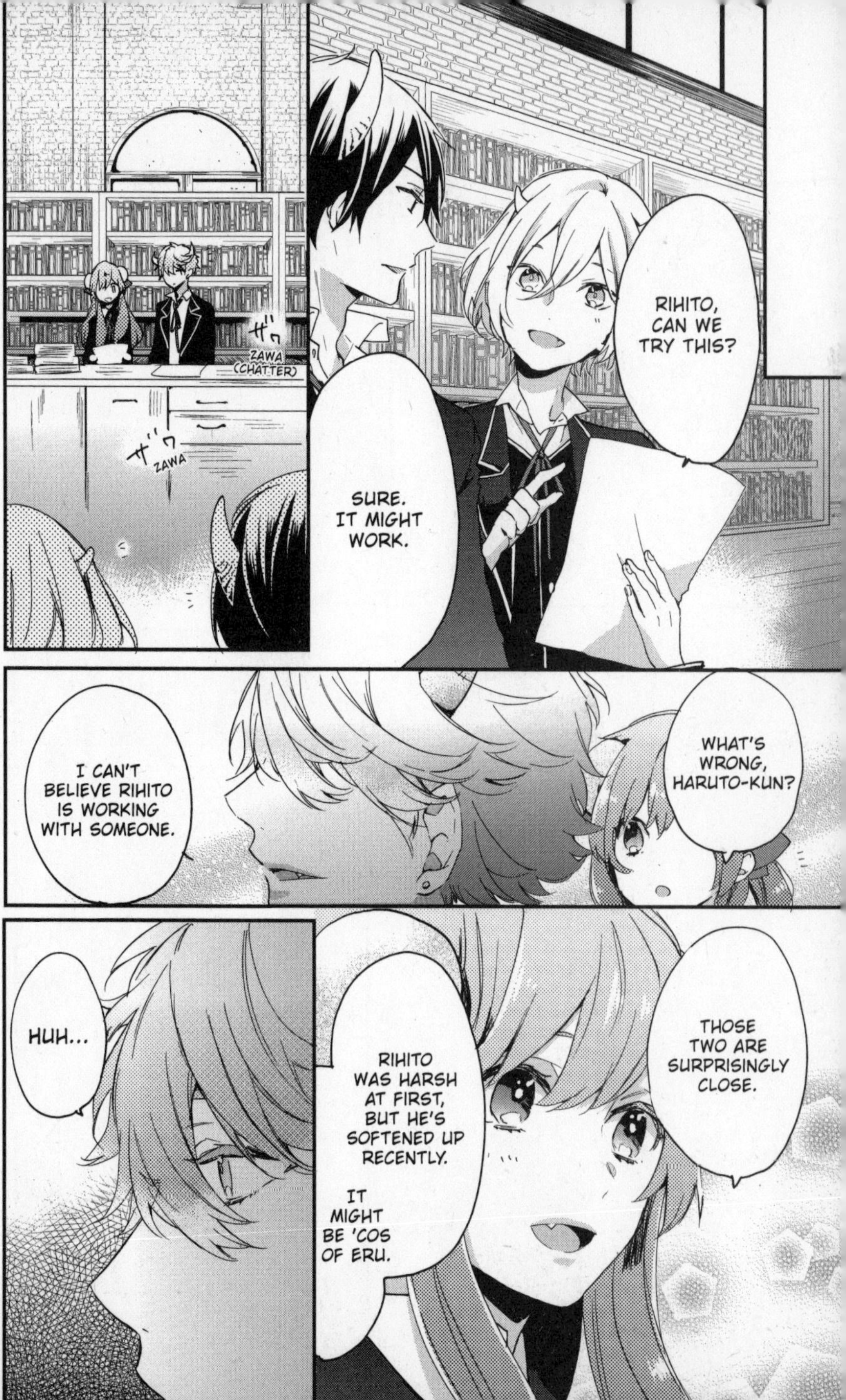
RIHITO, CAN WE TRY THIS?
SURE. IT MIGHT WORK.
ザワ ZAWA (CHATTER)
ザワ ZAWA
WHAT'S WRONG, HARUTO-KUN?
I CAN'T BELIEVE RIHITO IS WORKING WITH SOMEONE.
THOSE TWO ARE SURPRISINGLY CLOSE.
RIHITO WAS HARSH AT FIRST, BUT HE'S SOFTENED UP RECENTLY.
IT MIGHT BE 'COS OF ERU.
HUH...

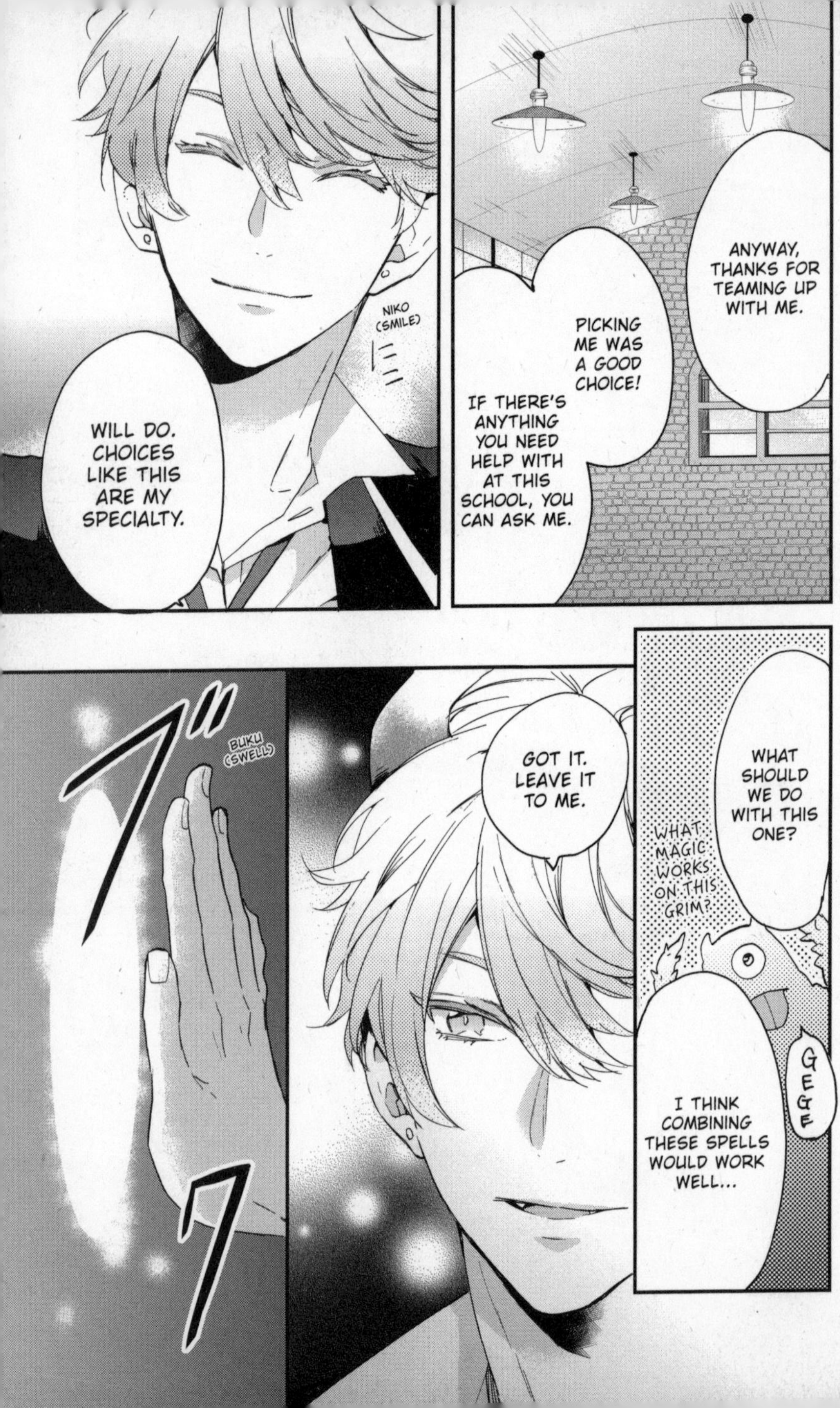
ANYWAY, THANKS FOR TEAMING UP WITH ME.
PICKING ME WAS A GOOD CHOICE!
IF THERE'S ANYTHING YOU NEED HELP WITH AT THIS SCHOOL, YOU CAN ASK ME.
NIKO (SMILE)
WILL DO. CHOICES LIKE THIS ARE MY SPECIALTY.
WHAT SHOULD WE DO WITH THIS ONE?
WHAT MAGIC WORKS ON THIS GRIM?
GEGE
I THINK COMBINING THESE SPELLS WOULD WORK WELL...
GOT IT. LEAVE IT TO ME.
BUKU (SWELL)

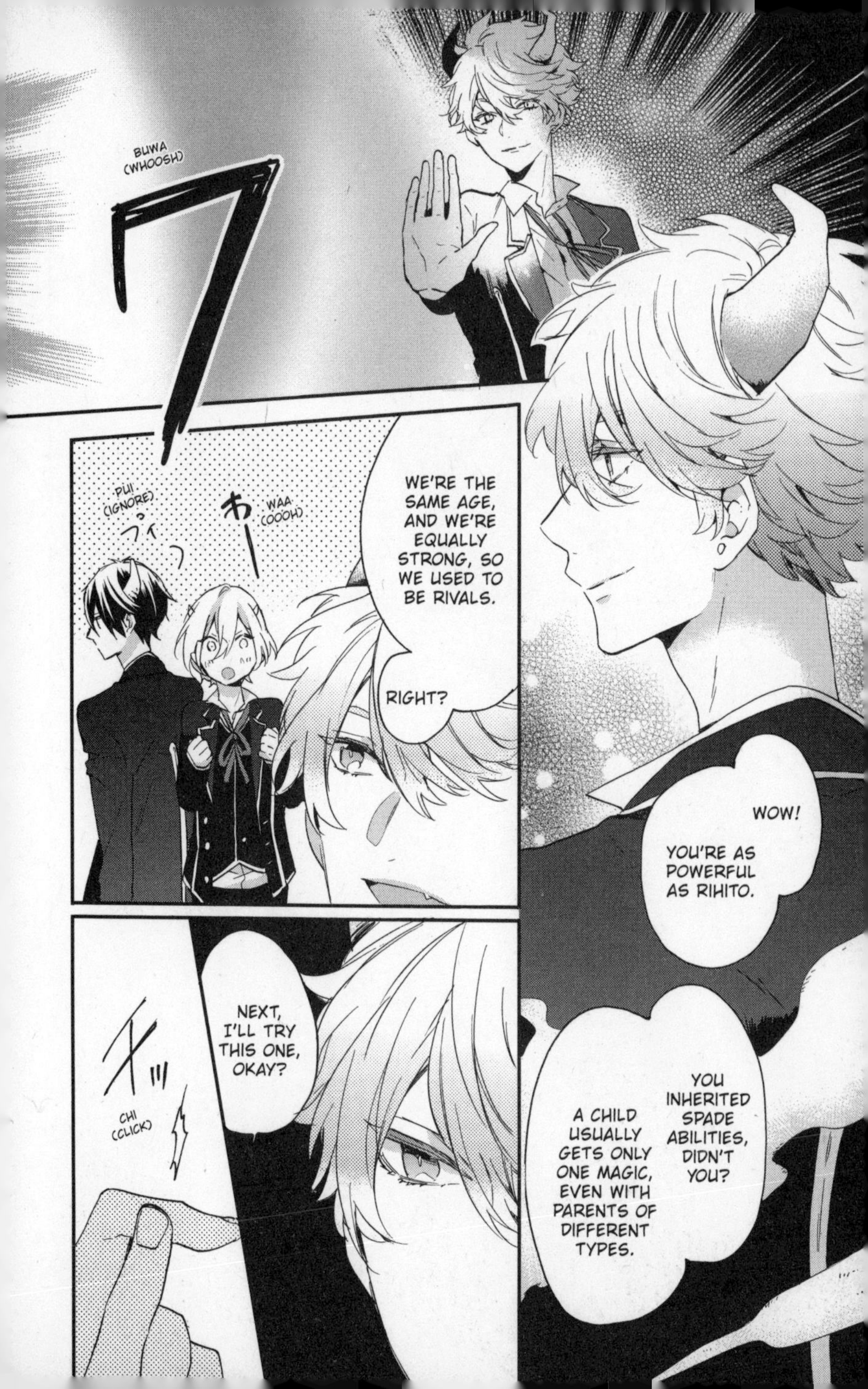
BUWA (WHOOSH)
WOW!
YOU'RE AS POWERFUL AS RIHITO.
YOU INHERITED SPADE ABILITIES, DIDN'T YOU?
A CHILD USUALLY GETS ONLY ONE MAGIC, EVEN WITH PARENTS OF DIFFERENT TYPES.
WE'RE THE SAME AGE, AND WE'RE EQUALLY STRONG, SO WE USED TO BE RIVALS.
RIGHT?
WAA (OOOH)
PUI (IGNORE)
NEXT, I'LL TRY THIS ONE, OKAY?
CHI (CLICK)

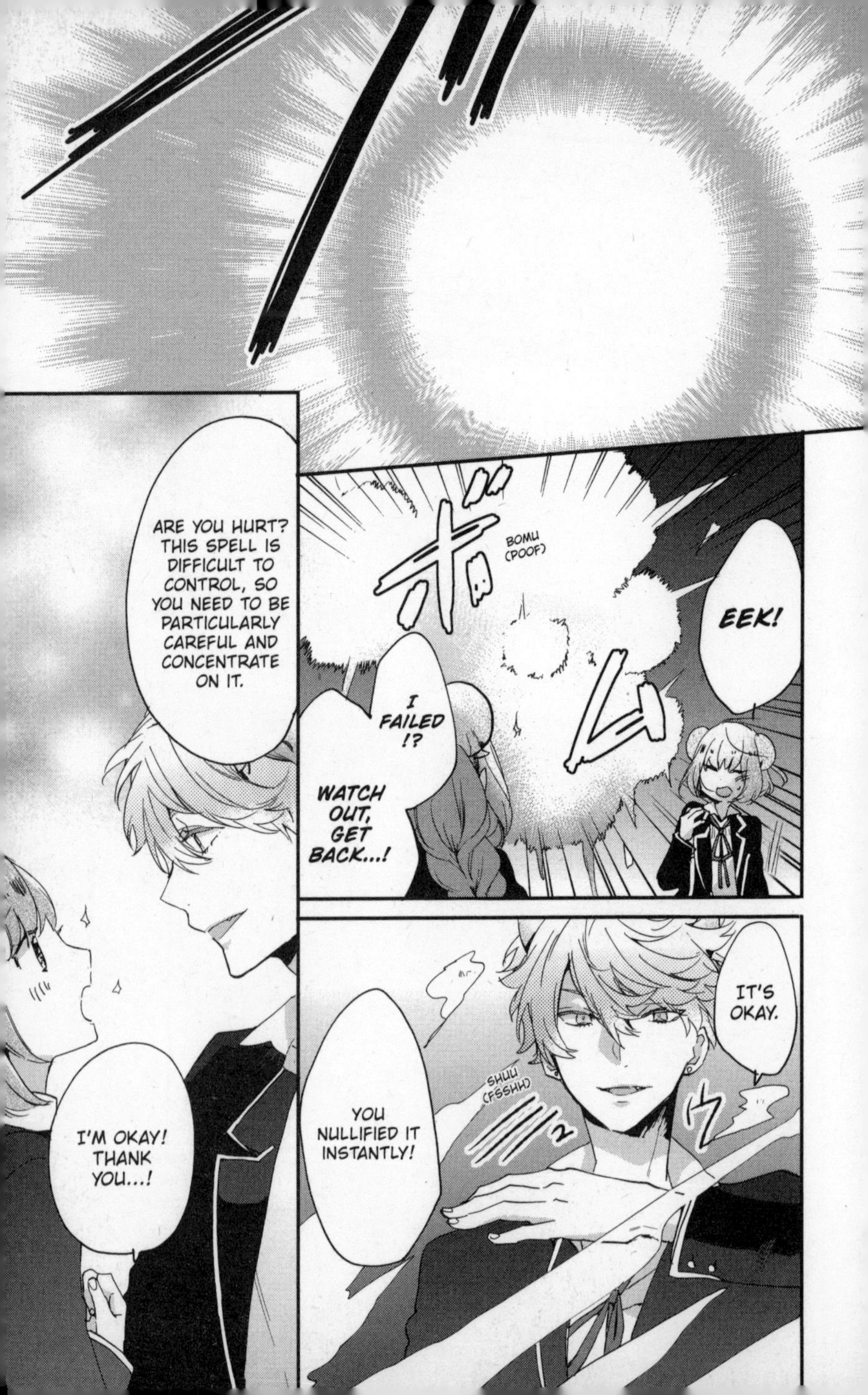
EEK!
BOMU (POOF)
I FAILED!?
WATCH OUT, GET BACK...!
IT'S OKAY.
SHUU (FSSHH)
YOU NULLIFIED IT INSTANTLY!
ARE YOU HURT? THIS SPELL IS DIFFICULT TO CONTROL, SO YOU NEED TO BE PARTICULARLY CAREFUL AND CONCENTRATE ON IT.
I'M OKAY! THANK YOU...!

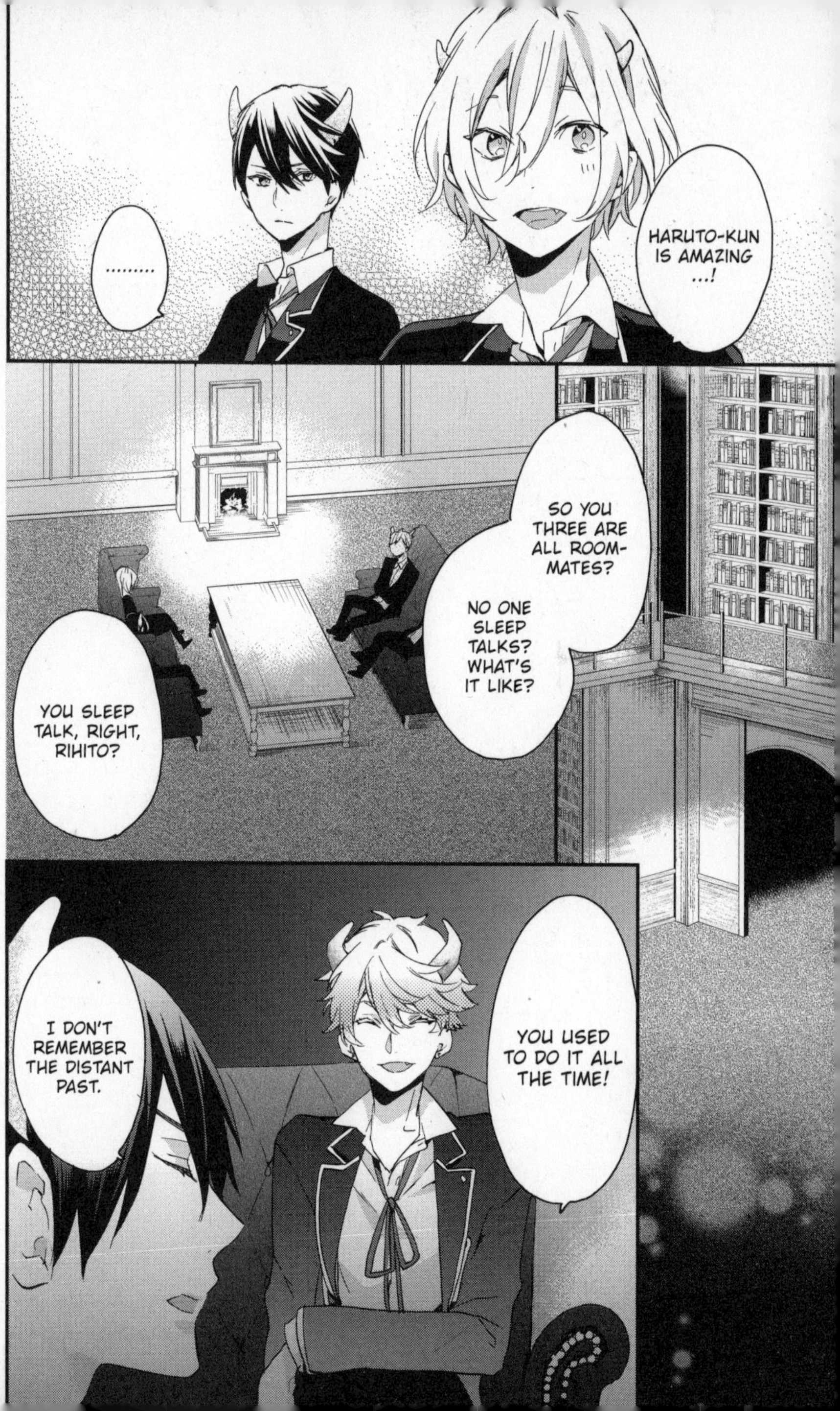
HARUTO-KUN IS AMAZING ...!
....
SO YOU THREE ARE ALL ROOM-MATES?
NO ONE SLEEP TALKS? WHAT'S IT LIKE?
YOU SLEEP TALK, RIGHT, RIHITO?
YOU USED TO DO IT ALL THE TIME!
I DON'T REMEMBER THE DISTANT PAST.

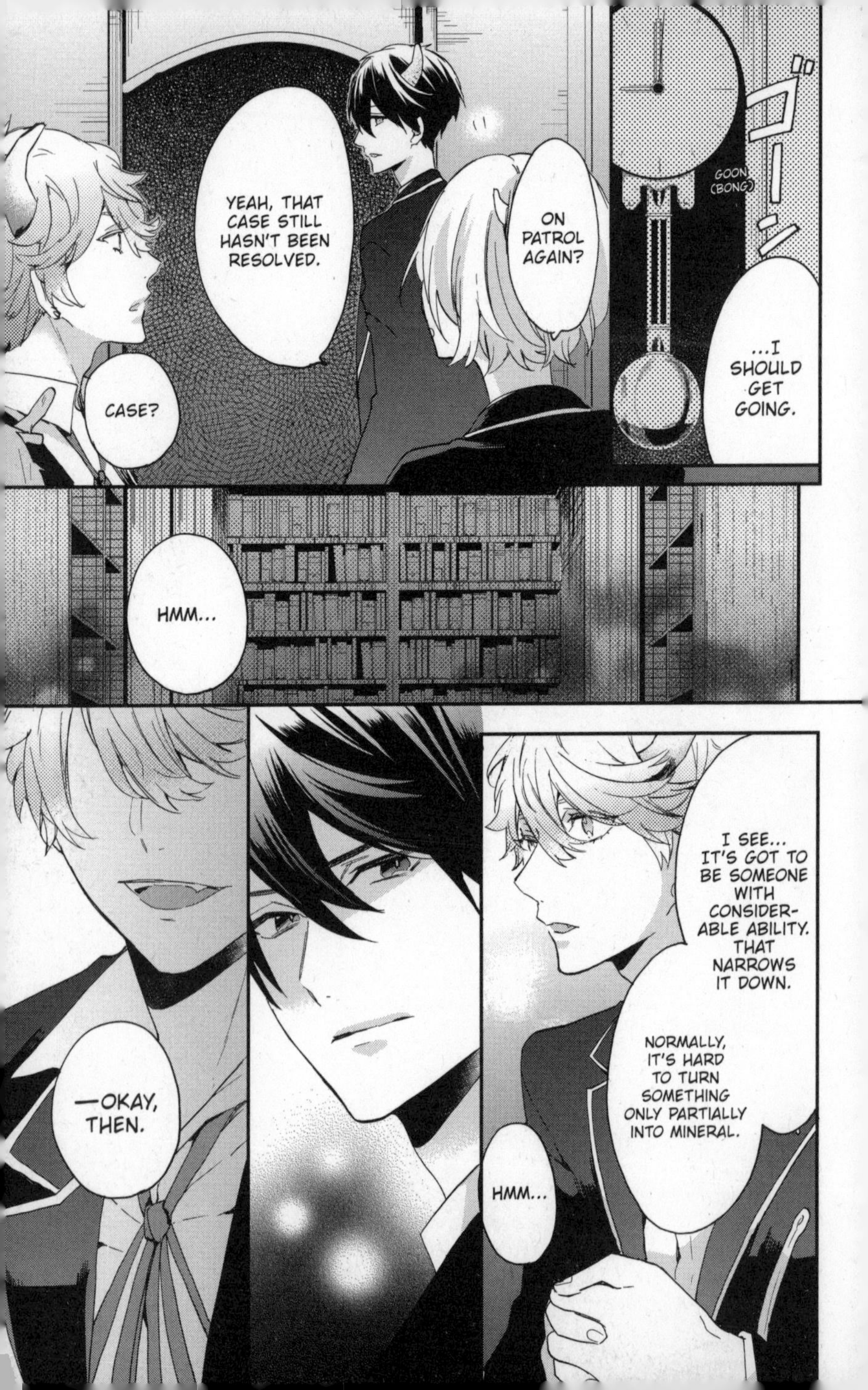
ゴーン
GOON (BONG)
...I SHOULD GET GOING.
ON PATROL AGAIN?
YEAH, THAT CASE STILL HASN'T BEEN RESOLVED.
CASE?
HMM...
I SEE... IT'S GOT TO BE SOMEONE WITH CONSIDER-ABLE ABILITY. THAT NARROWS IT DOWN.
NORMALLY, IT'S HARD TO TURN SOMETHING ONLY PARTIALLY INTO MINERAL.
HMM...
—OKAY, THEN.

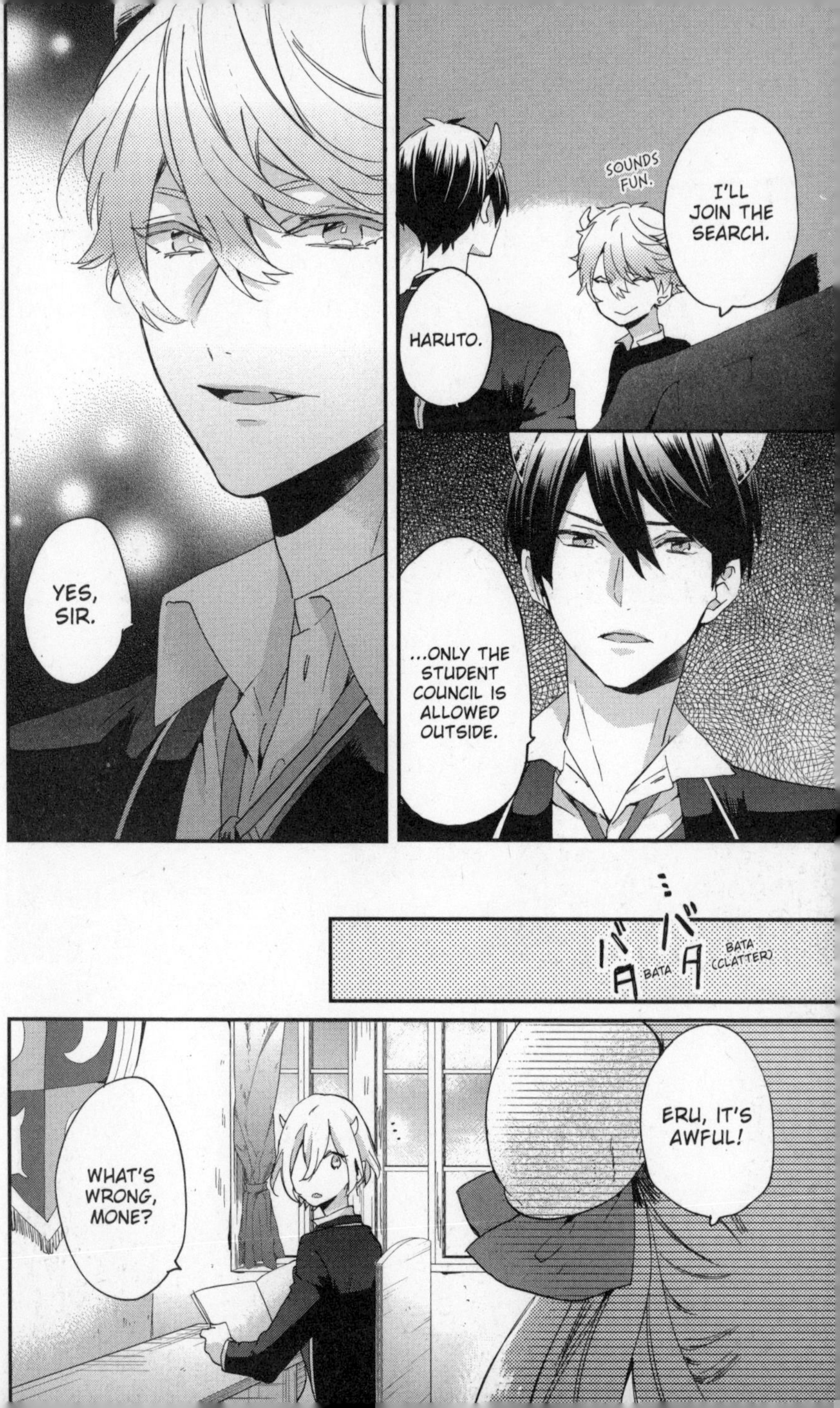
I'LL JOIN THE SEARCH.
SOUNDS FUN.
HARUTO.
...ONLY THE STUDENT COUNCIL IS ALLOWED OUTSIDE.
YES, SIR.
BATA (CLATTER)
BATA
ERU, IT'S AWFUL!
WHAT'S WRONG, MONE?

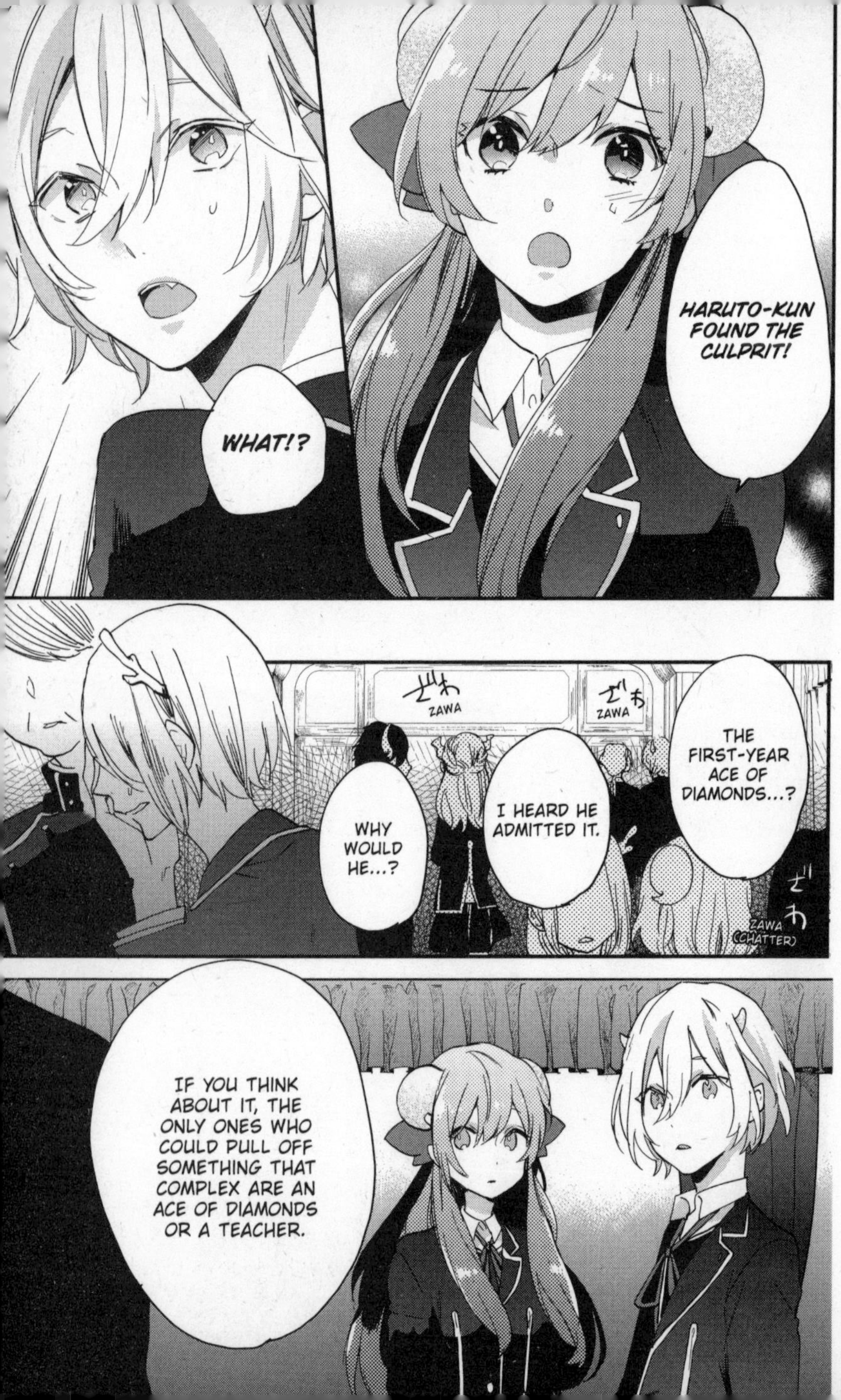
HARUTO-KUN FOUND THE CULPRIT!
WHAT!?
THE FIRST-YEAR ACE OF DIAMONDS...?
ざわ ZAWA
ざわ ZAWA
I HEARD HE ADMITTED IT.
WHY WOULD HE...?
ざわ ZAWA (CHATTER)
IF YOU THINK ABOUT IT, THE ONLY ONES WHO COULD PULL OFF SOMETHING THAT COMPLEX ARE AN ACE OF DIAMONDS OR A TEACHER.

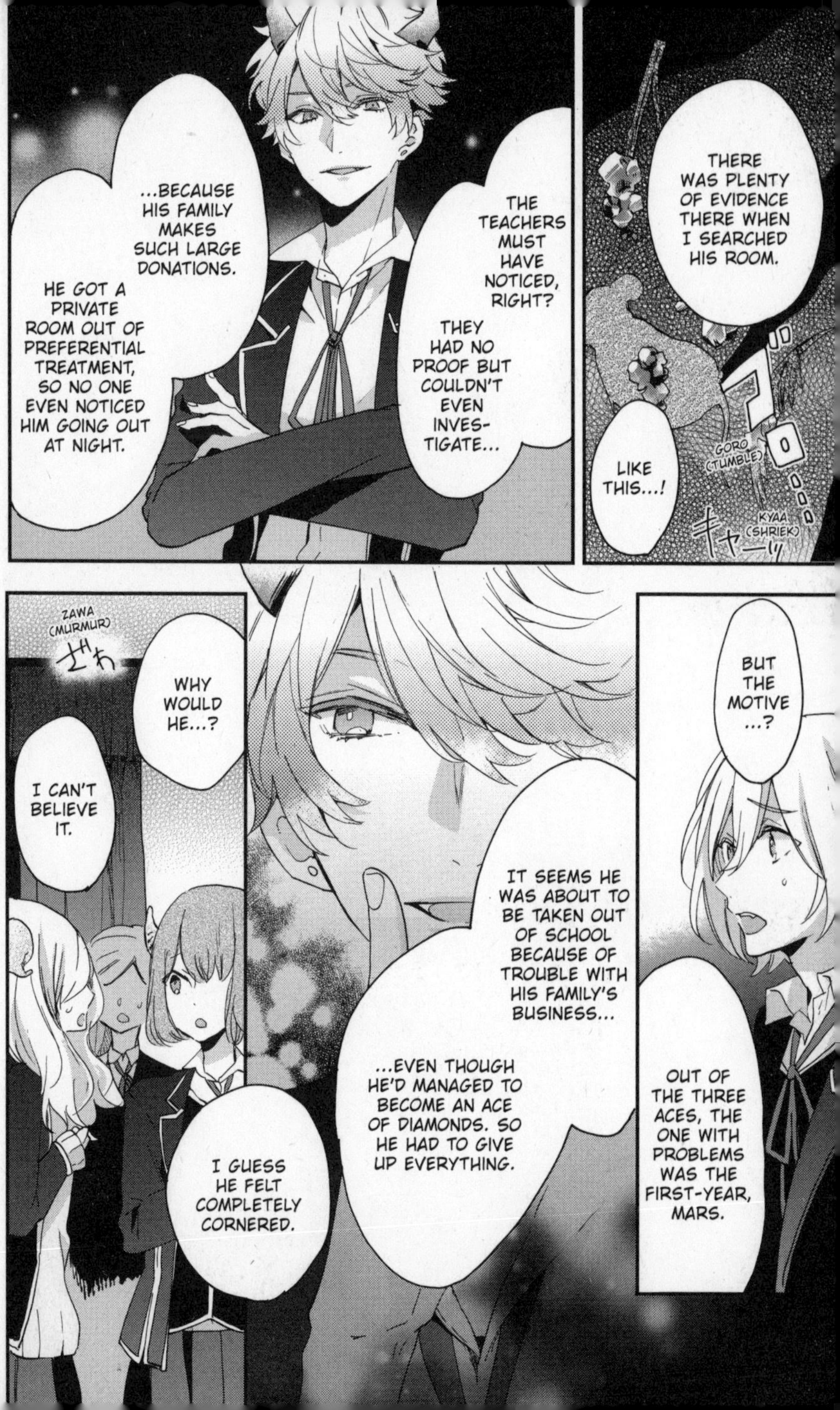
THERE WAS PLENTY OF EVIDENCE THERE WHEN I SEARCHED HIS ROOM.
GORO (TUMBLE)
LIKE THIS...!
KYAA (SHRIEK)
THE TEACHERS MUST HAVE NOTICED, RIGHT?
THEY HAD NO PROOF BUT COULDN'T EVEN INVES-TIGATE...
...BECAUSE HIS FAMILY MAKES SUCH LARGE DONATIONS.
HE GOT A PRIVATE ROOM OUT OF PREFERENTIAL TREATMENT, SO NO ONE EVEN NOTICED HIM GOING OUT AT NIGHT.
BUT THE MOTIVE ...?
OUT OF THE THREE ACES, THE ONE WITH PROBLEMS WAS THE FIRST-YEAR, MARS.
IT SEEMS HE WAS ABOUT TO BE TAKEN OUT OF SCHOOL BECAUSE OF TROUBLE WITH HIS FAMILY'S BUSINESS...
...EVEN THOUGH HE'D MANAGED TO BECOME AN ACE OF DIAMONDS. SO HE HAD TO GIVE UP EVERYTHING.
ZAWA (MURMUR)
WHY WOULD HE...?
I CAN'T BELIEVE IT.
I GUESS HE FELT COMPLETELY CORNERED.

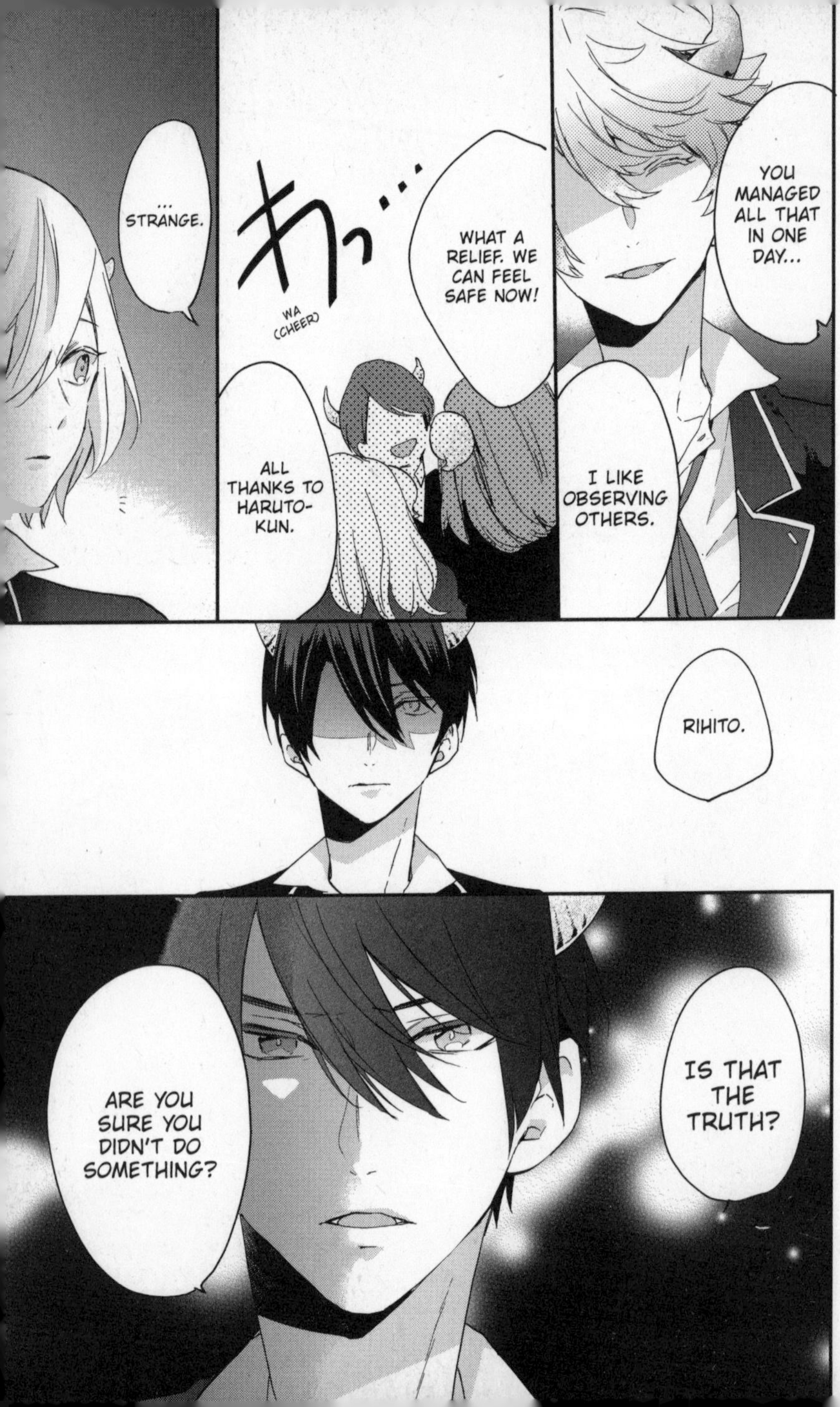
YOU MANAGED ALL THAT IN ONE DAY...
I LIKE OBSERVING OTHERS.
WHAT A RELIEF. WE CAN FEEL SAFE NOW!
わっ…
WA (CHEER)
ALL THANKS TO HARUTO-KUN.
...STRANGE.
RIHITO.
IS THAT THE TRUTH?
ARE YOU SURE YOU DIDN'T DO SOMETHING?

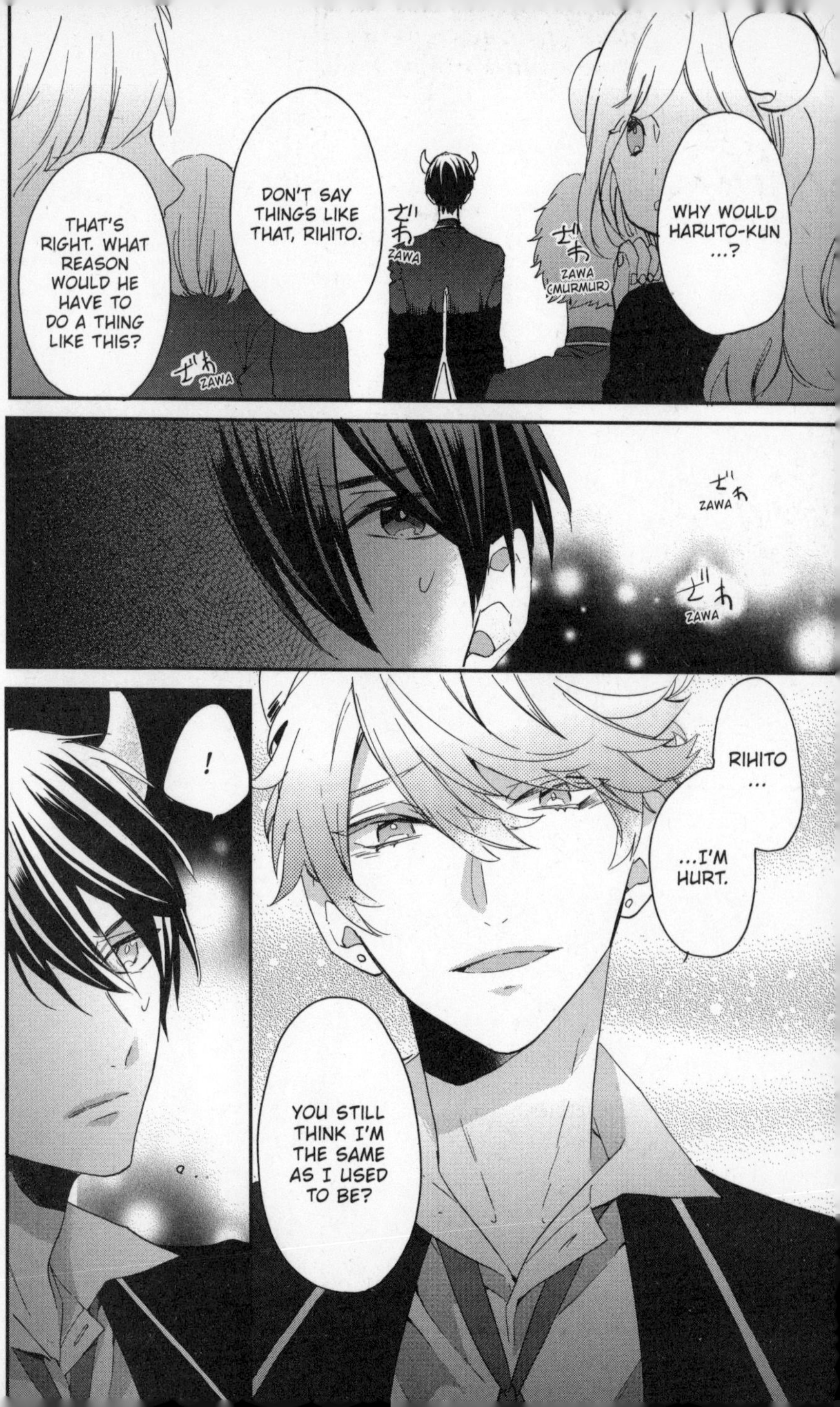
WHY WOULD HARUTO-KUN ...?
ZAWA (MURMUR)
DON'T SAY THINGS LIKE THAT, RIHITO.
ZAWA
THAT'S RIGHT. WHAT REASON WOULD HE HAVE TO DO A THING LIKE THIS?
ZAWA
ZAWA
ZAWA
RIHITO ...
...I'M HURT.
!
YOU STILL THINK I'M THE SAME AS I USED TO BE?

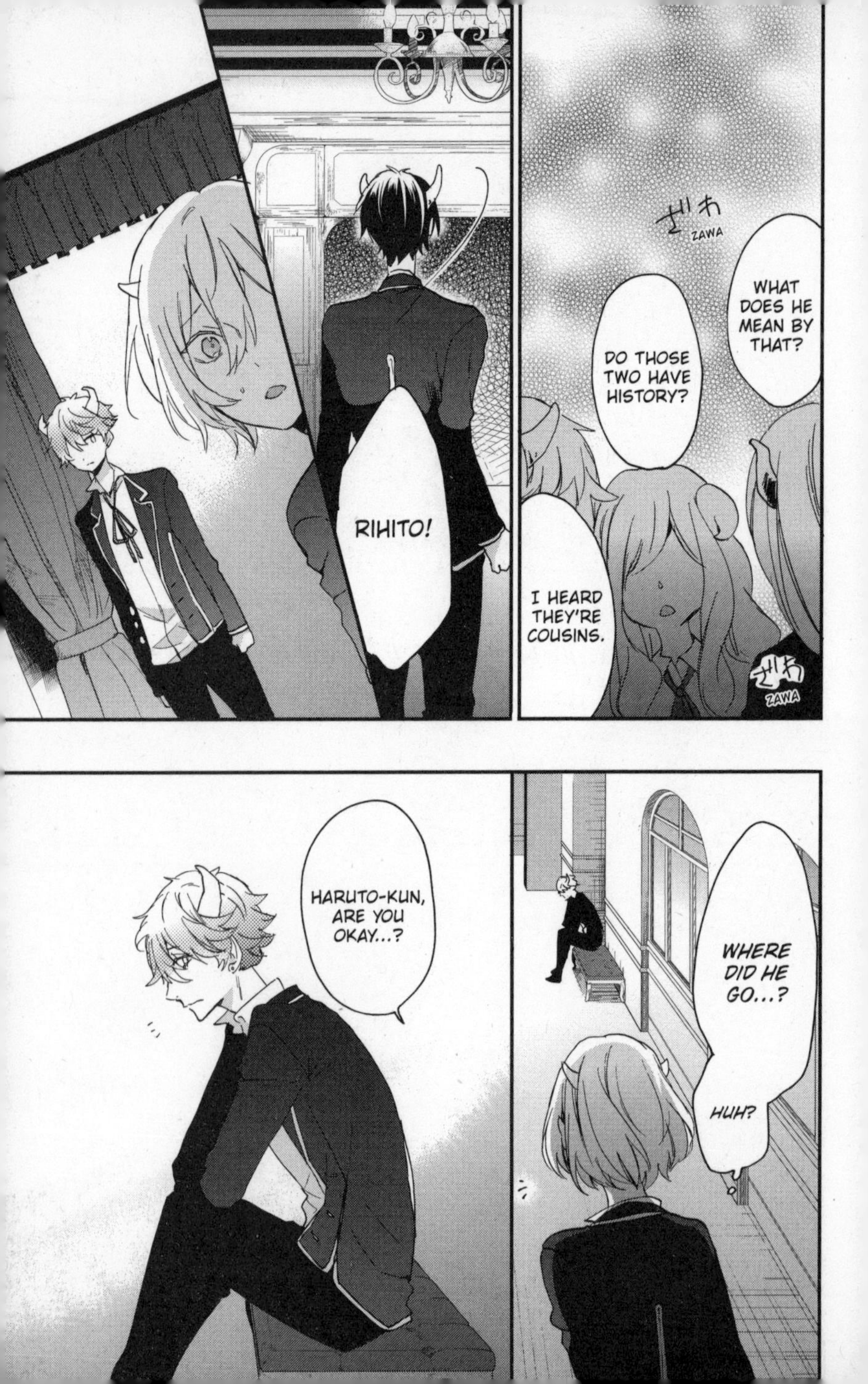
ざわ
ZAWA
WHAT DOES HE MEAN BY THAT?
DO THOSE TWO HAVE HISTORY?
I HEARD THEY'RE COUSINS.
ざわ
ZAWA
RIHITO!
WHERE DID HE GO...?
HUH?
HARUTO-KUN, ARE YOU OKAY...?

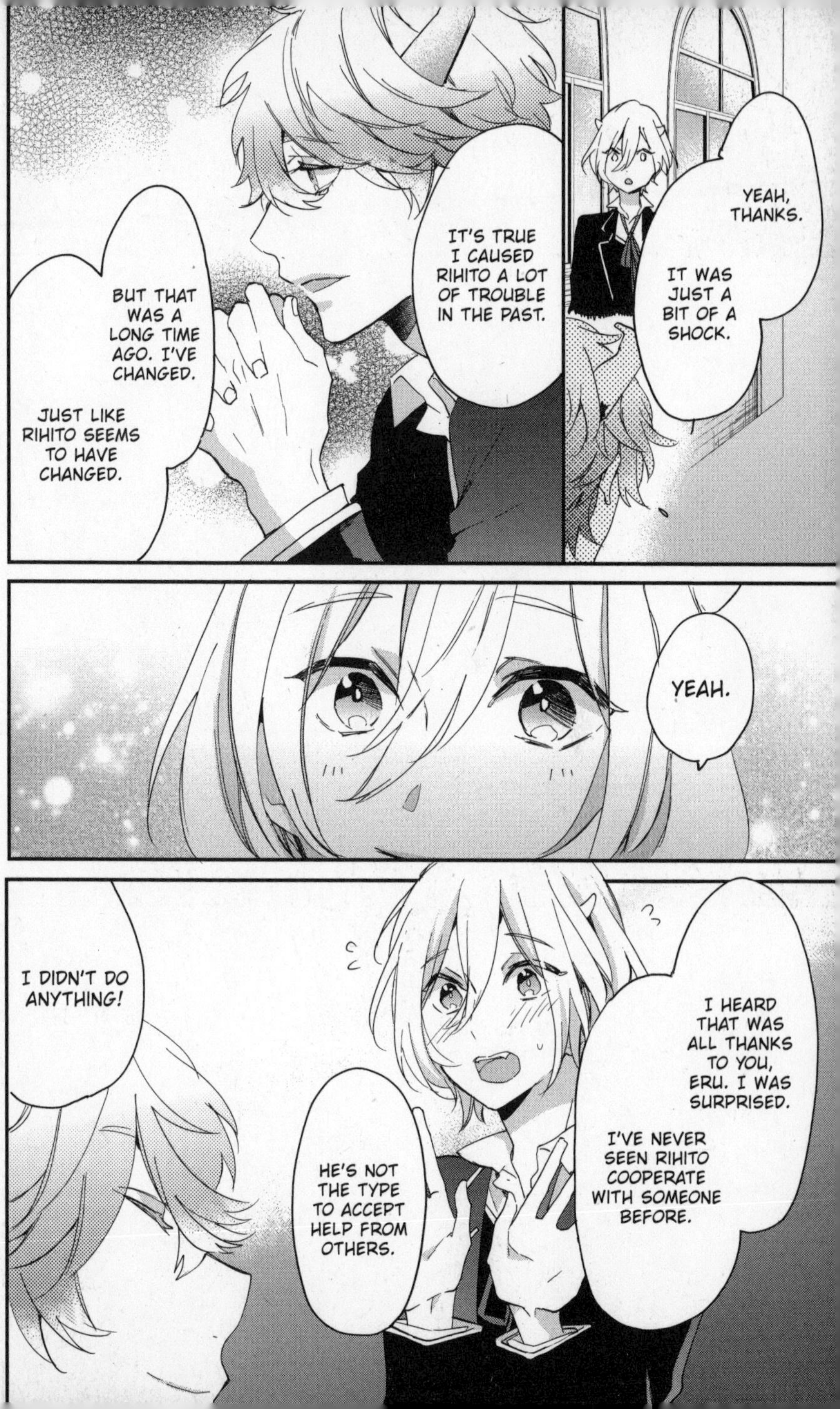
YEAH, THANKS.
IT WAS JUST A BIT OF A SHOCK.
IT'S TRUE I CAUSED RIHITO A LOT OF TROUBLE IN THE PAST.
BUT THAT WAS A LONG TIME AGO. I'VE CHANGED.
JUST LIKE RIHITO SEEMS TO HAVE CHANGED.
YEAH.
I HEARD THAT WAS ALL THANKS TO YOU, ERU. I WAS SURPRISED.
I'VE NEVER SEEN RIHITO COOPERATE WITH SOMEONE BEFORE.
HE'S NOT THE TYPE TO ACCEPT HELP FROM OTHERS.
I DIDN'T DO ANYTHING!

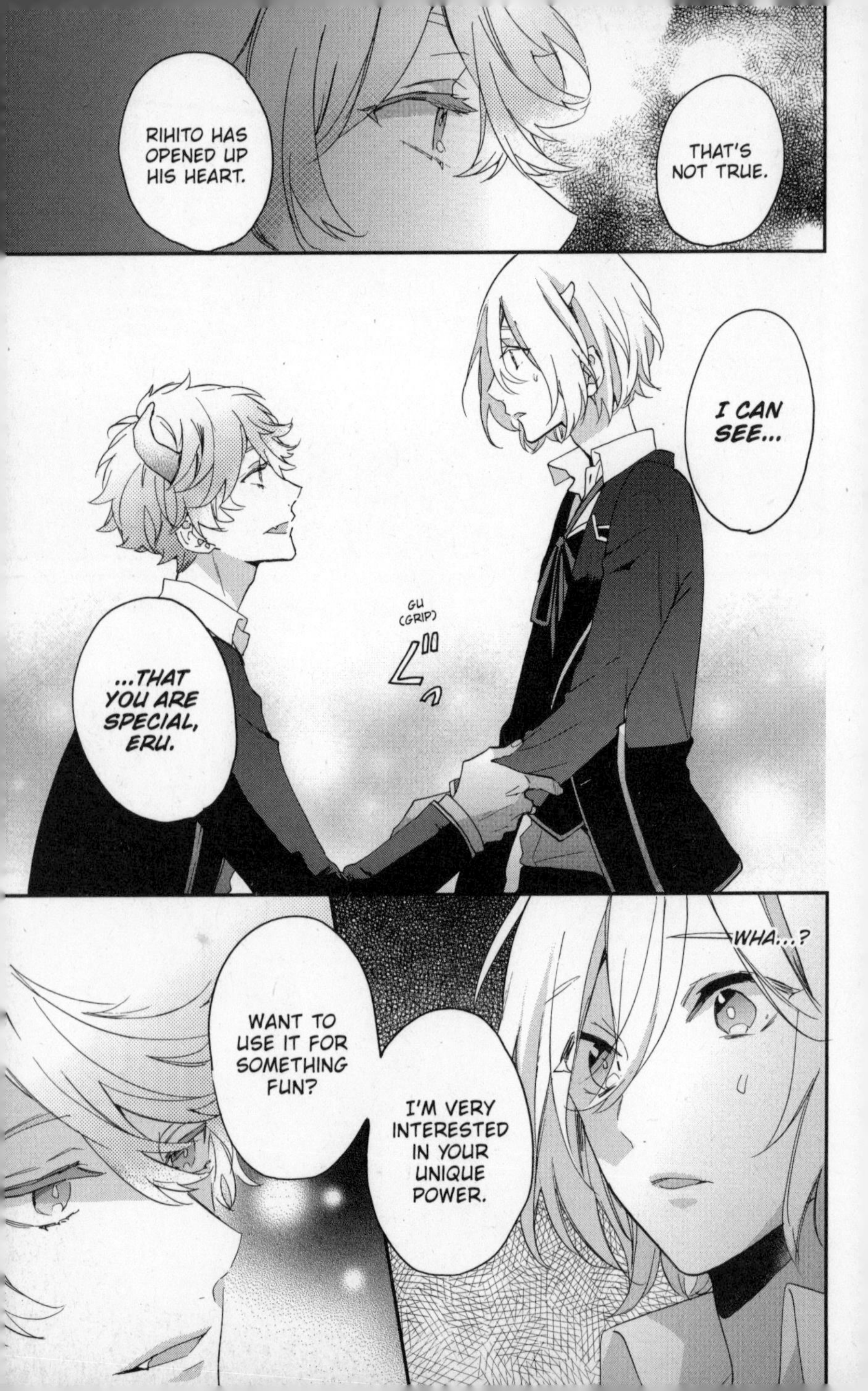
THAT'S NOT TRUE.
RIHITO HAS OPENED UP HIS HEART.
I CAN SEE...
GU (GRIP)
...THAT YOU ARE SPECIAL, ERU.
WHA...?
I'M VERY INTERESTED IN YOUR UNIQUE POWER.
WANT TO USE IT FOR SOMETHING FUN?

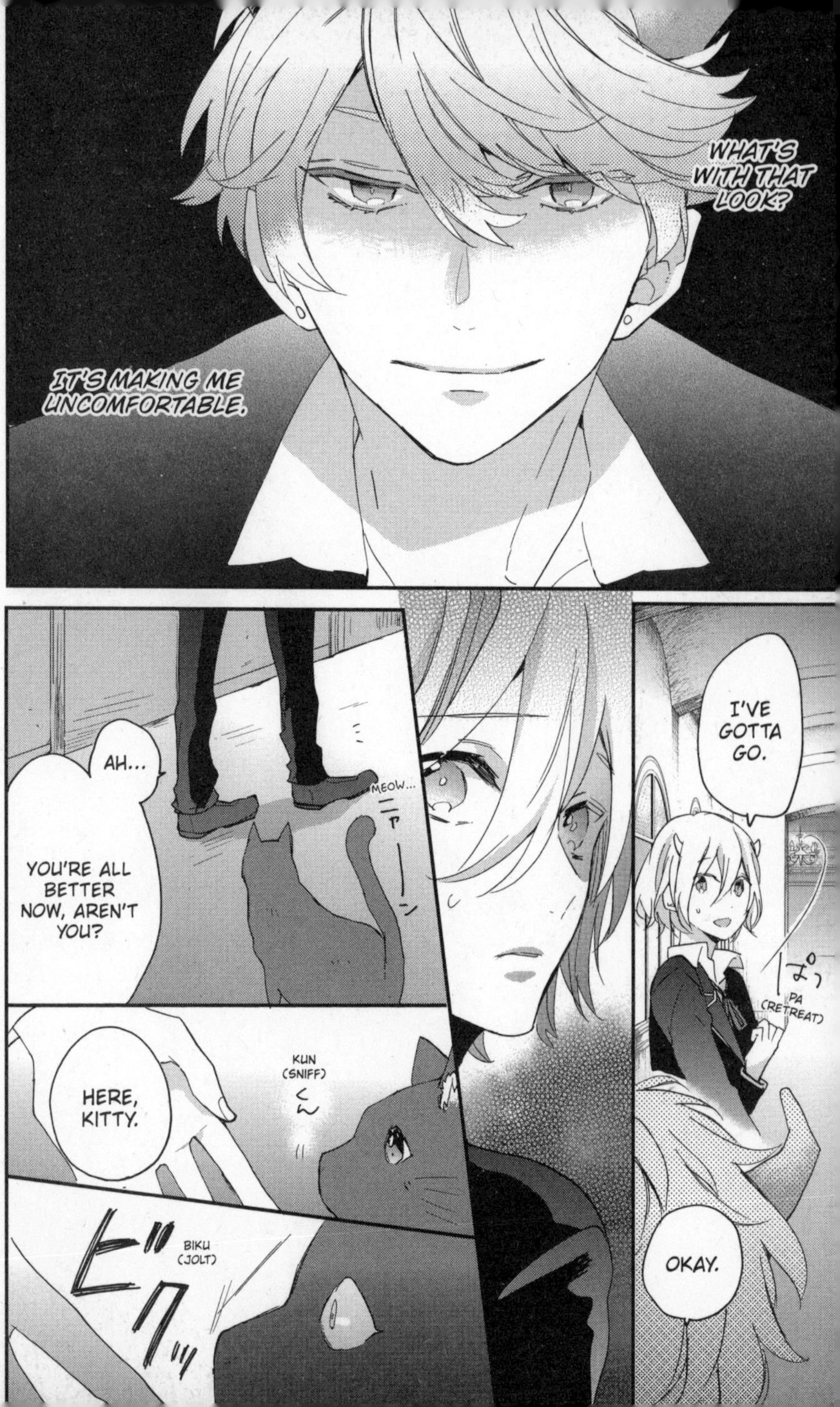
WHAT'S WITH THAT LOOK?
IT'S MAKING ME UNCOMFORTABLE.
I'VE GOTTA GO.
ぱっ
PA (RETREAT)
OKAY.
AH...
YOU'RE ALL BETTER NOW, AREN'T YOU?
ニァーン
MEOW...
HERE, KITTY.
くん
KUN (SNIFF)
ビクッ
BIKU (JOLT)

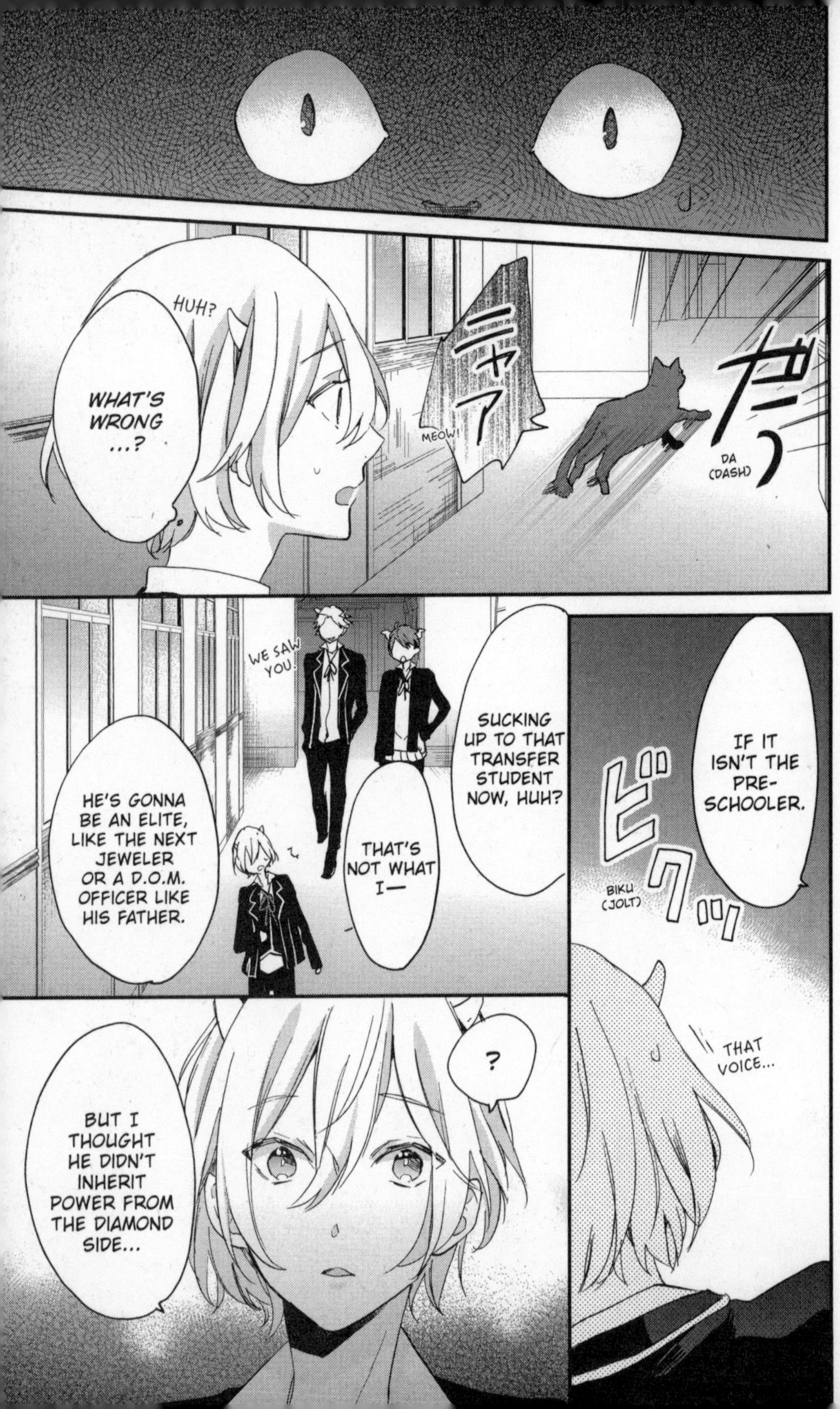
ダッ
DA (DASH)
ニャア
MEOW!
HUH?
WHAT'S WRONG ...?
IF IT ISN'T THE PRE-SCHOOLER.
ビクッ
BIKU (JOLT)
THAT VOICE...
SUCKING UP TO THAT TRANSFER STUDENT NOW, HUH?
WE SAW YOU.
THAT'S NOT WHAT I—
HE'S GONNA BE AN ELITE, LIKE THE NEXT JEWELER OR A D.O.M. OFFICER LIKE HIS FATHER.
?
BUT I THOUGHT HE DIDN'T INHERIT POWER FROM THE DIAMOND SIDE...

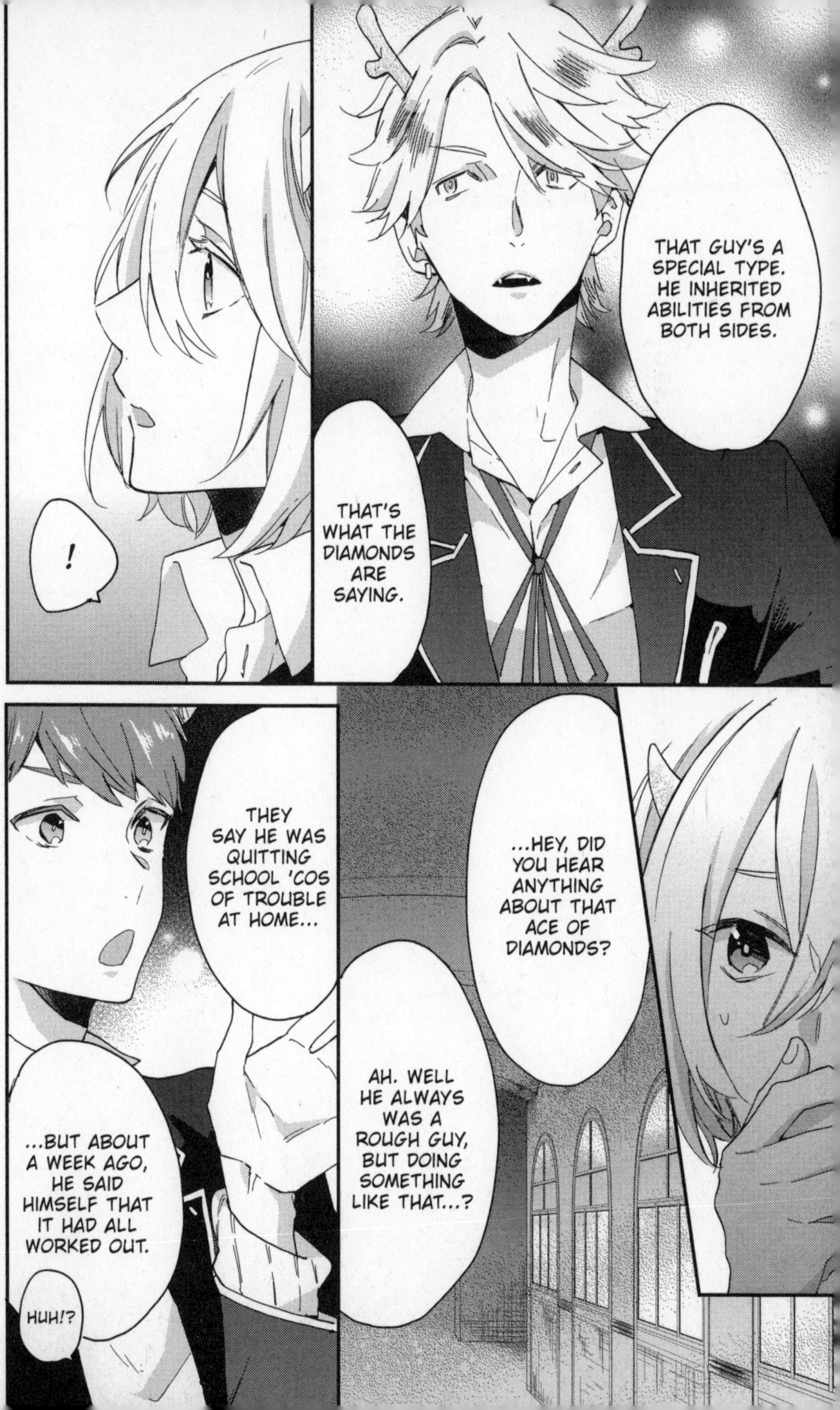

THAT GUY'S A SPECIAL TYPE. HE INHERITED ABILITIES FROM BOTH SIDES.
THAT'S WHAT THE DIAMONDS ARE SAYING.
!
...HEY, DID YOU HEAR ANYTHING ABOUT THAT ACE OF DIAMONDS?
AH. WELL HE ALWAYS WAS A ROUGH GUY, BUT DOING SOMETHING LIKE THAT...?
THEY SAY HE WAS QUITTING SCHOOL 'COS OF TROUBLE AT HOME...
...BUT ABOUT A WEEK AGO, HE SAID HIMSELF THAT IT HAD ALL WORKED OUT.
HUH!?

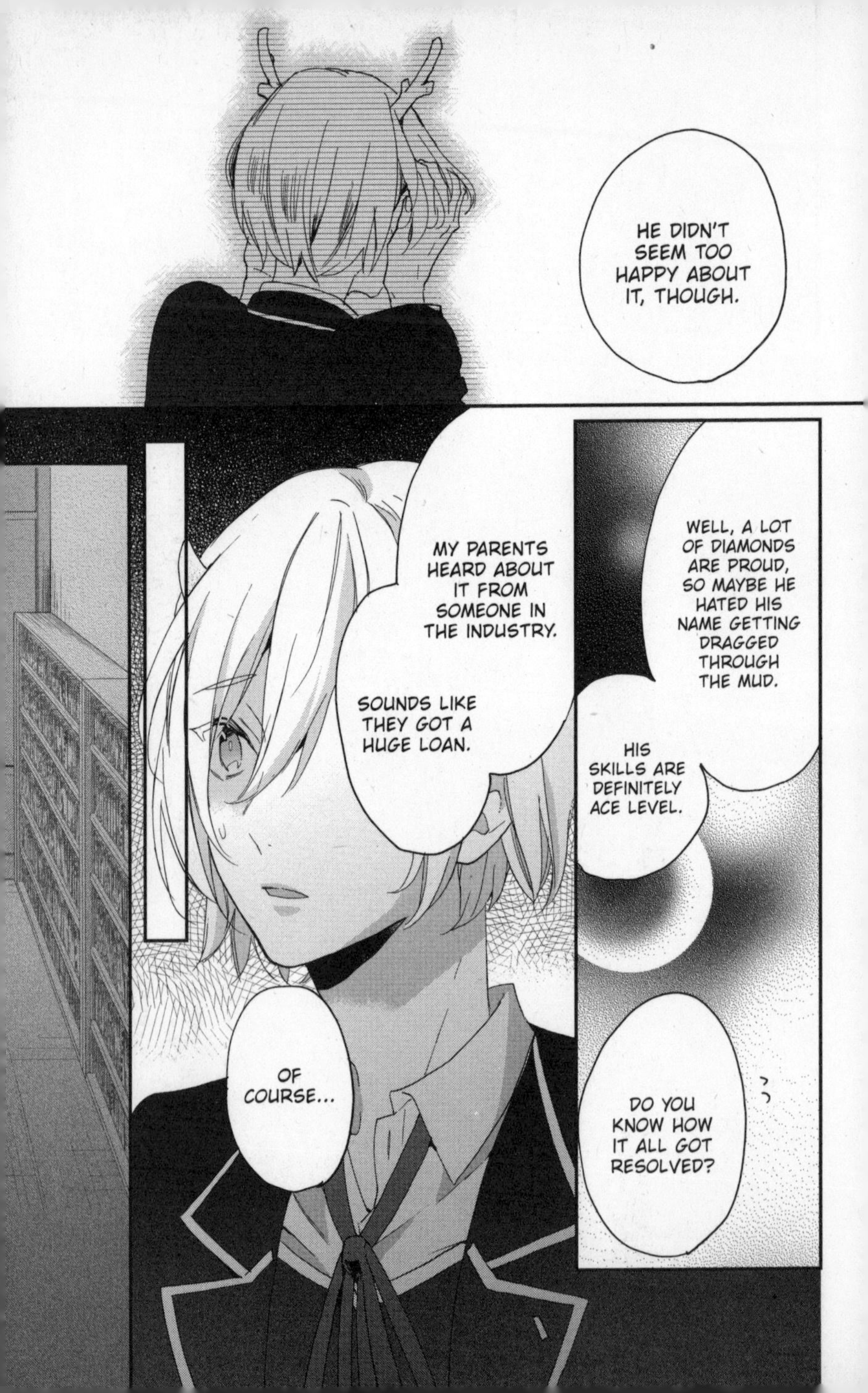
HE DIDN'T SEEM TOO HAPPY ABOUT IT, THOUGH.
WELL, A LOT OF DIAMONDS ARE PROUD, SO MAYBE HE HATED HIS NAME GETTING DRAGGED THROUGH THE MUD.
HIS SKILLS ARE DEFINITELY ACE LEVEL.
DO YOU KNOW HOW IT ALL GOT RESOLVED?
MY PARENTS HEARD ABOUT IT FROM SOMEONE IN THE INDUSTRY.
SOUNDS LIKE THEY GOT A HUGE LOAN.
OF COURSE...

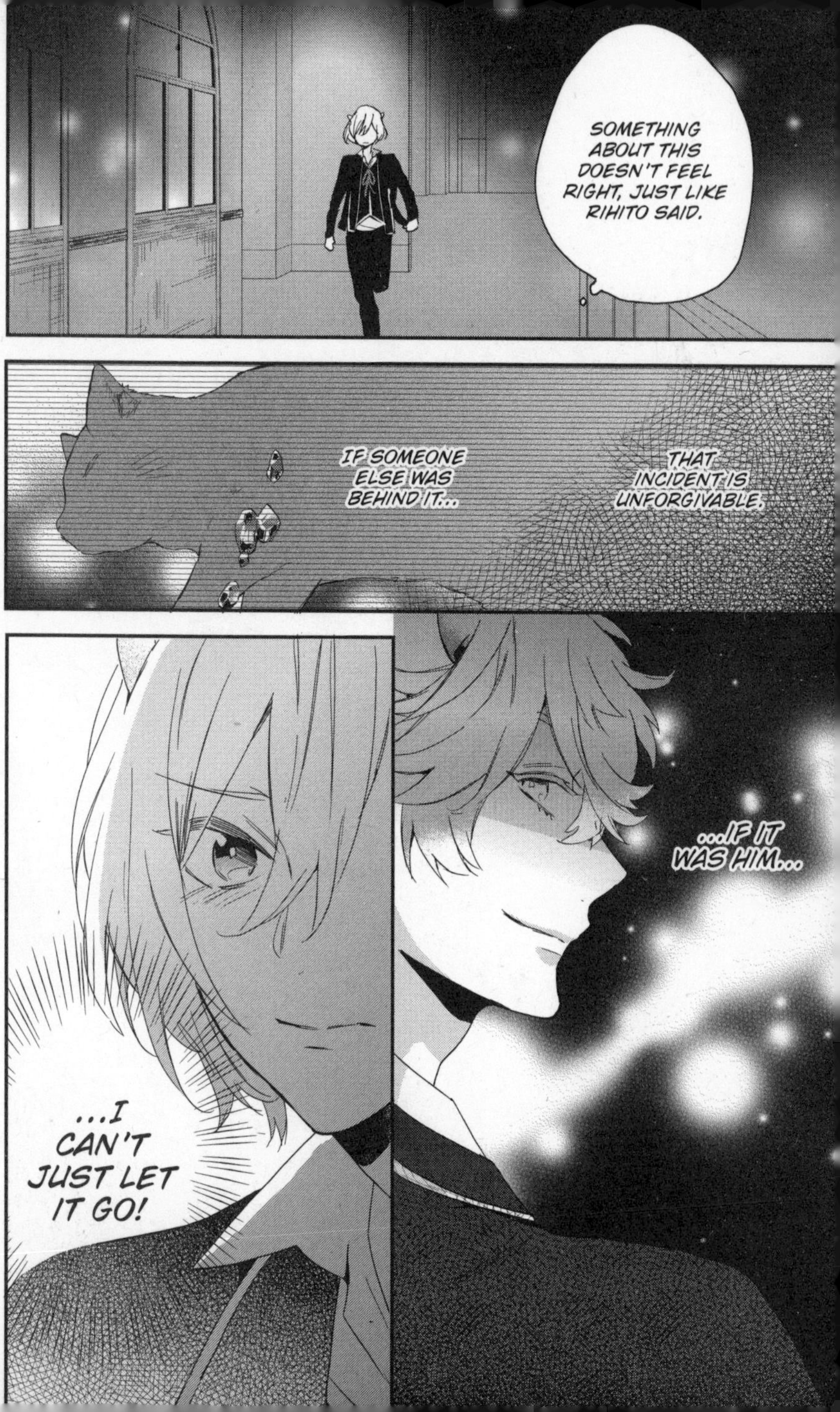
SOMETHING ABOUT THIS DOESN'T FEEL RIGHT, JUST LIKE RIHITO SAID.
THAT INCIDENT IS UNFORGIVABLE.
IF SOMEONE ELSE WAS BEHIND IT...
...IF IT WAS HIM...
...I CAN'T JUST LET IT GO!

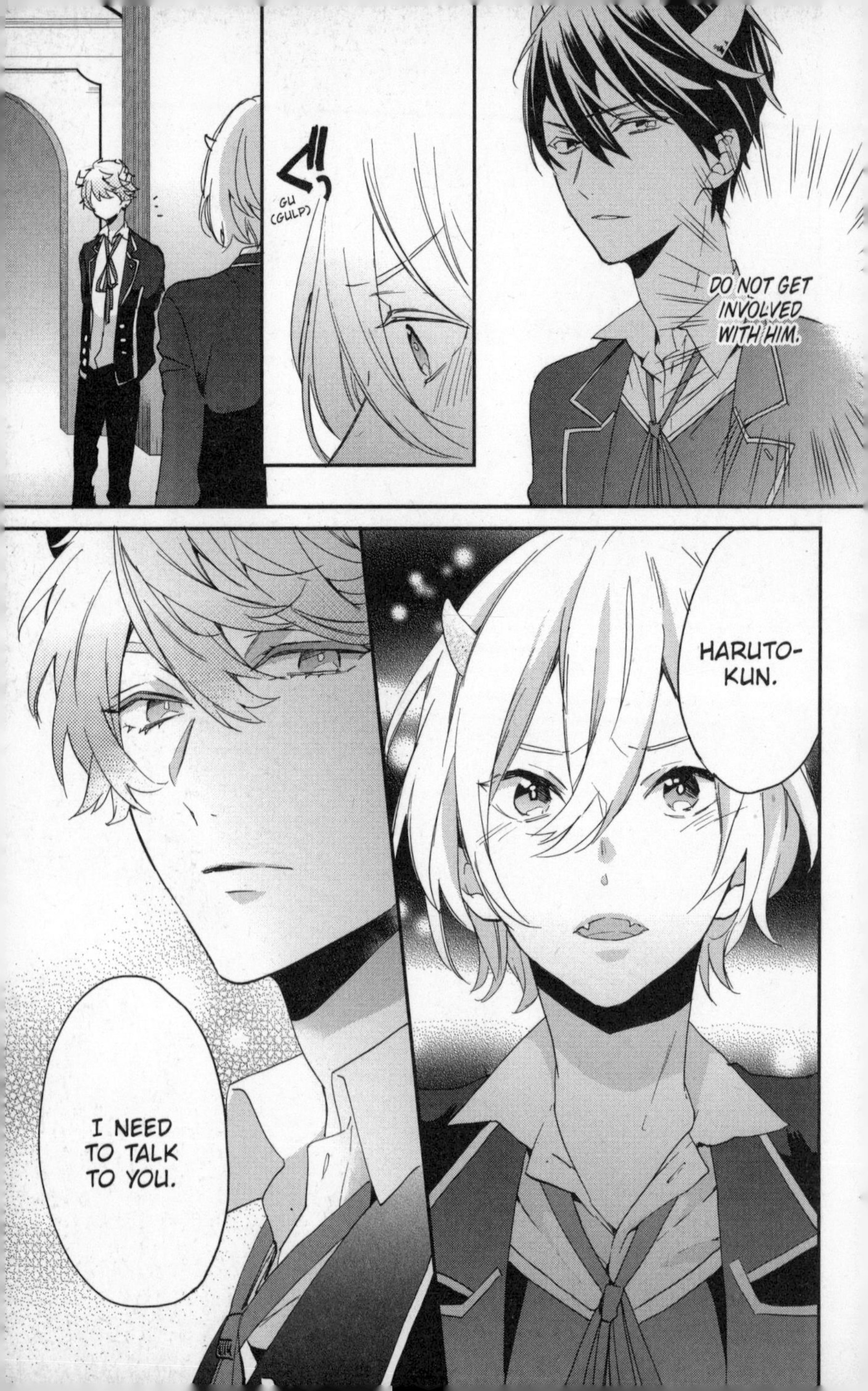
DO NOT GET INVOLVED WITH HIM.
GU (GULP)
HARUTO-KUN.
I NEED TO TALK TO YOU.

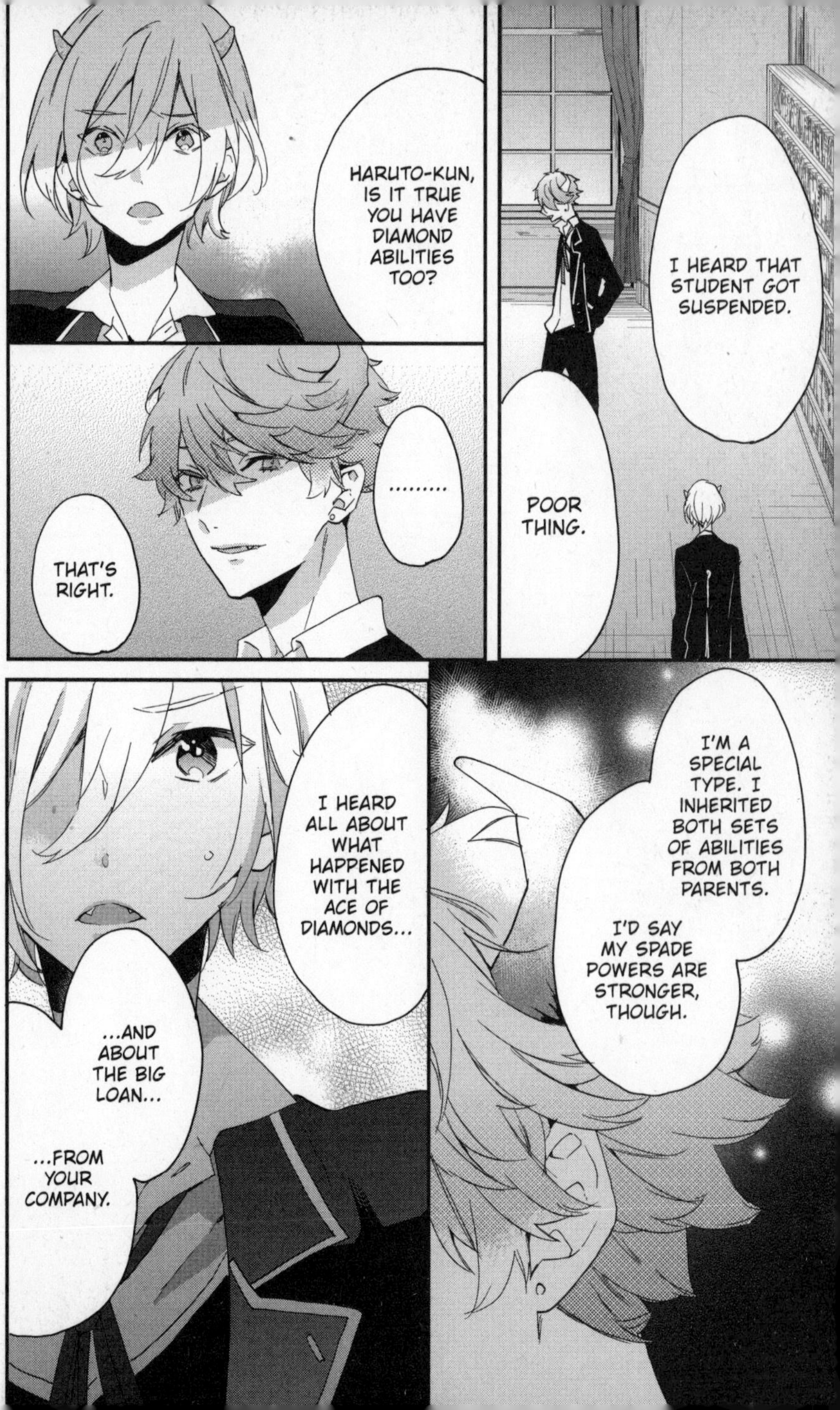
I HEARD THAT STUDENT GOT SUSPENDED.
POOR THING.
HARUTO-KUN, IS IT TRUE YOU HAVE DIAMOND ABILITIES TOO?
....
THAT'S RIGHT.
I'M A SPECIAL TYPE. I INHERITED BOTH SETS OF ABILITIES FROM BOTH PARENTS.
I'D SAY MY SPADE POWERS ARE STRONGER, THOUGH.
I HEARD ALL ABOUT WHAT HAPPENED WITH THE ACE OF DIAMONDS...
...AND ABOUT THE BIG LOAN...
...FROM YOUR COMPANY.

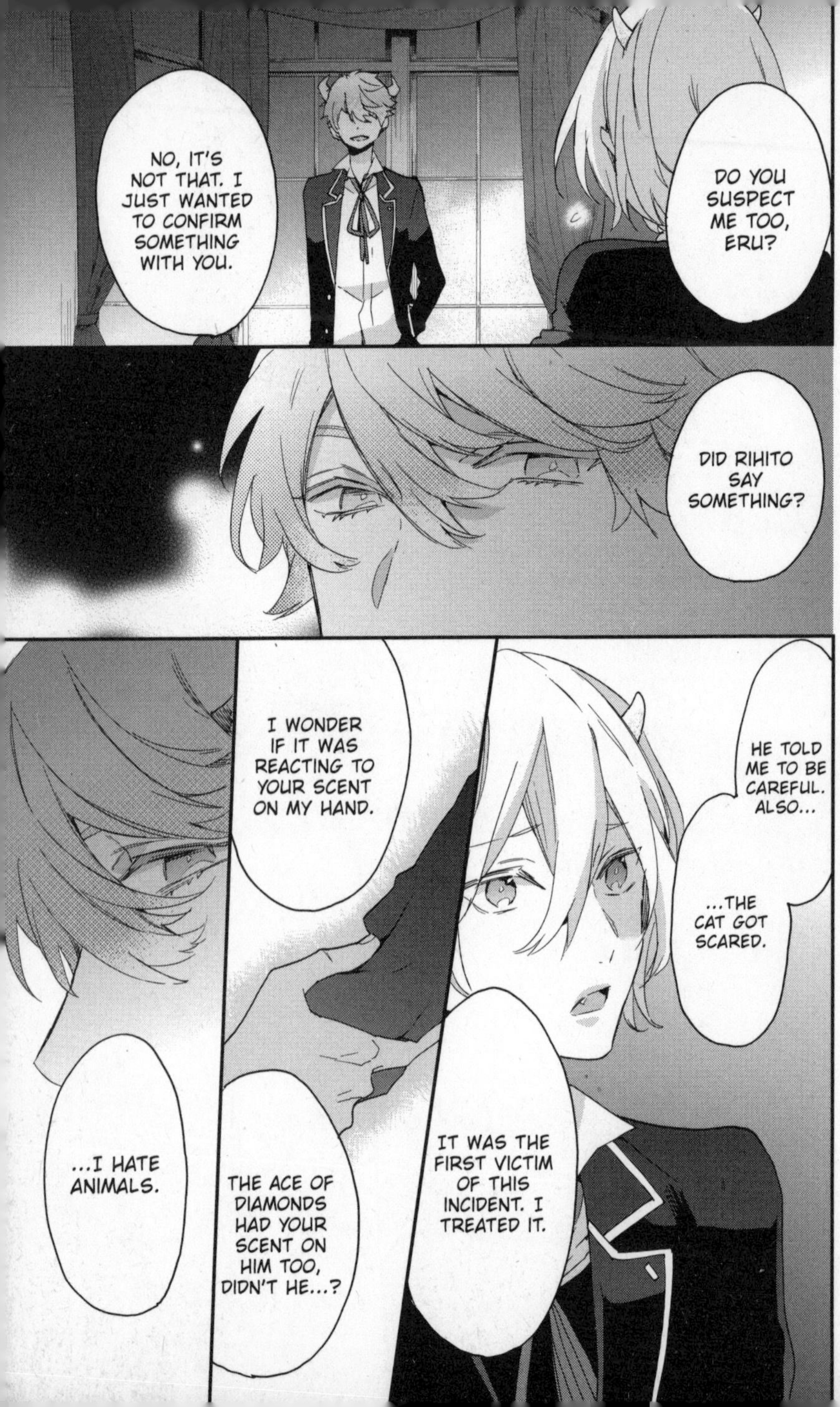
DO YOU SUSPECT ME TOO, ERU?
NO, IT'S NOT THAT. I JUST WANTED TO CONFIRM SOMETHING WITH YOU.
DID RIHITO SAY SOMETHING?
HE TOLD ME TO BE CAREFUL. ALSO...
...THE CAT GOT SCARED.
IT WAS THE FIRST VICTIM OF THIS INCIDENT. I TREATED IT.
I WONDER IF IT WAS REACTING TO YOUR SCENT ON MY HAND.
THE ACE OF DIAMONDS HAD YOUR SCENT ON HIM TOO, DIDN'T HE...?
...I HATE ANIMALS.

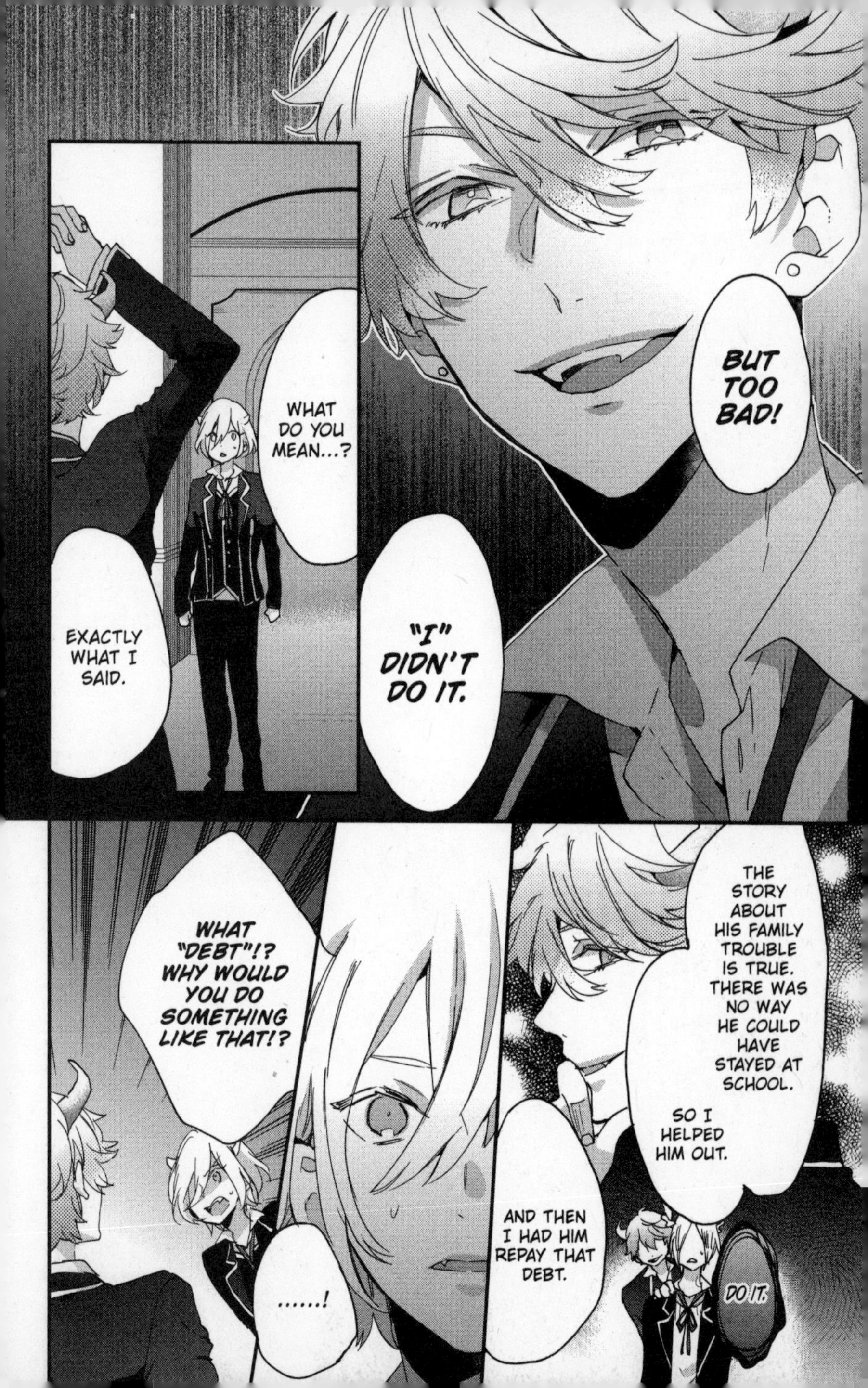
BUT TOO BAD!
"I" DIDN'T DO IT.
WHAT DO YOU MEAN...?
EXACTLY WHAT I SAID.
THE STORY ABOUT HIS FAMILY TROUBLE IS TRUE. THERE WAS NO WAY HE COULD HAVE STAYED AT SCHOOL.
SO I HELPED HIM OUT.
AND THEN I HAD HIM REPAY THAT DEBT.
DO IT.
......!
WHAT "DEBT"!? WHY WOULD YOU DO SOMETHING LIKE THAT!?

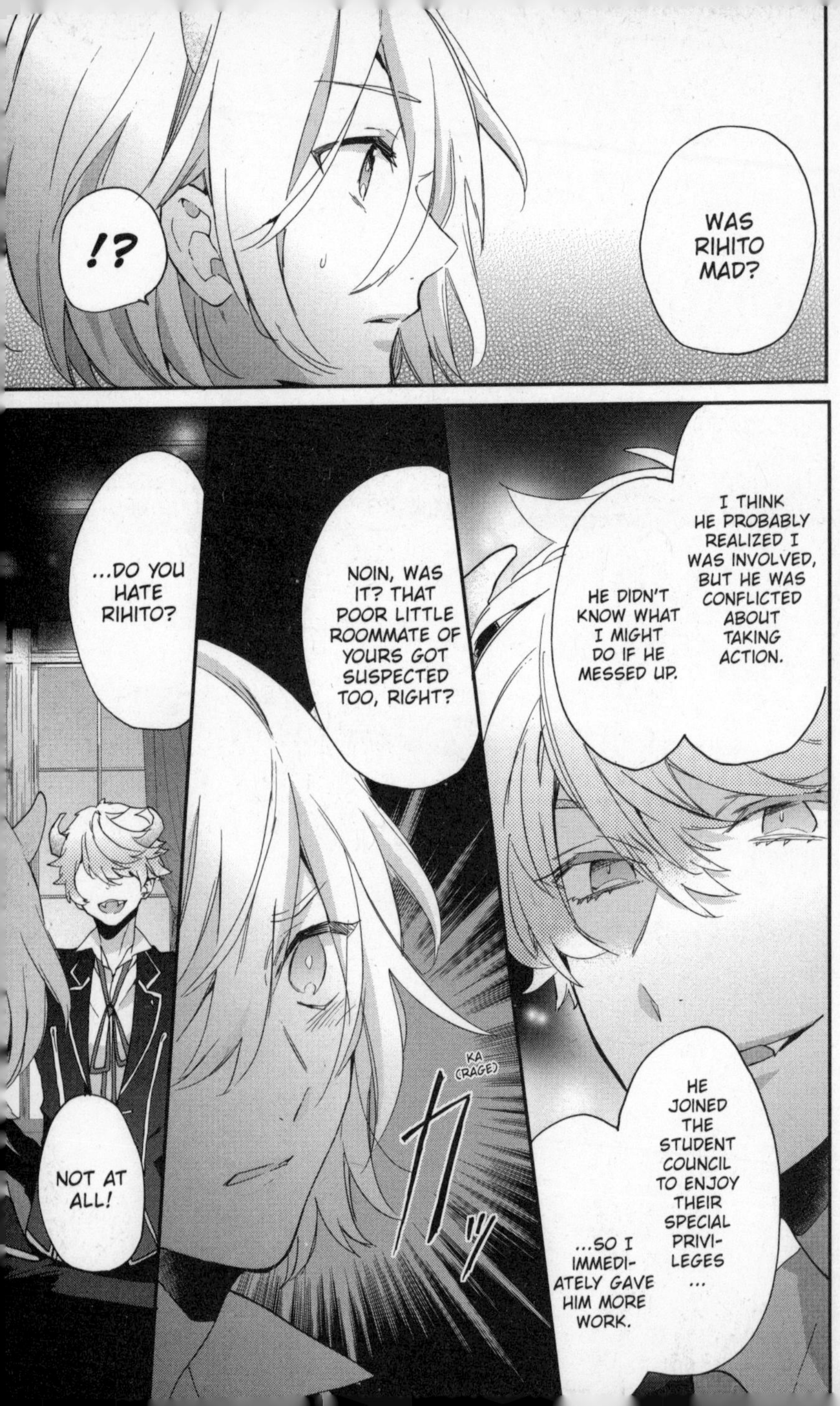
WAS RIHITO MAD?
!?
I THINK HE PROBABLY REALIZED I WAS INVOLVED, BUT HE WAS CONFLICTED ABOUT TAKING ACTION.
HE DIDN'T KNOW WHAT I MIGHT DO IF HE MESSED UP.
HE JOINED THE STUDENT COUNCIL TO ENJOY THEIR SPECIAL PRIVI-LEGES ...
...SO I IMMEDI-ATELY GAVE HIM MORE WORK.
NOIN, WAS IT? THAT POOR LITTLE ROOMMATE OF YOURS GOT SUSPECTED TOO, RIGHT?
KA (RAGE)
...DO YOU HATE RIHITO?
NOT AT ALL!

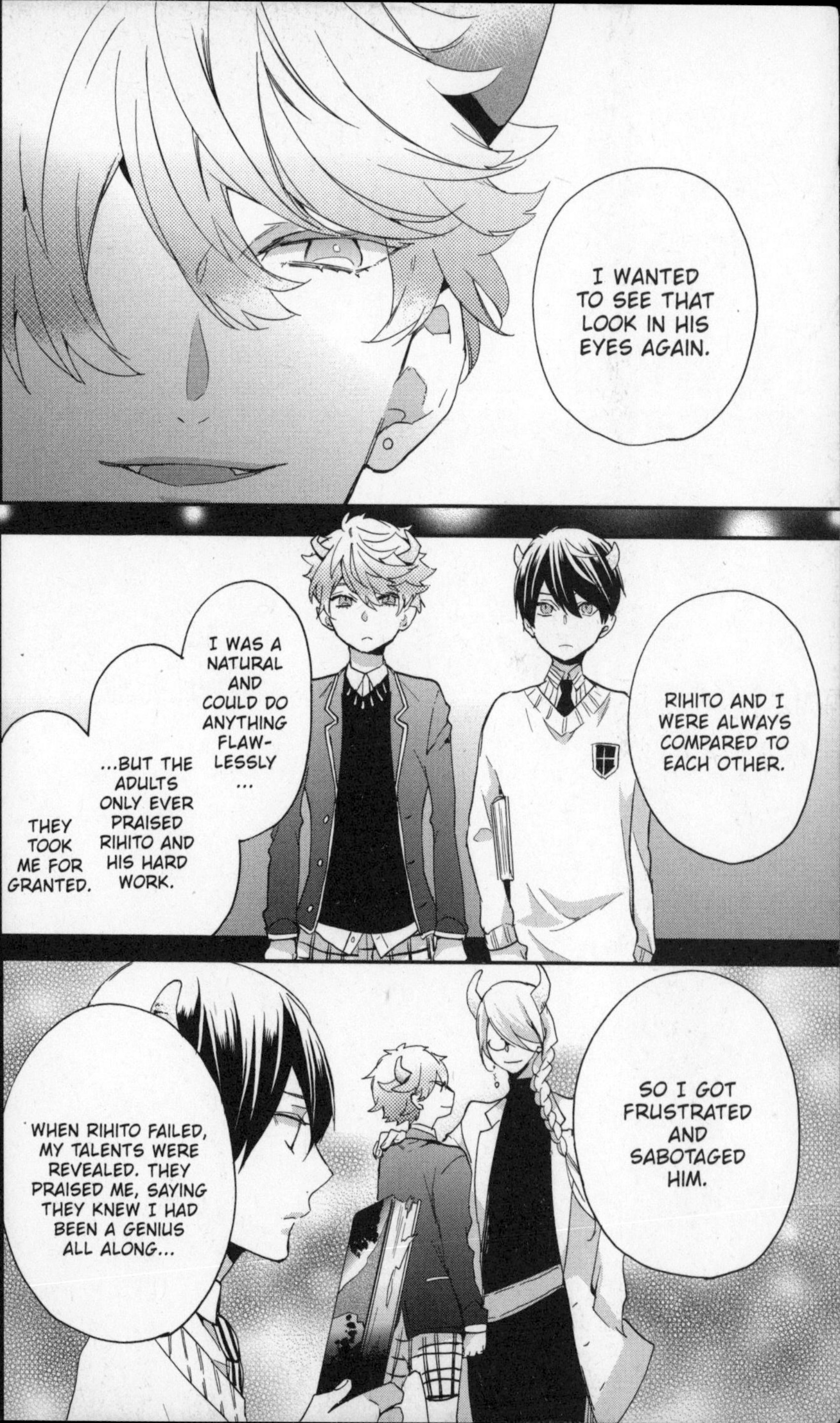
I WANTED TO SEE THAT LOOK IN HIS EYES AGAIN.
RIHITO AND I WERE ALWAYS COMPARED TO EACH OTHER.
I WAS A NATURAL AND COULD DO ANYTHING FLAW-LESSLY ...
...BUT THE ADULTS ONLY EVER PRAISED RIHITO AND HIS HARD WORK.
THEY TOOK ME FOR GRANTED.
SO I GOT FRUSTRATED AND SABOTAGED HIM.
WHEN RIHITO FAILED, MY TALENTS WERE REVEALED. THEY PRAISED ME, SAYING THEY KNEW I HAD BEEN A GENIUS ALL ALONG...

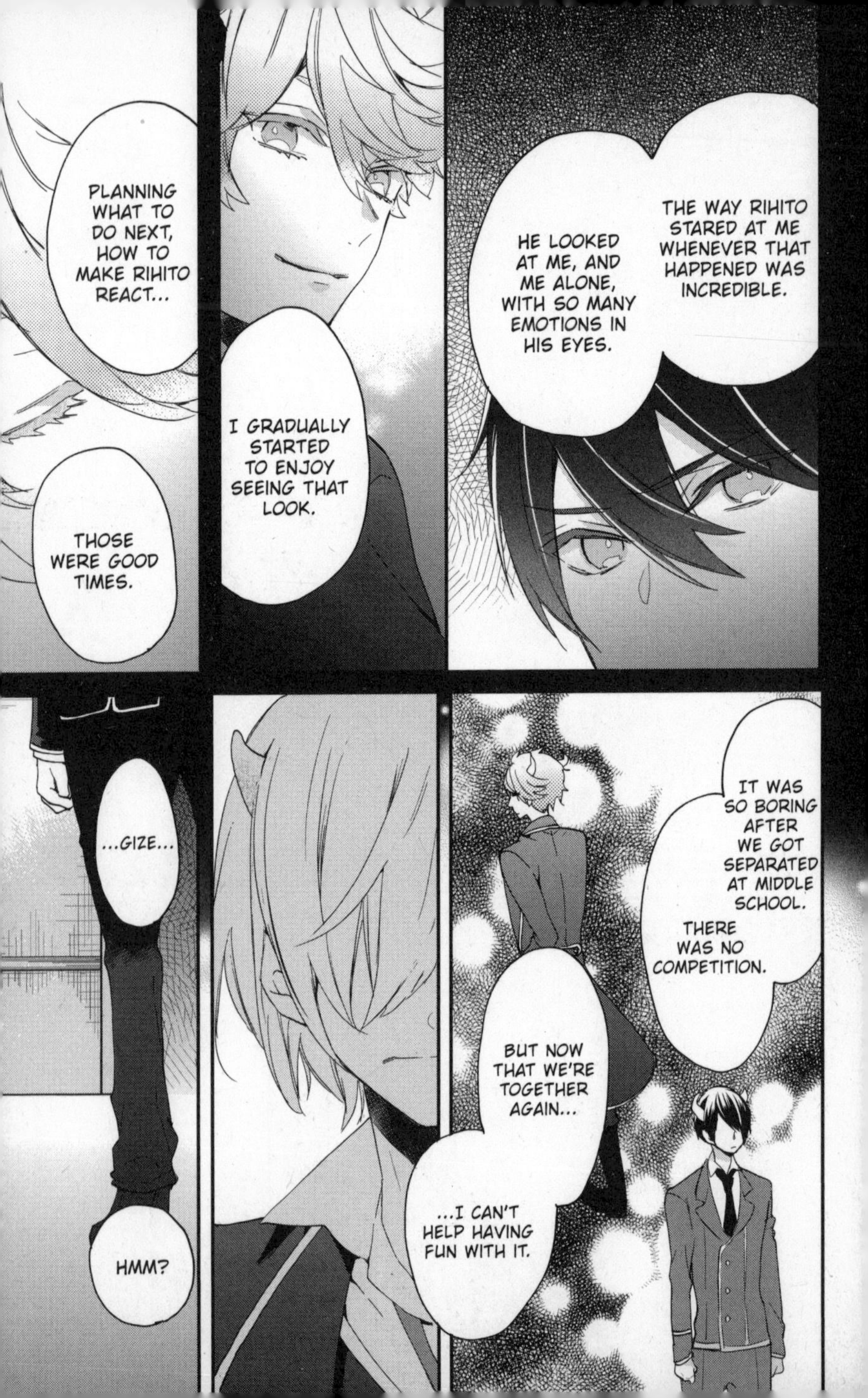
THE WAY RIHITO STARED AT ME WHENEVER THAT HAPPENED WAS INCREDIBLE.
HE LOOKED AT ME, AND ME ALONE, WITH SO MANY EMOTIONS IN HIS EYES.
I GRADUALLY STARTED TO ENJOY SEEING THAT LOOK.
PLANNING WHAT TO DO NEXT, HOW TO MAKE RIHITO REACT...
THOSE WERE GOOD TIMES.
IT WAS SO BORING AFTER WE GOT SEPARATED AT MIDDLE SCHOOL.
THERE WAS NO COMPETITION.
BUT NOW THAT WE'RE TOGETHER AGAIN...
...I CAN'T HELP HAVING FUN WITH IT.
...GIZE...
HMM?

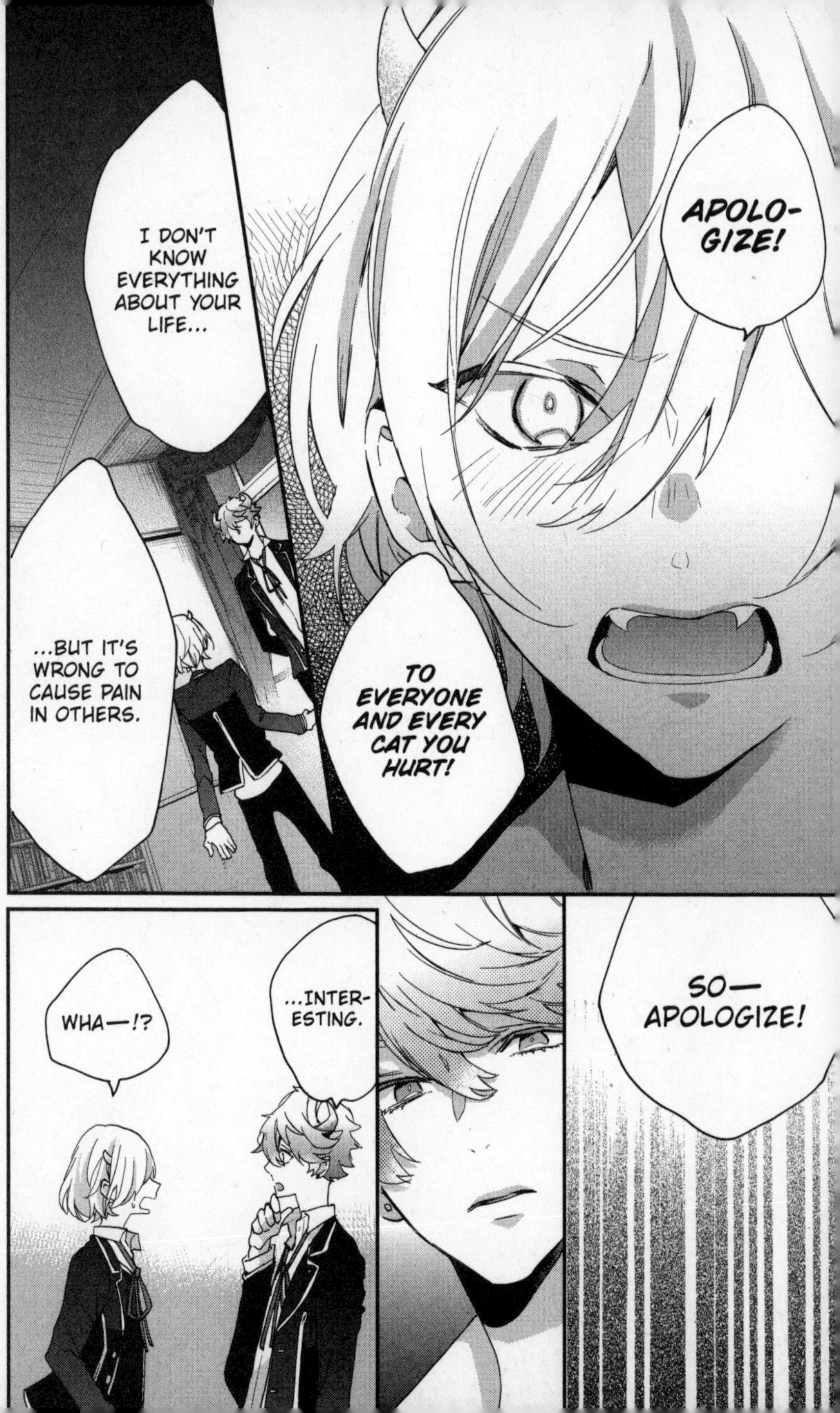
APOLO-GIZE!
TO EVERYONE AND EVERY CAT YOU HURT!
I DON'T KNOW EVERYTHING ABOUT YOUR LIFE...
...BUT IT'S WRONG TO CAUSE PAIN IN OTHERS.
SO— APOLOGIZE!
...INTER-ESTING.
WHA—!?

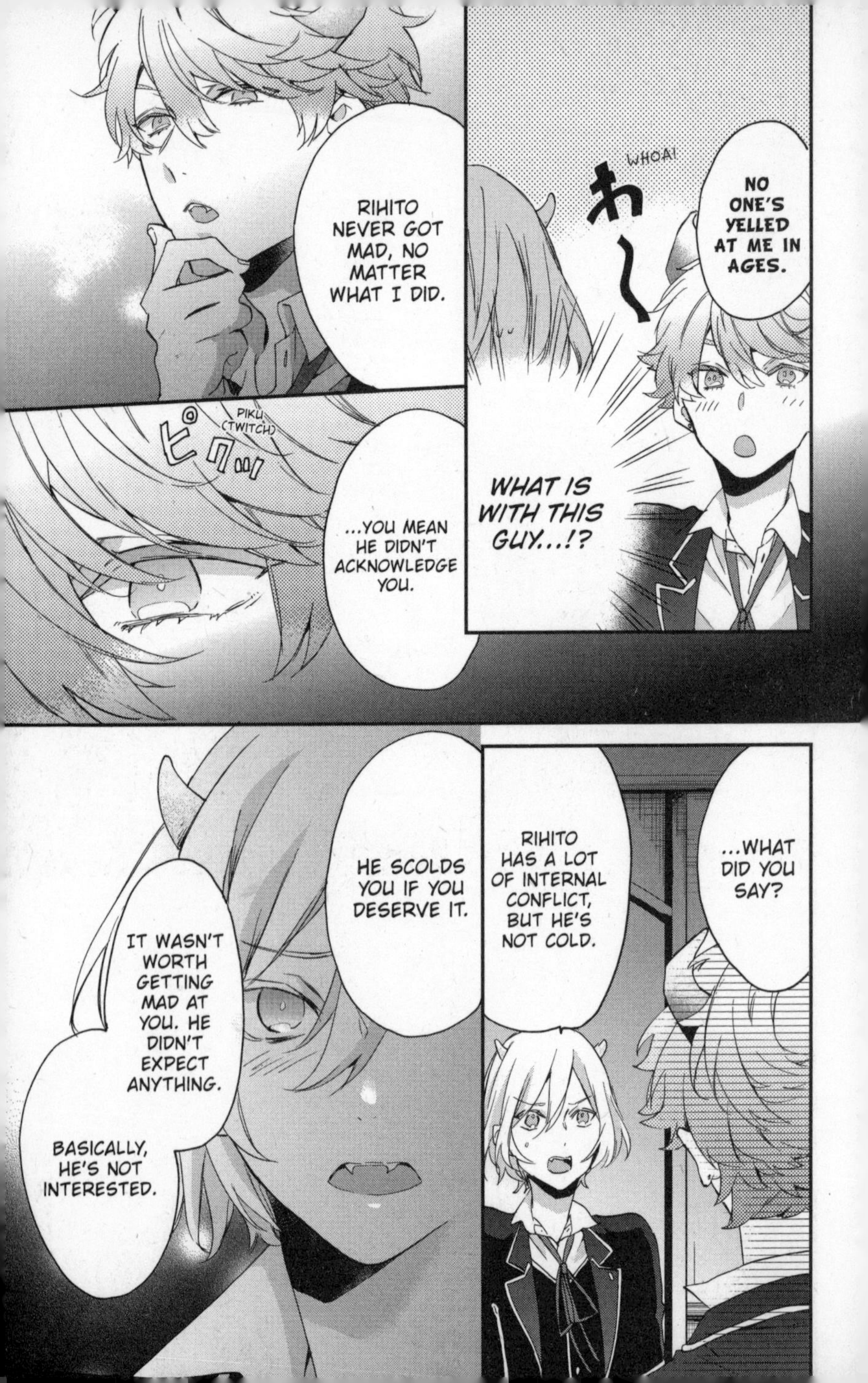
NO ONE'S YELLED AT ME IN AGES.
わ〜
WHOA!
WHAT IS WITH THIS GUY...!?
RIHITO NEVER GOT MAD, NO MATTER WHAT I DID.
...YOU MEAN HE DIDN'T ACKNOWLEDGE YOU.
ピクッ
PIKU (TWITCH)
...WHAT DID YOU SAY?
RIHITO HAS A LOT OF INTERNAL CONFLICT, BUT HE'S NOT COLD.
HE SCOLDS YOU IF YOU DESERVE IT.
IT WASN'T WORTH GETTING MAD AT YOU. HE DIDN'T EXPECT ANYTHING.
BASICALLY, HE'S NOT INTERESTED.

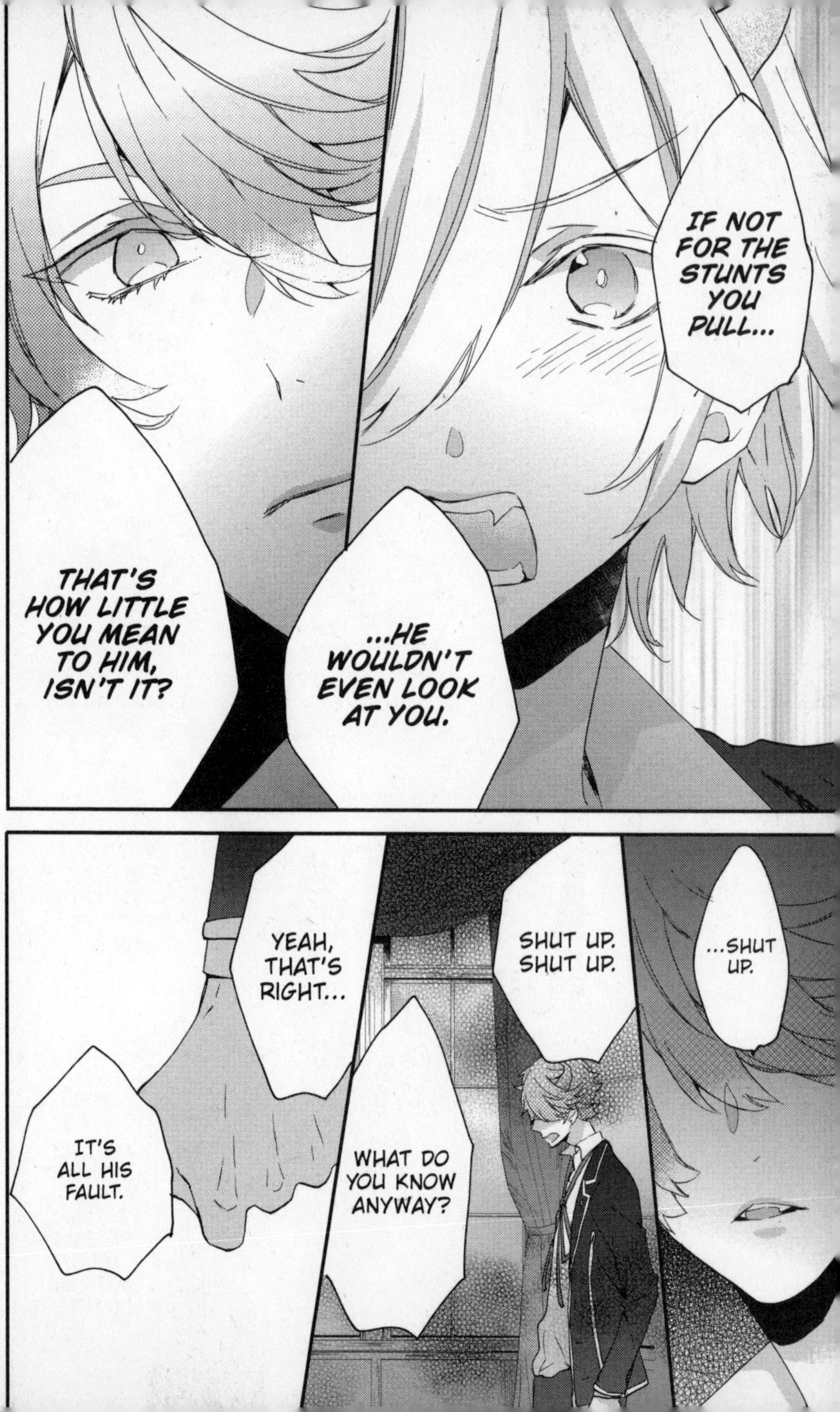
IF NOT FOR THE STUNTS YOU PULL...
...HE WOULDN'T EVEN LOOK AT YOU.
THAT'S HOW LITTLE YOU MEAN TO HIM, ISN'T IT?
...SHUT UP.
SHUT UP. SHUT UP.
WHAT DO YOU KNOW ANYWAY?
YEAH, THAT'S RIGHT...
IT'S ALL HIS FAULT.

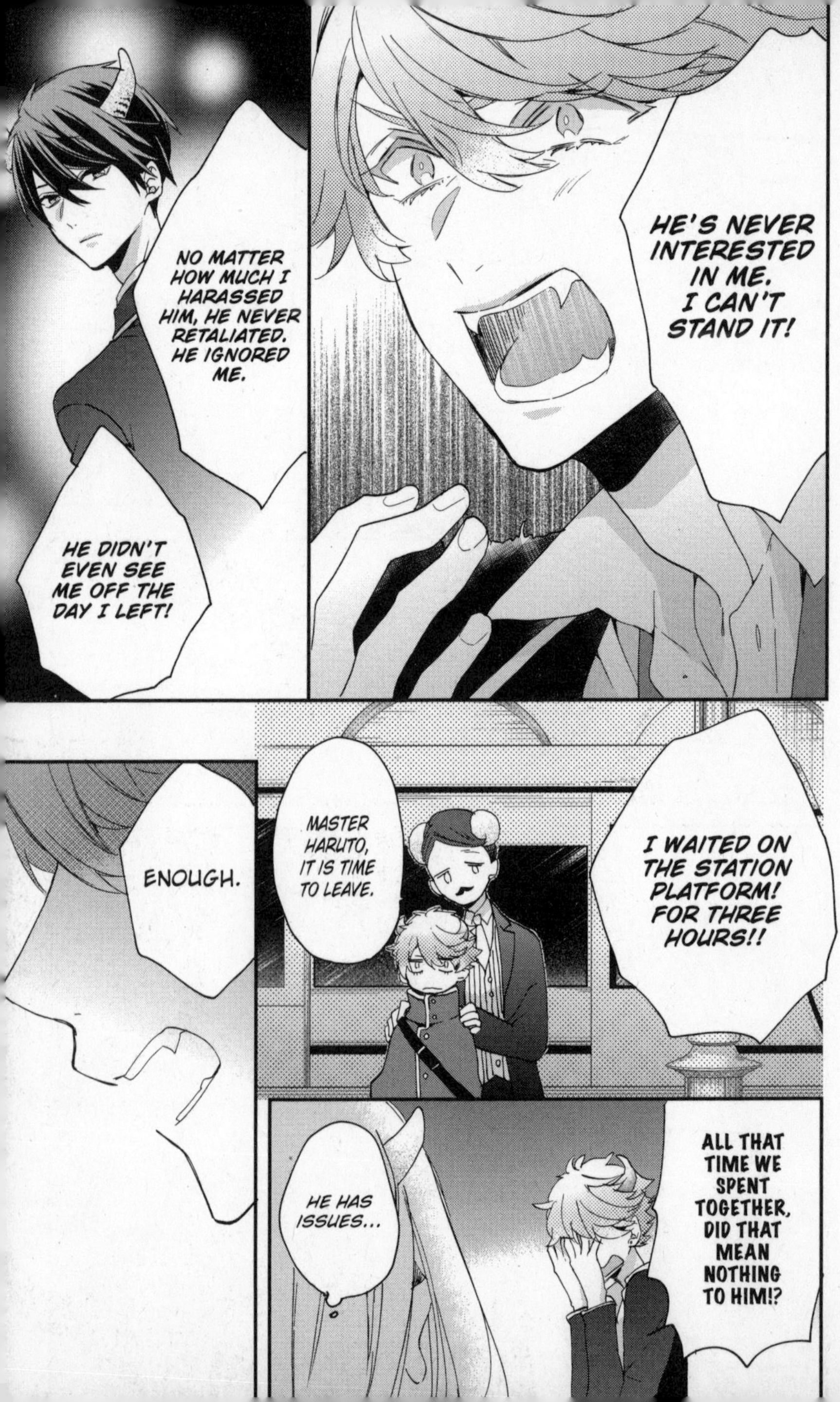
HE'S NEVER INTERESTED IN ME. I CAN'T STAND IT!
NO MATTER HOW MUCH I HARASSED HIM, HE NEVER RETALIATED. HE IGNORED ME.
HE DIDN'T EVEN SEE ME OFF THE DAY I LEFT!
I WAITED ON THE STATION PLATFORM! FOR THREE HOURS!!
MASTER HARUTO, IT IS TIME TO LEAVE.
ALL THAT TIME WE SPENT TOGETHER, DID THAT MEAN NOTHING TO HIM!?
HE HAS ISSUES...
ENOUGH.

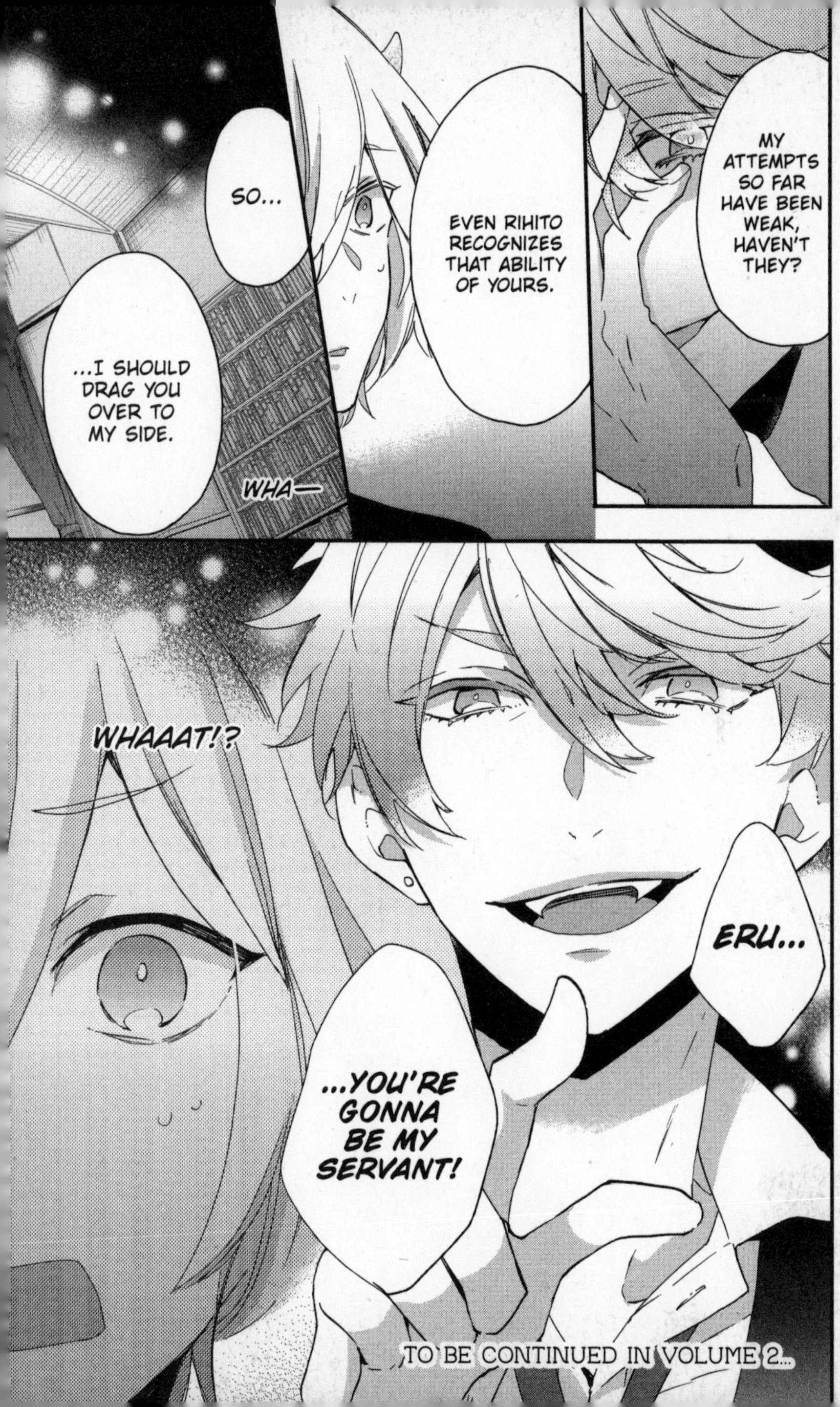
MY ATTEMPTS SO FAR HAVE BEEN WEAK, HAVEN'T THEY?
EVEN RIHITO RECOGNIZES THAT ABILITY OF YOURS.
SO...
...I SHOULD DRAG YOU OVER TO MY SIDE.
WHA—
ERU...
...YOU'RE GONNA BE MY SERVANT!
WHAAAT!?
TO BE CONTINUED IN VOLUME 2...

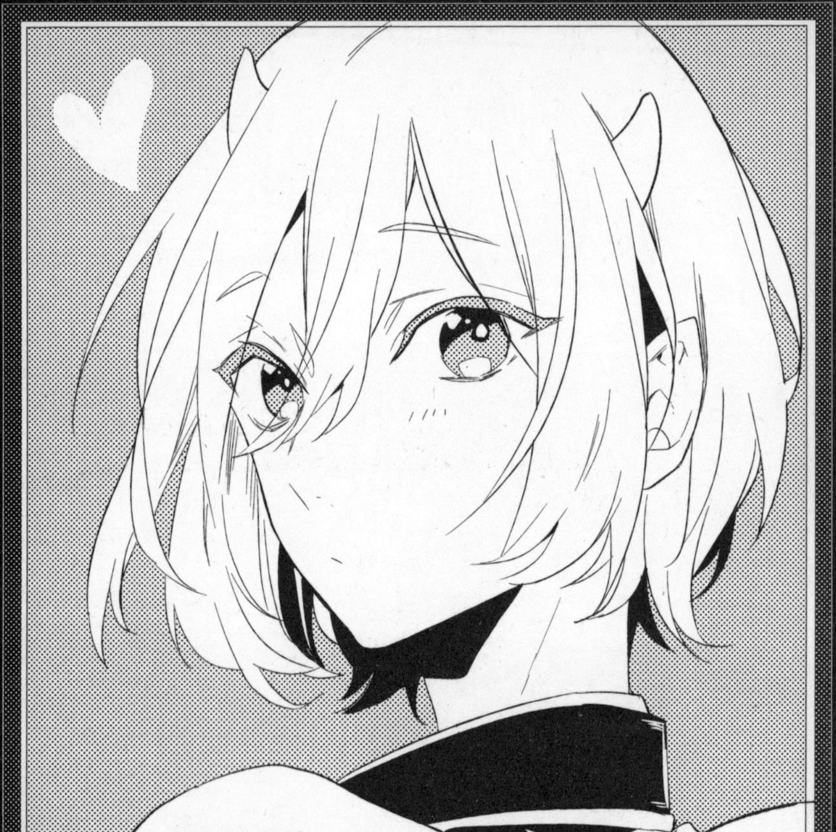
I hope you enjoyed this book!! Thank you!!!
!! Special Thanks !!
To my editor, all the editorial staff, my designer, Uto-san, Tadano-san, Saho-san, everyone involved in this book, and everyone reading this. Thank you!
mito.

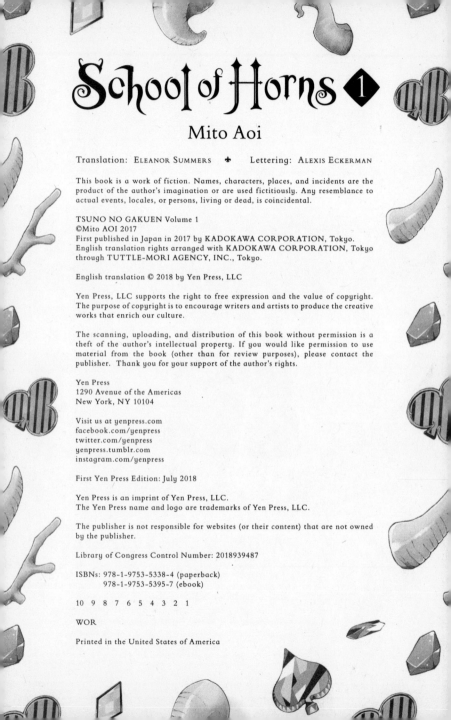

School of Horns 1

Mito Aoi

Translation: ELEANOR SUMMERS ✦ Lettering: ALEXIS ECKERMAN

TSUNO NO GAKUEN Volume 1
©Mito AOI 2017
First published in Japan in 2017 by KADOKAWA CORPORATION, Tokyo.
English translation rights arranged with KADOKAWA CORPORATION, Tokyo through TUTTLE-MORI AGENCY, INC., Tokyo.

English translation © 2018 by Yen Press, LLC

Yen Press
1290 Avenue of the Americas
New York, NY 10104

Visit us at yenpress.com
facebook.com/yenpress
twitter.com/yenpress
yenpress.tumblr.com
instagram.com/yenpress

First Yen Press Edition: July 2018

Yen Press is an imprint of Yen Press, LLC.
The Yen Press name and logo are trademarks of Yen Press, LLC.

The publisher is not responsible for websites (or their content) that are not owned by the publisher.

Library of Congress Control Number: 2018939487

ISBNs: 978-1-9753-5338-4 (paperback)
       978-1-9753-5395-7 (ebook)

10 9 8 7 6 5 4 3 2 1

WOR

Printed in the United States of America

Two girls, a new school, and the beginning of a beautiful friendship.

Volumes 1-5 available now

Kiss & White Lily for My Dearest Girl

In middle school, Ayaka Shiramine was the perfect student: hard-working, with excellent grades and a great personality to match. As Ayaka enters high school she expects to still be on top, but one thing she didn't account for is her new classmate, the lazy yet genuine genius Yurine Kurosawa. What's in store for Ayaka and Yurine as they go through high school...together?

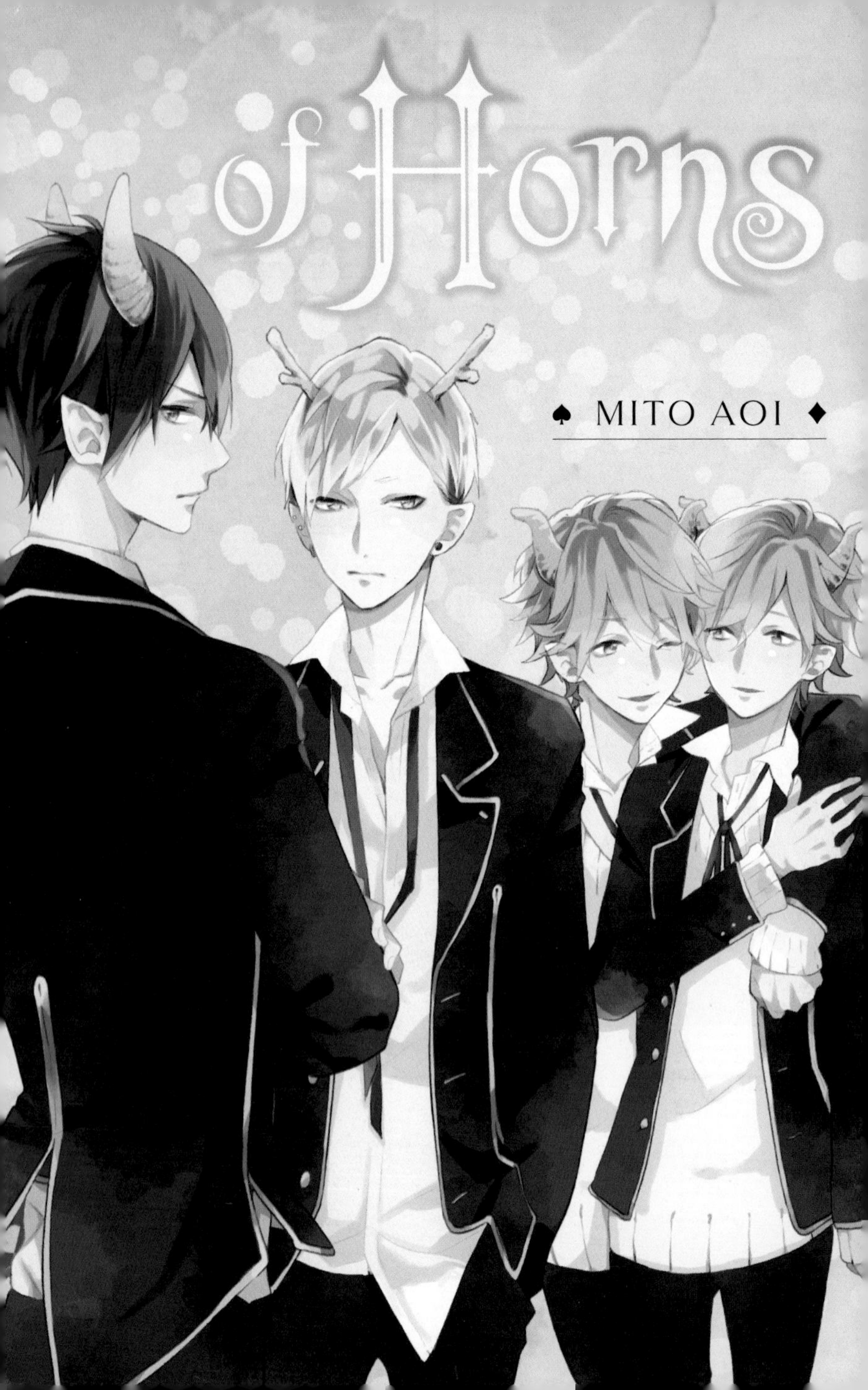
of Horns
♠ MITO AOI ♦

CHAPTER 1

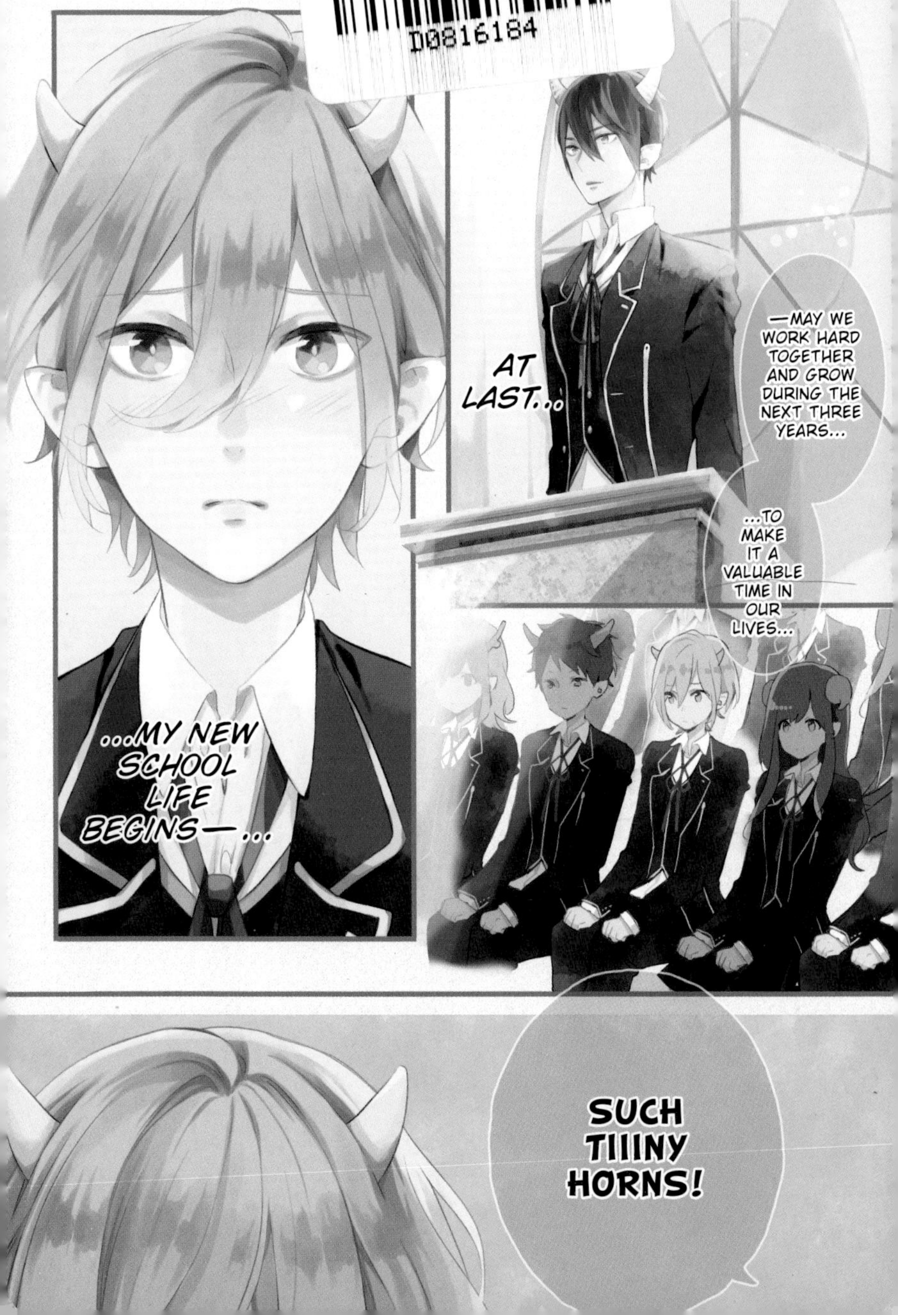
—MAY WE WORK HARD TOGETHER AND GROW DURING THE NEXT THREE YEARS...
AT LAST...
...TO MAKE IT A VALUABLE TIME IN OUR LIVES...
...MY NEW SCHOOL LIFE BEGINS—...
SUCH TIIINY HORNS!

Table of Statutes

Table of Statutory Instruments

Introduction

'Boundaries are notorious troublemakers'
Lloyd v *Stanbury* [1971] 2 All ER 267, 271 per Brightman J

'O wall, O sweet, O lovely wall,
That standest between her father's ground and mine'
Midsummer Night's Dream, William Shakespeare

'Good fences make good neighbours'
North of Boston. Mending Wall, Robert Frost

Questions and disputes about the boundaries of private properties can arise in many legal contexts. They are relevant to allegations of trespass, nuisance and breach of contract. They arise not only between neighbours, but also between vendor and purchaser and between landlord and tenant. The rules and presumptions on this subject, and the statutory provisions relating to it, do not fall into any readily definable category of law, so they can be difficult to trace. In this book, they are brought together to give a readily available source of reference.

The law is stated as at 1 April 1986.

Chapter 1

Determining Boundaries

1 Construing title deeds

(a) Description of parcels

Parcels of land in separate ownership may be divided horizontally, vertically or in any other way (Law of Property Act 1925, s 205 (1)(ix)). As this power is unrestricted, the first consideration in determining boundaries is to look at the acts of the owners of the different parcels as revealed by the title deeds. A clear definition in the deeds will normally be conclusive. To this general rule there are a number of exceptions.

First, adverse occupation by a squatter for a sufficient time to acquire title under the Limitation Act 1980 may alter the boundary. Secondly, an act of the landowner or one of his predecessors in title, although not varying the boundary shown on his deeds, may estop him from taking action in respect of the infringement. Thirdly, if the title deeds to the adjoining properties conflict, then reference will have to be made to the deeds showing the original division.

The limitation on the commencement of title in s 44 of the Law of Property Act 1925 (as amended by the Law of Property Act 1969, s 23), applies to matters between vendor and purchaser, and would not bar an older deed being adduced in evidence in a boundary dispute. Similarly, because of the general rule that Land Registry plans do not necessarily show precise boundaries, reference may need to be made in cases of registered title to pre-registration deeds.

Fourthly, a deed containing an error by both parties to it, or not accurately representing their prior agreement, will normally be rectified by the court, unless the applicant has disentitled himself to equitable relief (eg, by laches). Fifthly, the boundary may subsequently be varied by statute, although evidence of this should have been placed with or indorsed upon the deeds.

(b) Ambiguous descriptions

If the definition of the parcels is clear, and yet some further erroneous description is added to it, the latter may be disregarded, applying the maxim *falsa demonstratio non nocet*. An example of this is where a deed defines boundaries by reference to existing physical objects, and also states the area of the land, and the two descriptions disagree. The description by physical objects will prevail. Thus, if a lease of land describes the premises by admeasurement and adds 'with the houses now erected or being erected thereon' and the foundations have already been laid and extend beyond the boundaries according to the measurements, the description by measurements is disregarded and the boundaries extend to include the foundations (*Manning* v *Fitzgerald* (1859) 29 LJ Ex 24). The maxim applied in that case to reject the first description.

Another example of the application of the maxim is provided by a case where land was described in a tabulated schedule to a conveyance. The second column, headed 'description' referred to a plan which clearly showed an area conveyed of 27 perches. The fourth column of the schedule gave the area as 34 perches. The larger figure, coming second, was treated as erroneous and disregarded (*Llewellyn* v *Earl of Jersey* (1843) 11 M & W 183).

Should there be a number of conflicting descriptions, however, the maxim *falsa demonstratio non nocet* is not available to permit all but the first to be discarded. The order is not in that case paramount (*Eastwood* v *Ashton* [1915] AC 900). In such a case it is a question of construction of the deed which description prevails, and there are no general presumptions.

It is sometimes possible to admit extrinsic evidence of the parties' intentions, eg, that both landlord and tenant meant to include a rear storeroom when they only referred to a shop (*I S Mills (Yardley) Ltd* v *Curdworth Investments Ltd* (1975) 119 SJ 302).

(c) Descriptive words

Certain words have acquired a technical meaning, and where they occur in a description of property they can assist in defining the boundaries. 'Messuage' and 'house' both pass a dwellinghouse with its curtilage, attached garden and buildings appurtenant to it. 'Dwellinghouse' is not limited to the part of the building that happens to be occupied for residential purposes (*Grigsby* v *Melville* [1974] 1 WLR 80). 'Curtilage' means land that belongs with a house in the physical sense, and the term can be used for the land that goes with a church (*Re St John's Church, Bishop's Hatfield* [1967] P 113). Land is sometimes described as having a building erected on it 'or on some part thereof'. This implies that more than the mere site of the building is referred to (*Bisney* v *Swanston* (1973) 225 EG 2299).

'Farm' passes the farmhouse and the land held with it. 'Water' passes the right to water and fishing, but not the land beneath it. 'Pool' passes both the water and its bed.

Where it is clear that the intention of the deed is to convey the whole of the grantor's holding, evidence of the extent of that holding will be admitted to construe the deed (*Maxted* v *Plymouth Corporation* [1957] CLY 243). If all but a small part of the grantor's land is conveyed and no intention to retain any has been displayed (as where the title deeds are handed over), the whole plot with its original boundaries will be presumed to be conveyed, in the absence of contrary evidence.

The position of a fence may itself determine the interpretation in the context of a 'close' or 'curtilage' (*Walsh* v *Allweather Mechanical Grouting Co Ltd* [1959] 2 QB 300: not a case interpreting a title deed).

(d) General words

The general words implied into the description of the parcels in a conveyance by s 62 of the Law of Property Act 1925 can extend the amount of property which appears to be conveyed, and therefore affects its boundary. In a case where the parcels were described in the deed and shown coloured on a plan, part of a yard which was not coloured was conveyed, because one of the general words was 'yard' and was held to include it (*Willis* v *Watney* (1881) 51 LJ Ch 588).

(e) Plans

A plan referred to may be drawn on or annexed to the deed, form part of another deed or be independent of the title, eg, an Ordnance Survey or tithe map. If the plan is to be of assistance, it will have to be sufficiently clear and detailed to be self-explanatory. Two points of general application in interpreting plans may however be mentioned.

First, it is Ordnance Survey practice, where there are boundary features such as hedges or fences between parcels of land, to draw the boundary line down the middle of these features. General presumptions, which may suggest that the boundary should lie down one side or the other, are ignored. This will apply to plans which do not explicitly state that they are extracts from, or based upon, the Ordnance Survey, but which can be seen to be so (eg, because the Ordnance Survey parcel numbers are given).

Secondly, there is the practice of defining the ownership of boundary features, or the responsibility for their maintenance, by the insertion of 'T' marks. The convention is that the 'T' is written, with its cross stroke parallel to the boundary and its down stroke touching it, on the side of the boundary on which lies the property with which the feature is included. There is no authority to suggest that this is anything more than a convention. If, as sometimes happens, 'T' marks appear on the plan without any reference to them in the deed, they can be no more than persuasive evidence of the ownership of the boundary features. Since 1962 'T' marks have been shown on the filed plan of land with registered title in certain circumstances (p 17). This does not, however, invest them with any greater significance than they would have when considering the precise position of the boundary of unregistered land.

Occasionally, an 'H' mark will be found, but much less frequently than 'T' marks. The 'H' is written so that its vertical strokes are parallel to the boundary, one on each side of it, so that it is, in effect, two 'T' marks joined. This is intended to indicate a party wall. Because of the ambiguity of that expression (see Chapter 4), and because 'H' marks are not used frequently enough for a universal practice to have been established, they cannot be regarded as of any evidential value if they appear without any verbal explanation.

(f) Interrelation of plans and parcels

Where the verbal description of premises in a deed is incomplete, it may be supplemented by reference to any plan to which the deed refers. Indeed, where the wording of the conveyance is ambiguous, a plan annexed to the conveyance, even if not referred to, may be considered (*Leachman* v *L & K Richardson Ltd* [1969] 1 WLR 1129). Where the conveyance plan did not accord with the fencing round the site of a new house, the plan prevailed even though stated to be 'for the purpose of identification only'; because there was no clear verbal description. The land was referred to as 'plot No . . .' and the word plot suggests a reference to a plan, and the surrounding circumstances made it appropriate (*Spall* v *Owen* (1981) 44 P & CR 36).

Should the verbal description of the parcels and the plan disagree, it is a question of construction of the deed's reference to the plan, to determine which will prevail. It may be possible to adduce extrinsic evidence (*Scarfe* v *Adams* [1981] 1 All ER 843). When the words are not clear, but go on to define the property as 'more particularly described' on the plan, the latter will prevail (*Eastwood* v *Ashton* [1915] AC 900). The phrase 'more particularly delineated in' has the same effect (*Wallington* v *Townsend* [1939] Ch 588). On the other hand, a plan referred to 'for identification only' cannot overrule a description in words (*Hopgood* v *Brown* [1955] 1 WLR 213, 228). The function of such a plan is to show roughly where the land is located, not to define its boundaries (*Moreton C Cullimore (Gravels) Ltd* v *Routledge* (1977) 121 SJ 202). But it can supplement and elucidate a description which does not by itself clearly describe the land (*Wiggington & Milner Ltd* v *Winster Engineering Ltd* [1978] 1 WLR 1462). If, in such a case, the verbal description is vague, the surrounding circumstances can be taken into consideration, eg, the position of a boundary pegged out on the ground (*Wilson* v *Greene* [1971] 1 WLR 635). A plan stated to be 'for the purpose of delineation only' is one which is not true to scale (*Re Freeman and Taylor's Contract* (1907) 97 LT 39).

The plan may influence the construction of the words of the deed. A house described as 'comprising that portion of Terrant Monkton House which was formerly known as the Old Rectory' was not restricted to what had been the Old Rectory when more was shown on the plan. 'Comprising' was construed as 'including' (*Smout* v *Farquharson* (1973) 226 EG 114). Where there is no conflict between the description and the plan, even a plan for identification can supplement the verbal description (*Tebaldi* v *Wiseman and Kemp* (1983) 133 NLJ 1042: the plan on a lease of a basement flat showed that the internal staircase down to it was included in the demise).

The maxim *falsa demonstratio non nocet* can apply here also. Where the deed's description makes it clear that the boundary runs along the centre line of a hedge, but adds 'which said piece of land is delineated on the plan drawn hereon' and the plan shows the boundary lines at the foot of the hedge, the plan is ignored and the boundary is in the middle of the hedge (*Maxted* v *Plymouth Corporation* [1957] CLY 243). On the other hand, if, as a matter of construction, the description of the property in the parcels of a conveyance is to be read as a whole, dimensions given in the verbal description can prevail over an inaccurate plan (*Boyd Gibbins Ltd* v *Hockham* (1966) 199 EG 229). Where the title to land is registered, a conflict between the verbal description of the land and the filed plan for that title number, or the general map, may be resolved by the Land Registry, subject to an appeal to the High Court (Land Registration Rules 1925, r 285).

2 Presumptions in certain cases

Where the boundaries of land are defined by reference to, or in fact follow, certain physical features, advantage may be taken of legal presumptions applicable to land bounded by such features, which will apply unless or until rebutted by contrary evidence (*Beaufort (Duke)* v *Swansea Corporation* (1849) 3 Exch 413). It must be emphasised that these presumptions may be modified or excluded where the title to the land is registered, and reference should be r ade to pp 16–17. Assistance may also be gained from statutory rules where the adjoining property is used for certain purposes. Listed alphabetically below are a number of features by which boundaries may be defined, with particulars of whether, and if so, what special rules apply in each case.

(a) Beach

'Beach' is not a term of art. When used to define a boundary it may prima facie have the same meaning as 'seashore' (*Government of State of Penang* v *Beng Hong Oon* [1972] AC 425). However, it can extend further, to include land in apparent continuity with the beach at high water mark, ie, until there is a change of vegetation, a physical barrier, or a road (*Tito* v *Waddell (No 2)* [1977] Ch 106, 263).

(b) Canals

Artificial waterways are not subject to the presumptions noted below in respect of certain rivers, where the riparian lands extend to the centre of the stream, because they must have been originally dug by a person on his own land or on land acquired from the adjoining owners for the purpose. Land bordering a canal is bounded by it, so minerals beneath the canal do not pass on a conveyance of the bordering land which does not expressly include the canal, or some part of it, even though they belong to the transferor (*Chamber Colliery Co* v *Rochdale Canal Co* [1895] AC 564).

(c) Flats

Where part of a house, divided horizontally or vertically, is leased, the demise includes the external walls enclosing the part so demised unless there are provisions to the contrary in the lease. A covenant by the landlord to do external repairs is not sufficient to displace this presumption (*Sturge* v *Hackett* [1962] 1 WLR 1257). The outside of a flat can be expressly excluded from a demise of it, but that does not prevent the external walls from constituting its exterior for the purposes of the landlord's implied repairing obligations (*Campden Hill Towers Ltd* v *Gardner* [1977] QB 823).

(d) Foreshore

See *(q) Seashore*, below.

(e) Forests

The boundaries of the royal forests—most of which were vested in the Minister of Agriculture and Fisheries (now the Minister of Agriculture, Fisheries and Food) by the Forestry Act 1945—were finally fixed, after considerable friction between the Crown and its subjects, by the Delimitation of Forests Act 1640. This necessarily also fixed the boundaries of the private lands adjoining the forests. Since then, however, considerable areas have been disafforested by special statutes, private inclosure acts, and letters patent, and these have mostly passed into private ownership.

(f) Hedges and ditches

Where two fields are separated by an artificial ditch alongside a bank, with or without a hedge or fence on it, there is a presumption that the boundary is along the edge of the ditch furthest from the bank (*Fisher* v *Winch* [1939] 1 KB 666). This arises from the assumption that the landowner digs his drainage ditch on the extreme edge of his property and throws up the earth on to his own side of the ditch to avoid committing a trespass against his neighbour, so forming the bank upon which he plants a hedge or erects a fence. The presumption only applies to a single hedge (or fence or bank) and ditch. If there is one without the other, or two hedges or two ditches, no such presumption operates, because the original landowner's actions in digging the ditch or planting the hedge cannot be logically deduced. Similarly, because the presumption is based on a landowner's action in digging the ditch, it probably does not apply where the ditch is natural and not artificial (*Marshall* v *Taylor* [1895] 1 Ch 641, 647).

Ordnance Survey practice is to take the centre line of the hedge as the boundary. A conveyance which describes the land conveyed by express reference to the Ordnance Survey will rebut the presumption, in favour of the Ordnance Survey practice (*Rouse* v *Gravelworks Ltd* [1940] 1 KB 489 (at first instance); *Davey* v *Harrow Corporation* [1958] 1 QB 60). It is thought, however, that the presumption would still be applied where the conveyance plan was based on the Ordnance Survey for convenience, without expressly incorporating the Survey map.

(g) Highways

If a highway is fenced on both sides, it will be presumed to extend up to both fences (or hedges) if, but only if, it can be shown that the fences were erected (or hedges planted) to separate the adjoining closes from the highway (*Attorney-General* v *Beynon* [1970] Ch 1). This presumption extends to land between other boundary features, eg, banks, whether natural or man-made (*Naydler* v *Hampshire County Council* (1973) 226 EG 176).

There are said to be two occasions on which a presumption arises as to the boundary of land adjoining a highway. First, the boundary of land adjoining a highway is presumed to be a line drawn down the middle of the highway, and land 'adjoins' a highway for this purpose although separated from it by a public right of way not being part of the street (*Ware Urban District Council* v *Gaunt* [1960] 1 WLR 1364). This presumption only applies where the conveyancing history of the land and the road is unknown (*Giles* v *County Building Constructors* (*Hertford*) *Ltd* (1971) 22 P & CR 978, 981).

For the purpose of making up and adopting private roads, road charges are normally imposed on the owners of property 'fronting' (which includes 'adjoining': Highways Act 1980, s 203(3)) the street (s 205). An upper maisonette, separated from the highway by a twenty-five foot garden belonging to the lower maisonette, does not adjoin the highway for this purpose (*Buckinghamshire County Council* v *Trigg* [1963] 1 WLR 155). But leaving a twelve foot strip of land between a housing development and the road, to accommodate future widening, does not prevent the houses fronting the road (*Warwickshire County Council* v *Adkins* (1967) 112 SJ 135).

The second case in which there may be a presumption is on the conveyance of land forming part of a building estate. It can include half the road, even though it clearly describes the property as excluding any part of the road. Very little now seems to be needed to rebut this presumption (*Giles* v *County Building Constructors* (*Hertford*) *Ltd*, supra).

The surface of that part of the land comprising the highway is not normally vested in the adjoining owner, but the boundary is important in passing the ground beneath the surface with its minerals and possible basement accommodation. In such a case, the ownership of growing trees remains in the owner of the subsoil, although the management and control of them may be assumed by the highway authority (*Russell* v *London Borough of Barnet* (1984) 271 EG 699).

The boundary also needs to be considered where a stopping-up order is obtained so that the surface reverts to private ownership. In some cases where the land was conveyed to the highway authority (not dedicated), a stopping-up order will only extinguish the public rights over the surface, the land remaining vested in the highway authority. The boundaries are then unaffected. Where only part of a highway is affected by a stopping-up order it is thought that this does not affect the position of the boundary, which thereafter need not be in the centre of the remaining road. The boundary is fixed on the first conveyance of the land, and all that is changed are the rights that may be exercised over part of the surface of the plot. Where it is not practicable to trace the original conveyance, such evidence of the facts as is available will have to be relied upon. Statutory declarations as to the practice in the past made by independent persons would normally be accepted in a conveyancing transaction; evidence admissible in court is considered below, at pp 29–33.

In the case of registered land the half of the highway is excluded from the registration of the title of the adjoining land if adopted by the local authority. This was started as an application of the general boundaries rule (p 16), and applied even in cases of an express conveyance of half the roadway. However, as it is now clear that where the highway authority has the surface vested in it, it acquires a legal estate (*Tithe Redemption Commission* v *Runcorn Urban District Council* [1954] Ch 383). It would not be proper in such cases to do otherwise. The presumption still applies to the subsoil.

The presumption of ownership of half an adjoining highway is displaced by evidence showing an intention not to include any part of the road. In one case, the presumption did not apply where a sewer was to be laid under the road by the authority leasing the adjoining land, and there was even doubt whether they had power to include it (*Mappin Brothers* v *Liberty & Co Ltd* [1903] 1 Ch 118).

(*h*) *Houses*

Where a house is conveyed or demised there is a presumption that it passes in its entirety, including projecting eaves and footings (although not shown on the plan referred to), but not the air space between them (*Truckell* v *Stock* [1957] 1 WLR 161). On the other hand, a conveyance of property by reference to the ground plan of a building will include part of a neighbouring building which overhangs above it (*Laybourne* v *Gridley* [1892] 2 Ch 53). A conveyance of a dwellinghouse by description passed with it a void under the ground floor, even though the only access to that basement was from the adjoining property, with which it had previously been enjoyed (*Grigsby* v *Melville* [1974] 1 WLR 80).

Walls which are shared by two properties (eg, those between semidetached or terraced houses) may belong to one of the adjoining houses exclusively if there is clear evidence that the wall is on one side of the boundary line. It is usual, however, for these to be party walls (Chapter 4), and in the absence of contrary evidence there is a presumption that the boundary runs down the middle of the wall.

Where land is conveyed described as bounded by a house, or something else to which title would normally be made independently, the boundary object is completely excluded.

(i) Islands

Ownership of the bank of a non-tidal river does not carry with it islands up to a line midway between the two banks. The riparian owner's boundary is in the middle of the stream between the bank and the island (*Great Torrington Commons Conservators* v *Moore Stevens* [1904] 1 Ch 347). There is no settled presumption, however, on the line of the boundary round the ends of the island facing up and down stream.

The boundary of an island is similarly in the middle of the stream. If the title to the island is registered, with the boundary shown at the water's edge, the presumption applies, and is not displaced by a claim to a corporeal fishery over more than half the stream, because being land it would itself have to be registered (*Hesketh* v *Willis Cruisers Ltd* (1968) 19 P & CR 573).

It is otherwise when islands are formed by the water suddenly cutting off what was formerly part of the bank, or laying bare land formerly covered by water; such islands belong to the riparian owners, the boundary being drawn where it was before the islands were formed. In tidal rivers islands created by uncovering the river bed (even if only at low tide), or to which the riparian owners or some other person cannot make title, belong to the Crown. If part of a riparian owner's land is suddenly cut off by the waters of a tidal river, his boundary remains unaltered and extends round the island.

There are no presumptions relating to islands in lakes.

(j) Lakes

There is no settled presumption about the position of the boundary between properties in different ownership separated by a lake. The question of whether a rule similar to that for rivers applies, was left undecided in a nineteenth-century case (*Marshall* v *Ulleswater Steam Navigation Co Ltd* (1863) 3 B & S 732, 742). Evidence of exclusive possession will normally be conclusive. A lake wholly within the boundaries of a parcel of land will pass without special reference, unless expressly excluded. Equally, a lake could be conveyed separately from any surrounding property, when its boundaries, if not defined, would probably be the water's edge at the normal water level.

Where land adjoining a lake is conveyed, the lake forms its boundary. Gradual accretions to the land, as a result of natural forces, become part of it. The boundary moves to the position of the edge of the lake for the time being (*Southern Centre of Theosophy Inc* v *State of South Australia* [1982] AC 706). Presumably, the same applies, in reverse, if the lake shore is eroded.

(k) Pipe-lines

The grant of an easement for a pipe or wire may give exclusive rights of use. The boundaries of the land over which the easement is granted do not extend beyond the physical extent of the pipe, etc, unless otherwise stated, but such an easement will automatically carry ancillary rights of entry for inspection, cleaning, repair and replacement (*Jones* v *Pritchard* [1908] 1 Ch 630). Land through which passes a pipe-line authorised by the Pipe-lines Act 1962 may have been acquired by the pipe-line owner, or he may only have rights of user. A plan showing the route and extent of a pipe-line authorised to be laid or diverted under the Act must be deposited with the local authorities of the areas affected: s 35. This plan is open for inspection by anyone at all reasonable times without fee.

(l) Railways

No special presumption applies to railways, the boundary being where it appears to be and not in the centre of the track, because the land on which the railway is built had to be acquired from the adjoining owner and became a separate plot at that date. Adjoining landowners are not therefore automatically entitled to minerals under the railway (*Thompson* v *Hickman* [1907] 1 Ch 550). However, conveyances under the Railways Clauses Consolidation Act 1845, s 77, do not pass the mines and minerals unless expressly included, and they therefore remain vested in the grantor who may well be the adjoining owner. This section is taken to apply to Land Registry transfers where appropriate.

The boundary of a railway will usually be such as to include the boundary fence with the railway, by reason of the fencing obligations imposed on railway companies by the Railways Clauses Consolidation Act 1845, s 68. These obligations may not, however, apply: see p 56.

(m) Rights of way

Where a private right of way forms a boundary, the same presumption arises as for highways, ie, the centre line of the path or roadway is the boundary (*Lang* v *House* (1961) 178 EG 801). But in this case the land up to the half-way line remains vested in the adjoining owners (subject only to the rights of way), and will not be excluded from a registered title.

(n) Rivers

In the case of non-tidal rivers, the boundary of the riparian lands is presumed to be in the centre of the stream.

. . . Where land adjoining . . . [an] inland river is granted, the prima facie presumption is, that the parties intended to include in the grant a moiety . . . of the river bed . . .; and that such general presumption ought to prevail, unless there is something to indicate a contrary intention (*Dwyer* v *Rich* (1871) Ir Rep 6 Ch 144, 149).

This applies not only on the conveyance of freehold land bounded by a river, but also on the grant of a lease of such land (*Tilbury* v *Silva* (1890) 45 Ch D 98, 109 per Kay J). The same rule applies to the limits of riparian owners' fishing rights in Scotland (*Fothringham* v *Kerr* (1984) 48 P & CR 173). The presumption is not displaced by the fact that the grantor owns both banks of the river nor by facts which only came to light later which, had they been known, might have induced him to reserve the river bed (*Mickelthwait* v *Newlay Bridge Co* (1886) 23 Ch D 133).

If there are gradual, imperceptible accretions to either bank in the ordinary course of nature, the additional land belongs to that riparian owner and the boundary in the centre of the stream is automatically adjusted, even though the original boundary may still be ascertainable (*Foster* v *Wright* (1878) 4 CPD 438). If, however, the river suddenly completely changes its course, the boundary remains where it was immediately before the diversion (*Ford* v *Lacy* (1861) 7 H & N 151). Where there is evidence that the river and its bed belong to some person other than the riparian owners, so rebutting the presumption, the boundary is the water line when the river is in its natural state, disregarding seasonal fluctuations. Evidence of independent ownership would be either normal conveyancing evidence of title, long possession as of right, or acts of ownership (*Jones* v *Williams* (1837) 2 M & W 326).

The soil of the bed of a river where it is tidal prima facie belongs to the Crown (being managed by the Crown Estate Commissioners (Coast Protection Act 1949), except in the cases of the rivers Thames and Tees), and continues to do so although the river may gradually change course (*Carlisle Corporation* v *Graham* (1869) LR 4 Ex 361). The boundary on each side is medium high water. Accordingly, the fishing on such stretches of river does not pass with the riparian lands, as it normally does on non-tidal waters.

(o) Roads

See (g) *Highways*, above.

(p) Rooms

Where a room is demised without any precise definition of its boundaries, the position varies according to whether its walls constitute outside walls of the building, or partition walls. The whole of any outside wall is included, but only an undefined part of a partition wall passes with the room (*Phelps* v *City of London Corporation* [1916] 2 Ch 255, 263).

(q) Seashore

The technical name for the seashore is 'foreshore', but in an appropriate context, where this is meant, these words are synonymous (*Mellor* v *Walmesley* [1905] 2 Ch 164). The boundary between the seashore and the adjoining land is presumed to be the line of medium high tide between the ordinary spring and neap tides (ibid). The lower boundary of the seashore is the medium low water mark. In Scotland, the rule is that the boundary lies at the high water mark of the ordinary spring tides (*Musselburgh Real Estate Co Ltd* v *Musselburgh Provost* [1905] AC 491).

A conveyance of land described as bounded by the seashore, but containing measurements making it clear that there is a strip of land between that conveyed and the seashore, estops the grantor denying the grantee access to the seashore over that strip, but does not convey the strip (*Mellor* v *Walmesley*, supra). If the medium high tide line moves, the boundary of land described as bounded by the seashore moves with it. This is a moveable freehold (*Scratton* v *Brown* (1825) 4 B & C 485; *Smart & Co* v *Suva Town Board* [1893] AC 301). This is the effect of imperceptible accretions to the shore, which add to the land in private ownership, or of gradual erosion which returns land to the ownership of the Crown (*Re Hull and Selby Railway* (1839) 5 M & W 139). The common law treats the land as if it had always, since the limit of legal memory, been as it now is (*Mercer* v *Denne* [1905] 2 Ch 538).

Whether land conveyed is in fact bounded by a moveable line, or whether the boundary is fixed in the place to which the tide came when the deed was executed, is a question of construction of the document (*Baxendale* v *Instow Parish Council* [1982] Ch 14). The fact that there are physical markers showing the boundary line in its original position does not necessarily prevent the boundary being altered by natural forces (*Attorney-General* v *M'Carthy* [1911] 2 IR 260).

Land reclaimed by the owner of land bounded by the sea does

not belong to him, but to the Crown (*Attorney-General of Southern Nigeria* v *John Holt and Company (Liverpool) Ltd* [1915] AC 599).

(r) *Waste land*

Where a fenced close adjoins waste land, there is a presumption that the fence belongs to the owner of the close (*White* v *Taylor* (*No 2*) [1960] 1 Ch 160).

3 Other evidence of boundaries

Other forms of evidence of the position of boundaries may be available. These are discussed in Chapter 3 in relation to boundary disputes, where their admissibility in accordance with the strict rules of evidence is considered.

4 Horizontal boundaries

(a) *Minerals*

Although mines and minerals are readily severable from the surface of the land, there is normally no definition of the boundary between them and the surface. It would appear that the owner of the minerals can work any substance which comes within the definition of minerals and to which he is entitled (not, eg, coal), so long as it is below the surface. It may be noted that certain conveyances (including Land Registry transfers) exclude mines and minerals unless they are expressly included (under the Railways Clauses Consolidation Act 1845, s 77, and the Waterworks Clauses Act 1847, s 18).

(b) *Highways*

The rights of the public to use a highway extend only to the surface of it. '"Street" . . . includes the surface and so much of the depth as may be not unfairly used, as streets are used' (*Coverdale* v *Charlton* (1878) 4 QBD 104, 121, per Brett LJ). This defines the extent of the property of which the highway authority can make use. It does not permit the use for other amenities, such as underground public conveniences, even though constructed by the highway authority (*Tunbridge Wells Corporation* v *Baird* [1896] AC 434). Statute may, however, confer rights on the highway or other authorities to construct under highways these and other amenities (eg, car parks) which the common law would not permit. The highway authority has a legal estate in so much of the surface land as is vested in it for highway purposes. This is a determinable fee simple, lasting only while the use as a highway continues (*Tithe Redemption Commission* v *Runcorn Urban District Council* [1954] Ch 383).

(c) Streams

Although running water is not capable of being owned, a stream may be vested in a different person from its bed. A stream may, eg, be a public sewer, and so vested in the water authority (Public Health Act 1936, s 20), while the bed remains the property of the riparian owners. The boundary between the bed and the stream above it is not subject to any legal presumption, but must be the place at which the liquid of the stream physically meets the solid substance of the bed.

(d) Basements

Basements of premises adjoining streets built extending under the street can extend up to the horizontal boundary between the highway and the subsoil ascertained as above. Where the basement has existed for some time this will be excellent evidence of the lowest possible limit of the surface in cases where the highway authority later wishes to extend its occupation downwards. Although roads adopted by the local authority are excluded from registered titles, basements under them will be included in the registration if the position is made clear to the Land Registry. Where they have not been so included, they are taken to pass on dispositions of the registered land under the Land Registration Rules 1925, r 251, which passes all rights, etc, enjoyed with the land.

(e) Flats and maisonettes

There are no settled presumptions determining the horizontal boundary of a flat (or maisonette) from the one above or below it. However, 'it is the general expectation of anyone who takes the lease of a flat that he acquires the space between the floor of his flat and the underneath of the floor of the flat above' (*Graystone Property Investments Ltd* v *Margulies* (1983) 47 P & CR 472, 474, per Griffiths LJ).

The Court of Appeal has accepted that the upper boundary is not lower than the underside of the floor joists to which the ceiling is fixed, but it left undecided the question whether in fact the flat extends upwards to half-way through the joists, or even to the upperside of them (*Sturge* v *Hackett* [1962] 1 WLR 1257, 1266). In particular circumstances, a flat included a void created by false suspended ceilings which were lower than the original ceilings (*Graystone Property Investments Ltd* v *Margulies*, supra). The demise of a top floor flat may, but does not necessarily, include the roof above it.

Whether it does is a matter of construction of the document (*Cockburn* v *Smith* [1924] 2 KB 119).

Where the lower boundary is not defined at least some part of the floor is included (*Phelps* v *City of London Corporation* [1916] 2 Ch 255, 264).

The divisions are sometimes referred to as 'party floors' or 'party ceilings'. In the case of party walls there is a presumption in the absence of contrary evidence that the boundary runs down the middle, but it is doubtful whether this applies to floors and ceilings. The provisions of the Law of Property Act 1925, s 38, relating to party walls certainly do not apply, as they do not envisage hollow structures which most floors and ceilings are, and they also only deal with a vertical division. Some of the special legislation relating to inner London does apply to floor partitions, but only in cases of parts of buildings approached by separate staircases or separate entrances from outside. This would normally exclude flats, but some maisonettes are included.

5 Registered land

(a) General boundaries

In the absence of special notes on the register, dealt with below under the heading (*b*) *Fixed boundaries*, the boundaries on the Land Registry general map and filed plans of particular titles indicate only general boundaries (Land Registration Rules 1925, r 278). That is to say, although it may be clear that some physical feature is followed—say a wall or a ditch—the exact position of the line on the plan does not indicate who owns the feature, or whether the boundary actually runs down one of the sides or down the middle of it. As the Land Registry maps and plans often consist of or are based on Ordnance Survey maps, the boundary lines will normally be drawn down the middle of the physical features in accordance with the Ordnance Survey practice. A broken line is often used on the Registry plans to indicate a boundary where no physical feature yet exists, as where a fence is still to be erected. Nevertheless, Land Registry plans are as precise as possible and no great variation from the boundary shown comes within the rule. *Lee* v *Barrey* [1957] Ch 251, where the Court of Appeal held that a divergence of ten feet was within the general boundaries rule, is considered exceptional. That particular filed plan bore an endorsement that it was subject to revision after the erection of fences, implying that it gave no more than a general indication of the boundaries.

Without being technically fixed boundaries, certain boundary features may be recorded on the register as either included in or excluded from the title. These precise indications are effective, but leave the general rule unaffected as far as the rest of the boundaries are concerned.

The filed plan may show 'T' marks in two circumstances. First, when they are referred to in restrictive covenants, or in positive covenants imposed with restrictive ones and reproduced on the register with them. Secondly, in cases where they appeared on a plan referred to in a pre-registration deed, but without any explanation in the deed of their significance, and the applicant for first registration specifically requests their inclusion. In the latter case, the fact that the marks were not referred to in the deed will be recorded on the register. Before 1962 such 'T' marks were not reproduced on filed plans.

(b) Fixed boundaries

Only where there is a note in the property register that the boundaries have been fixed, and also on the filed plan or general map, will the boundaries be precise and fixed: Land Registration Rules 1925, r 277. The obvious advantages are that those boundaries can be relied upon, and are guaranteed so that even the slightest adjustment by rectification could be the basis of an indemnity claim under the Land Registration Act 1925, s 83 (except in certain cases of acquisition by adverse possession). Application for registration with fixed boundaries must be made specifically to the Chief Land Registrar (there is no prescribed form), and may apply to part only of the boundary of a plot of land. Upon receipt of the application the Chief Land Registrar must give notice of the intention to ascertain and fix the boundaries, with a plan or description of the land, to the owners and occupiers of the adjoining lands (Land Registration Rules 1925, r 276). They will also require to be deduced to them the freehold and leasehold titles of the owners of all adjoining lands to which the title is not registered. A comprehensive and very accurate survey will then be undertaken. Disputes or questions of doubt may be resolved by hearings before the Chief Land Registrar, with a right of appeal to the High Court. An application for fixing boundaries can be extremely and disproportionately expensive, and the applicant can and will be called upon to pay all costs involved in serving notices, examining titles and surveying. There is no limit on this liability, even in areas of compulsory registration, and an advance payment on account is normally required. Probably for this reason, and because fixed boundaries do not often offer practical advantages, applications to have boundaries fixed are extremely rare.

6 Commons

The registration of common land and town and village greens under the Commons Registration Act 1965 involved a determination of their boundaries, and consequently the boundaries of the adjoining private properties. Registrations are by reference to plans, and the documents are open to public inspection. The register is conclusive evidence of the matters registered, as at the date of registration (s 10). This includes the extent of the land. The boundary of land to be registered as waste land of a manor does not alter, when bounded by the sea, when gradual imperceptible accretions change the shore line (*Baxendale* v *Instow Parish Council* [1982] Ch 14).

See the presumption as to the boundary of waste land (p 14).

7 Variation of boundaries

(a) *By agreement*

Adjoining landowners may fix or alter their boundaries by agreement. An agreement varying boundaries amounts to an assurance of the land involved. A deed is therefore necessary (Law of Property Act 1925, s 52), and if the title is registered the prescribed form of Land Registry transfer must be used. The only restrictions on the power of a landowner to agree to alter his boundaries are those general restrictions on any disposition of land imposed on certain bodies, or persons under a disability.

If, however, the boundary was previously in doubt, and the agreement is a genuine attempt to state what is thought always to have been the position, neither a deed, nor even writing, is necessary because no land changes hands. For the same reason the agreement is not registrable as an estate contract under the Land Charges Act 1972, unless it intends to vary a boundary (*Neilson* v *Poole* (1969) 20 P & CR 909). The settlement is sufficient mutual consideration to make the agreement enforceable (*Penn* v *Lord Baltimore* (1750) 1 Ves Sen 444). Clearly, however, a deed accurately recording the settled boundaries for the future is more satisfactory.

(b) *Limitation Act*

An encroachment upon neighbouring land which lasts for twelve years and which fulfils the requirements of the Limitation Act for adverse possession inconsistent with the owner's title, completely extinguishes the former owner's right to the land (unless the title is registered) (Limitation Act 1980, s 15(1)). That varies the boundary (*Williams Bros Direct Supply Ltd* v *Raftery* [1958] QB 159). This applies even if the owner's right to recover possession is subject to statutory restriction (eg, under the Rent Act): *Moses* v *Lovegrove* [1952] 2 QB 533. Acquisition by prescription can vary the presumptions to which reference may be made when determining boundaries (eg, where there is a hedge and a ditch) (*Marshall* v *Taylor* [1895] 1 Ch 641). But if the acts of purported ownership are not sufficient to establish adverse possession, a fence can lawfully be re-erected along the original boundary (*Dear* v *Woods* (1984) 9 CSW 728).

The Limitation Act extends the twelve year period in certain cases (Sched 1, Pt 2). The Crown or a spiritual or eleemosynary corporation sole has thirty years to bring an action. This is extended to sixty years for an action by the Crown to recover foreshore.

Where the title to the land concerned is registered, the former owner remains registered proprietor, holding in trust for the squatter: Land Registration Act 1925, s 75. Upon application, the register will be rectified to show the squatter as proprietor, and the plans will be varied as necessary. Until this is done the boundaries of the registered properties remain unaltered. A purchaser of registered land should accordingly inspect the property in the usual way before contracting: he cannot assume that all the land included in a registered title is occupied, or even beneficially owned, by the registered proprietor.

(c) Estoppel

A landowner may be estopped by an act of his or his predecessor's in title from taking action in respect of an encroachment upon his boundaries, which has the practical effect of varying them, at any rate as between those parties and persons deriving title under them. So where a company which owned one of two adjacent plots agreed with the owner of the other to build a house and garage on it in such a position that the garage encroached upon the company's plot by between two and three feet, the company's successor in title could not maintain an action for trespass against a subsequent owner of the garage (*Hopgood* v *Brown* [1955] 1 WLR 213).

(d) Rectification

Where the parties to a binding agreement purport to carry it into effect by a document which is not in accordance with the agreement, that document can be rectified. This principle can apply to vary boundaries of land defined by a conveyance, if they do not accord with what the parties agreed in their prior contract (*Craddock Brothers Ltd* v *Hunt* [1923] 2 Ch 136).

(e) Inclosure Acts

The inclosure of commons, which necessarily involves the definition of new boundaries, is not a subject that can be dealt with here. It must be mentioned, nevertheless, that a valuer appointed under the Inclosure Act 1845 has power, with the consent of adjoining owners, to straighten fences or define new boundaries of the lands to be inclosed or regulated, and to give directions for the fencing of the new boundary: s 45. This procedure is, however, virtually obsolete because it is extremely elaborate, including calling local meetings and promoting a private Act of Parliament. Other provisions in the many statutes governing inclosure can affect boundaries. They are administered by the Department of the Environment, who may be able to give help.

(f) Registered land

The boundaries of land to which title is registered can be varied only if the alteration is shown on the register, and this can be done only by the Chief Land Registrar under his powers of rectification (in default of a normal transfer). This power is conferred by the Land Registration Act 1925, s 82, to give effect to orders of the court, to alter entries obtained by fraud, to give effect to an agreement of all interested parties and to correct any error or omission. As has been noted, there is also power to give effect to an acquisition by adverse possession under the Limitation Act 1980. Cases of dispute will be dealt with in Chapter 3. Where all parties are in agreement, rectification of the register may well prove to be more simple than drawing the necessary deeds for an unregistered title, where the mapping is generally less accurate. Cases of errors in boundaries on the part of the Registry will give rise to claims for indemnity, unless they are so slight as to come within the general boundaries rule where that applies. This rule is not thought to permit any substantial variation from the line shown, although there is no definite scale that can be applied and presumably the latitude allowed would vary according to the circumstances of the case (eg, greater variation could be expected on open moorland than in a built-up city). Where the Ordnance Survey map of the area is revised, the Land Registry maps based on it will normally be revised too, and a claim might also arise unless it was a case of showing more accurately the facts which always existed.

(g) Natural forces

The gradual effects of wind and tide can alter the position of a boundary which is defined by reference to a physical feature such as a river bank or seashore. This does not apply where a single unusually violent natural phenomenon drastically and suddenly alters the position of a river bed (*Ford* v *Lacey* (1861) 7 H & N 151), but merely to imperceptible accretions. Those accretions can, however, be large enough to provide an easily measurable difference over, say, a year (*R* v *Lord Yarborough* (1824) 3 B & C 668).

The change in the position of the boundary applies equally to accretions and to erosion. Accretions to land bounded by the sea belong to the owner of that land (*Government of the State of Penang* v *Beng Hong Oon* [1972] AC 425), and erosion returns the land to Crown ownership (*Re Hull and Selby Railway* (1839) 5 M & W 139). The action of wind in blowing sand has been treated in the same way as alluvial accretions (*Southern Centre of Theosophy Inc* v *State of South Australia* [1982] AC 706).

Chapter 2

Sale of Land

1 Searches and enquiries

It is customary for prospective purchasers to make preliminary enquiries of the vendor as to the ownership of boundary features, and as to disputes which will include boundary disputes. Failure to disclose a dispute in reply to a preliminary enquiry can be a misrepresentation justifying the subsequent rescission of the contract (*Walker* v *Boyle* [1982] 1 WLR 495). Conveyancing contracts normally seek to restrict the purchaser's right to rescind on the ground of misrepresentation (eg, National Conditions of Sale, 20th ed, cond 17(1); Law Society's General Conditions of Sale, 1984 rvsn, cond 7). How far such a condition is effective depends on the circumstances of each case. It must satisfy the test of reasonableness, ie, the term must be a fair and reasonable one to be included having regard to the circumstances which were, or ought reasonably to have been, known to or in the contemplation of the parties when the contract was made (Misrepresentation Act 1967, s 3; Unfair Contract Terms Act 1977, ss 8(1), 11(1)).

Other pre-contract searches that can be important in relation to boundary features are:

(*a*) Ownership of fences adjoining a railway line: pp 56–7;

(*b*) Whether the local planning authority has made a direction under art 4 of the Town and Country Planning General Development Order 1977, restricting the general permission given for the erection of fences etc (pp 60–1). One of the standard enquiries of local authorities to accompany local land charge searches refers to this, but it should be noted that it relates only to directions made by the council. In appropriate circumstances, a direction can be made by a joint planning board, an urban development corporation or an enterprise zone authority.

2 Title

(a) *Proof of extent of property*

A purchaser has a right to a marketable title to the property sold by the contract, subject to any contrary terms in the contract. That involves establishing first the extent of what the vendor contracts to sell, and secondly the boundaries of the land to which he deduces title. A contract normally defines the land sold in the particulars, and may refer to a plan. Even a plan which is not referred to in the contract may be used to determine what is sold, if it is handed to the purchaser with that intention (*Re Lindsay and Forder's Contract* (1895) 72 LT 832).

The courts are loath to deprive the purchaser of his right to insist that the property to which title is offered is the same in extent as that which the vendor contracted to sell. Contractual conditions which could prejudice that right are narrowly construed. In one case where the descriptions of the property in the various title deeds differed, and none was the same as the contract description, there was a condition of sale, 'that no further evidence of the identity of the parcels shall be required, than what is afforded by the abstract, or the deeds, instruments, or other documents therein abstracted'. Although the purchaser could call for no further evidence, because of the effect of that condition, the vendor had not fulfilled his obligation to identify what he was selling and so could not oblige the purchaser to complete (*Flower* v *Hartopp* (1843) 6 Beav 476). In another case, the contract provided that 'the purchaser is not to require any further proof of identity than is furnished in the title deeds themselves', but the deeds did not identify the property. Again, the purchaser could not require further evidence, but the vendor could not oblige him to buy (*Curling* v *Austin* (1862) 2 Dr & Sm 129).

Condition 13(1) of the National Conditions of Sale, 20th ed, reads:

The purchaser shall admit the identity of the property with that comprised in the muniments offered by the vendor as the title thereto upon the evidence afforded by the descriptions contained in such muniments, and of a statutory declaration, to be made (if required) at the purchaser's expense, that the property has been enjoyed according to the title for at least twelve years.

This condition, appearing verbatim in the 17th ed, was considered in *Re Bramwell's Contract, Bramwell* v *Ballards Securities Investments Ltd* [1969] 1 WLR 1659. The contract description of the property sold and the parcels in the root of title could only be reconciled as a matter of probability. As the deeds did not contain what could properly be called a description of the property for the purpose of the condition, it did not have any effect.

The Law Society's General Conditions of Sale, 1984 rvsn, provide that the vendor shall produce such evidence as may reasonably be necessary to establish the identity and extent of the property. In default, if the purchaser reasonably requires, the vendor must at his own expense provide a statutory declaration in an agreed form (cond 13).

(b) Ownership of boundary features

Whether or not the vendor owns the fences, etc, surrounding the property sold will only have a very small effect on the extent of the property sold, although disputes about ownership of and the responsibility to maintain boundary features can lead to considerable acrimony. Both the National Conditions of Sale, 20th ed, cond 13(2), and the Law Society's General Conditions of Sale, 1984 rvsn, cond 13(1), absolve the vendor from any obligation to prove ownership of fences, ditches and walls.

(c) Deducing title

A plan referred to in an abstracted deed is an integral part of the deed and the vendor must supply a copy of it at his own expense (*Llewellyn* v *Earl of Jersey* (1843) 11 M & W 183). This is subject to the qualification that the plan must be necessary for properly identifying the property or correctly interpreting the deed. The Council of the Law Society decided that a purchaser at auction of 20 acres of land, which the vendor had purchased as part of an estate of 275 acres, was only entitled to a copy of that part of the original conveyance plan which related to the land he had bought (*Law Society's Digest*, vol 1, Opn 84, 1900).

The extent of registered land is briefly defined on the register, with a reference to the filed plan. Both the verbal description and the plan are therefore needed to determine the boundaries of the property (subject always to the general boundaries rule: p 16). A purchaser is always entitled to require the vendor to furnish a copy of the subsisting entries on the register and of the filed plan, whatever the contract says (Land Registration Act 1925, s 110(1)). Unless the contract otherwise provides, the purchaser pays for the copies when the purchase price exceeds £1,000. The Council of the Law Society recommends, as a matter of good conveyancing practice, that the copies supplied should be office copies rather than plain copies (*Law Society's Digest*, vol 1, 4th cum supp, Opn 316(i), 1968). The Law Society's General Conditions of Sale, 1984 rvsn, place a duty on the vendor to supply office copies (cond 12(*b*)(i)).

(d) Not enough land

When the examination of title discloses that the vendor is not in a position to sell all the land which he has contracted to, the purchaser's remedies will depend on the terms of the contract. Under an open contract, or in the absence of express conditions of sale referring to the matter, the purchaser is entitled to rescind if the extent of the property differs substantially from that contracted to be sold. Where the boundary is only slightly different, the purchaser's only remedy is compensation. This must be claimed before completion, otherwise he is taken to have waived his rights.

A deficiency in area of 40 per cent justifies rescission (*Watson* v *Burton* [1957] 1 WLR 19). Where a property was described as including a wall and tradesman's entrance, but actually excluded the wall and gave no indefeasible right to use the entrance, the right also arose (*Brewer* v *Brown* (1884) 28 Ch D 309). Even though the purchaser is entitled to rescind, he may nevertheless insist on taking a conveyance at a reduced price, the compensation being assessed at a fair figure, not a penal one.

The National Conditions of Sale, 20th ed, cond 17, and the Law Society's General Conditions of Sale, 1984 rvsn, cond 7, both contain provisions with the object of eliminating claims for compensation where discrepancies are immaterial, and restricting the purchasers' rights to compensation rather than rescission in more substantial cases. Whether the right to rescind is successfully excluded in any particular case depends on whether the condition satisfies the test of reasonableness (Misrepresentation Act 1967, s 3; Unfair Contract Terms Act 1977, ss 8(1), 11(1)).

3 Conveyance

(a) Unregistered land

The purchaser is entitled to have the land conveyed to him by a modern description. This need not be the description by which it was conveyed to the vendor (*Re Sansom and Narbeth's Contract* [1910] 1 Ch 741), nor need it be identical to the contract description. The purchaser can insist on the inclusion of measurements, even when there was none in the contract description of the property, if this will avoid litigation which would be likely without them (*Monighetti* v *Wandsworth Borough Council* (1908) 73 JP 91).

On the other hand, the purchaser can require that the contract description is repeated in the conveyance, if the alternative would be to exclude part of the land he contracted to buy (*Lloyd* v *Stanbury* [1971] 1 WLR 535).

A purchaser can generally insist on the conveyance referring to a plan if the verbal description is not adequate. When the words give a sufficient and satisfactory identification of the land sold, fixing all its boundaries, no plan is necessary (*Re Sharman's Contract* [1936] 1 Ch 755). A whole island off the coast was satisfactorily described by naming it and referring to two other islands by name, and without referring to a plan showing an outline and measurements (*Collector of Land Revenue, Singapore* v *Hoalim* [1978] AC 525).

If the verbal description is not adequate, the purchaser is entitled to a plan. That plan must be to an adequate scale (*Scarfe* v *Adams* [1981] 1 All ER 843). For a house, a scale of 1:1250 will generally suffice (*R* v *Secretary of State for the Environment exp Norwich City Council* [1982] QB 808). The only exceptions are where a plan would be particularly complicated and might itself induce litigation. The duty to provide a plan applies even if the contract did not refer to one. Even though the contract plan was stated to be for reference only and without any guarantee of accuracy, the purchaser can insist on its being used without those qualifications, if the plan is required to complete a satisfactory definition of the property conveyed (*Re Sparrow and James' Contract* [1910] 2 Ch 60).

(b) Registered land

Although the same principles apply to describing the land comprised in a registered transfer as apply in the case of a conveyance of unregistered land, problems are necessarily much rarer. When the whole of the land registered under a particular title is transferred, a reference to that registration is all that is needed. In the rare case in which part of the land has passed to a third party who has acquired a squatter's title, or the title to extra land has been acquired, the purchaser would be entitled to have the property transferred by reference to a modern description, with a revised plan if necessary.

On the transfer of part of the land comprised in a title, the rules require a reference to a plan, unless the extent of the land can be clearly defined by a verbal reference to the filed plan or the general map (Land Registration Rules 1925, r 79). A transfer plan must be signed by the vendor and by or on behalf of the purchaser. The same thing applies to a transfer of mines and minerals separately from the surface of the land, or one of the surface without the mines and minerals, and to a transfer, grant or lease of an easement defining the dominant or servient tenement (r 113).

Chapter 3

Boundary Disputes

1 Types of action

In default of agreement to submit them to arbitration, boundary disputes can be brought before the courts for determination in a number of ways. If the position of the boundary is the only question in issue a declaration may be sought.

An action for a declaration may be brought in the High Court under RSC, Ord 15, r 16, without asking for any other relief. This jurisdiction is discretionary. There must be nothing to disentitle the plaintiff to relief, and the defendant must previously have asserted some right or formulated some specific claim. The court will not usually entertain an action where the subject matter is under £10 in value (*Westbury-on-Severn Rural Sanitary Authority* v *Meredith* (1885) 30 Ch D 387). Where the question in issue is the interpretation of a deed, will or other document, which may well be the case in a boundary dispute, any person interested may apply for a declaration of the rights of all the persons interested by originating summons under RSC, Ord 15, r 13. The application in boundary disputes, as matters of title, will be to the Chancery Division using the 'inter partes' form of originating summons: see RSC, Ord 7, r 2.

The county court has the same jurisdiction as the High Court to make declarations relating to land, where the rateable value of the land does not exceed £1,000 (County Courts Act 1984, s 22). The particulars of claim must contain a statement of the land in question and its rateable value, or if it has no separate value, the rateable value of the hereditament of which it forms part or if none its yearly value (CCR, Ord 6, rr 3, 4).

An application for a declaration is usually linked with some other form of action, even in the High Court. The appropriate form where one party alleges infringement of his boundary and occupation of part of his land by the other is trespass. It is nuisance where the infringement consists of allowing such things as tree roots to spread past his boundary. The exact position of a boundary may be

27

important in other actions too, for example under the rule in *Rylands* v *Fletcher* (1868) LR 3 HL 330, straying animals, contract and recovery of road charges.

An action for damages may be appropriate, where the violation of a boundary has deprived the plaintiff of the use of some of his land. Particulars of special damage must be given (*Ilkiw* v *Samuels* [1963] 1 WLR 991). A claim for damages can be small provided it is genuine (*Hatt & Co (Bath) Ltd* v *Pearce* [1978] 1 WLR 885).

Boundary disputes may, by an agreement made either at the time of the difference or before, be referred to arbitration, when the Arbitration Acts will apply.

Registered land

Where the title to land of which the boundary is in dispute is registered, application may be made by one party to the Chief Land Registrar for rectification of the register. In default of agreement, rectification may be ordered in cases of fraud, error or mistake (Land Registration Act 1925, s 82). This would cover, for instance, misinterpretation of deeds when the title was investigated for first registration. Where, however, a strip of land is, by a mistake, conveyed twice and the second purchaser registered as proprietor of it, justice may prevent rectification to adjust the boundary once the registered land has changed hands again (*Epps* v *Esso Petroleum Co Ltd* [1973] 1 WLR 1071).

The application is made in writing: there is no prescribed form. There is a hearing before the Chief Land Registrar if the matter is not settled. Appeal against the order of the Chief Land Registrar is by notice of motion to the Chancery Division under RSC, Ord 93, r 10, and is heard by a single judge whose decision is final unless leave to appeal is granted either by him or the Court of Appeal. Notice of any appeal should be given to the Chief Land Registrar as soon as possible, so that a notice of it may be entered on the register to warn purchasers.

This form of proceedings is not, however, completely satisfactory for settling disputes as it may not provide a final determination of the issues between the parties. For instance, it seems that the Chief Land Registrar (and the court on appeal from him) may construe a title deed to decide its effect upon the entries on the register, but it will still be open to the court to construe the same deed in a different sense in subsequent proceedings between the same parties where more evidence is available (*Re Dances Way, West Town, Hayling Island* [1962] Ch 490). Disputes affecting registered land may be brought before the courts in the usual way and, should the boundary be found to be different from that shown on the register, the court may order the Land Registry to effect the necessary rectification.

2 Evidence of the position of boundaries

The primary evidence available in boundary disputes is the title deeds to the properties. Extrinsic evidence is not available to vary a clear description given in a deed, but it may be called to lay before the court the information that the parties had at the time of the execution of the deed. It is also admissible in cases of ambiguity, even if only latent, ie, only apparent when the deed is read by a person with knowledge of the facts. Evidence can be called to show the boundaries of the land as used prior to the grant, to prove what was meant to have been conveyed.

Evidence of reputation is only admissible where matters of general or public interest are concerned (*Evans* v *Merthyr Tydfil Urban Council* [1890] 1 Ch 241; *Mercer* v *Denne* [1905] 2 Ch 538). This would include boundaries of towns and parishes, and would only be of use in private boundary disputes where the extent of the land is defined by reference to such public boundaries. When admissible, such evidence may be oral or documentary. It may also consist of the verdict of a jury in a previous action between different parties (*Evans* v *Rees* (1839) 10 Ad & El 151).

(a) Civil Evidence Act 1968

Under this Act, a statement in a document may be admitted as evidence of the fact stated if certain conditions are satisfied (s 4 (1)). These are: (i) the fact must be one of which direct oral evidence would be admissible; (ii) the document must be, or be part of, a record compiled by a person acting under a duty; and (iii) it must have been compiled from information supplied by a person having, or who might reasonably be supposed to have, personal knowledge of the matters dealt with. If the information was not supplied directly, each intermediary must have been acting under a duty. This provision has been applied to admit a tithe apportionment survey in evidence (*Knight* v *David* [1971] 1 WLR 1671). A copy of the document rather than the original may be admitted in evidence if authenticated in a manner approved by the court (s 6(1)).

This enactment may well overlap with the older provisions relating to the admissibility of evidence dealt with below.

(b) Public documents

The contents of public documents may generally be proved as evidence of the facts in them. Examples of such documents that have been received in evidence to prove boundaries include Domesday Book (being a record of a public survey) (*Alcock* v *Cooke* (1829) 5 Bing 340;

Duke of Beaufort v *John Aird & Co (1904)* 20 TLR 602); a survey made under a statutory duty, eg, a tithe map and tithe apportionment survey (*Knight* v *David* [1971] 1 WLR 1671); an ancient survey of Crown lands (*Doe d William IV* v *Roberts* (1844) 13 M & W 520); and a map drawn by authority of a royal commission (*New Romney Corporation* v *New Romney Sewers Commissioners* [1892] 1 QB 840). The survey must normally have been made with the intention that it should be available for public inspection, and the person undertaking it must be a public officer with a quasi-judicial duty to inquire into the matters recorded. It should be produced from proper custody.

Surveys not intended for public inspection, or made under private auspices, are not available as public documents. This includes Crown surveys made for private or temporary purposes such as a survey by the Augmentation Office for the Crown as a private owner (*Phillips* v *Hudson* (1867) 2 Ch App 243), and a seventeenth-century survey of coastal castles to consider whether repairs were necessary (*Mercer* v *Denne* [1905] 2 Ch 538). Such documents may, however, be admissible on other grounds: see (*h*) *Declarations of deceased persons*, below.

(c) Ancient documents

Ancient documents produced from proper custody which on the face of them deal with questions of ownership may be admitted in evidence to prove boundaries. Examples are leases, or documents showing that a person in occupation successfully protected his right to possession. There is a presumption relating to such documents produced from proper custody which are over twenty years old, in favour of their validity: erasures and interlineations are presumed to have been made before execution. This includes documents in the keeping of a person to whom they came in the natural course.

(d) Title deeds

The title deeds of the properties divided by a disputed boundary will be most important as evidence, and in an action a party is entitled to discovery of deeds in the other party's possession which either contain evidence of the joint title, or tend to substantiate the case of the party seeking discovery. A party may resist discovery in boundary cases only if the deeds relate exclusively to the case of the party resisting or are immaterial (which is unlikely in this type of case). Even then, a person who has been responsible for confusing the boundaries cannot resist discovery. In disputes between landlord and tenant, when the tenant has confused his own land with that demised to him, the tenant must produce his own title deeds to the landlord. A third party called as a witness is entitled to refuse to produce his title deeds, unless he or his predecessor in title has given an acknowledgment for production to the party calling him, or his predecessor in title. A solicitor holding deeds for a client who is not a party to the action cannot be compelled to produce them, even by subpoena, if the client objects.

(*e*) *Ecclesiastical terriers*

An ecclesiastical terrier is a schedule of the temporal possessions of a parish church. They are made from time to time. If produced from proper custody, they are admissible in evidence, and may be of use in proving the boundaries of glebe or adjoining lands. Proper custody would be the diocesan record office, the bishop's or the archdeacon's registry or the chest of the parish church.

(*f*) *Ordnance Survey*

Authority to carry out a complete survey of Britain and publish maps was first conferred by the Ordnance Survey Act 1841. The powers are now exercised by the Minister of Agriculture, Fisheries and Food. Section 12 of the Act expressly provided that the powers conferred did not extend to ascertaining or altering private boundaries, and that private titles should remain unaffected. As such, the Ordnance Survey is not therefore of evidential value. It may, however, be adopted in private deeds, and often is, in which case it is deemed to be incorporated in them and must be referred to. Superseded editions of the Survey are not generally available for purchase. Some are kept in county record offices. All are available in the Map Room of the British Library, and copies may be obtained, subject to receiving the authority of the Director-General of the Ordnance Survey, Romsey Road, Southampton SO9 4DH, and paying a fee, where the copyright has not expired. The Library will inform practitioners when authority is required.

The Ordnance Survey will prepare, for production in court, an authoritative statement on questions arising from an ordnance map. They will also nominate an expert witness to give evidence about Ordnance Survey mapping practices. A charge is made, which varies according to the time spent and expenses incurred. It is likely to exceed £50.

(*g*) *Other maps*

Private boundaries may not be proved by maps attached to inclosure awards, which, although they may prove a road to be a highway, do not conclusively delineate its boundaries.

A map drawn, accepted or acted upon by a party to the proceedings or his predecessor in title, might be available as an admission of the facts shown, though not admissible as a public document. General maps and atlases may be adduced as evidence of facts within public knowledge.

It is unlikely that Land Registry plans would be used in evidence (except where the entries on them are directly in issue) because the boundaries shown are not normally precise. Filed plans are only available for inspection by registered proprietors, persons authorised by them, or under an order of the court (Land Registration Act 1925, s 112). If it is desired to produce any plan filed in the Registry, an office copy is admissible to the same extent as the original (ibid, s 113).

(*h*) *Declarations of deceased persons*

In three cases relevant to boundary disputes the declarations of persons since deceased may be admitted in evidence: when against his pecuniary or proprietary interests; when made in the course of duty (*Price* v *Earl of Torrington* (1703) 1 Salk 285); and when as to public rights. In the first case the declaration must have been against the declarer's interests at that time, and have been so to his knowledge. To be admissible as made in the course of duty, the statement must concern his normal business, and be made in its normal course at or about the time to which it relates. This includes not only statements of a man holding permanent office, but also a professional man (eg, a surveyor) employed on an ad hoc basis for the particular job concerned (*Mellor* v *Walmesley* [1905] 2 Ch 164). It is necessary for it to be apparent from the document that it was recorded as personal knowledge (not hearsay) and contemporaneously (*Mercer* v *Denne* [1905] 2 Ch 538). Declarations as to public rights must have been made before any controversy arose. They must concern rights exercisable by the whole community (such as public rights of way) or a substantial part of it (such as a right of common), and such declarations must directly assert or deny the existence of the rights.

The effect of these provisions is to admit some documents that would otherwise be excluded. For example, surveys of Crown property made for the Crown's private purposes do not come within the definition of public documents for the purposes of admissibility, but if of some antiquity (so that the death of the author can be presumed without further proof, by reason of the normal life span) they will be available as evidence, by virtue of being a declaration made by a deceased person in the course of his duty.

(*i*) *Acts of ownership*

Evidence may be given of acts of ownership of property to establish boundaries. Acts which have been admitted include tree planting and felling, cutting grass, grazing cattle, fishing, turning off strangers or preventing them from removing soil. The perambulation of his boundaries by the lord of the manor is evidence of the extent of his manor.

If the dispute concerns the ownership of an existing boundary feature, or the question is whether the boundary is down one side or the other of it or down the middle, evidence of acts of ownership exercised over the feature is admissible. Such acts are clipping and trimming a hedge, repairing a fence or wall, or clearing a ditch.

Acts of ownership are not conclusive evidence, particularly if they are relatively slight and for the convenience of the person doing them. He might not have been under a legal obligation, or even have had the right, to do them. Acts carried out without the contesting neighbour's knowledge, and therefore without his acquiescence, are not good evidence (*Henniker* v *Howard* (1904) 90 LT 157).

(j) Mode of construction of boundary features

It is customary to build brick walls and close-boarded fences so that the piers and upright supports protrude onto the land of the owner of the wall or fence. This is so that the wall or fence may go right up to the boundary; if the protrusions were to project into the neighbour's property they would constitute a trespass which the owner could be made to remove. (Nevertheless, the foundations of party walls can project in certain cases: see p 42.) Accordingly, the mode of construction of this type of wall or fence is prima facie evidence of its ownership. But it is not conclusive, because owners are not compelled to build in this way: they may set the wall or fence back very slightly to avoid trespassing. A fence reversing the usual method of construction has the advantage that repairs can be carried out from the owner's side.

(k) Local custom

Occasionally local custom may help to establish the position of a boundary. For example, in one case it was alleged, but not established, that private properties which adjoined a common were always considered to extend four feet on the common side of their hedges so that a fence could be erected to protect the hedge from animals grazing on the common (*Collis* v *Amphlett* [1918] 1 Ch 232; [1920] AC 271).

3 Vendor and purchaser

Under an open contract, or in the absence of express conditions of sale referring to this question, the purchaser is entitled to rescind if the property differs substantially from that contracted to be sold. Where the boundary is only slightly different, the purchaser's only right is compensation. This must be claimed before completion, otherwise the purchaser is taken to have waived his rights. A deficiency in area of 40 per cent justifies rescission (*Watson* v *Burton* [1957] 1 WLR 19), and where a property is described as including a wall and tradesmen's entrance, but excludes the wall and gives no indefeasible right to use the entrance, the right also arises (*Brewer* v *Brown* (1884) 28 Ch D 309). Even though the purchaser is entitled to rescind, he may nevertheless insist on taking a conveyance at a reduced purchase price, the compensation being assessed at a fair figure, not a penal one.

Provision is made as to this in both the National Conditions of Sale, 20th ed, cond 17, and The Law Society's Conditions of Sale, 1984 rvsn, cond 7, with the object of eliminating claims for compensation where discrepancies are immaterial, and restricting the parties' rights to compensation rather than rescission in more substantial cases. The extent to which the right to rescind is successfully restricted depends on whether the condition satisfies the reasonableness test (Misrepresentation Act 1967, s 3; Unfair Contract Terms Act 1977, ss 8(1), 11(1)).

4 Landlord and tenant

As the tenant who impugns his landlord's title gives the landlord grounds for forfeiture of his lease, boundary disputes, which are normally disputes as to title, are rare between landlord and tenant. The relationship of landlord and tenant itself imposes an obligation upon the tenant to preserve the boundaries of the demised premises, and to prevent their being destroyed so that the landlord's property cannot be delimited (*Attorney-General* v *Fullerton* (1813) 2 Ves & B 263). Where the tenant has confused the boundaries by merging adjoining premises, the landlord may apply to the court to have the boundary ascertained, even during the term of the demise (*Spike* v *Harding* (1878) 7 Ch D 871). To give jurisdiction, the plaintiff must show by evidence, or the defendant's admission, that he has legal title to the land, that the boundaries are confused and that the tenant is in possession of part at least. The application is to the Chancery Division and the practice is to direct an enquiry in chambers to ascertain the boundary. If at the end of the term of a lease the boundaries are so confused that the tenant cannot render up precisely the landlord's property, he is bound to restore land of equal value. This is ascertained as fairly as may be, but doubts are resolved against the tenant, because he is at fault.

5 Crown lands

Formerly, special provisions applied to the settlement of disputes relating to Crown lands, and arbitration awards had to be enrolled in the Office of Land Revenue Records and Enrolments (now housed with and superseded by the Public Record Office, Chancery Lane, London

WC2A 1LR). These provisions were repealed by the Crown Estates Act 1961. In all Crown leases there is now inserted a provision for the Crown Estate Commissioners to settle boundary disputes. The address of the Commissioners is Crown Estate Office, 13–15 Carlton House Terrace, London SW1Y 5AH.

6 Duchy of Cornwall lands

The Duke of Cornwall (or, during his minority, the Sovereign or other person appointed by her, on his behalf), with the previous consent of the Treasury, may make any arrangement to settle a boundary dispute affecting Duchy lands. The agreement must be enrolled in the Office of the Duchy of Cornwall, after which it is conclusive and binding on the Duke of Cornwall and all other interested parties. In the case of dispute as to the terms of such an agreement, the Duke of Cornwall may, with Treasury consent, agree to refer the matter to arbitration. The award must be enrolled in the Duchy Office, when it will be binding.

Enrolment is effected at the Duchy Office which is at 10 Buckingham Gate, London SW1E 6LA, to which documents may be sent by post. Enrolment must be within six months of the date of the document, but enrolments out of time made nunc pro tunc may be permitted on reasonable cause being shown. A certificate of enrolment is admissible in all courts as proof of the original instrument and its enrolment.

Chapter 4

Party Walls

1 What is a party wall?

The term 'party wall' is now applied to walls dividing properties in different ownership in three situations : first, where the wall is divided vertically in half, each neighbour owning the half on his side; secondly, where the wall is entirely the property of one adjoining owner, but is subject to easements or rights in favour of the other to have it maintained dividing the properties; thirdly, and most common, where the wall is divided vertically, but each part is subject to cross-easements in favour of the other. These different situations will be examined separately below. Before 1926 party walls were often held by the adjoining owners as tenants in common, but in abolishing this form of joint ownership at law, the Law of Property Act 1925 substituted a division of the wall with cross-easements.

Party walls in London are subject to certain special rules, and indeed special definitions, which are dealt with below. Further, part only of a wall may be a party wall, the remainder—either above or to one side—being in one ownership and not subject to easements.

(a) Vertically divided walls

A boundary wall which is built so that its centre exactly follows the dividing line will fall into this first class, being divided vertically into halves each owned by the landowner adjoining it (*Matts* v *Hawkins* (1813) 5 Taunt 20). Even though it may be built at the joint expense of the neighbours it is not subject to joint ownership. Whether the wall is built exactly astride the boundary is a question of fact, but minor inaccuracies will be ignored (*Reading* v *Barnard* (1827) Mood & M 71).

(b) Walls in single ownership

Where a boundary wall is built exclusively on the land of one owner it belongs to him in the absence of agreement to the contrary. The adjoining owner may acquire rights over it by agreement or prescription. (An easement of support may be acquired under the Prescription Act 1832 by user as of right for twenty years, provided that the owner of the servient tenement has not during the period been under a disability, or forty years notwithstanding such disability.) Long use of a wall as part of a building on his land does not give the adjoining owner title to the wall (as it will not normally amount to exclusive possession of it adverse to the owner), but may give him an easement of support for his roof (*Waddington* v *Naylor* (1889) 60 LT 480). Acquisition of a wall by adverse possession can be avoided by fixing a notice to it visible to the public stating to whom it belongs.

(*c*) *Divided walls subject to cross-easements*

Walls expressly made subject to a tenancy in common, or since 1925 to the Law of Property Act 1925, s 38, or other walls not exclusively on one person's property (and not within the first class above), come within this class. In cases of doubt before 1926, there was a presumption that a tenancy in common existed. This applied, for instance, when the circumstances of building the wall and how much land each adjoining owner contributed were not known (*Cubitt* v *Porter* (1828) 8 B & C 257). Similarly, where both parties used the wall, this was sufficient prima facie evidence for the presumption to operate (ibid).

Since 1925, cases where previously a tenancy in common existed or would have been created, and walls which are or are expressed to be party walls, are covered by the Law of Property Act 1925, s 38. This provides that they shall be regarded as severed vertically, each part enjoying such rights of support and user over the other as would have subsisted if a valid tenancy in common of it had existed. These rights vary according to the circumstances, but normally extend to permitting the use of the wall by either adjoining owner for any purpose contemplated when the grant of the wall was made (eg, support of a roof) without interference. A person interested in a party structure affected by the section may apply to the court for a declaration of the rights and interests of those interested, when the court may make such order as it thinks fit (Law of Property Act 1925, s 38(2)). Although the section refers to 'walls or structures', its provision for dividing them vertically prevents it applying to ceilings and floors between flats and maisonettes in separate ownership.

2 Rights and duties of adjoining owners

(*a*) *Support*

An easement of support for one part of a party wall by another in separate ownership may be acquired by grant, express or implied, or by prescription. In the absence of acquisition by any of these methods, there is no right of support (*Peyton* v *London Corporation* (1829) 9 B & C 725). If support is withdrawn by the adjoining owner no action lies for the resulting damage. This remains so even if the building owner has covenanted with the neighbour who withdraws the support to keep his building in repair, and the withdrawal makes it impossible to comply with his covenant (*Colebeck* v *The Girdlers Company* (1876) 1 QBD 234).

Cases now falling under s 38 of the Law of Property Act 1925 will have such an easement, and where part of a wall is granted by the owner to his neighbour with the intention of making it a party wall, the grant and reservation is implied of such cross-easements as are necessary to carry out the parties' intentions for the joint use of the wall (which will vary according to the facts of each case) (*Jones* v *Pritchard* [1908] 1 Ch 630, 635). This right binds a local authority which demolishes the servient tenement under a clearance order, even though it acts under a statutory duty, and accordingly it must provide alternative support (*Bond* v *Norman, Bond* v *Nottingham Corporation* [1940] Ch 429). Where the ownership of the wall is split vertically without mutual rights, neither half is entitled to support from the other. Rights of support exist only where houses adjoin, so the demolition of the next but one house in a terrace is not an actionable withdrawal of support (*Solomon* v *Vintners' Co* (1859) 5 H & N 585). Nevertheless, in cases where no easement of support exists, an action in negligence may be maintained where damage is caused by the adjoining owner's failure to observe a proper standard of care (*St Anne's Well Brewery Co* v *Roberts* (1928) 140 LT 1).

Where support is wrongfully withdrawn, no action can be maintained until actual damage is sustained, except in suitable cases for injunction proceedings where damage is imminent. The action will be for nuisance, see p 40. Even where damage has been suffered, the adjoining owner is not liable for merely failing to keep his building or part of the wall in repair, only for positive acts resulting in the withdrawal of support (*Sack* v *Jones* [1925] Ch 235). In these cases he is equally liable for the acts of independent contractors engaged by him (*Bower* v *Peate* (1876) 1 QBD 321). The adjoining owner who is liable continues to be so even though he may sell his property before some or all of the resulting damage becomes apparent. The occupier who succeeds him is not liable (*Hall* v *Duke of Norfolk* [1900] 2 Ch 493).

In the case of a boundary wall in single ownership there will be an easement for natural support, but this relates only to the support of the soil. A withdrawal of support for the wall is in such a case, therefore, only actionable if it is such as to cause a greater than minimal fall of soil, whatever the effect on the wall. In addition, there may be an easement for the support of the wall itself, acquired by grant or prescription. Such an easement is extinguished if the dominant owner alters the use of the wall in a way substantially to prejudice the enjoyment of the servient tenement (*Ray* v *Fairway Motors (Barnstaple) Ltd* (1969) 20 P & CR 261).

(b) Repairs

An easement of support does not cast upon the joint owner of a party wall any positive obligation to keep his part of the wall in repair. Similar duties may nevertheless arise as a result of the law of nuisance, see section (*c*) *Nuisance*. If a party wall collapses because of neglect by one owner, the other has no right of action (*Sack* v *Jones* [1925] Ch 235). The other owner need not, however, sit by and watch the wall crumble, but may enter his neighbour's property in order to carry out repairs (*Bond* v *Nottingham Corporation* [1940] Ch 429, 439). Where the easement is one of support only, without any additional repairing obligation, there is no right to reimbursement for the cost of repairs to someone else's wall (*The Highway Board, etc, of Macclesfield* v *Grant* (1882) 51 LJQB 357).

One property owner protected his building from exposure to the weather through a party wall, following the demolition of the neighbouring building, by building eaves out over the neighbour's land. He successfully resisted an application for a mandatory injunction to remove the eaves, because the court exercised its discretion taking into account the neighbour's conduct (*Tollemache & Cobbold Breweries* v *Reynolds* (1983) 268 EG 52).

An adjoining owner is entitled to make use of a party wall for the purpose originally intended. If in doing so the neighbouring property is damaged, he is not liable (*Jones* v *Pritchard* [1908] 1 Ch 630). If one of the owners demolishes and rebuilds for such purposes, he is bound to see that the operations are carried out with reasonable care, skill and speed, whether he does them personally or through independent contractors (*Murly* v *M'Dermott* (1838) 8 Ad & El 138; *Murray* v *Hall* (1849) 7 CB 441). Positive action in shoring up the remaining property is not required if the wall is wholly owned by the person demolishing it (*Southwark and Vauxhall Water Co* v *Wandsworth Board of Works* [1898] 2 Ch 603, 612).

If a party wall to which s 38 of the Law of Property Act 1925 applies is damaged by a third party, each adjoining owner can only recover half of the cost of its repair, as each now only owns half the wall. In so far as one adjoining owner suffers a withdrawal of support for his half by damage done to the wall by the other adjoining owner's tenant, his remedy is against the owner, not the tenant, because the Act places the burden of the easement upon him (*Apostal* v *Simons* [1936] 1 All ER 207).

(c) Nuisance

One neighbour may be liable to the other in nuisance as a result of disrepair to a party wall. This can effectively create repairing obligations where otherwise none exists. Where dry rot spread through a party wall, the owner on whose side it started was held liable in damages, because she should reasonably have appreciated the danger and there were preventative steps she could reasonably have taken (*Bradburn* v *Lindsay* [1983] 2 All ER 408). An action in nuisance was also successful when subsidence caused damage to a party wall, because the demolition of the house on one side caused the clay soil to dry out. The nuisance was an interference with the easement of support (*Brace* v *South Eastern Regional Housing Association* (1984) 270 EG 1286).

3 The London Building Acts

Party walls in inner London and the rights of adjoining owners are governed by special rules contained in Pt VI of the London Building Acts (Amendment) Act 1939. These provisions apply to the City of London and to the following London boroughs: Camden, Greenwich, Hackney, Hammersmith, Islington, Kensington and Chelsea, Lambeth, Lewisham, Southwark, Tower Hamlets, Wandsworth and Westminster (London Government Act 1963, s 43). For this purpose 'party wall' is defined as a wall forming part of a building constructed so that the wall is standing on lands in different ownership (to a greater extent than artificial supports, such as piers or buttresses) and a wall (even though wholly on one person's land) separating buildings in different ownership (1939 Act s 44). The rules apply also to a 'party fence wall' which is a boundary wall not forming part of a building but standing on lands in different ownership (to a greater extent than only its artificial supports), and to 'party structures', which extends the term 'party wall' to include floor partitions or other structures separating buildings or parts of buildings approached by separate staircases or separate entrances from without (s 4). This appears to mean that, when parts of one building are separate, each must have direct access to the open air at ground level, and so many divided buildings do not come within the definition.

For the purposes of the Act 'owner' includes every person in possession or in receipt either of the whole or any part of the rents and profits of the property, and every person in occupation otherwise than as a tenant at will or from year to year or for a lesser term (London Building Act 1930, s 5). It includes a long leaseholder, even though he has sublet for a term longer than from year to year (*Hunt* v *Harris* (1865) 19 CB (NS) 13).

The 1939 Act does not generally apply to the property of the Crown, the Duchies of Lancaster and Cornwall (s 151) or the Inns of Court (s 152).

The operation of the Act is to give rights to adjoining owners who comply with its provisions as to the giving of notices, etc. There is no compulsion to comply with the procedure in the case of existing party structures, but in default the landowner is not entitled to exercise the rights which can be of considerable value. The service of notices in connection with new party structures is, however, obligatory.

Forms of notice for use in the course of the statutory procedure are published by the Royal Institute of British Architects, 66 Portland Place, London W1N 4AD.

To fail within a reasonable time to make good damage occasioned to adjoining property by the exercise of rights conferred by the Act is an offence, and on summary conviction a maximum fine of £200, plus £20 per day during such failure, may be imposed. Contravention of any other provision or requirement of the Act mentioned below is an offence, subject to a maximum fine of £200, plus £20 per day while it lasts, on summary conviction (s 148(2) (xix), (xxxix); Greater London Council (General Powers) (No 2) Act 1978, s 7, Sched 2).

(a) Existing party structures

Where there already exists a building or a party fence wall over the boundary of adjoining lands in different ownership, extensive rights are given to the building owner to carry out works on the structure (1939 Act, s 46), subject (unless he has the adjoining owner's and occupier's written consent) to his serving notices on the adjoining owner. First, where the wall is in want of repair or defective, he may repair, thicken or underpin it, make it good or demolish and rebuild it, although not to a lower height (*Gyle-Thompson* v *Wall Street (Properties) Ltd* [1974] 1 WLR 123). Secondly, where he wishes to build against the party structure and it is of insufficient height or strength, he may rebuild to a specification suitable for his purpose, subject to making good all damage to adjoining premises (including internal finishings and decorations), and raising all chimney stacks or flues on or against it belonging to the adjoining owner. He is also authorised to do all incidental works necessary to connect the party structure with adjoining premises, including cutting back projecting parts of it, and may convert a party fence wall into part of an adjoining building. Thirdly, partitions, rooms or buildings in different occupation and arches over public ways or passages owned by others, may be demolished if not in conformity with the London Building Acts (or the byelaws thereunder) and rebuilt so as to comply. A structure, but not a building, which existed at the date of the commencement of the Act (1 January 1940), is deemed to conform with the Act and the bye laws if it was in conformity with the legislation governing it at the date of its erection (Building (Inner London) Regulations 1985, Sched 4).

(b) New party structures

Where an owner wants to build a wall (either as part of a building or as a party fence wall) on a boundary of his land hitherto unbuilt on, he must serve a notice of his intention on the adjoining owner (s 45). This must specify whether he wishes to build wholly on his own land or astride the boundary. In the latter case, if the adjoining owner gives his written consent, the wall will be a party wall, the expenses of building it being shared by both owners in proportions fixed with regard to the use to be made of it by each, and the cost of labour and materials when use is made. In default of the adjoining owner's written consent, the wall must be built exclusively on the builder's land. In any case where the wall is solely on the land of one owner, he may, between one and six months after serving his notice, build at his own expense projecting footings or foundations below ground level in his neighbour's land, compensating the owner and/or occupier for any damage done. Foundations reinforced with steel rods or beams are not authorised by this section dealing with new party structures.

(c) Notices

A building owner wishing to exercise any rights in connection with an existing party structure must serve written notice on the adjoining owner specifying the nature and details of the work proposed. Where foundations reinforced with steel rods or beams ('special foundations') are proposed, plans must also be served. Where a party fence, wall or special foundations are concerned, notice must be served at least one month before the date given in the notice for work to commence; for other party structures two months' notice must be given. The notice is ineffective unless work is commenced within six months after the service of the notice and prosecuted with diligence (s 47).

The adjoining owner may serve a counter-notice within twenty-one days in respect of special foundations or one month in other cases. In the case of special foundations, the counter-notice may require them to be of greater strength and/or greater depth to accommodate a proposed new building that the adjoining owner has in contemplation. In other cases it may require the building of chimneys, flues, copings, piers or recesses for the adjoining owner's convenience. In every case plans of the works specified must accompany the notice. The building owner upon whom the counter-notice is served must comply with its requirements unless they would be injurious to him, cause him unnecessary inconvenience, or unnecessarily delay the works (s 48).

(d) Execution and cost of works

A building owner may not exercise the rights conferred on him by the Act in such a way or at such a time as to cause unnecessary inconvenience to the adjoining owner or occupier. Where the work involves laying open part of the adjoining land or building, the building owner responsible for the works must at his own expense maintain a proper hoarding or shoring as necessary for the protection of the land or building and the security of the occupier (s 51). For the purpose of carrying out the works, the Act confers upon the building owner, his servants, agents and workmen a power of entry on any premises, with power to remove any furniture and fittings if necessary. If the building is closed, those with rights of entry may break open any fences or doors in order to enter, if accompanied by a police officer. Fourteen days' notice of intention to enter must be given, except in case of emergency (s 53).

Works which are for the benefit of both owners—the rebuilding or repair of defective party structures or those contravening the London Building Acts—are carried out at their joint expense, the cost being shared in proportions fixed having regard to the use each makes of the party structure. The building owner bears the expense of works for his sole benefit, such as strengthening a wall to incorporate it into a new building of his own (s 56). The adjoining owner may by notice in writing before the works begin require the building owner to give security for expenses in a sum agreed, or in default of agreement determined by the county court (s 57).

(e) Disputes

The Act provides machinery for the settlement of all disputes between two adjoining owners, and a difference is deemed to have arisen if the recipient of a party structure notice or a counter-notice does not give his consent in writing within fourteen days (s 49). To settle the dispute the parties must either agree upon the appointment of one surveyor, or each appoint his own surveyor, and these two then appoint a third, the three acting together. All appointments are in writing, and detailed provision is made for cases where one of the surveyors is unable or unwilling to act. The award in settlement of the dispute is made by the agreed surveyor, or the majority of the three surveyors, or if no two of them agree by the third surveyor appointed by the parties' surveyors. The work may not commence until the award is made. The costs of the award and supervision of the work are dealt with by the award.

Within fourteen days of the delivery of the award either party may appeal to the county court (procedure: CCR Ord 3, r 6) but if the sum involved (exclusive of costs) is more than £100, the appellant may apply for a stay of the county court proceedings and prosecute his appeal in the High Court, subject to giving security approved by the county court. Any costs incurred in the county court are then deemed costs in the High Court proceedings (s 55).

Chapter 5

Duty to Fence

1 No general duty

A landowner is not, simply by reason of his owning property, under any obligation to fence his boundaries. There are, however, many cases where there will be such a duty, owed either to certain persons only or to the public at large. The circumstances in which the duty arises are dealt with in detail below. They fall into the following general categories: obligations imposed by agreement; arising by prescription; imposed because of the nature of the land, its situation or the use to which it is put; and special statutory obligations. Where no obligation exists there can be no liability for damage sustained solely by reason of the lack of a fence. However, where a fence has been erected even though there is no obligation to do so, and it is in a dangerous condition, its owner may be liable for damage resulting from its condition. In appropriate circumstances an action could be maintained in nuisance (where there is detriment to a neighbour's enjoyment of his land: *Harrold* v *Watney* [1898] 2 QB 320), in negligence (where damage is caused to a person who must have been in the landowner's contemplation and to whom he owes a duty of care: *Tarry* v *Ashton* (1876) 1 QBD 314), independently of these causes of action if the damage flows naturally from the defective fence (*Firth* v *Bowling Iron Co* (1878) 3 CPD 254), or against a landlord who has undertaken to repair (Defective Premises Act 1972, s 4).

2 Obligations on freehold owners

(a) Covenants on conveying freeholds

A covenant to erect and/or maintain a fence contained in a conveyance of freehold property is valid and enforceable between the parties to the conveyance, subject only to the usual limitation period of twelve years from the date of the breach of covenant for suing on an agreement under seal. There is, however, no completely satisfactory way to ensure that the obligation to fence will bind every person into whose hands the land comes. Normal conveyancing practice is for the covenantor to obtain an indemnity from his successor in title against loss suffered by him because of a future breach of the covenant, but this does not make the covenant directly enforceable against the new owner. At common law the burden of covenants never passed with the land. Equity modified this in the case of restrictive covenants (*Tulk* v *Moxhay* (1848) 2 Phil 774), but a covenant to fence is a positive covenant and is not therefore affected (*Jones* v *Price* [1965] 2 QB 618). The benefit of the equitable rules cannot be obtained by phrasing in negative form what is in effect a positive covenant.

A number of possible methods of attaching a fencing obligation to a freehold may be mentioned, although some are rather involved and therefore only likely to be employed in cases where the need is particularly pressing. Proposals for reform have been put forward by the Law Commission (see Appendix).

The first involves the creation of an estate rentcharge issuing out of the land on which the obligation is to be imposed. This form of rentcharge was introduced by the Rentcharges Act 1977, s 2. The amount of the rentcharge cannot exceed a nominal sum, except to the extent that it pays for maintenance or repairs to the fence. It is not subject to compulsory redemption (s 8 (4)).

The covenant to fence is made one of the covenants entered into with the owner of the rentcharge. A right of re-entry may be reserved to the owner of the rent when it is created, which would be exercisable on breach of covenant, and should be an adequate sanction. The right to exercise it need not be confined to the perpetuity period (Perpetuities and Accumulations Act 1964, s 11 (1)). A similar, more limited, provision means that the right does not have to be confined to the perpetuity period in a conveyance of Crown lands by the Crown Estate Commissioners (Crown Estates Act 1961, s 3 (8)).

A second way to enforce a fencing covenant is to reserve a right of re-entry in favour of the owner of retained land, when selling part of a holding. A vendor does not have to retain a reversion in the land sold in order to do that. The drawback is that unless any default complained of is grave and wilful, it is unlikely that equitable relief will be granted (*Shiloh Spinners Ltd* v *Harding* [1973] AC 691).

It has also been suggested that the principle of *Halsall* v *Brizell* [1957] Ch 169, could be employed here: anyone taking advantage of benefits granted by a deed must comply with obligations which it imposes to contribute to costs. That case related, amongst other benefits, to sea walls. Presumably, therefore, there is no difficulty in establishing that a purchaser takes the benefit of a fence or wall, even though the enjoyment of it is essentially passive. However, it is not clear whether the principle extends beyond making an obligation to pay money binding, to enforcing a positive obligation to do work.

The last possibility is, instead of conveying the freehold, for the vendor to grant to the purchaser a lease for at least 300 years at a peppercorn rent and without a proviso for re-entry, so that the purchaser can convert it into a fee simple by deed poll under s 153 of the Law of Property Act 1925. The obligations created by the covenants in such a lease do not come to an end when the term is enlarged into a freehold, but continue to attach to the freehold (subs (8)). Accordingly, if the covenant that was required as to fencing was inserted in the lease originally, the obligation would be imposed on successive owners of the freehold. The drawback of this method, which in any event would hardly be suitable for widespread use on the development of an estate, is that it is not clear what measure of damages (if any) would be recoverable in an action for breach of covenant. A landlord normally recovers the amount of the damage to his reversion, but here he has no reversion. It may therefore be that there is no effective sanction to support this obligation.

The Lands Tribunal has held that it has no jurisdiction to discharge a positive covenant to fence, under s 84 of the Law of Property Act 1925, because it is a purely personal covenant (*Re Blyth Corporation's Application* (1963) 14 P & CR 56 (LT)). If a covenant is satisfactorily made to bind successors in title, it is an open question whether it could be varied. The section refers to a 'restriction', and it may be that that would never be apt to include a positive covenant.

(b) Damages on breach of covenant

On a failure to erect a boundary wall in accordance with a covenant to do so, the convenantee who owns the adjoining land can recover damages equal to the cost of carrying out the work on his own land. The amount of damages is not limited to the loss of value resulting from the lack of a wall, nor to the cost of erecting the cheapest possible fence in its place (*Radford* v *De Froberville* [1977] 1 WLR 1262). Damages which amount to the cost of the work when judgment is given, even if this is greater than it would have been at the date the work should have been done, can be recovered by a plaintiff who could not reasonably have done the work earlier (*Dodd Properties (Kent) Ltd* v *Canterbury City Council* [1980] 1 WLR 433).

3 Landlord and tenant

(a) *Express covenants*

Covenants to erect and/or maintain fences are often found in leases, and they may be by either party. This is certainly one of the matters that a lease should deal with explicitly wherever possible. If there is a covenant to repair the demised premises, it is necessarily a question of construction whether a boundary wall forms part of the demised premises. If it does not, the covenant does not apply to it (*Blundell* v *Newlands Investment Trust* (1958) 172 EG 855).

If the lease is silent, certain obligations will be implied in the case of a tenancy for a term of years (see below), and these may not accord with the parties' wishes. If the tenancy is from year to year or at will, no obligations will attach to either party, which makes the position clear but not satisfactory. The Law of Property Act 1925, ss 141 and 142, provides that the benefits of tenants' covenants and the burden of landlord's covenants, where they have reference to the subject-matter of the lease, run with the reversion, so benefiting and binding whomsoever is in the position of landlord. Covenants which 'touch and concern' the land demised run with the land at common law, binding the tenant for the time being, and the benefit of the landlord's covenants runs similarly. Fencing covenants fall within both these definitions, and so remain valid and enforceable against and by the persons then concerned with the land, although one or both of the original parties to the lease have disposed of their interests. There is one possible exception. It may be that a covenant to erect a new fence or boundary wall (rather than merely to repair), in a lease executed prior to 1926, will not bind the tenant's successors in title unless he expressly covenanted for himself and his assigns (*Spencer's Case* (1583) 5 Co Rep 16a). No difficulty arises in the case of covenants to repair only.

There is no limit to the period for which a fencing covenant in a lease can be effective (the rule against perpetuities not being applicable), so the covenant settles the question of fencing for the duration of the term. Although, formerly, a fencing covenant in a lease could only be enforced by the other party to the lease, a landlord's responsibility for a fence in a dangerous condition is in effect extended by the Defective Premises Act 1972, s 4. Anyone who might reasonably be expected to be affected by defects and who suffers injury or damage, has a remedy against a landlord who knew, or ought to have known, of the defect. A landlord who has reserved a right of entry to repair is, for this purpose only, treated as having covenanted to repair.

(b) Covenants implied by statute

Where the terms on which an agricultural holding is let do not expressly deal with fences and walls, certain covenants are implied (Agriculture (Maintenance, Repair and Insurance of Fixed Equipment) Regulations 1973, Sched). The landlord must execute all repairs and replacements of walls and fences of open and covered yards and garden walls (para 1). The tenant has a duty to repair and leave in good repair, order and condition, various parts of the property, but only to the extent that the matters are not already covered by a landlord's covenant. The tenant's responsibility extends to fences, hedges, field walls, stiles, gates and posts (para 5 (1)). Also, he must cut, trim or lay a proper proportion of the hedges each year so as to maintain them in good and sound condition (para 9). These implied covenants are displaced by any written agreement placing responsibility on the other party (*Burden* v *Hannaford* [1956] 1 QB 143). In determining the extent of the implied obligation, regard must be had to the age, character and condition of the property at the beginning of the tenancy (*Evans* v *Jones* [1955] 2 QB 58).

In default, the other party may do the work and recover the reasonable cost from the other, although the amount the tenant can recover is limited to the smaller of £500 and the annual rent (paras 4 (2), 12 (2)). Breach of a covenant to maintain fences can also be the foundation of a notice to quit under the Agricultural Holdings (Notices to Quit) Act 1977, s 2 (3), Case D (*Shepherd* v *Lomas* [1963] 1 WLR 962).

It is unlikely that a garden wall or fence belonging to a residential property will fall within the landlord's repairing covenant implied into short lettings by the Landlord and Tenant Act 1985, s 11 (*Hopwood* v *Cannock Chase District Council* [1975] 1 WLR 373).

(c) Covenants implied at common law

Apart from express provisions in the lease and the statutory provisions relating to agricultural holdings, the occupier of premises let for a term of years is liable to repair fences, but tenants from year to year or at will are not. This is because only tenants for years are liable for permissive waste. The landlord can maintain an action against the tenant where the repairs are not carried out, on the ground of damage to his inheritance (*Cheetham* v *Hampson* (1791) 4 Term Rep 318), and if the fences fall down by reason of excavations in breach of covenant a mandatory injunction may be granted to renew them (*Newton* v *Nock* (1880) 43 LT 197). Provided the landlord has not undertaken to repair the fences and (unless the tenant has agreed to put them in good repair) they were not dilapidated at the start of the term, the occupier is liable to any third party injured because of the want of repair.

For the performance of his obligations the occupier is entitled to fell timber (ie, oak, ash and elm over twenty years old, and possibly other wood by local custom), the felling of which is generally waste. The use is known as 'estovers', but only felling for immediate fencing requirements is permitted.

(d) Compensation

Compensation is payable to the outgoing tenant of an agricultural holding in respect of improvements taking the form of the making or removal of permanent fences (Agricultural Holdings Act 1948, Scheds 3, 4). If the improvement was begun before 1 March 1948 (an 'old improvement'), the landlord's consent must have been obtained. For later improvements (a 'new improvement'), the tenant must either have the landlord's consent or the Minister's approval. A tenant who is aggrieved by his landlord withholding consent may apply to the Agricultural Land Tribunal (s 50). The amount of compensation for an old improvement is such sum as fairly represents its value to an incoming tenant (s 37). For a new improvement, compensation equals the increase in the value of the holding attributable to the improvement, having regard to the character and situation of the holding and the average requirements of tenants reasonably skilled in husbandry (s 48).

4 Fencing easements

A landowner may acquire an easement that his neighbour shall fence the boundary between their properties, or shall maintain a hedge along it (*Jones* v *Price* [1965] 2 QB 618). This is not, however, an easement which is covered by the Prescription Act 1832, and accordingly title to the right must be made in other ways, eg, under the Law of Property Act 1925, s 62, on a conveyance by the former owner of the dominant and servient tenements (*Crow* v *Wood* [1971] 1 QB 77), or by prescription at common law. The latter theoretically involves proof that the right dates back to the limit of legal memory, 1189, although in practice a long period of exercise of the right is accepted if there is no definite proof that the right previously did not exist. Alternatively, the court may be asked to apply the doctrine of the lost modern grant: ie, the presumption that the duty must have been imposed by a document now lost. In either case proof of twenty or thirty years' undisputed exercise of the right is likely to succeed in the absence of evidence to the contrary. Such a right may normally be established by proof that the owner of the servient tenement and his predecessors in title have been in the habit of carrying out all necessary repairs to the fence at their own expense, and doing so on receiving notice to do so from the owner of the dominant tenement and his predecessors.

By way of example it is interesting to contrast two cases. Evidence that the owners of one piece of land had repaired a certain fence for fifty years was held insufficient to establish an easement, in the absence of any evidence that they did so as a result of an obligation (*Hilton* v *Ankesson* (1872) 27 LT 519). On the other hand, evidence that a fence had been repaired by one party and his predecessors for forty years was held sufficient, when combined with the fact that for the last nineteen years they had done so on notice from those claiming the benefit of the easement (*Lawrence* v *Jenkins* (1873) LR 8 QB 274).

The landowner subject to the obligation is not entitled to notice of the want of repair. He is liable for all damage resulting therefrom, including escape of his neighbour's cattle, even though he was ignorant of the need for repair. He is not liable for the results of damage to the fence by act of God or vis major. Where the servient tenement is let, the action in cases of non-repair is against the tenant, not the landlord (*Lawrence* v *Jenkins*, supra).

No obligation can arise by prescription whereby one owner has to maintain a wall merely to protect his neighbour's building against penetration of the weather. This is not a right susceptible of constituting an easement (*Phipps* v *Pears* [1965] 1 QB 76). If, however, a wall is laid bare in the course of demolition, the local authority may require that the demolisher make it weatherproof (Public Health Act 1961, s 29).

A prescriptive obligation to fence comes to an end if the dominant and servient tenements come into the same ownership, in such a way that the estate for which each is held is identical.

5 Obligations arising from particular circumstances

(a) Land adjoining a highway

At common law there was no duty to fence a boundary with a highway.* This formerly meant that there was no liability for damage caused by animals straying on to the road. Now, however, the normal rules apply (Animals Act 1971, s 8). There are exceptions. Merely placing animals on unfenced land does not,

---

* In fact from the reign of Edward I to that of George III it was forbidden to maintain a dyke, tree or bush within 200 feet of either side of a highway, as a protection against highwaymen.

without more, constitute a breach of duty if the person had the right to place animals on the land and that land is common land, is situated in an area where fencing is not customary, or is a town or village green. The keeper of any horses, cattle, sheep, goats or swine—the person in whose possession they are—commits an offence if they stray onto the highway, except where it passes over common, waste or unenclosed ground. Maximum fines are: £20 (first offence), £50 (thereafter) (Highways Act 1980, s 155).

The Highways Act 1980, s 165, imposes an obligation upon the owner of land adjoining a street (which includes inter alia a highway, lane, footpath or passage, whether a thoroughfare or not) adequately to fence anything thereon which is a source of danger to persons using the street (as, for example, a building in the course of demolition). This is enforced by the local authority serving on the owner notice to execute the necessary works and, subject to an appeal to the magistrates' court, on his failure to comply the authority may carry out the work at the owner's expense. Where the only source of danger is the difference in level between the road and the adjoining land, the owner cannot be compelled to fence because the danger does not exist in or on his land (*Myers* v *Harrow Corporation* [1962] 2 QB 442). There are also statutory obligations to fence certain objects of danger within certain distances of a road, such as steam engines, windmills and dangerous quarries.

Where a fence has been erected adjoining a highway, liability will arise if it is allowed to fall into such a state of dilapidation that it is a nuisance, and any person using the highway is injured as a natural result (*Harrold* v *Watney* [1898] 2 QB 320). This can also be a nuisance which magistrates, on the complaint of a local authority, can order to be abated (Public Health Act 1961, ss 24, 25).

Where the land adjoining a highway is fenced with barbed wire, or the fence contains barbed wire, which is a nuisance to the highway (ie, if it is likely to be injurious to persons or animals lawfully using the highway), the highway authority can serve a notice on the occupier to abate the nuisance within a specified time (not less than one month nor more than six months) (Highways Act 1980, s 164). If the highway authority is itself the occupier any ratepayer can initiate similar action.

A fence which is dangerous to persons lawfully using the highway can also lead to a civil action for nuisance. Actions have been brought successfully where the injury was caused by wire (*Stewart* v *Wright* (1893) 9 TLR 480) and by spikes (*Morrison* v *Sheffield Corporation* [1917] 2 KB 866).

Where a hedge, tree or shrub overhangs any road or footpath to which the public has access and endangers, obstructs or interferes with the passage or view of vehicle drivers or pedestrians or the light from a public lamp, the appropriate authority may require it to be lopped within fourteen days or (subject to an appeal to the magistrates' court) do it themselves at the owner's or occupier's expense (Highways Act 1980, s 154).

No door, gate or bar on any premises may open outwards on a street, except in the case of a public building with the consent of the local authority and the highway authority. An owner may be given eight days in which to alter an offending door, and in default is subject to a fine of £25 (Highways Act 1980, s 153).

It is an offence (carrying a fine of up to £50) to erect a fence or plant a hedge in a highway which consists of or comprises a carriageway for vehicles (Highways Act 1980, s 138). A person interested in land adjoining or near a highway may enter into an agreement with the highway authority restricting or regulating the use of the land, and in particular what grows on it. The agreement is registrable as a local land charge (Highways Act 1980, s 253).

Vaults, arches and cellars under streets must be kept in good repair. In default, the local authority may do necessary work and recover the expense (Highways Act 1980, s 180 (6), (7)). A person injured has no action against a defaulter (*Scott* v *Green & Sons* [1969] 1 WLR 301).

A highway authority may, and in some circumstances must, fence the highway. If a fence protecting highway users from a dangerous drop, or a stream, is part of the highway—which is a question of fact as to whether it is built on land originally dedicated or acquired for the highway—it is repairable with the highway (*R* v *Whitney* (1835) 7 C & P 208). Where the authority, or its predecessors in title, have fenced a dangerous place, it may be liable for damage resulting from removal of the fence (*Whyler* v *Bingham Rural Council* [1901] 1 KB 45). A highway authority may erect and maintain a fence to prevent access to a road. This power may not, however, be exercised in such a way as to interfere with a gate used for agricultural purposes, a public right of way, or a means of access to the road for which planning permission has been granted or for which it was not needed because it existed on 1 July 1948 and did not contravene the earlier legislation (Highways Act 1980, s 80). In any area of the countryside where walls of a particular construction are a feature, the highway authority's powers and duties relating to fences can apply to walls of that construction (Wildlife and Countryside Act 1981, s 72 (12)). A special road authority may stop up private means of access to special roads (eg, motorways) and provide alternative means of access to adjoining premises (1980 Act, s 125).

(b) Land accessible to the public

A local authority has power to require works, which may include fencing, to remove the danger from an excavation on land accessible to the public from a highway, or on a place of public resort. In default, or where the authority does not know the identity of the owner or occupier of the land, it must carry out the work required (Local Government (Miscellaneous Provisions) Act 1976, s 25).

(c) Land adjoining a common

An owner of land adjoining a common may, by prescription, become liable to fence his property against the beasts grazing on the common, although only with a fence capable of keeping out the type which usually graze there (*Coaker* v *Willcocks* [1911] 2 KB 124). Breach of such an obligation gives rise to at least a claim for nominal damages by the owner of cattle which stray off the common (*Egerton* v *Harding* [1975] QB 62).

(d) Animals

The owner of livestock (cattle, horses, asses, mules, hinnies, sheep, pigs, goats, poultry, deer not in the wild state, and captive pheasants, partridges and grouse) is liable for any damage to land or property that it causes when it strays on to someone else's land (Animals Act 1971, s 4). The owner is also liable for the cost of maintaining the livestock before it is restored to him. For this purpose, the person who has possession of the livestock is liable as owner. There is no liability where the animals stray from the highway, provided their presence there was a lawful use of the highway (s 5 (5)).

The fact that the land on to which the animals strayed was not fenced is not of itself a defence. But the livestock owner is not liable if he can establish that the animals would not have strayed but for a breach of a duty to fence by someone interested in the land (s 5 (6)). The duty to fence does not have to be owed to the livestock owner. It could be an obligation attached to the freehold or a covenant in a lease.

A landowner has a duty of care to users of an adjoining highway to prevent stock known to be on the land from straying. But when a heifer strayed from land let on a grass keep agreement and caused an accident, the landowner was not liable because there was no evidence that he knew the fencing to be inadequate (*Hoskin* v *Rogers* (1985) *The Times* 25 January).

If any horses, cattle, sheep, goats or swine are found straying or lying on or at the side of the highway, their keeper (the person in whose possession they are) is liable to a fine of up to £20 (first offence) or £50 (thereafter) (Highways Act 1980, s 155). This does not apply where the highway crosses common, waste or unenclosed land, and is without prejudice to any right of pasture on the side of the highway. However, there was an offence where a cow strayed from common land onto a road and went 300 yards along the road away from the common, where a car collided with it (*Rees* v *Morgan* (1960) *The Times* 14 February).

(e) Dangerous objects and operations

The occupier of land used for dangerous operations or for the storage of dangerous objects must consider fencing obligations from two points of view: to prevent the escape from his land of dangerous things, or objects made dangerous by the activities on his land, and to prevent the entry of persons who are likely to be harmed there.

The rule in *Rylands* v *Fletcher* (1868) LR 3 HL 330 imposes upon the occupier of land a strict liability for the results of the escape from that land of dangerous objects not normally there, or accumulated there in unnatural quantities. No negligence is necessary. Act of God, statutory authority, act of a third party and consent or default of the injured party are defences.

Apart from this an occupier may be liable under the general law of negligence for the results of the escape of something from his land, such as a golf ball (*Castle* v *St Augustine's Links* (1922) 38 TLR 615), or a football (*Hilder* v *Associated Portland Cement Manufacturers Ltd* [1961] 1 WLR 1434). This is not an absolute liability; it depends upon whether he could reasonably have foreseen what happened, which is a question of fact. The number of times similar things have happened before and the cost of preventing it are relevant (*Bolton* v *Stone* [1951] AC 850).

The Occupiers' Liability Act 1957, s 2, imposes upon the occupier of premises the duty to take such care as in all the circumstances of the case is reasonable to see that a visitor will be reasonably safe using the premises for the purpose for which he has been invited or permitted to be there. As permission to enter will be assumed in cases where people habitually use the premises, although not expressly authorised, the obligation will probably only be discharged by the erection and maintenance of fences to exclude them where the premises are themselves inherently dangerous (such as a deep gravel pit). The Act expressly states as an example that, in assessing whether a degree of care is reasonable in any case, consideration should be given to the fact that children are less careful than adults, and accordingly it may be more necessary to fence against them. Where premises are occupied for business purposes, the occupier cannot exclude his liability for breach of this common duty of care in so far as it results in death or personal injury, and can only do so in the case of other loss if in all the circumstances it is reasonable (Unfair Contract Terms Act 1977, ss 1, 2).

6 Statutory obligations

(a) Railways

The Railways Clauses Consolidation Act 1845, s 68, imposed upon railway companies acquiring land compulsorily the obligation to fence it in perpetuity as part of the accommodation works. This duty persists and now falls on British Rail. Indeed, it even continues after the land has ceased to be used for railway purposes (*R Walker & Son* v *British Railways Board* [1984] 1 WLR 805).

The extent of the duty to fence is limited. The obligation is to mark the limit of railway property. There is no general duty to fence in such a way as to exclude adult or child trespassers (*Proffitt* v *British Railways Board* (1985) *The Times* 4 February).

The original acquiring companies were, however, empowered to pay compensation in return for a release from their fencing obligations where the vendor agreed. Many such releases were in fact effected. It is not always clear today, however, whether or not this happened in respect of any particular stretch of line, because the railways do still maintain some fences where they are not obliged to. Normally where a release was granted it was stated in the conveyance of the land to the railway company, but even if a duplicate or counterpart conveyance was executed then, it may be that because of the lapse of time, no record of the release now appears on the title. It is therefore wise to make enquiries about this when buying or taking a lease of land bordering a railway. Failing other sources, enquiry may be made of British Rail Property Board, sending a plan showing the name of the parish and Ordnance Survey plot numbers of the adjoining land concerned. They reserve the right to charge a production fee, but may not do so.

Enquiries should be addressed to the Regional Estate Surveyor and Manager, British Rail Property Board, of the region concerned, as follows:

> Southern Region (*South of the Thames and West to include Dorset and Wiltshire*): Denison House, 296/298 Vauxhall Bridge Road, London SW1V 1AG. Tel: (01) 928 5151.
>
> South Western Region (*English counties West of Dorset and Wiltshire and North to mid-Wales*): Temple Gate House, Temple Gate, Bristol BS1 6PS. Tel: Bristol (0272) 24191.
>
> Eastern Region (*North of the Thames and West and North to include Oxfordshire, Cambridgeshire and parts of Leicestershire and*

Lincolnshire): Great Northern House, 79/81 Euston Road, London NW1 2RT. Tel: (01) 837 4200.

Midland Region (*The Midlands, North to but excluding Merseyside and the Northern half of Wales*): Stanier House, 10 Holliday Street, Birmingham B1 1TG. Tel: (021) 643 4444.

North Eastern Region (*East of the Pennines and North to the Scottish border*): Hudson House, Toft Green, York YO1 1HP. Tel: York (0904) 53022.

North Western Region (*West of the Pennines and North to the Scottish border*): 34 High Street, Manchester M4 1QB. Tel: (061) 228 2141.

(b) Parsonages

Church of England incumbents are required, by order of the Parsonages Board or the Diocesan Board of Finance, to carry out repairs, specified by the diocesan surveyor, to the walls, fences and gates of the parsonage house and any former parsonage house while vested in them (Repair of Benefice Buildings Measure 1972, ss 2–6; Endowments and Glebe Measure 1976, s 33).

(c) Churchyards and burial grounds

In any particular parish the duty to maintain the fences round the churchyard may, by custom from time immemorial, be cast upon the owner of a particular piece of land or upon the incumbent. In default the duty lies on the parochial church council (Parochial Church Council (Powers) Measure 1921, s 4). Since the abolition of the compulsory church rate, this has ceased to be a legal obligation. A cemetery company is bound to maintain the boundary walls and fences of a cemetery in good repair and, in the absence of special provisions, these must be substantial walls or iron railings at least eight feet high (Cemeteries Clauses Act 1847).

The parochial church council or the burial board, as the case may be, must maintain the boundary walls and fences of a disused churchyard or burial ground. Upon their certifying the cost of the repairs, they are entitled to repayment from the general rates, except where there is another fund legally chargeable with the expense (Burial Act 1855, s 18; Parochial Church Councils (Powers) Measure 1921; Rating and Valuation Act 1925, s 4).

(d) Disused mines

The owner of an abandoned mine, or one that has not been worked for twelve months, must fence it, to prevent injury to persons or animals falling down the shaft (Mines and Quarries Act 1954, s 151).

(e) Local legislation

In some areas, local authorities have powers under local Acts to oblige owners to repair boundary walls and fences. In Manchester, eg, a district council can require the repair, replacement or renewal of a party or boundary wall or fence of any house, if it has collapsed, is in danger of collapsing, or is in a ruinous or dilapidated condition (Greater Manchester Act 1981, s 43(1)).

7 Rights of entry for fencing

There is no general right to enter on neighbouring property to repair a boundary fence, even if that is the most convenient, or even the only practicable, means of doing it (*Kwiatkowski* v *Cox* [1970] EGD 9). An owner who enters to repair without authority can be restrained by injunction (*John Trenbarth Ltd* v *National Westminster Bank Ltd* (1969) 39 P & CR 104). The Law Commission has recommended reforms to tackle this problem (see Appendix).

A right of access to repair can arise by prescription, even if that means that the use to which the neighbour can put the strip of land along the boundary is thereby restricted (*Ward* v *Kirkland* [1967] Ch 194). In the same case it was suggested, although somewhat tentatively, that the doctrine that a person may not derogate from his grant would also apply. So that where part of a property is sold off, including a wall on the boundary common to the vendor and the purchaser, the purchaser may enter the retained land to maintain his property. It may not, however, be necessary to rely upon this doctrine, as the Law of Property Act 1925, s 62, implying the general words into a conveyance, will have the effect of vesting a right of entry in the purchaser (ibid).

Where a landowner is under an obligation to his neighbour to fence their common boundary, and the only means of complying with the obligation is to go on the neighbour's property, it is thought that a right of entry for that purpose must necessarily be implied. This would not, however, be the case if repair from the side owned by the person undertaking it was perfectly possible.

Where a right of entry to fence is expressly granted as an easement, but does not take effect as a legal easement—either because it is not granted in fee simple or for a term of years absolute, or because it is not granted by deed—it should be protected as an equitable easement by registration as a land charge class D (iii), or by the registration of a caution at the Land Registry.

A landlord who covenants in a lease to repair fences has an implied right of entry to carry out such repairs.

Certain statutory rights of entry are conferred by the London Building Acts (p 41), and the joint owner of a party wall can exercise a right to enter to repair (p 39).

8 Obligation not to fence

Some conveyances and leases contain covenants not to fence specified boundaries. This is common enough on modern housing estates laid out with open plan front gardens. A mandatory injunction is the appropriate remedy for the removal of a fence erected in contravention of such a covenant, but it will not be issued in every case (*Shepherd Homes Ltd* v *Sandham* [1971] Ch 340). However, there is no need to show that the plaintiff has suffered loss, or that the defendant has made a profit, before a mandatory injunction will be issued (*Harlow Development Corporation* v *Myers* (1979) 249 EG 1283 (cc).

Chapter 6

Miscellaneous

1 Planning

The erection of walls and fences is an operation that is within the definition of development in the Town and Country Planning Act 1971, s 22, and accordingly permission is necessary before it can lawfully be done. General permission is, however, given for the erection of certain fences, etc, by the Town and Country Planning General Development Order 1977. This deems permission to have been given for the erection of gates, fences, walls and other means of inclosure that do not exceed one metre in height when abutting upon a road used by vehicles, or two metres in height in other cases. There seems to be no authority as to how far back from the road a side wall has to be before it can be said not to abut the road. An inspector hearing an appeal against an enforcement notice decided that a fence 38cm (1ft 3in) back from a highway abutted it (T/APP/5337/C/82/1995/G4). To be covered by this provision, the wall must serve to enclose property. But if, in addition, it has another purpose (eg, retaining banked soil) that does not prevent the consent from applying (*Prengate Properties Ltd* v *Secretary of State for the Environment* (1973) 25 P & CR 311).

The permission granted by the General Development Order may be removed in certain cases by a direction of the local planning authority confirmed by the Secretary of State. One of the agreed standard enquiries to accompany local land charges searches to all local authorities asks whether such a direction applies to the property in question. A condition imposed on a planning consent can also have the effect of negating the general permission.

The formation or laying out of means of access to highways is also an operation that requires planning permission. This applies to access, whether private or public, for vehicles or pedestrians. It extends to all streets, but the General Development Order gives an automatic consent where the road is not a classified one and the work is required in connection with development for which permission has been given.

2 Settled land

(a) Duty to fence

In the absence of a direction in the trust instrument, a tenant for life is not bound, by virtue of his position as such, to erect or repair fences on the boundaries of the settled property (*Re Cartwright* (1889) 41 Ch D 532; *Woodhouse* v *Walker* (1880) 5 QBD 404), except where the settled land is leasehold and the lease casts the obligation on the tenant. As occupier of the property, however, he has the normal obligations under the general law, outlined in Chapter 5. On the other hand, unless the trust instrument expressly gives him an interest 'without impeachment of waste' the tenant for life is liable for 'voluntary waste', which would include the positive action of destroying a boundary fence. Damages are recoverable for the injury done by an act of waste, and any person interested under the settlement may apply for an injunction to prevent it, and may sue under RSC, Ord 15, r 13, on behalf of himself and all persons having the same interest.

(b) Erection of fences

The erection of a fence is one of the improvements that a tenant for life for the purposes of the Settled Land Act 1925 may carry out and have paid for from capital money without being called upon to repay by instalments. The scheme for improvements does not have to be submitted by the tenant for life for prior approval by the trustees or the court. The trustees are authorised to pay out the money on the certificate of the tenant for life's engineer or surveyor. The settled land may be mortgaged to raise money for this purpose.

Appendix

Proposal for reform

The Law Commission has put forward reform proposals in two areas which affect matters dealt with in this book.

Enforcing positive covenants

The fact that the law does not provide a satisfactory way to make the burden of positive covenants run with freehold land affected by them is a well recognised defect. It prevents covenants to erect and maintain a boundary fence being effectively imposed to bind future owners.

The Commission's report *The Law of Positive and Restrictive Covenants* (Law Com No 127), published in 1984, recommends the creation of 'land obligations' as a new interest in land. They would supersede both positive and restrictive covenants: the benefit and burden of them would run with the dominant and servient tenements, much as easements do.

Two different types of land obligation are proposed. 'Neighbour obligations' would be suitable for the simple case of a covenant made by the owner of one piece of land in favour of the owner of another piece. The permitted categories of neighbour obligation would be specified. One would be 'an obligation requiring the carrying out on the servient land or the dominant land of works which benefit the whole or any part of the dominmant land'. This would clearly include a duty to fence.

The other types of land obligation would be 'development obligations'. These would cover a substantial area of land, so that they could be enforced by all owners within that area against each other. It would also be possible to appoint a manager to provide services at the common expense. Although perhaps principally aimed at blocks of flats, this type of arrangement would be suitable for a housing estate. Among the permitted types of development obligation would be positive obligations to do work, equivalent to the neighbour obligation, and reciprocal payment and reimbursement obligations. The latter could impose a duty to pay on account towards expenditure to be incurred in carrying out works or to repay a manager who has done work. This could cover an obligation to pay for fencing work which someone else has had to do.

Power of entry

Without special provision, no property owner is entitled to enter the adjoining property to repair his own boundary wall, even though that is the only reasonable, or only possible, way to do it. This is strictly in accordance with the principles of property ownership, and the law of trespass which protects it. Nevertheless, it is inconvenient, to say the least, for the owner of the property in need of repair.

The Law Commission makes proposals to alleviate this in its report *Rights of Access to Neighbouring Land* (Law Com No 151), published in 1985. The recommendation is that the owner of the building in need of repair should be entitled to apply to the county court for an 'access order', entitling him to go in to do the work, in any case in which it would be substantially more difficult or expensive to do it without entering the next door property.

Safeguards are proposed for the owner of the property entered. First, the court would have to be satisfied that the proposed works were reasonably necessary for the preservation of the land. Secondly, the order would specify the period during which entry was authorised, and it could impose terms and conditions designed to avoid or minimise loss, damage or injury, and inconvenience or loss of privacy.

Access orders would not supersede arrangements for entry by consent, whether by advance agreement or by negotiation when the need for entry arises. Indeed, the existence of the court jurisdiction as an ultimate possibility might well stimulate the parties to come to an amicable arrangement. On the other hand, it might also suggest that greater care should be taken in drafting the terms of transfers selling off new houses on estates, where at present rights of entry are often given without specific safeguards for the owner of the property to be entered.

Index

Accretions, effect of, 11, 21
Agricultural holdings, 49–50
Ancient documents, 30
Animals, 28, 51–2, 54–5

Basements, 15
Beaches, 6
Boundaries—
 agreement, fixing by, 18
 customary, 33
 determination of, 1–21
 disputes as to, *see* Disputes
 horizontal, 14–16
 presumptions as to, 5–14
 registered land, *see* Registered land
 variation of, 1, 18–21
 vertical division, 1
Building estate, 8
Burial grounds, 57

Canals, 6
Cemeteries, 57
Commons, 18, 20, 31, 54
Compensation, 25, 33–4, 50
Crown, 12, 19, 32, 34–5, 40
Custom, 33

Damages, action for, 28, 47–8, 61
Declaration—
 action for, 27
 deceased person, of, 32
Deeds—
 construction, 1–5
 evidence, as, 1, 29–33
 plans, *see* Plans and maps
 rectification, 1, 19
 variation of boundaries, 1, 18
Disputes—
 action, types of, 27–9
 arbitration, 27–8, 34
 Crown land, 34–5
 evidence, admissible, 1, 14, 29–33

Disputes— *(cont)*
 landlord and tenant, 34
 party structures, as to, 43–4
 registered land, 28–9
 sale of land, 25, 33–4
Ditches, 7, 8, 16, 24, 33
Documents—
 deeds, *see* Deeds
 evidence, as, 29–32
Duchy—
 Cornwall, of, 35, 41
 Lancaster, of, 41

Easements, 11, 36–9, 50–1, 58
Ecclesiastical terriers, 31
Erosion, 21
Estate rentcharges, 46
Estoppel, 1, 19
Evidence, 1, 14, 29–33

Farms, 3
Fences—
 agricultural holdings, 49–50
 animals, 51–2, 54–5
 barbed wire, 52
 burial ground, 57
 business premises, 55
 churchyard, 57
 common land, adjoining, 54
 covenants as to—
  freehold property, 45–7, 59, 63
  leases, in 48–50, 59
 dangerous, 45, 48, 52, 58
 dangerous objects etc, where, 55–6
 easements, 50–1
 erection of—
  duty, extent of, 45–59
  planning permission, 22, 60–1
  unlawful, remedy, 59
 excavation, around, 54
 highway, 7, 51–3
 mines, disused, at, 57